ROMAN LITURGY AND FRANKISH CREATIVITY

This incisive, in-depth study unearths the significance of a neglected group of early medieval manuscripts, those which transmit the *Ordines Romani*. These texts present detailed scripts for Christian ceremonies that narrate the gestures, motions, actions and settings of ritual performance, with particular orientation to the Roman Church. While they are usually understood as liturgical, and thus lacking any particular creative flair, Arthur Westwell here foregrounds their manuscript permutations in order to reveal their extraordinary dynamism. He reflects on how the Carolingian Church undertook to improve liturgical practice and understanding, questioning the accepted idea of a 'reform' aimed at uniformity led by the monarch. Through these manuscripts, Westwell reveals a diversity of motivations in the recording of Roman liturgy and demonstrates the remarkable sophistication of Carolingian manuscript compilers.

ARTHUR WESTWELL is a research assistant in the Faculty for Catholic Theology at the University of Regensburg. His individual research project, in which he investigates Carolingian liturgical manuscripts, is supported by the Deutsche Forschungsgemeinschaft. He has held fellowships at the Pontifical Institute for Medieaeval Studies in Toronto, funded by the Mellon Foundation, and at the University of Trier, with the Humboldt Stiftung.

Cambridge Studies in Palaeography and Codicology

FOUNDING EDITORS

Albinia de la Mare[†]

Rosamond McKitterick *Sidney Sussex College, University of Cambridge*

GENERAL EDITORS

David Ganz

Teresa Webber *Trinity College, University of Cambridge*

This series has been established to further the study of manuscripts from the Middle Ages to the Renaissance. It includes books devoted to particular types of manuscripts, their production and circulation, to individual codices of outstanding importance, and to regions, periods and scripts of especial interest to scholars. The series will be of interest not only to scholars and students of medieval literature and history, but also to theologians, art historians and others working with manuscript sources.

RECENT TITLES

Charles F. Briggs *Giles of Rome's* De regimine principum: *Reading and Writing Politics at Court and University, c.1275 – c.1525*

Leslie Brubaker *Vision and Meaning in Ninth-Century Byzantium: Image as Exegesis in the Homilies of Gregory of Nazianzus*

Lisa Fagin Davis *The Gottschalk Antiphonary: Music and Liturgy in Twelfth-Century Lambach*

Albert Derolez *The Palaeography of Gothic Manuscript Books: From the Twelfth to the Early Sixteenth Century*

Yitzhak Hen and Rob Meens, editors *The Bobbio Missal: Liturgy and Religious Culture in Merovingian Gaul*

Alison I. Beach *Women as Scribes: Book Production and Monastic Reform in Twelfth-Century Bavaria*

Marica S. Tacconi *Cathedral and Civic Ritual in Late Medieval and Renaissance Florence: The Service Books of Santa Maria del Fiore*

Anna A. Grotans *Reading in Medieval St. Gall*

Alexandra Gillespie and Daniel Wakelin, editors *The Production of Books in England 1350–1500*

Susan Rankin *Writing Sounds in Carolingian Europe: The Invention of Musical Notation*

Margaret Connolly *Sixteenth-Century Readers, Fifteenth-Century Books: Continuities of Reading in the English Reformation*

David Rundle *The Renaissance Reform of the Book and Britain: The English Quattrocento*

Lawrence Nees *Illuminating the Word in the Early Middle Ages*

Arthur Westwell *Roman Liturgy and Frankish Creativity: The Early Medieval Manuscripts of the* Ordines Romani

ROMAN LITURGY AND FRANKISH CREATIVITY

The Early Medieval Manuscripts of the Ordines Romani

ARTHUR WESTWELL
University of Regensburg

Shaftesbury Road, Cambridge CB2 8EA, United Kingdom

One Liberty Plaza, 20th Floor, New York, NY 10006, USA

477 Williamstown Road, Port Melbourne, VIC 3207, Australia

314–321, 3rd Floor, Plot 3, Splendor Forum, Jasola District Centre, New Delhi – 110025, India

103 Penang Road, #05–06/07, Visioncrest Commercial, Singapore 238467

Cambridge University Press is part of Cambridge University Press & Assessment, a department of the University of Cambridge.

We share the University's mission to contribute to society through the pursuit of education, learning and research at the highest international levels of excellence.

www.cambridge.org
Information on this title: www.cambridge.org/9781009360487

DOI: 10.1017/9781009360500

© Arthur Westwell 2024

This publication is in copyright. Subject to statutory exception and to the provisions of relevant collective licensing agreements, no reproduction of any part may take place without the written permission of Cambridge University Press & Assessment.

First published 2024

A catalogue record for this publication is available from the British Library.

A Cataloging-in-Publication data record for this book is available from the Library of Congress

ISBN 978-1-009-36048-7 Hardback

Cambridge University Press & Assessment has no responsibility for the persistence or accuracy of URLs for external or third-party internet websites referred to in this publication and does not guarantee that any content on such websites is, or will remain, accurate or appropriate.

For my Mother, Chantry Westwell

Contents

List of Figures		*page* ix
Acknowledgements		x
List of Abbreviations		xii
	Introduction	1

PART I   COMPILATION AND CONTENT OF THE MANUSCRIPTS   17

1	The 'Roman' Collection of *Ordines* in Metz, Lorsch and Tours	19
2	The 'Frankish' Collection of *Ordines* in Verona, Regensburg, Nonantola and Corbie	40
3	Unique Collections of the *Ordines* from Worms, Wissembourg, St Amand and St Gallen	52
4	Liturgical 'Usefulness' and Reading the *Ordines Romani*	69

PART II   THE ARRANGEMENT OF RITES   101

5	Orders for the Stational Mass in Frankish Cities and Monasteries	103
6	The *Ordo Romanus* of the Baptismal Scrutinies	140
7	*Ordines* for Special Occasions, Ordination and the Ember Days: The Contribution of Arn of Salzburg	178

PART III   FORMAT AND SCRIPT OF THE MANUSCRIPTS   205

8	Layout, Script and Language of the *Ordo Romanus* Manuscripts	207

viii   *Contents*

Conclusion: Who Copied the *Ordines Romani,* and Why?   236

Bibliography   257
Index   281

Figures

2.1	Verona Biblioteca Capitolare XCI fol.62v. By permission of Verona Biblioteca Capitolare.	*page* 43
8.1	Biblioteca Apostolica Vaticana Pal.lat.487 fol.1r. By permission of Biblioteca Apostolica Vaticana, with all rights reserved.	213
8.2	Bayerische Staatsbibliothek München, Clm 14510, fol.41v.	215
8.3	BIblioteca Apostolica Vaticana Reg.lat.1127, fol.52v. By permission of Biblioteca Apostolica Vaticana, with all rights reserved.	216
8.4	Bayerische Staatsbibliothek München, Clm 14510, fol.46r.	217
8.5	Biblioteca Apostolica Vaticana Pal.lat.574, fol.156v. By permission of Biblioteca Apostolica Vaticana, with all rights reserved.	218
8.6	Herzog August Bibliothek Wolfenbüttel, Weissenburg 91, fol.42v. © Herzog August Bibliothek Wolfenbüttel http://diglib.hab.de/mss/91-weiss/start.htm.	219
8.7	Herzog August Bibliothek Wolfenbüttel, Weissenburg 91, fol.54r. © Herzog August Bibliothek Wolfenbüttel http://diglib.hab.de/mss/91-weiss/start.htm.	220
8.8	Herzog August Bibliothek Wolfenbüttel, Weissenburg 91, fol.58r. © Herzog August Bibliothek Wolfenbüttel http://diglib.hab.de/mss/91-weiss/start.htm.	230
8.9	Herzog August Bibliothek Wolfenbüttel, Weissenburg 91, fol.70v. © Herzog August Bibliothek Wolfenbüttel http://diglib.hab.de/mss/91-weiss/start.htm.	231
8.10	Verona Biblioteca Capitolare XCI fol.5r. By permission of Verona Biblioteca Capitolare.	232

Acknowledgements

This book is a substantial reimagining of my doctoral thesis, undertaken at the University of Cambridge under the stewardship of Rosamond McKitterick. Rosamond first suggested the topic of the *Ordines Romani* to me with characteristic insight during a chat in her Sydney Sussex office. Initially, the subject was principally a way to allow me to continue to work with manuscripts, my fascination with them only deepened by Rosamond's reflections. This initial pointer has led me into the rich and fascinating early medieval liturgy, which I have not subsequently left, and I have Rosamond to thank for that. Our meetings were always a source of rich inspiration and invaluable help. Throughout the process and now for some years subsequently, she has been an incredible mentor and colleague. My examiners, Susan Rankin and Els Rose, offered patient and helpful feedback, pointing me in the right direction on many accounts where otherwise I would have gone astray. Both have been valued colleagues in the years since. Claudine Moulin in Trier and the wonderful community at the Pontifical Institute of Mediaeval Studies in Toronto have provided warm and welcoming settings for my further wrangling. Harald Buchinger in Regensburg has been an inordinately generous host and colleague in the years which have now seen the turning of that thesis into what I hope is a more polished study.

The generosity and kindness of scholars of the Early Middle Ages and of manuscript studies have made it clear what a great community of people choose to work in these fields. I would single out the help of David Hiley, Eric Palazzo, Ingrid Rembold, Carine van Rhijn and Sarah Hamilton. David Ganz and Tessa Webber were of special help in the final editing stages. The anonymous peer reviewer was patient with what was still a rough version, and gave me some very good suggestions to improve it. Thank you Emily Hockley, of Cambridge University Press, for getting this over the finishing line and to Llinos Edwards for the copy-editing.

Acknowledgements

I am grateful for funding provided by the Bibliographical Society, the H.M. Chadwick Fund, Queens' College Cambridge, the Humboldt Foundation, the Deutsche Akademischer Austauschdienst, the Deutsche Forschungsgemeinschaft and the Neil Ker Memorial Fund at the British Academy.

One of the great privileges of studying this stock of texts has been the chance to visit the great libraries and collections of Europe. The staff have been universally welcoming, and sincerely interested in discovering what I will do with their manuscripts. For all their help, my gratitude goes to the staff at the Biblioteca Apostolica Vaticana, the Bibliothèque national de France, the British Library in London, Cambridge University Library, the Österreichische Nationalbibliothek in Vienna, the Zentralbibliothek, Zurich, the Bayerische Staatsbibliothek in Munich, Milan's Biblioteca Ambrosiana, the Biblioteca Nazionale di Roma, the Biblioteca Alessandrina in Rome, the Biblioteca Capitolare of Verona, the Dombibliothek of Cologne, the Bibliothèque Municipale of Albi, the Bibliothèque de la Faculté de Médecine, Montpellier, the Staatsbibliothek zu Berlin, the Biblioteca dell'Abbazia di Montecassino, the Staatliche Bibliothek, Regensburg, as well as the countless other institutions which have kindly put their treasures online and those who have enabled them to do so. The British School at Rome provided me with a home away from home, and gave me a wonderful community during my stay there, enabled by the Trust of Roger and Ingrid Pilkington.

Jessica and Jana, you have been wonderful friends to me, in Cambridge and since. Jana, thank you for helping with the Introduction. Without my family, none of my academic career could have happened. George, Anna and Thomas, you are an incredible support base at home. Dad, I appreciate your support through these years more than is easy to say. Andi, I love you and you have made me very happy. Life would not be the same without you. Finally, my mother, Chantry Westwell, to whom I dedicate this book in its entirety. You have always been my inspiration.

Abbreviations

AfL	*Archiv für Liturgiewissenschaft*
BAV	*Biblioteca Apostolica Vaticana*
Bischoff, *Katalog*	Bernhard Bischoff, *Katalog der festländischen Handschriftendes neunten Jahrhunderts (mit Ausnahme der wisigotischen)*, 4 vols. (Wiesbaden, 1998–2017)
BM	*Bibliothèque municipale*
BnF	*Bibliothèque nationale de France*
BSB	*Bayerische Staatsbibliothek*
Cap.	*Capitularia, Legum Sectio II, Capitularia Regum Francorum*, A. Boretius and V. Kraus (eds.), 2 vols. (Hanover, 1883–97)
CCCM	*Corpus Christianorum, Continuatio Medievalis*
CCSL	*Corpus Christianorum, Series Latina*
CLA	*Codices Latini Antiquiores*, E. A. Lowe (ed.), 12 vols. (Oxford, 1934–1971)
CLLA	Klaus Gamber, *Codices Liturgici Latini Antiquiores*, 2nd ed., 2 vols. (Freiburg, 1968) + Supplement (Freiburg, 1988)
Conc.	*Concilia, Legum Sectio III, Concilia I*, F. Maassen (ed.)(Hanover, 1893); *Concilia II*, A. Werminghoff (ed.) (Hanover, 1906–1908); *Concilia V*, W. Hartmann, I. Schröder and G. Schmitz (eds.) (Hanover, 2012)
EphLit	*Ephemerides Liturgica*
Epp.	*Epistolae* II, L. Hartmann (ed.), *Gregorius I Papae Registrum Epistolarum* (Hanover, 1890); IV–VII, *Karolini Aevi* (Hanover 1895–1932)
HAB	Herzog August Bibliothek

List of Abbreviations

HBS	Henry Bradshaw Society
Les Ordines	Michel Andrieu (ed.), *Les Ordines Romani du haut moyen âge*, 5 vols., *Spicilegium Sacrum Lovaniense, Études et Documents*, 11, 23–24, 28–29 (Louvain, 1931–1961)
MGH	*Monumenta Germaniae Historica*
ÖNB	*Österreichische Nationalbibliothek*
PL Patrologia Latina:	J.-P. Migne (ed.), *Patrologiae Cursus Completus, Series Latina*, 221 vols. (Paris, 1841–1864)
RevBen	*Revue Bénédictine*
UB	*Universitätsbibliothek*

Introduction

This book is a study of a group of early medieval texts, known today as the *ordines romani* (Roman Orders), and of the manuscripts which carry them, written across the Carolingian realms between the years 750 and 900. Though often categorised straightforwardly as 'liturgical' texts, the *ordines* reveal plainly the limitations of this modern category, and they have a great deal more historical value than this categorisation might, from our modern perspective, immediately suggest. First and foremost, these manuscripts reflect the sophistication of early medieval book culture: complex scribal practices of compilation and formatting, choices of individual texts and accessory material, deployment of varied scripts and languages. Evident in the manuscripts are also diverse practices of reading and 'use' of manuscripts once they lay in the possession of individuals and communities, which strict terms such as 'liturgical' limit our ability to fully grasp.[1] The categorisations which modern scholars have used to understand such manuscripts, including the category of 'liturgical' itself, are in many respects anachronistic. A 'liturgical' manuscript might have had many potential uses, both those conceived by its original compilers and those reenvisaged by later owners and users.[2]

Additionally, the manuscripts of the *ordines romani* are themselves products of widely felt imperatives to improve ecclesiastical practice and the education of clergy in the Carolingian era. They are an important source for understanding how these impulses were promulgated and shared. Initially, the texts expressed the ideals and purposes of certain circles of high-ranking and highly educated clergymen of the Carolingian Church, above all bishops who were personally familiar with Rome,

---

[1] Helen Gittos and Sarah Hamilton (eds.), 'Introduction', in *Understanding Medieval Liturgy: Essays in Interpretation* (Aldershot, 2015), pp.4–7.

[2] *Ibid.*, p.9: 'Medieval manuscripts of liturgical rites were rarely if ever intended simply as a prescription of how service should be conducted'; Edoard Henrik Aubert, 'When the Roman Liturgy Became Frankish: Sound, Performance and Sublation in the Eighth and Ninth Centuries', *Études Grégoriennes*, 40 (2013), p.85.

2   Introduction

accustomed to reading and using liturgy in highly sophisticated ways, and eager to raise the quality of practice and understanding of ritual. The gathering of *ordines* in collections, copied in surviving manuscripts, was an important innovation accomplished by such men, a kind of liturgical book which was entirely new, and reflected their ambitious goals for their own churches and devotional lives, as well as for those whom they guided and taught. The text type *ordo* and books containing collections of *ordines* are both distinctive achievements of these Carolingian churchmen. They are expressions of genuine creativity and dynamism in an age that is often seen as derivative, and within a genre of text, the medieval liturgy, often presented as entirely uncreative.

Widespread reception and copying of these new collections, which took place in monastic communities as well as episcopal churches, demonstrate to us that the complex resonances of these texts could then be further reframed to shape ritual comprehension in new, local settings. The flexible *ordines romani* were thus perfectly suited to accomplishing such positive change in distinctly Carolingian ways, and they give us an invaluable view of the methods and results of this process. This guides us beyond the previous understanding of the texts as primarily the tool and expression of a straightforward top-down 'liturgical reform'.[3] According to the traditional understanding, the monarchs of the Carolingian dynasty, principally Pippin III and Charlemagne, had taken the initiative in appealing to Rome for authoritative books and texts.[4] The monarchs aimed for uniformity in the cultural life of the Empire, and liturgy was an important means to achieve this. They thus imposed authoritative Roman books upon their subjects in order to eliminate the diversity previously characteristic of the Western liturgy. This narrative was built upon predetermined understandings of how liturgical reform worked, through which the scanty evidence available was interpreted. It has also sometimes been argued that the *ordines romani* were, in some sense, imposed by Pippin III, though there exists no evidence of this.[5]

---

[3] Julia Barrow, 'The Ideas and Application of Reform', in Julia M. H. Smith and Tom Noble (eds.), *The Cambridge History of Christianity*, vol. III, *600–1100* (Cambridge, 2008), pp.345–362; Arthur Westwell, Carine van Rhijn and Ingrid Rembold (eds.), *Rethinking the Carolingian Reforms* (Manchester, 2023), especially van Rhijn, 'Introduction', pp.1–31.

[4] Cyrille Vogel, 'La réforme liturgique sous Charlemagne', in Bernhard Bischoff (ed.), *Karl der Große Lebenswerk und Nachleben*, vol. II, *Das geistige Leben* (Dusseldorf, 1966), pp.217–32; Theodor Klauser, 'Die liturgischen Austauchsbeziehungen zwischen der römischen und der fränkisch-deutschen Kirche vom achten bis zum elften Jahrhundert', *Historisches Jahrbuch*, 53 (1933), pp.169–189, on the *ordines romani*, p.176.

[5] Yitzhak Hen, *The Royal Patronage of Liturgy in Frankish Gaul to the Death of Charles the Bald (877)*, HBS, Subsidia 3 (London, 2001), pp.62–64.

Introduction

Despite important critiques, reform in the sense of uniformity according to the Roman model has remained the principal means of understanding and evaluating the Carolingian period's effects on liturgy. When the actual fact of continued or even increased manuscript diversity in this period is confronted, it has led to the assumption that Carolingian liturgical reform must have failed, or even that they inaugurated a period of 'liturgical anxiety and confusion'.[6] But treatments of 'reform' or 'Romanisation' can be demonstrated to have the matter the wrong way round in their belief that the drive to improve liturgy was the product of, and strictly limited by, imperial and conciliar directives on the subject.[7]

Legal and conciliar sources were highlighted because they conformed to expectations of what was perceived as top-down 'reform', but they really give only a narrow picture of Carolingian culture.[8] In fact these central directives were the response from above to a movement already flourishing at every level of society, which we are better able to recognise if we begin with the manuscripts. This cultural movement went further and in many more directions than the narrow and specific purview of the legal and political interventions. This is a much more collaborative model for sharing liturgy that potentially involved many rather different, but mostly harmonious, priorities and visions.[9] This would also mean seeing the 'Carolingian effect' on the liturgy playing out over the whole period in many different places in different ways, rather than confined to one decisive moment of exertion on the part of the monarchs. It is in the

---

[6] Frederick S. Paxton, 'Researching Rites for the Dying and the Dead', in Gittos and Hamilton (eds.), *Understanding Medieval Liturgy*, p.49; Yitzhak Hen, 'When Liturgy Gets Out of Hand', in Elina Screen and Charles West (eds.), *Writing the Early Medieval West* (Manchester, 2018), pp.203–212.

[7] Marco Mostert, '"... but they pray badly using corrected books": Errors in the Early Carolingian Copies of the *Admonitio Generalis*', in Rob Meens, Dorine van Espelo, Bram von den Hoven van Genderen, Janneke Raaijmakers, Irene van Renswoude and Carine van Rhijn (eds.), *Religious Franks: Religion and Power in the Frankish Kingdoms* (Manchester, 2017), pp.112–127; Daniel DiCenso, 'Revisiting the Admonitio Generalis', in Daniel DiCenso and Rebecca Maloy (eds.), *Chant, Liturgy and the Inheritance of Rome: Essays in Honour of Joseph Dyer* (London, 2017), pp.315–372; Raymond Kottje, 'Einheit und Vielfalt des kirchlichen Lebens in der Karolingerzeit', *Zeitschrift für Kirchengeschichte*, 76 (1965), pp.335–340; Wolfgang Steck, '"Secundum usum romanum": Liturgischer Anspruch und Wirchlichkeit zur Karolingerzeit', in Christian Schäfer and Martin Thurner (eds.), *Mittelalterliches Denken: Debatten. Ideen und Gestalten im Kontext* (Darmstadt, 2007), pp.15–28.

[8] For example, Arnold Angenendt, 'Keine Romanisierung der Liturgie unter Karl dem Großen?: Einspruch gegen Martin Morards "Sacramentarium immixtum" et uniformisation romaine', *AfL*, 51 (2009), pp.96–108, argues for the principle of liturgical uniformity chiefly based on the writings of Boniface and the assumption that Charlemagne must have imposed the Gregorian Sacramentary, with little attention to manuscripts.

[9] Karl Morrison, 'Know Thyself: Music in the Carolingian Renaissance', in *Committenti e produzione artistico-letteriaria nell'alto medioevo occidentale*, Settimane, 39 (Spoleto, 1992), pp.369–481.

4 Introduction

manuscripts that were produced through the whole period in response to these many divergences that we actually see the trajectories and horizons of how people understood the liturgy, the wealth of what was allowed and the boundaries of what was not.

Ordines and the 'Arrangement' of the Liturgy

The importance of the *ordines romani* for our comprehension of early medieval ritual life and the medieval understanding of what that ritual did and meant should not be underestimated. In many cases, they present the first and only detailed description of what might have occurred during the key rituals of the Christian tradition in the Early Middle Ages. But more fundamentally and perhaps more truthfully (since the translation of the written description to ritual practice remains obscure and was likely not straightforward), the *ordines* are an invaluable pointer to how those rituals were framed and understood by those who participated in them. Their setting in manuscripts is a vital part of the evidence they provide.

The texts categorised as *ordines* take many forms and appear in various contexts.[10] They differ hugely in their length and their detail, and, thus, in their exact relation to the performance of ritual. The common description of them as 'stage directions' for ritual is overly simplistic.[11] It is not true that *ordines* described (even in their earliest form) only the gestures, actions and non-spoken elements of ritual, or properly dealt with only a single liturgical event each.[12] They are not in any simple way the counterpart or inextricable accompaniment of a book of prayers like the Sacramentary, which equally does not 'only' or 'merely' contain the words said in ritual. A number of *ordines* interact with the spoken, sung or read elements of liturgical ceremony in various ways, and the Sacramentary is actually a significant presence in the transmission of some of the most important individual *ordines*.

The term *ordo* was applied by contemporaries to both individual texts and full books in this period. It is best to think of *ordo* in terms of an 'arrangement' of a liturgical rite. Indeed, the idea of 'arrangement' allows a better appreciation of the ambiguity of the relation of the written *ordo* to

---

[10] Aimé-Georges Martimort, *Les Ordines, les ordinaires et les cérémoniaux*, Typologie des sources du moyen âge, 56 (Turnhout, 1991); Roger Reynolds, 'Ordines', in Joseph Strayer (ed.), *Dictionary of the Middle Ages*, vol. IX (New York, 1987), p.269; Eric Palazzo, *Histoire des livres liturgiques: Le Moyen Âge des origins au XIIIe siècle* (Paris, 1993), pp.196–197.

[11] Henry Parkes, *The Making of Liturgy in the Ottonian Church: Books Music and Ritual in Mainz 950–1050* (Cambridge, 2015), pp.12, 219.

[12] Cyrille Vogel, *Medieval Liturgy: An Introduction to the Sources*, trans. William G. Storey and Niels Krogh Rasmussen (Washington, DC, 1986), p.135.

Ordines *and the 'Arrangement' of the Liturgy* 5

the performed ritual as it would be acted out. It is not at all clear that *ordines* were written as 'scripts', to be followed mechanically step by step. Many address preconditions of ritual, including the proper understanding of the ritual prior to the performance. When viewed in their manuscript context by their medieval users, they invited reflection and the participation of their readers in working out the potential of how the recorded text could guide the acted out liturgical ceremony. Thus, understanding any given *ordo* as the 'standard' guide to the performance of a ritual across the whole Carolingian Empire, or even the sufficient and complete account of how it would invariably be performed in a single church, misses the potential for a significant level of individual and dynamic involvement on the part of both compilers and readers in the use of such texts.

This is particularly visible in a subset of the texts which were edited as the *ordines romani*. *Ordines romani* are distinguished by a particular orientation towards the Roman Church, often in describing rituals as they were performed, or envisaged to be performed, by the hierarchy around the Pope and on the streets and sacred locations of the city. The terminology of *ordo romanus* goes back at least to the ninth century, and was applied then to individual texts as well as to complete books (or booklets), but was not used systematically. We can see this, for example, in ninth-century book lists from Reichenau and St Gall.[13] Individual texts are variously titled: *Ordo Romanorum*, *Ordo Qualiter Romanae Ecclesiae* and so on. The modern designation of this kind of text as the *ordines romani* stems from a long tradition of editorial selection. Jean Mabillon divided up and numbered a particularly influential set, and his designations were employed in some of the older treatments.[14] Other liturgists and historians followed suit in identifying and editing various texts from some early manuscripts, Gerbert and Duchesne among them.[15] When presented in this way, the conviction was held that such texts were the accurate representations of Roman norms, and had been created by Roman pens for the purposes of putting the liturgical rites so described into practice in Rome itself. Their presence and purposeful configuration in Frankish manuscripts copied from the ninth century onward were not therefore discussed in any depth.

---

[13] For example Gustav Becker, *Catologi bibliothecarum antiqui*, vol. I (Bonn, 1885), p.51: 'Ordo Romanus in duobus quaternionibus. Item aliud in quaternionibus'; p.63: 'Romanus Ordo'.

[14] Jean Mabillon, *Museum Italicum*, vol. II (Paris, 1689), reprinted in *PL* 78, cols.851–1408; concordance in Vogel, *Medieval Liturgy*, pp.194–197.

[15] Martin Gerbert, *Monumenta veteris liturgiae alemannicae* (St-Blaise, 1779); Louis Duchesne, *Origines du culte chrétien*, 5th ed. (Paris, 1920), pp.475–504; English translation, *Christian Worship: Its Origins and Evolution*, trans. L. McClure (London, 1919), pp.455–464, and discussion at pp.146–150.

6   Introduction

By cataloguing the manuscripts which carried *ordines*, Michel Andrieu's monumental edition made significant strides to making that discussion possible.[16] Andrieu identified and selected a particular selection of fifty *ordo romanus* texts. Each one was given a number, which this book will continue to use. His editions in five volumes have a lucid commentary that presents a pertinent 'state of the question' for liturgical research on the many different rituals which the texts address. In general, the focus is on Rome and what we can know about the Roman Church's practices, from the *ordines* and complementary sources such as papal letters and councils. But Andrieu also made it clear for the first time how many of the texts that had been previously published as *ordines romani* showed a significant level of Frankish adaptation. Details in the language used and the rituals described reveal that, even where the rites ostensibly are depicted as taking place in Rome, they were still written by Frankish authors. Among these, a number still maintain accurate descriptions of real and historical Roman practice so far as Andrieu could tell.[17] But many others introduce rituals and elements of rituals that were not, or could not, have been undertaken in the Roman Church.[18] Andrieu made great efforts to distinguish one from another, but his method was to draw a sharp distinction between 'authentically' Roman elements and what he deemed to be 'tendentious' Frankish fraud in a way that does not seem to capture the roles which the texts can be shown to play in their complex manuscripts.[19] He based this on his particular conception of what receiving Roman liturgy would have meant. In his view, any adaptations of Roman liturgy had to be an unwilling compromise on the part of 'reformers' to the sensibilities of greater part of the people and clergy, rather than an intrinsic and valid response that was quite normal and expected in the period's liturgical culture.[20] He wrote, for example, of one *ordo* (*Ordo* 15) and of its author (the 'zealous romaniser'):

> It represents a sort of compromise between the Roman and the Gallican mass ... to suppress abruptly the Gallican tradition would have been too difficult. The void thus created would have disconcerted most of the faithful and the majority of the clergy. The latter were all the more attached to their traditional customs as their lack of education and their lack of an overarching view made them less sensitive to the state of anarchy of the Gallican liturgy

[16] *Les Ordines*; Vogel, *Medieval Liturgy*, pp.135–197.
[17] For example, *Ordo* 1, 2, 14, 20, 34, 40, 42.
[18] For example, *Ordo* 3, 5, 9, 10, 28, 29, 30, 31, 32, 37, etc.
[19] *Les Ordines*, vol. II, pp.153–154: 'une contrefaçon tendancieuse'.
[20] *Ibid.*, pp.xlvii–xlviii: '[Collection B] témoigne d'une sorte de compromis. On n'avait pas voulu heurter trop brusquement les vieilles coutumes indigènes.'

Ordines *and the 'Arrangement' of the Liturgy*

and the need for reform. Also, our zealous romaniser, after having proposed to the bishops, whom he considered enlightened enough to adopt it and powerful enough to impose it, a quite strictly Roman model of the Mass, had believed it necessary to compromise in order to win to his cause the lower clergy.[21]

Thus, the 'reformers' really wanted a complete adoption of the 'Roman rite' wholesale, exactly as the modern Catholic Church would require, but were forced to make compromises that were not in line with their real goals by the parlous state of clerical education. This was a common perspective on the reception of Roman liturgical forms in Francia, closely linked to the modern idea of 'reform': for example, Andrieu also viewed the Mass Book known as the Gelasian Sacramentary of the Eighth Century in the same terms, not as a real act of Frankish creativity and individuality but as an unsatisfactory compromise made out of necessity.[22] It is unclear, however, if Carolingian liturgists really understood the 'Roman rite' as unitary, in the way the printing press and centuries of consolidation have made it today.

It is also true that even more of the texts than Andrieu suspected were in fact created by Frankish hands, and his defence of their Roman origin does not in every case convince.[23] His singular focus on the reconstruction of an 'original' form tended to allow less attention on the new forms they took in the surviving manuscripts, which were evidence of ongoing creativity in adaptation beyond the initial act of writing the 'original' text. Notably, such later adaptations also belie his presentation of much of the Carolingian Church as poorly educated, hopelessly traditional and unable to accept change. Seeing 'anarchy' in the so-called Gallican liturgy

---

[21] *Les Ordines*, vol. III, p.79: '[*Ordo* 15] une sorte de compromise entre la messe romaine et la messe gallicane ... La supprimer brusquement eut été trop hardi. Le vide ainsi créé eût déconcerté le commun des fidèles et la majeure partie du clergé. Celle-ci était d'autant plu attachée à ses coutumes traditionnelles que son peu d'instruction, son manque de vues générales lui rendaient moins sensibles l'état d'anarchie de la liturgie gallicane et la nécessité d'une réforme. Aussi notre zélé romanisant, après avoir proposé aux évêques, qu'il estimait assez éclairés pour l'adopter et assez puissants pour l'imposer, un modèle de messe assez strictement romaine, a-t-il cru nécessaire de transiger pour gagner à sa cause le clergé inférieur.'

[22] Michel Andrieu, 'Quelques remarques sur le classement des sacramentaires', Jahrbuch für Liturgiewissenschaft, 11 (1931), pp.46–66, at pp.55–56. For the more updated evaluation of these books: Bernard Moreton, *The Eighth-Century Gelasian Sacramentaries. A Study in Tradition* (Oxford, 1976).

[23] Indicated already by Aimé-Georges Martimort, 'Recherches recentes sur les Sacramentaries', *Bulletin de literature ecclésiastique*, 63 (1962), p.38; Stephen J. P. van Dijk, 'The Medieval Easter Vespers of the Roman Clergy', *Sacris Erudiri*, 19 (1969–70), pp.261–363 (on *Ordo* 27); Arthur Westwell, 'The Content and the Ideological Construction of the Early Pontifical Manuscripts', *Mélanges de l'École française de Rome – Moyen Âge*, 132 (2020), pp.233–251 (on *Ordo* 35).

8   Introduction

(the scholarly construction of an indigenous liturgical tradition of France) was another precondition for understanding the Carolingian age as one of reform, so that it had been necessary to correct a decadent past. The actual vitality of Merovingian liturgical life was a casualty to this understanding.[24]

Andrieu gave a significant and pertinent presentation of the range of manuscripts in which the texts appear. He identified a number of 'Collections', which represented the self-conscious selection and juxtaposition of a number of different *ordines* together in a single book. Two of these collections, which Andrieu designated as Collection A the 'Roman Collection' and Collection B the 'Frankish Collection', are present in a number of different manuscripts; several other Collections are only found in a single manuscript (e.g. the Collection of St Amand, the Collection of St Gall and the *Capitulare* Collection).[25] As the names he gave the first two imply, Andrieu read ideological function into the gathering and presentation of the sets of *ordines*. But this aspect was dealt with only cursorily in his editions. Describing the Collections as respectively 'Roman' and 'Frankish' identified these designations as wholly distinct; Andrieu saw the texts they contained as purely one or the other, when the relation to the Roman liturgy of both Collection A and B was much more ambiguous than this would suggest. Nor did Andrieu go into how the individual manuscripts of each of the Collections reinterpreted what he identified as the original content: each one contains additional *ordines*, and additional liturgical and non-liturgical texts. These additions bear witness to a complex and individualised phenomenon of individual Frankish writers using the Roman texts for their own purposes. Andrieu's understanding of wholesale 'liturgical reform' based on the *ordines* was not principally aimed at recovering this nuance.

Likewise, Andrieu's conception of what a 'liturgical book' was and how it was intended to be used meant that he imposed a further distinction between the manuscripts of the Collections. He differentiated between 'real' liturgical books, in particular an important set that were identified as precursors to the genre of the 'pontifical', and those that were not 'really' liturgical because they were not designed for use in church. In Andrieu's presentation, only a manuscript whose entire content was orientated towards liturgical use could be properly deemed liturgical. Thus, they would be without any subsidiary content which precluded a manuscript from being considered 'liturgical' in the same way (most notably the addition of *expositiones* and

---

[24] Yitzhak Hen, 'Unity in Diversity: the Liturgy of Frankish Gaul before the Carolingians', *Studies in Church History*, 32 (1995), pp.19–30.
[25] Vogel, *Medieval Liturgy*, pp.144–155.

Ordines *and the 'Arrangement' of the Liturgy*   9

study texts on liturgy).[26] In practice, very few manuscripts obey these rules. This understanding plainly projected the characteristics of modern liturgical books back onto medieval liturgical manuscripts which have a much more complex relationship to practice. The *ordines romani* manuscripts, in fact, allow us to mount one of the more lucid challenges to a frame of interpretation which has been assumed for study of liturgical sources. 'Using' an *ordo* as a framework for the physical performance does not seem to have been the simple transaction that has hitherto been envisaged. Unlike Mass prayers, chants or lections, the principal utility of *ordines* did not lie in their being read and used during the ceremony itself. Since they describe an 'arrangement' of how the ceremony could proceed, we come closer to their utility if we imagine them being read beforehand, pondered and rehearsed, or consulted if ever questions arose. Such nuances are important when it comes to the question of what a 'liturgical' manuscript was originally designed to do and in what other ways it may have been used over time. Both the placement of *ordines* in manuscripts and the ongoing processing of them as they were copied show that copyists did not envisage that 'using' an *ordo* simply meant replicating its instructions. Instead, 'using' an *ordo* would have involved far more of the preconditions, understanding and intentions of the people involved in setting up and enacting it, individuals who are not really a presence at all in Andrieu's reconstruction. What did they intend the rite described by a particular *ordo* to do, and what did it mean to them? Questions such as these would have strongly affected the shape the actual ritual took, with the *ordo's* text certainly contributing but likely not having the final word. In the same way, the presentation of the *ordo* in the manuscript, with other material (whether that was non-liturgical or liturgical in these strict terms) was certainly intended to help guide how the *ordo* itself was interpreted, and thus what form the 'use' of the *ordines* would take. Such presentation likewise suggests a much greater role for the user and reader, who was expected to actively interpret the text, than was assumed in the more traditional analysis of Andrieu.

This is even more pertinent in the specific case of the *ordines romani*. It would not be simple to translate the narrative of a complex ceremonial in an *ordo romanus* set in Rome and practised by the Pope into a ceremony undertaken in a Frankish church or monastery. Rome's abundance of churches and special hierarchy are often displayed in the *ordines romani*, which revel in their presentation

---

[26] For example, *Les Ordines*, vol.I, p.476: 'Un tel volume est fait pour l'étude. On le lit dans une bibliothèque, mais on ne l'emporte pas à l'église.'

Introduction

of the exotic richness of Rome's ecclesiastical resources. It would take a certain imaginative leap to see one's own Frankish cathedral as St Peter's Basilica, described in the *ordo*, for example. But rather than this being than an obstacle to the use and dissemination of the texts, the *ordines romani* seem to be designed to effect exactly such an imaginative leap. This appears to be key to understanding why the texts were widely shared and copied. The potential to see in one's own liturgical ceremonies the precious and prized enactment of such an intimate mental link to Rome and the papacy allowed the *ordines romani* to act as both a framework for a ceremony and a guide to then seeing the ceremony in progress as a physical, dynamic expression of this desirable connection to Rome. Thus, the copying of *ordines* should be considered in tandem with the other methods the Franks employed to express and embody their link to Rome: the copying of Roman architectural forms in basilica churches, the fevered search for Roman relics to found their churches upon; pilgrimage to Rome to rest at the threshold of the apostles; and the presentation of Frankish history as continuous with the history of the papal church.[27] As we will see, the churchmen who can be linked to the transmission of *ordines* can in almost every case also be seen to have undertaken initiatives of these other kinds. They integrated the *ordines* into their broader agendas, which made use of Rome for the sophisticated consolidation of their own authority and as a measure of their understanding of what was correct, orderly and right.

The *ordo romanus* manuscript, by acting as the 'guidebook' for such processes, would also partake of and represent a special connection to the city of Rome in the same way as a manuscript of the Roman Gregorian Mass Book did, which, in addition to its obvious liturgical function

---

[27] On architecture '*more romano*': Judson Emerick, 'Building *more romano* in Francia During the Third Quarter of the Eighth Century: The Abbey Church of Saint-Denis and its Model', in Claudia Bolgia, Rosamond McKitterick and John Osborne (eds.), *Rome Across Time and Space: Cultural Transmission and the Exchange of Ideas, c.500–1400* (Cambridge, 2011), pp.127–150; Carol Heitz, '*More romano*: problèmes d'architecture et liturgie carolingiennes', in *Roma e l'età carolingia. Atti della giornale di studio 3–8 Maggio 1976 a cura dello Istituto di Storia dell'arte dell'università di Roma* (Rome, 1976), pp.27–34; on Roman relics: Julia M. H. Smith (ed.), 'Old Saints, New Cults: Roman Relics in Carolingian Francia', in *Early Medieval Rome and the Christian West: Essays in Honour of Donald A. Bullough* (Leiden, 2000), pp.317–340; on Roman history: Rosamond McKitterick, 'Les Perceptions Carolingiennes de Rome', in Woljciech Falkowski and Yves Sasser (eds.), *Le monde carolingien: Bilan, perspectives, champs de recherches, Actes de colloque international de Poitiers, Centre d'Études Supérieures de civilisation médiévale, 18–20 novembre* (Turnhout, 2009), pp.83–102; Rosamond McKitterick, 'Rome and the Popes in the Construction of Institutional History and Identity in the Early Middle Ages: The Case of Leiden UB Scaliger MS 49', in Valerie Garver and Owen Phelan (eds.), *Rome and Religion in the Early Medieval World: Studies in Honor of Thomas F. X. Noble* (Farnham, 2014), pp.207–234.

Ordines *and the 'Arrangement' of the Liturgy*

carrying prayers of the Mass, also acted as a 'book relic' of the city.[28] Like the *ordines*, the Gregorian Sacramentary (the most widely copied form of Mass Book in the Carolingian period) presented to its readers a 'mental map' of Rome, as also reading and pondering the influential history of the popes, the *Liber Pontificalis*, did.[29] The Gregorian Mass Book was organised according to the stational liturgy of Rome, and it thus gave notice of the churches in which the Pope would celebrate on a given day, something consumed and pondered by the priests and celebrants who used the book.[30] It allowed one to feel that one was celebrating 'in the person of the Pope', mapping out in one's own church or city a similar sacred topography, just as the *ordines* described the Pope and his clergy's gestures and movements in the course of a ritual event, which the same celebrant might also imitate.

Indeed, as we will see, a distinct number of *ordines* seem to have begun life as what we term travel documents, descriptions by a traveller of the exotic ceremonies of Rome and the urban stage on which they unfolded, for an audience at home. They thereby take place in a long history of Frankish 'liturgical tourism', going back to the Pilgrimage of Egeria in the fourth-century Holy Land, which described the Jerusalem liturgy at length and first-hand, as it existed at the time of her visit.[31] Such texts met the thirst of readers for descriptions of the sacred places, allowing them to envisage and imagine what they might not have been able to have seen for themselves, and trace the paths the pilgrim took in their minds. They might indeed inspire new ritual practices, but we should be clear that surviving Carolingian descriptions and itineraries of Rome were not

---

[28] Rudolf Schieffer, '"Redeamus ad fontem". Rom als Hort authentischer Überlieferung im früheren Mittelalter', in Arnold Angenendt and Rudolf Schieffer (eds.), *Roma – Caput et Fons. Zwei Vorträge über das päpstliche Romo zwischen Altertum und Mittelalter* (Opladen, 1989), pp.62–63. On the Gregorian: Vogel, *Medieval Liturgy*, p.64ff; edition: *Le sacramentaire grégorien: ses principales formes d'après les plus anciens manuscrits*, Jean Deshusses (ed.), 3 vols., Spicilegium Friburgense 16, 24, 28, 3rd ed. (Freiburg, 1971–1982).

[29] Rosamond McKitterick, *Rome and the Invention of the Papacy* (Cambridge, 2020), pp.41–61.

[30] On the stational liturgy: John F. Baldovin, *The Urban Character of Christian Worship*, Orientalia Christiana Analecta, 228 (Rome, 1987); Angelus Albert Häußling, *Mönchskonvent und Eucharistiefeier. Eine Studie über die Messe in der abendländischen Klosterliturgie des frühen Mittelalters und zur Geschichte der Meßhäufigkeit*, Liturgiewissenschaftliche Quellen und Forschungen, 58 (Münster, 1973); Rosamond McKitterick, 'Charlemagne, Rome and the Management of Sacred Space', in R. Große and M. Sot (eds.), *Charlemagne: les temps, les espaces, les hommes. Construction et déconstruction* (Turnhout, 2018), pp.165–79.

[31] Egeria, *Itinerarium*, in Aet Franceschini and R. Weber (eds.), *Itineraria et alia geographica*, Corpus Christianorum Series Latina, 175 (Turnhout, 1965), pp.27–103; also in Pierre Maraval, *Égérie. Journal de voyage (Itinéraire)* (Paris, 1982); English translation in Anne McGowan and Paul F. Bradshaw (eds.), *The Pilgrimage of Egeria* (Collegeville, Minnesota, 2018).

12   Introduction

entirely distinct texts from the *ordines*, and both furnish the same attempts to make Rome visible, in a way which isolating the *ordines* as purely 'liturgical' obscures.

Participation in these processes necessitated at least some acquaintance with Roman custom and norms. Certain ceremonies and elements of ceremonies described in the *ordines romani* were specifically restricted to the Pope alone, and the Franks were interested in understanding which ones they were, and why. In particular, the history of liturgical usages was plainly a subject of a very keen interest in the period, and compilers combed the records of papal letters, councils and histories to find the origin and meaning of the practices which animated their religious life. Walahfrid Strabo's *Libellus de exordiis*, a particularly striking and thorough examination of liturgical history, is the most famous example, but, although Walahfrid is often presented as singular, the same preoccupation can be much more widely demonstrated, not least in the manuscripts of the *ordines*, which extract from historical documents the most useful and pertinent documents to give context to their liturgical descriptions.[32] Such texts helped make the image of Rome a dynamic, almost timeless one, in which the city's sacred history, as much as its topographical present, was a resource on which the reader could draw.

The Creativity of the Carolingian Liturgy

The focus of much liturgical scholarship on recovering purer, more authentic originals (which could be linked to 'reform' movements, or to the purity of the antique liturgy of Rome) has meant that the techniques and priorities of individual, most often anonymous scribes and compilers were not generally interrogated, being obstacles to the kind of research such liturgists really wanted to do, that is, uncover the 'pure' original. The set ideas of what a liturgical book was for, and of the genres into which it was to be placed, also made it difficult to access Carolingian ingenuity.

Once identified as the best representatives of what reform movements aimed to accomplish, official 'types' were edited and presented in grand synthetic editions, like that of Andrieu. Since these editions were much more accessible and usable than a diverse and diffuse manuscript tradition, they tended to accrue ever more authority as the 'truer' representation of how liturgy was understood in the given period. Therefore, such

---

[32] Walahfrid Strabo, *Libellus de exordiis et incrementis quarundam in observationibus ecclesiasticis rerum*, Alice Harting-Correa (ed.), Mittellateinische Studien und Texte, 19 (New York, 1996).

The Creativity of the Carolingian Liturgy   13

reconstructions have tended to deemphasise the possibility of any significant individual or local input into the process of liturgical change. A sense of how creative individual scribes could be with liturgical material has not always reached the broader treatments of medieval culture. Liturgy is not often permitted to contribute to broader discussions of medieval practices of compiling and presenting knowledge, or of manuscript organisation. A manuscript might organise and present liturgical material in a way that is not easily recognisable in the modern 'type'. It might seem to have never been copied afterwards or to have had any lasting observable impact. But it is still an equally valuable expression of how scribes were able to experiment with organising a form of knowledge that had a particular malleability. Examined as a particular product of a particular milieu, manuscripts can reveal 'human stories' of how individuals responded to the liturgy and made use of it.[33]

Under the Carolingians, a new liturgical synthesis was certainly achieved.[34] We cannot understand the appearance and copying of the *ordines* without taking into account the simultaneous appearance of new ways of representing and sharing liturgical knowledge. New types of books were placed in circulation, and new types of texts were incorporated in them. New techniques of organisation and compilation appeared. We find in this period the earliest examples of gatherings of liturgical material into books that would later become standard elements of the liturgical arsenal, such as what we call today the 'pontifical', the book for a bishop's liturgical usage.[35] By looking to individual manuscripts as the products of specific local needs, we can get closer to the picture of a creative liturgical culture capable of making such innovations at every level, rather than one which simply copied what it was given by rote.[36]

The Franks also began the large-scale interpretation of the liturgy as a form of knowledge which presented and continually re-enacted the truths

---

[33] Parkes, *Making of Liturgy*, p.2.

[34] Rosamond McKitterick, *The Frankish Church and the Carolingian Reforms 789–895* (London, 1977), pp.116–154; Eric Palazzo, 'La liturgie carolingienne: vieux débats, nouvelles questions, publications recentes', in Falkowski and Sasser (eds.), *Le monde carolingien*, pp.219–241.

[35] Vogel, *Medieval Liturgy*, pp.226–230; Sarah Hamilton, 'The Early Pontificals: Anglo-Saxon Evidence Reconsidered from a Continental Perspective', in David Rollason, Conrad Leyser, and Hannah Williams (eds.), *England and the Continent in the Tenth Century* (Turnhout, 2011), pp.415–420; Westwell, 'Content and the Ideological Construction'; Arthur Westwell, 'Three Ninth-Century Liturgical Fragments Identified as Pontificals in Heidelberg, Douai and Innsbruck', *RevBen*, 131 (2021), pp.387–406.

[36] Another vital innovation was the invention of musical notation: Susan Rankin, *Writing Sounds in Carolingian Europe: The Invention of Musical Notation* (Cambridge, 2019). As Rankin argued, neums are misinterpreted when seen purely and judged as antecedents of modern musical notation, but rather should be understood within their own context, interacting with memorisation.

of the Christian faith. Texts that we term *expositiones* and which explain the meaning and history of various ritual acts, most notably Mass and baptism, flourish in this period.[37] The proliferation of this genre in the ninth century caused an efflorescence of different interpretations, taking different methods to different conclusions. They address people at all levels of society and with every conceivable level of sophistication. Among the vast stock of the anonymous texts, the popular synthetic treatment by Amalarius of Metz in the *Liber Officialis* is noteworthy. In the manuscript tradition, it has a particularly close relation to the *ordines romani*.[38] In the majority of such explanations, the ritual that is explained is not identical to any surviving liturgical description at all. The *expositiones* challenge our assumptions by revealing even more diversity in how rituals could be put into practice, far beyond what the liturgical books tell us. When seeking the meaning of rites, *expositiones* go far beyond liturgical texts themselves. They described rituals before these were ever actually openly recorded in liturgical texts. They show the wide range of possible ideas that could enter into thinking about the liturgy, and into putting it into practice. Such texts would form part of the mental foundations with which readers would approach the translation of a liturgical text into a performance, and how they understood the latter. It is therefore important that the manuscripts which carry such *expositiones* (and which often transmit them alongside liturgical texts like *ordines*) do not offer only one example each as the only 'correct' way to understand rituals like the Mass or baptism, but, as a matter of course, offer several different versions for the reader to compare and contrast. Such manuscripts should be understood as the principal way that thinking about the liturgy was disseminated to clergy at every level. They show how the Carolingian Church saw in the liturgy a potential for a broad range of understandings and uses.[39]

---

[37] André Wilmart, 'Expositio Missae', in Fernand Cabrol and Henri Leclercq (eds.), *Dictionnaire d'archéologie chrétienne et de liturgie*, vol. V (Paris, 1922), col. 1014–1027; Susan Keefe, *Water and the Word, Baptism and the Education of the Clergy in the Carolingian Empire*, 2 vols. (Notre Dame, 2002); Christopher Jones, 'The Book of the Liturgy in Anglo-Saxon England', *Speculum*, 73 (1996), pp.659–702.

[38] Amalarius' *Liber Officialis*, Jean Michel Hanssens (ed.), *Amalarii episcopi opera liturgica omnia*, vol. II (Vatican City, 1948); English translation by Erik Knibbs (ed.), *On the Liturgy*, 2 vols. (Cambridge, MA, 2014).

[39] Carine van Rhijn, 'The Local Church, Priests' Handbooks and Pastoral Care in the Carolingian Period', in *Chiese locali e chiese regionali nell'alto Medioevo*, Settimane di Studio del Centro Italiano di Studi Sull'Alto Medioevo, 61 (Spoleto, 2014), pp.689–709; Carine van Rhijn, 'Manuscripts for Local Priests and the Carolingian Reforms', in Steffen Patzold and Carine van Rhijn (eds.), *Men in the Middle: Local Priests in Early Medieval Europe* (Berlin, 2016), pp.177–198; Steffen Patzold, *Presbyter. Moral, Mobilität und die Kirchenorganisation im Karolingerreich* (Stuttgart, 2020).

The Creativity of the Carolingian Liturgy

We see in these texts how the Frankish idea of Rome acted as the spur to innovation, and that Frankish compilers and liturgists at every level thought deeply and acted resourcefully in ways that made their model work for them. Because the *ordines romani* appear as something entirely new in the Carolingian era, and because their organisation into discrete manuscripts represents a real innovation in book formatting, this corpus of texts allows us to examine the techniques of compilation and presentation in a judicious way. They simultaneously allow us to discuss the broader liturgical context, and how liturgy really changed in the Early Middle Ages. Likewise, because of their relation to the 'arrangement' of liturgical feasts, '*ordines* lent themselves to conscious propagandizing' more than most kinds of liturgical texts, as Bullough has observed.[40] We thus have a particularly direct access to the thought and agendas of individual compilers who were working on the ground, enacting their own visions of appropriating Roman liturgical actions and Rome itself.

Some liturgical scholars focused exclusively or overwhelmingly on the 'Roman rite' and its history. Yet we must stress the extent to which what we categorise today as 'Roman' liturgy was for the first time written down and organised in recognisable forms by Frankish copyists. Given the confessional orientation of liturgical studies, the question of the Roman-ness of *ordines*, and what form a Roman original would have taken, has been the paramount concern. Frankish adaptations were noted principally as a way 'through' the texts to the supposed purer and more valuable Roman original. In scholarship, the role of the Carolingian Church in liturgical history has been consistently downplayed by the focus on the authority and purity of Rome's tradition, and on the presentation of 'reform' as the almost unthinking reception and replication of that tradition. This study aims to redress the balance, by making known how vital and lasting this Carolingian contribution was.

Part I establishes how compilers were not overly concerned with 'pure' presentations of only the verifiable Roman usages, but rather allowed Roman and Frankish rituals to coexist in a single manuscript. Chapter 1 discusses a Collection of *ordines* visible in multiple manuscripts that Andrieu designated as 'Roman', showing that it developed much more gradually within Frankish monasteries and that compilers had numerous interests at work as they copied. The same is true in the 'Frankish collection', the subject of Chapter 2, which also contains many examples of the first manuscripts designated as 'pontificals', or books supposedly for the use of a bishop.

---

[40] Donald Bullough, 'Roman Books and Carolingian *Renovatio*', in *Carolingian Renewal: Sources and Heritage* (Manchester, 1991), p.9.

16 Introduction

Some of these manuscripts intensify their reference to Rome, others add Frankish rituals and customs, but all show an active and continual reinterpretation and recontextualisation of the *ordines*. Chapter 3 is concerned with even more unique collections, that survive in only one manuscript, and often seem to represent the project and interests of an individual even more clearly than in other cases. Finally, Chapter 4 considers how *ordines* were read in all these cases, presenting the evidence that liturgical usefulness and the abstract study of liturgy were not diametrically opposed visions, but coexist easily and seamlessly in *ordines* manuscripts. This chapter argues that projecting liturgical genres of the later period onto these manuscripts has obscured the individual character of each.

Part II probes the representation of individual rituals in the *ordines romani*. Chapter 5 discusses the Mass, showing how the Franks made use of the Roman stational Mass, and were deeply invested in understanding its peculiarities. Chapter 6 concerns itself with a single case study, demonstrating how a text hitherto taken as a Roman original, *Ordo* 11, concerned with baptism, was in fact a Frankish development taken out of the Sacramentary. Chapter 7 discusses the rites of ordination and Holy Week. Finally, Part III with its single Chapter 8 deals with the physicality and composition of the corpus of manuscripts, as representations of Carolingian innovations in format and presentation, discussing palaeography, layout and structure, what the use of these manuscripts could have been and by whom they were used. In the Conclusion, the *ordines* are placed within a circle of elite Carolingian churchmen who venerated Rome's sacredness and understood how to harnass and use the textual and ritual reference to the city, and linked to various other efforts to import Rome to a new context.

Given the manuscript-focused nature of the study, where relevant, I will indicate those manuscripts I was able to examine in person. Unfortunately, due to the impact of the Coronavirus (COVID-19) pandemic, not all planned research trips could take place. In these cases, I have availed myself of the excellent digitisations, particularly those provided by the St Gallen Stiftsbibliothek, St Gallen and the Herzog August Bibliothek, Wolfenbüttel, as well as the Bibliotheca Lareshamensis digital project.

Note on the Text

When making quotations from Latin texts, italics indicate words that are spoken, while bold text indicates text that is highlighted in the manuscript, or to which the author wishes to draw attention as the feature of an individual manuscript.

PART I

Compilation and Content of the Manuscripts

CHAPTER I

The 'Roman' Collection of Ordines in Metz, Lorsch and Tours

Texts identified and edited as *ordines romani* appear in various forms and in various contexts. In the definitions presented by Andrieu and Vogel, an *ordo* was conceived as a 'pure' representation of action and gesture, distinct from other elements of the narrative of liturgical ceremonial.[1] For example, in Vogel's influential handbook, they are described thus: 'an *Ordo* is a description of a liturgical action, a directory or guide for the celebrant and his ministers, setting forth in detail the arrangement of the entire ritual procedure and how to carry it out. As descriptive of the actual rite, the *ordines* are the indispensable complement to the Sacramentary'.[2] This counterpart, the Sacramentary or Mass Book, properly contained only prayers and spoken texts, and these were likewise supposed to be fully separable and extricable in their original conception. Yet it is rare to see any *ordo* of which one could say such a thing without qualification. In Andrieu's works, this idea of purity of content is implicitly linked to the purity of Roman origin: that is, his reconstruction of *ordines* that were created and used in Rome, and represented wholly the Roman liturgy before Frankish copyists began to adulterate and alter them. Originally, such *ordines* had been copied individually or in small booklets whose aim was to propagate Roman usages; all surviving manuscripts represented the movement away from this. Again, we might quote Vogel: 'Before they were gathered in Collections, each *Ordo* – which described a single *actio liturgica* or some part thereof – existed completely on its own . . . and were gathered for the first time only in Gaul.'[3] None of these hypothetical original settings of these texts has survived.

The idea that different books classified in the same genre might have different usages, or indeed that different components of the same book

---

[1] *Les Ordines*, vol. II p.xlvi–xlviii; Martimort, *Les Ordines, les ordinaries et les cérémoniaux*; Vogel, *Medieval Liturgy*, pp.135–224.
[2] *Ibid.*, p.135.   [3] *Ibid.*, p.138.

19

The 'Roman' Collection of *Ordines*

might have been read in different ways, and so help to interpret each other, was not integrated into this understanding of liturgical books, which employed a zero-sum understanding of this category of 'liturgical' (as being for ritual use). Such an understanding, however, is not evidenced in Carolingian attitudes to such books. For the Carolingians, texts we describe as 'liturgical' were comprehensible in various formats, and the *ordines* present this phenomenon particularly plainly. Carolingian manuscripts of the *ordines romani* raise questions concerning modern assumptions about the purpose and nature of the written liturgy, which, when addressed, allow a better understanding of the creative agency of manuscript creators and users, and ultimately the purposes of the *ordines* as copied and shared by them.

A great deal of background lay behind the assumed framings of Vogel and Andrieu. In the twentieth century, the history of liturgy was discussed in a certain way, with a certain background of assumed truths or 'laws' that still remain difficult to fully escape. One might, for example, quote Ellard's formulation that: 'the growth of liturgical ceremonial there operates first of all by that law of evolution where the rudimentary tends to perfection' (i.e. the medieval liturgy is perceived as the evolutionary antecedent to modern practices).[4] Scholars like Andrieu attained a deep acquaintance with the texts and the meaning of liturgy that is difficult to emulate, and were most often liturgical practitioners themselves. But analysing liturgy as a historical source which provides some insight into the mindset of manuscript compilers requires that we sometimes take a different approach from theirs.

In the following treatment, manuscripts of the 'collections' of *ordines* will be examined and, where possible, links to known figures and locations used to help explore the use and reinterpretation of the texts which they contain. Critical and new in Andrieu's study of the *ordines* were the discovery of Collections of the *ordines romani* that circulated in one or more manuscripts. In his editions, these were said to represent deliberate configurations of several *ordines* to a single purpose. Most widely witnessed were two to which Andrieu gave particular significance: Collection A or the 'Roman Collection', and Collection B or the 'Frankish Collection'.

Within the framing of the medieval liturgy and how it was changed, as delineated above, Andrieu's analysis assigned a reconstructed purpose and use to various manuscripts. The first of them, Collection A, he suggested, began life as the definitive attempt to establish purely Roman usages in

---

[4] Gerald Ellard, *Ordination Anointings in the Western Church Before 1000 AD* (Cambridge, MA, 1933), pp.3–4.

The 'Roman' Collection of Ordines

Francia.[5] Only the purest Roman *ordines* were selected for this purpose. Other scholars wondered consequently if Collection A could have been the product of an official 'reform' effort by Pippin III, or even if it was a work of the famous Alcuin of York (735–804).[6] The compilation was dated by Andrieu in around 750, and he inclined to somewhere in modern-day France as the place of compilation. Drawing a specific analogy to the Gregorian Sacramentary that Charlemagne received around 785, he suggested that Frankish churchmen soon found the Collection too specialised in its presentation of specifically Roman liturgical usages. Later copies should rather be interpreted as 'library copies' for study outside a liturgical context, entirely different in their conception from the first few. Collection A is given by Andrieu as:

> *Ordo Romanus* 1, the Papal stational Mass.[7] This is, more specifically, the so-called 'long recension' of the text.
>
> *Ordo Romanus* 11, baptismal ritual with preceding scrutinies.[8]
>
> *Ordo Romanus* 27, an *ordo* of Holy Week from Wednesday created by the fusion of pre-existing text *Ordo Romanus* 24 and 26, plus the Vespers for the week after Easter, which include Roman stations.[9]
>
> *Ordo Romanus* 42, the Roman order for depositing relics in a new church.[10]
>
> *Ordo Romanus* 34, the Roman order for ordinations to the grades of the church from acolyte to bishop.[11]
>
> *Ordo Romanus* 13A, an order of the sequence in which the non-Gospel Books of the Bible are to be read in the course of the year.[12]

No manuscript evidence for any of these individual components is known to survive from before the closing decades of the eighth century. Surviving manuscripts also suggest a more gradual process of compilation, with no definitive form of the Collection, and considerable freedom to add additional content.

Significant redating of several manuscripts, as well as more precise localisation of them, permits us to give new context to the Collections and individual manuscripts. This is mostly thanks to the verdicts of Bernhard Bischoff. Along with his *Katalog*, I have consulted his Nachlass in the Bayerische, Staatsbibliothek, ANA 553, in order to better understand

---

[5] *Les Ordines*, vol. I, p.467–470: 'La collection que nous venons de décrire était purement romaine.'

[6] Vogel, 'La réforme liturgique', p.218; Emmanuel Bourque, *Étude sur les sacramentaires romains*, vol. II pt. 2 (Rome, 1958), p.96; Hen, *Royal Patronage*, p.63.

[7] *Les Ordines*, vol. II, pp.3–108.

[8] *Ibid.*, pp.365–447; Keefe provides a helpful summary in English: Keefe, *Water and the Word*, vol. I, pp.43–44.

[9] *Les Ordines*, vol. III, pp.333–372.　　[10] *Les Ordines*, vol. IV, pp.359–384.

[11] *Les Ordines*, vol. III, pp.534–613.　　[12] *Les Ordines*, vol. II, pp.469–488.

22   The 'Roman' Collection of *Ordines*

and evaluate the reasoning behind these often very important decisions. The earliest available manuscript of Collection A is now identifiable as BAV, MS Pal.lat.487, which actually contains only *Ordines* I, II, 27 and 34, lacking two of the texts, *Ordines* 13A and 42.[13] It was written at Lorsch towards the end of the eighth century, and was often used as the 'best' manuscript for Andrieu's editions because it preserves a text of *Ordo* I and the others quite close to what Andrieu had reconstructed as the Roman 'original'. This suggests the importance of Lorsch as the node for the initial distribution of the Collection. The key to this importance is likely to be Lorsch's close links with the bishopric of Metz and notably Chrodegang of Metz, bishop of Metz 742/748 to 766, who took a decisive part in the founding of the monastery in 764.[14] He provided Lorsch with the relics of Nazarius, a Roman martyr, given to him by Pope Paul I, which became central to the monastery's liturgical identity.[15]

Another clue that elements of Collection A perhaps came to Lorsch via Metz and which provides a possible connection with Chrodegang is the manuscript Bern, Burgerbibliothek, MS 289, specifically the parts fols.1–19, which can be dated around the same period as the Lorsch manuscript, at the end of the eighth century.[16] This fragmentary manuscript gives us a partial text of *Ordo* I (nn.36–64), the key text of Collection A, which also opens the Lorsch manuscript. The state of the text of this *ordo* is closest to that of BAV Pal.lat.487. Since the end of the text is lost, and we cannot say what followed, it is quite possible other *ordines* were originally present – perhaps four *ordines* from Collection A, just as in Lorsch? Certainly, directly proceeding *Ordo* I in these fragments we find also the Rule of Chrodegang himself for the canonical clergy of his cathedral. Since the manuscript ends before the end of *Ordo* I, we cannot know if the manuscript originally contained the rest of Collection A, but perhaps this is not unlikely, since the version of the text otherwise can only be found with the other elements of that Collection. Can

---

[13] *Les Ordines*, vol. I, pp.319–321; Bischoff, *Katalog*, vol. III. 6532. p.414; Bernhard Bischoff, *Die Abtei Lorsch im Spiegel ihrer Handschriften* (Munich, 1974), pp.21–22; Digitised at http://bibliotheca-lauresamensis-digital.de/bav/bav_pal_lat_487/0001/image?sid=c3cb487033166a1c8a1a3b17aeb40cb3b.

[14] Josef Semmler, 'Chrodegang, Bishof von Metz 747–766', in Friedrich Knöpp (ed.), *Die Reichsabtei Lorsch: Festschrift zum Gedenken an ihre Stiftung 764*, vol.I (Darmstadt, 1973), pp.229–245; Marty A. Claussen, *The Reform of the Frankish Church: Chrodegang of Metz and the Regula Canonicorum in the Eighth Century* (Cambridge, 2004).

[15] Paul the Deacon, *Gesta Episcoporum Mettensium*, Georg Heinrich Pertz (ed.), *MGH Scriptores rerum Sangellensium. Annales, chronica historiae aevi Carolini* (Hanover, 1829), p.268. Later Mass Books of the monastery, such as the lavish fragment in Erlangen, UB MS 2000, highlight the martyr's name. This is digitised at: https://hs-lorsch.bsz-bw.de/cgi-bin/koha/opac-detail.PL?biblionumber=1123.

[16] *Les Ordines*, vol. I, p.90; *CLA*, vol. VII, p.861; Bischoff, *Katalog*, vol. I, p.121: 'Metz (1) VIII/IX Jh. (IX Jh. Anfang).'

The 'Roman' Collection of Ordines   23

we then uncover Chrodegang's role in the transmission of some early *ordines*, and link Lorsch's reception and copying of an early form of Collection A to its connections to the bishopric of Metz?

Of similar age to the Lorsch manuscript are the various fragments of a manuscript probably copied in Murbach monastery and taken to Regensburg, which are found today in Munich, Regensburg and in Sankt-Paul in Lavanttal, of which Andrieu knew only the latter fragment. This book seems to have originally contained only the same four texts as the Lorsch example (pieces survive of characteristic elements of *Ordo* 34 and *Ordo* 27).[17] An abbot of Murbach from 789 was called Simpert, and a bishop of the same name is found in Regensburg from 768 to 791. It is likely that these were the same man, particularly since Charlemagne himself then took over as abbot of Murbach from 792, presumably following the death of Simpert.[18] Clear evidence of the transmission of manuscripts from the Alsatian monastery of Murbach to Regensburg would support an identity of the two, and help to explain our manuscript's provenance.[19] Simpert, through his presence at the court of Charlemagne, was closely associated with the archchancellor and bishop of Metz, Angilram (bishop 777–791), successor to Chrodegang. Furthermore, Simpert of Regensburg went on campaign against the Avars in the company of Charlemagne and Angilram of Metz. Both Simpert and Angilram died during that campaign. Given that the Lorsch manuscript, the Bern fragments and also the Murbach fragments were all copied not in Chrodegang's lifetime but towards the end of the eighth century, Angilram of Metz emerges as another contender for involvement in the initial transmission of Collection A, at least in its original form with just four constituent texts (*Ordines* I, II, 27 and 34), not the six reconstructed by Andrieu.

In addition to his links with Simpert of Murbach and Regensburg, Angilram also had close relations with Lorsch, and consecrated the church

---

[17] On the Sankt Paul fragment 979 fol.1r–v (now perhaps lost), see *Les Ordines*, vol. I, pp.347–349. The four additional folios, now Munich, BSB, Clm 14659, Clm 14655 and Regensburg, Staatliche Bibliothek, fragm.2, are described and dated in Bernhard Bischoff, *Die Südostdeutschen schreibschulen und Bibliotheken in der Karolingerzeit*, vol.I, 3rd ed. (Wiesbaden, 1974), pp.197–198 and vol. II (Wiesbaden, 1980), pp.237–238, and Bischoff, *Katalog*, vol. II, 3239, p.261. I have seen all these fragments in person, except that in Sankt Paul.

[18] Simpert of Murbach is sometimes identified as the bishop of Augsburg of the same name (bishop, 778–807), but Charlemagne's acquisition of the abbacy in 792 is less easy to explain had Abbot Simpert still been alive. On Simpert of Augsburg, Wilhelm Volkert and Friedrich Zoepfl, *Die Regesten der Bischöfe und des Domkapitels von Augsburg*, vol. I (Augsburg, 1985), pp.20–29.

[19] A number of other manuscripts with script very similar to our fragments made the same journey: Munich, BSB, Clm 14082 and Clm 14379 and Würzburg, UB M.p.th.o.1 (*CLA*, vol. IX, p.1442); Bischoff, *Die südostdeutschen Schreibschulen*, vol. II, p.241.

24 The 'Roman' Collection of *Ordines*

there.[20] He was also interested in his predecessor's Rule, a copy of which forms part of the Bern manuscript, which was likely made during his episcopacy, and the text was adapted with Angilram's own additions.[21] There is also some evidence for a Metz connection, and one to Angilram specifically, in a late copy of Collection A, British Library, Add. MS 15222, produced in Besançon during the eleventh century, which undoubtedly goes back to a Metz archetype.[22] It contains the unique copy of an institute issued by Angilram recording how much he paid his clergy for various functions on high feasts, including a stational system for Lent in Metz described as 'iuxta consuetudinem sedis apostolicae'.[23] It is difficult to explain the text's presence in this manuscript without assuming a Metz exemplar probably before Angilram's own death, from which was copied (either directly or at one or more stages removed) the Besançon manuscript some centuries later. Since a restoration and extension of canonical life was being undertaken in Besançon at this time under Archbishop Hugh of Salins (bishop 1031–1066), and with particular attention to liturgy, a memory of Carolingian Metz's role in the institution of common life, and of Chrodegang and Angilram as founders, probably helps to explain why the Collection was copied there.[24] A connection between Angilram of Metz, canonical life in a cathedral city, Roman stational usages, and Collection A of the *ordines romani* seems to still have been alive in Besançon in the eleventh century.

The complete Collection A, as Andrieu reconstructed it, had two additional texts however, *Ordines* 13A and 42, which deal with the Matins biblical readings of the liturgical year and with church dedication respectively. Andrieu's own 'best' example of this complete Collection and the first to carry all six *ordines*, Montpellier, Bibliothèque de la Faculté de Médecine, MS 412, is from the first quarter of the ninth century, and was written at Tours.[25] The two additional texts which were added to the Collection in this example, *Ordo* 13A at the opening of the Collection and *Ordo* 42 at the closing of it, are notably also witnessed in manuscripts

---

[20] Otto Gerhard Oexle, 'Die Karolinger und die Stadt des heiligen Arnulf', *Frühmittelalterliche Studien*, 1 (1967), pp.250–364, at p.296.

[21] Jerome Bertram (ed.), *The Chrodegang Rules* (Aldershot, 2005), pp.39, 67.

[22] *Les Ordines*, vol. I, pp.142–144; Westwell, 'Content and Ideological Construction', pp.233–251; I have examined this manuscript in person.

[23] Michel Andrieu, 'Règlement d'Angilramne de Metz (768–793) fixant les honoraires de quelques fonctions liturgiques', *Revue des sciences religeuses*, 10 (1930), pp.349–369; see Chapter 3.

[24] Maurice Ray, *Les Diocèses de Besançon et de Saint-Claude* (Paris, 1977), pp.30–32.

[25] *Les Ordines*, vol. I, pp.467–468; Bischoff, *Katalog*, vol. II, n.2873, p.209: 'Tours, [IX. Jh., 1./2. Viertel].'

The 'Roman' Collection of Ordines 25

that are independent of the same Collection, indicating differing provenance. *Ordo* 42 can also be found in Albi, Bibliothèque Municipale, MS 42, which has some connection to Reims.[26] Though Albi 42 also included *Ordo* 1 (fols.60r–68r), it has a form of that text that has some independence from Collection A, perhaps representing an earlier version.[27] It also contains *Ordines* 24 and 26, the principal sources for Collection A's *Ordo* 27 but not that text itself. Despite its late date, Albi 42 therefore gives the impression of being a copy of an older archetype, a possibility that we will subsequently explore. But in this case, it indicates availability of *Ordo* 42 in France independently of Collection A.

Ordo 13A appears in a number of other manuscripts besides those containing Collection A, of which ninth- and tenth-century examples include: Douai, BM, MS 14; Vercelli, Archivio Capitolare, MS 183; St Gallen, Stiftsbibliothek, MS 225; Reims, BM, MS 1; Munich, BSB, Clm 6398 and 14470; Rouen, BM, MS 26; and BAV, MS Vat.lat.6018.[28] In some of these cases, *Ordo* 13A was added on spare folios of manuscripts of various kinds.[29] The St Gallen and Vercelli examples are the oldest, and date to the end of the eighth century, which demonstrates that this *ordo* already existed before its incorporation in the Collection.[30] They both include the *ordo* among patristic extracts, which suggests an understanding of the text as an authoritative one among the 'Fathers'.[31] However Reims 1, Douai 14 and BAV Vat.lat.6018 are the only three of these manuscripts to include a particular textual addition (*Ordo* 13A, nn.3–5) that is also found in manuscripts of Collection A which contain that *Ordo*, such as

---

[26] *Les Ordines*, vol. I, pp.32–34, 487; Bischoff, *Katalog*, vol. I, n.24 p.11: 'Nördliches Frankreich (Reimser Umkreis?).' A Reims connection and evidence of *terminus post quem* are also found in the copy of the 852 Capitulary of Hincmar of Reims and a letter of the monk Almannus of the monastery of Hautvillers in that diocese. I have examined this manuscript in person.

[27] *Les Ordines*, vol. II, pp.21–22: 'des traditions antérieures á l'établissement des deux collections A (Coll. Romaine) et B (Coll. Gallicanisée)'.

[28] *Les Ordines*, vol. II, p.470.

[29] In Munich, BSB, Clm 6398, following the text of Priscian's *Institutiones Grammaticae*; in Reims 1 added after the Book of Kings. In BAV Vat.lat.6018 it was added on the final folio, fol.129r–v, of a manuscript containing the Chronicle of Isidore and the *Decretum Gelasianum De libris recipiendis ac non recipiendis*, for which see *Les Ordines*, vol. I, p.304; digitised at: https://digi.vatlib.it/view/MSS_Vat.lat.6018/0191.

[30] On St Gallen 225: *Les Ordines*, vol. I, p.330; Gustav Scherrer, *Verzeichnis der Handschriften der Stiftsbibliothek von St. Gallen* (Halle, 1875), pp.80–81; digitised at: www.e-codices.unifr.ch/en/list/one/csg/0225; on Vercelli 183: *Les Ordines*, vol. I, p.367.

[31] In Vercelli 183, it follows directly the text of *De institutione divinarum litterarum* of Cassiodorus. It is also among patristic semons and homilies at fol.73r–74r in Munich, BSB, Clm 14470, a ninth-century manuscript from Saint-Emmeram in Regensburg (digitised at: www.digitale-sammlungen.de/de/view/bsb00022361?page=1). The text is found in a similar setting in Rouen 26 (from Jumièges): *Les Ordines*, vol. I, p.324.

Montpellier 412. Douai 14 is closest to Collection A in other details.[32] Two of these manuscripts come from Reims. Both are biblical: Reims 1 is part of the Bible presented by Archbishop Hincmar (845–822) to the Cathedral, and Douai 14 is an Old Testament manuscript, located to Reims by Bischoff.[33] Therefore, the circulation of *Ordo* 13A, like *Ordo* 42, in Northern France can be securely established, as well as its presence in numerous centres elsewhere. When combined with the evidence of *Ordo* 42's presence in Northern France, it was probably in this region that Collection A, having come from Metz, was enhanced with these two additional *ordines*.

Our earliest known copy of the full Collection is Montpellier, Faculté de Medecine, MS 412, copied at the abbey of St Martin, Tours, in the Loire valley. The only other ninth-century manuscript with the same full collection is Copenhagen, Kongelige Bibliotek, MS Gl. kgl. 3443, dating to the boundary between the ninth and tenth century, locatable to France.[34] This rather late manuscript is, in fact, the only one which carries Andrieu's Collection A apparently without the addition of any other *ordines* (leaves are now missing, the final item ending partway through *Ordo* 13A). Such evidence is not at all conducive to regarding the accomplishment of Collection A as already completed by the year 750, as Andrieu did.[35] We should probably therefore trace Collection A's creation on the basis of the surviving manuscripts, uncovering an initial collection of four distinct *ordines* towards the end of the eighth century in Metz, and an enhancement of this with two additional *ordines* around the beginning of the ninth, possibly in Northern France. The second, enhanced version also came to form the source for Collection B, probably redacted in Alemannia or Northern Italy, as we will see.

So, we come to the key question: did the compilers and copyists of the Collection A see themselves as copying a 'Roman collection', and were they selecting specifically and purely Roman *ordines* for the role, as Andrieu assumed? In the original collection, as transmitted in the Lorsch and Murbach manuscripts, which I attributed to Angilram of Metz, none of the four *ordines* were actually composed by Romans.

Ordo 1 has long been held to be a Roman document, but no knowledge of the text can be demonstrated in Rome. The assertion of Roman origin has tended to go together with the assumption of an early date for the text,

---

[32] *Les Ordines*, vol. II, p.471.　　[33] Bischoff, *Katalog*, vol. I, p.223: 'Reims, IX Jh., 3. Viertel.'
[34] *Les Ordines*, vol. I, pp.114–116; Bischoff, *Katalog*, vol. I, p.412: 'Etwa Ostfrankreich.'
[35] *Les Ordines*, vol. I, pp.468–470.

The 'Roman' Collection of Ordines

around 750. This latter assumption is perilous, since the text cannot be evidenced in any way so early. However, even those who maintain Roman origin for the 'long recension' of *Ordo* I concede the 'short recension', found in one manuscript, to be Frankish.[36] But if we accept Andrieu's argument that the 'long recension' is based on the 'short', as I do, and that the 'short recension' was known in Francia and used before the 'long recension' was known there, the Frankish origin of the latter can likely also be assumed.[37] The precise origin of this text, however, is less important for this study, which is focused on the purpose or purposes for which manuscript copies were made. However, in Chapter 4, I will present additional evidence against Andrieu's belief that *Ordo* I constitutes an accurate representation of Roman liturgical practice, namely a blatant error in the discussion of the *immixtio* in the text, for which the 'short recension' presents a more accurate description of Roman practice than the 'long'. The more it becomes clear that the Romans did not record texts such as *Ordo* I, and that the *ordines romani* are Frankish documents, the more the evidence is weighed to the probability that *Ordo* I was a Frankish document too. To this effect, I will also argue below that *Ordo* II, the baptismal text and another key element of Collection A, was not a Roman text at all, but was almost entirely written by Franks to begin to fill in very sparse rubrics in the Sacramentary.[38]

Of the four texts in the Lorsch manuscript, *Ordo* 34 has the strongest claim to be a Roman document, but this too becomes more problematic upon closer examination. This text describes the ordinations of the clerical orders from acolyte to subdeacon. The terminology and procedures are accurate for practice at Rome: all are undertaken by the *domnus apostolicus* (the Pope) and the episcopal ordination takes place in the 'aulam beati Petri apostoli' (*Ordo* 34, n.18). Nevertheless, in one key intervention, the text includes the note (*Ordo* 34 n.16) that the women called *ancilla dei sacrata* in Rome are called nuns by the Franks ('quae a Francis nonnata dicitur').[39] This indicates that a Frankish audience was also in mind. This part of the *ordo* also cites, it seems, the true Roman wording of the interrogation *quattuor capitulis secundum canones* (four things the bishop

[36] John Romano, 'The Fates of Liturgies: Towards a History of the First Roman Ordo', *Antiphon*, 11 (2007), pp.43–77.

[37] Peter Jeffrey's forthcoming new edition of *Ordo* I will argue for a Frankish origin for both recensions (as reported orally in his presentation at Leeds International Medieval Congress 2020).

[38] See Chapter 4; Antoine Chavasse, *Le sacramentaire gélasien (Vaticanus Reginensis 316): Sacramentaire presbyteral en usage dans les titres romains au VIIe siècle* (Tournai, 1957), pp.166–168.

[39] *Les Ordines*, vol. III, p.607.

28   The 'Roman' Collection of *Ordines*

must not have done), but also interprets the complex vocabulary and Greek terms which the Romans seem to have used for them, again it would seem for a non-Roman (and presumably Frankish) audience.[40]

Andrieu assumed that the text had been redacted by a cleric in the Lateran Basilica in Rome, but the intervention directly addressed to Franks makes it more likely that a foreign cleric present in Rome, who observed ordinations, carefully recorded the text for a Frankish audience, with much the same care as we see in *Ordo* 1. This suggestion should not be dismissed simply because, as Andrieu has put it, the ordination rites were not directly applicable in the Frankish realms, for it is evident that the Franks were interested in the rites they themselves could not do (as we shall see in the Frankish manuscript witnesses to *Ordines* 1 and 26 below).[41] Andrieu also adduced as evidence in support of his argument that Pope Hadrian I had cited 'toute au long notre document' ('quoted our document throughout'), in a letter to Charlemagne of 790–791.[42] However, although Hadrian's description accords in general with *Ordo* 34 and secures its general accuracy in describing Roman practice, he did not directly cite the text at all, nor indicate its availability in Rome. He spoke only in very general terms of his interrogation of the newly elected bishop, without citing any of the details of the ritual surrounding it which are described in *Ordo* 34.[43] This corresponds generally with the interrogation by the Pope on the *quattuor capitula* described by *Ordo* 34, n.16.[44] In fact, the only one of the questions to the bishop that Hadrian quoted directly (perhaps from memory) – 'Vide ne aliquam promissionem cuiquem aut dationem fecisses, quia simonicum et contra canones est?' – is not found in *Ordo* 34's narrative of the interrogation.[45] Hadrian's citation supports in a broad way the general accuracy of *Ordo* 34, but not the availability of the text itself to him, and thus its assumed redaction in the Lateran. *Ordo* 34 could thus also most likely be a work of a Frankish pilgrim who had observed papal ceremony closely.[46]

---

[40] *Ibid.*: 'Tunc domnus apostolicus praecipit sacellario vel nomenculatori, ut eum ad archidiaconum dirigat et eum inquirat de quattuor capitulis secundum canones, id est: arsenoquita, quod est masculo; pro ancilla Dei sacrata, quae a Francis nonnata dicitur; pro IIII pedes et pro muliero viro alio coniuncta; aut si coniugem habuit ex alio viro, quod a Grecis dicitur deuterogamia.'

[41] *Les Ordines*, vol. III, pp.594–595, and n.4: 'où beaucoup de ses prescriptions eussent été inapplicables'.

[42] *Les Ordines*, vol. III, p.539; letter at *MGH* Epp. III [Karol. aevi, t. 1], p.634.

[43] *MGH* Epp. III (Karol.aevi I), p.634: 'enucleatius eum de singulis indagantes capitulis, singillatim orthodoxae fidei atque divinorum voluminum interrogamus habere peritiam'.

[44] *Les Ordines*, vol. III, p.604.

[45] *Les Ordines*, vol. IV, pp.81–82: 'Do you swear that you have not made any promise or gift to them, for that is simony and against the canons?' A similar question can be found uniquely in *Ordo* 35B, a later redaction, in an eleventh-century manuscript: Rome, Biblioteca Universitaria Alessandrina, MS 173.

[46] Andrieu found it also in a manuscript he identified as ninth-century, Cambrai, BM, MS 465, fols.51v–53r: *Les Ordines*, vol. III, p.536, n.1, but Bischoff reports this as part of an eleventh-century addition to that manuscript: Bischoff, *Katalog*, vol. I, p.175.

The 'Roman' Collection of Ordines   29

The next *ordo* in the collection, *Ordo* 27, is the product of the merging and adaptation of the pre-existing *Ordo* 24 and *Ordo* 26, themselves found in three Frankish manuscripts important for the pre-history of the *ordines* prior to Collection A: Albi 42 already mentioned, also Brussels, Bibliothèque royale, MS 10127–10144 and St Gallen, Stiftsbibliothek, MS 614. *Ordo* 24 deals with the Day Office of Holy Week, and *Ordo* 26 with the Night Office. The Brussels manuscript is the oldest of these, and secures the existence of these two sources for *Ordo* 27 probably before the end of the eighth century.[47] But, as we will see, the other two manuscripts were probably copied from exemplars that were just as old. *Ordo* 24 describes the Day Office of Holy Week, from the Wednesday before Maundy Thursday through to Easter, while *Ordo* 26 describes the Night Office. But, unlike other *ordines* (and just like *Ordo* 11), the main narrative of *Ordo* 24 evidently does not take place in Rome. The celebrant is a pontifex, and he is clearly distinct from the Pope: at *Ordo* 24, n.28, the pontiff prays for the 'apostolicus' (the Pope) on Good Friday, whereas the priests name their bishop.[48] The ceremonies unfold in various churches, but no Roman names were given to them: for example in *Ordo* 24, n.22: 'in ecclesia statuta infra urbem, non tamen in maiore ecclesia'.[49] None of Rome's exotic personnel appear, only *notarii* and the *secundus* and *magister scolae* (there is no equivalent to this latter position in Rome in *Ordo* 1). Finally, the fact that everyone communicates on Good Friday (*Ordo* 24, n.38: 'Et communicant omnes cum silentio') directly contradicts what Amalarius of Metz learned from the Roman clergy concerning the papal celebration in Rome, where no one communicated on that day at all.[50]

In contrast, *Ordo* 26 does describe a specifically Roman, papal usage, but presents it as differentiated from the normal usages and rather exotic. Rome was evidently viewed as foreign to the presumed reader: for example, in the first part, the Sunday before Holy Week is that 'which the apostolic see calls *mediana*'.[51] During the Easter Vigil, the text details that other cities

---

[47] *Les Ordines*, vol. I, pp.91–96; *CLA*, vol. X, p.1548: 's. VIII–IX'.

[48] *Les Ordines*, vol. III, p.293: 'Presbiteri uero ecclesiarum, sive de urbe seu de suburbanis, vadunt per ecclesias, ut hoc ordine cuncta ad vesperum faciant, hoc tantum mutantes, ut, ubi pontifex meminit apostolicum, ipsi nominent episcopum suum.'

[49] 'in the church chosen for this purpose, within the city, but not however in the main church (cathedral).'

[50] *Liber Officialis* I.15.1, Hanssens (ed.), *Opera omnia*, vol. II, p.107: 'In superius memorato libro, inveni scriptum ut duo presbiteri offerant post salutationem crucis corpus Domini, quod pridie reservatum fuit, et calicem cum vino non consecrato, quod tunc consecretur et inde communicet populus. De qua observatione interrogavi Romanum archidiaconum, et ille respondit "In ea statione ubi apostolicus salutat crucis, nemo ibi communicat".'

[51] *Ordo* 26, n.1.

The 'Roman' Collection of *Ordines*

beyond Rome ('forensibus civitatibus') undertook the blessing of the Easter candle as usual (the blessing is not described, but a pointer to the Sacramentary is given), but that 'the catholic church within the city of Rome' did not do this.[52] Instead, the archdeacon of the papal church made the *agnus dei* from blessed wax to be distributed to the people on the Octave of Easter.[53] This description conveys the flavour of one of the 'travel records'; it was, according to the very wording of the text, not a practice to be imitated, but one to be read and wondered about.

Three mentions of the use of a Sacramentary in the two *ordines* (a Sacramentary which was specifically not the Roman Gregorian but rather the Gelasian) – *Ordo* 24, n.2: 'in Sacramentorum continetur'; *Ordo* 24, n.23: 'ordine quod in Sacramentorum continetur'; *Ordo* 26, n.5: 'ordine quod in Sacramentorum continetur'; and the specific note that a prayer 'pro rege Francorum' (*Ordo* 24, n.3) would be said on the Wednesday of Holy Week – would incline one to believe the two texts were describing a particular Frankish ceremony of Holy Week, with the interlude of the Roman practice of the *Agnus Dei* on Holy Saturday in *Ordo* 26 as a clearly indicated digression. Was the setting, in fact, Metz? Andrieu admitted the possibility, at least, that *Ordines* 24 and 26 had been redacted by Frankish observers of the Roman liturgy, but still preferred to argue for a Roman origin by proposing that these were created for the churches 'suffragen' to Rome, still partaking of the Roman liturgy, and that they described truly papal ceremonies.[54] However, this statement relies on Chavasse's theory that the Old Gelasian Sacramentary was originally compiled for use in the liturgies celebrated by a priest in one of Rome's titular churches, thus ingeniously explaining divergences from what we know of papal practice by hypothesising a distinctive 'presbyterial' Rite in Rome.[55] These theories have been strongly criticised, and it does not seem that the Old Gelasian can really be located to the titular churches of Rome at all, or seen as a presbyterial counterpart to the Gregorian's papal liturgy.[56] Further discussion on the origin of *Ordo* 24 and *Ordo* 26 as part of a set of *ordines* that can be specifically linked to Chrodegang of Metz, and which includes the 'short recension' of *Ordo* 1 (as witnessed, for example, by St Gallen 614),

---

[52] *Ordo* 26, n.6: 'Et hic ordo cerei benedicendi in forensibus civitatibus agitur. Nam in catholica ecclesia infra civitatem romanam non sic benedicitur.'

[53] *Ordo* 26, nn.7–8.   [54] *Les Ordines*, vol. III, pp.281–283.

[55] Chavasse, *Le sacramentaire gélasien*; Vogel, *Medieval Liturgy*, pp.64–70.

[56] C. Coeburgh, 'Le sacramentaire gelasien ancien', *Archiv für Liturgiewissenschaft*, 7 (1961), pp.46–88; Matthieu Smyth, *La liturgie oubliée: la prière eucharistique en Gaule antique et dans l'Occident non romain* (Paris, 2003), pp.129–32.

The 'Roman' Collection of Ordines

will be detailed below. For now, we should note that the Holy Week *ordo* in Collection A, *Ordo* 27, combines two *ordines* that were not clearly of Roman manufacture, and made little claim to be describing Roman usages at all. Their combination was not done with much finesse.[57] Very little was added, except a formula for chrismation, which was specifically by an *episcopus*.[58] This combination of the *ordines*, at least, clearly took place within the Frankish kingdoms, as even Andrieu acknowledged.[59]

There was a third source for *Ordo* 27. *Ordo* 27, nn.67–94 was a different kind of text, a description of paschal Vespers for the week after Easter (entitled 'Ad vesperas die pasche sanctum') which originated in neither *Ordo* 24 nor 26. This was of immediately different character to the preceding texts. Roman personnel like the *parafonistis infantibus* appear at *Ordo* 27, n.70 and the *notario vicedomni* at *Ordo* 27, n.28. Quite particular Roman placenames are also a feature: at *Ordo* 27, n.76 'Ad sanctum Iohannem ad Vestem', or *Ordo* 27, n.77 'ad sanctum Andream ad Crucem', both oratories in the Lateran Baptistery, as well as the Lateran itself (*Ordo* 27, n.80, n.83).[60] A number of the chants are even delivered in Greek (singing in Greek took place within the liturgy in Rome, and was imitated in Frankish cities, as at Metz).[61] Andrieu was clear, this part, at least, was a 'true *ordo romanus*', that is, one that was redacted in Rome and able to tell us how the paschal Vespers really unfolded in Rome.[62] However, Van Dijk demonstrated plainly that the text in *Ordo* 27 is not, as Andrieu said, the accurate record of Rome's own ceremonies on these days.[63] In fact these texts are a clumsy Frankish adjustment of a more accurate Roman original text that survived elsewhere, given in the important *ordo romanus* manuscript, Wolfenbüttel, Herzog August Bibliothek, MS Weissenburgenses 91 (examined below) but perhaps originally transmitted in the Antiphoner, since pieces resembling it do certainly survive in the Antiphoner of Compiègne, a Carolingian copy of a Roman chant book.[64] The fact that this piece could be taken by Franks

---

[57] Laid out in *Les Ordines*, vol. III, pp.339–341.

[58] *Ordo* 27, n.65: 'Episcopus debet dicere, quando mittit chrisma in frontibus infantium: *In nomine patris et filii et spiritus sancti. Pax tecum.* Respondit: *Et cum spiritu tuo.*'

[59] *Les Ordines*, vol. III, p.341.

[60] *Le Liber Pontificalis: Texte Introduction et Commentaire*, Louis Duchesne (ed.) (Paris, 1886), vol. I, p.242: 'Hic fecit oraturia III in baptisterio basilicae Constantinianae, sancti Iohannis Baptistae et sancti Iohannis evangelistae et sanctae Crucis.'

[61] *Ordo* 30B, n.41; *Ordo* 28, Appendix, n.4; Andrieu, 'Règlement d'Angilramne de Metz', p.353.

[62] *Les Ordines*, vol. III, pp.342–343: 'sans aucun doute un veritable *Ordo romanus*'.

[63] Van Dijk, 'The Medieval Easter Vespers', pp.261–363.

[64] Wolfenbüttel Weissenburgenses 91, fols.69r–71r with unique title: 'QUALITER VESPERA DIE SANCTUM PASCHAE DICENDA SUNT'; Antiphoner of Compiègne: Paris BnF lat.17436 (fol.58r–v): 'INCIPIT ORDO AD VESPERES.'

32 The 'Roman' Collection of *Ordines*

from a Roman chant book adds to the range of sources of *ordines* and undermines Andrieu's conception of the texts as wholesale independent inventions in Rome. Rather, the forms the *ordines* take in Collection A are in many cases Frankish reinterpretations, constituting a new format invented principally for Frankish consumption. Before it was copied into Collection A, this text of the Easter Vespers had been clumsily adjusted in order to make space for a stational service on the Thursday of the week after Easter (nn.78–91). Having a stational service on the Thursday was a more recent innovation in Rome which the Roman Sacramentaries available to the Franks displayed but which the original text, representing an earlier stage of the Roman liturgy, did not.[65] As those like him were accustomed to do, the Frankish author 'borrowed' texts in order to fill out a stational ceremony which they knew occurred in Rome.

If we suggest a role for Angilram of Metz in the transmission of this initial Collection A, it is not at all clear that Angilram had intended to gather a purely 'Roman Collection'. *Ordines* 11 and 27 actually described, for the most part, Frankish usages and could be replicated in a Frankish cathedral like Metz without any difficulty. *Ordo* 1 and 34 described Roman usages, but both were observations by Frankish observers, and not truly Roman texts, in the sense Andrieu had conceived. A dynamic contrast between Roman and Frankish liturgies was thus a part of the *ordo romanus* tradition from the earliest gathering of the texts. The reader was clearly supposed to read this collection with a mind to what he might find useful and what he could or should not.

The final addition of *Ordo* 13A and 34 to a second enhancement of Angilram's original collection did strengthen the ties of the Collection to Rome. *Ordo* 13A is perhaps the only one of the *ordines* that can uncomplicatedly be attributed to Rome itself, and it very likely accurately describes the practice of the clergy of St Peter's, probably only within or after the reign of Pope Zacharias (741–752).[66] The Roman text is notably not concerned at all with the things Franks were interested in, in the *ordines* we know they wrote, which is to say topography, movement, gestures and arrangement of clergy. It is simply a list of readings. *Ordo* 42 is also entitled specifically as a Roman usage: 'In nomine Dei summi ordo quomodo in

---

[65] Michel Andrieu, 'Les messes des jeudis de carême et les anciens sacramentaires', *Revue des sciences religeuses*, 9 (1929), pp.343–375; Van Dijk, 'The Medieval Easter Vespers', pp.353–354.

[66] Peter Jeffrey, 'The Early Liturgy of Saint Peter's and the Roman Liturgical Year', in Rosamond McKitterick, John Osborne, Carol M. Richardson and Joanna Story (eds.), *Old Saint Peter's, Rome* (Cambridge, 2013), pp.157–176, at pp.167–176.

The 'Roman' Collection of Ordines

sancta romana ecclesiae reliquiae conduntur.'[67] Here the church was dedicated simply by the deposition of relics. In this case, there is nothing that would argue against Roman origin: the prayers and antiphons listed as part of the ceremony all belong to the Roman Gregorian Sacramentary and the Roman Antiphoner of Compiègne.[68]

The impression gained of a complex relation to Roman practice is strengthened when we examine anew the manuscript copies of Collection A. None of the manuscripts show plainly that the copyists of the collection prized only the Roman *ordines*. Instead, the three earliest manuscripts each carry an additional *ordo* from outside what Andrieu defined as his Collection A, all of Frankish manufacture. In the case of BAV Pal.lat.487 and the Murbach/Regensburg fragments, a second, alternative Holy Week *ordo* was added to the manuscript not long after it was copied.

In Lorsch, the manuscript of what was probably Angilram's collection (BAV Pal.lat.487) had an extra folio at the end, and this was used, a few decades after the manuscript had originally been written, to begin a new text, which was completed with the addition of a new quire (fols.25r–30v).[69] This text is a reworking of *Ordo* 27 as a new text, edited by Andrieu as *Ordo* 29. In substance, this is a repetition of many of the same rituals but it now takes place in a Frankish monastery rather than an urban setting.[70] A simple 'presbiter' undertakes the prayers on Wednesday and Friday.[71] We can tell that the Lorsch reworker of the text wished to emphasise two particular aspects. One was the Eucharistic customs on Maundy Thursday (*Ordo* 29, nn.24–26):

> Sacerdos vero, cum fregerit Sancta, mittat unam partem in calice et ex alia communicet ; porro tertiam altare dimittat et confirmetur a diacono de calice. Et illo tantummodo die, postquam confirmaverit sacerdotem, ponat calicem super altare et accipiat de manu subdiaconi patena maiore mittetque in eam de Sancta oblatas integras et ponat iuxta calicem, in sinistro latere, et duo subdiaconi veniant, unus cum patena et alius cum calice utrisque vacuis, et tollat diaconus de maiore patena ex oblatis, quantum sufficere possit ad communicandum populum, et de calice similiter et mittat in patenam et calicem quae subdiaconi tenent in manibus. Et statim illud quod remanet super altare cooperietur a duobus diaconibus utrumque sindone munda et de illa alia iuxta altare facit confractionem et post

---

[67] *Les Ordines*, vol. IV, p.397: 'In the name of God the Most High an Order how relics are interred in the Holy Roman Church.'

[68] *Ibid.*, p.393.

[69] Bischoff, *Die Abtei Lorsch*, p.22: 'von fol.24r an in jüngerem Stil, saec IX1, fortgesetzt'.

[70] *Les Ordines*, vol. III, pp.429–446.

[71] *Ordo* 29, n.4: 'Et presbiter dicat . . . deinde reliquas per ordinem.'

34 The 'Roman' Collection of *Ordines*

confractionem redeant ad sacerdotem et communicent ipsi et reliqui per ordinem. Et, data oratione post communionem, diaconus non dicat: *Ite missa est*, sed ipsa oratione finiantur universa.[72]

The other was the gradual extinguishing of lights on each of the days, or the *Tenebrae* ceremony (*Ordo* 29, n.12).[73] Both these aspects were highly symbolic and theatrical, and demonstrate what are clearly non-Roman embellishments. The Vespers portion of *Ordo* 27 (with the Roman place names and characters) is also entirely absent. On the one hand, then, we have a clear reworking of *Ordo* 27 to make it less Roman and more reflective of Frankish customs and peculiarities. This was, in general, how we might imagine Holy Week really unfolded in the monastery of Lorsch itself. At the end of the text, however, is an extract from what appears to be a longer letter, in which a person reports that they consulted Pope Hadrian himself about some specifics of the Holy Week Ceremony, specifically aspects on which *Ordo* 27 was unclear or silent:

> And we consulted therefore the Lord Apostolic Hadrian according to your orders, if on the Paschal Saturday we should genuflect when the readings are recited. And he responded that we should by all means do that. And when we said: And how are the priests and ministers and clerics able to prostrate themselves on the ground while wearing their stole and chasuble? He indicated that the priests, ministers and clerics need not wear their stoles and chasubles at this point, not until the 'new light' is introduced for the blessing of the candle. We then asked at what time on the Pentecost Saturday we should go in for the reading of the office, and he said to us that the sixth hour should be suitable.[74]

---

[72] *Les Ordines*, vol. III, p.441: 'But the priest, when he has broken the Host, places one part in the chalice and from the other communicates; but the third part he leaves on the altar and he is confirmed by the deacon from the chalice. And on the same day, after the priest has been confirmed, (the deacon) places the chalice on the altar and takes from the hand of the subdeacon the great paten and places the complete holy offerings upon it and he places it by the chalice, on the left side. Two subdeacons come, one with a paten, and the other with a chalice, both being empty, and the deacon takes from the great paten the Hosts, that will suffice to communicate the people, and (wine) from the chalice similarly, and he puts these in the paten and chalice which the subdeacons hold. And at once that which remains on the altar is covered by two deacons with a clean linen, and after the confraction they return to the priest and he communicates them and the rest in their order. And when the prayer after communion is given, the deacon does not say Ite missa est, but this prayer finishes the whole ceremony.' It was then used on Good Friday, *Ordo* 29, n.27: 'The offering which remained on the altar should stay covered, but serves on the next day according to custom.'

[73] On the *Tenebrae*, see Edmund Bishop, *Liturgica Historica* (Oxford, 1918), p.159; Duchesne, *Christian Worship*, pp.248–249.

[74] Appendix in Pal.lat.487, fol.30v, beginning: 'Et interrogavimus nihilominus domnum apostolicum Adrianum, secundum mandata vestra'; *Les Ordines*, vol. III, p.446.

The 'Roman' Collection of Ordines   35

The two answers of Pope Hadrian about Holy Week were actually incorporated into the preceding *Ordo* 29.[75] Bischoff's dating of the manuscript means that the Pope consulted must have been Pope Hadrian I (d.795), and not Hadrian II (867–872) or III (884–885), as Andrieu had assumed.[76] *Ordo* 29 shows the same complex adaptations of the *ordo* to diverse Frankish sensibilities. On the one hand, they pruned back Roman details and added new elaborations to the ceremony, which probably had a long history in Francia. On the other hand, the Pope was still an ultimate arbiter and judge in matters of liturgical confusion. The question of who wrote this letter remains unanswered. Presumably it was a Frank who travelled to Rome and who was a cleric of sufficient standing to be admitted to Pope Hadrian's presence, but on the other hand, they were clearly tasked to ask about these liturgical matters by a superior (their abbot or Bishop Angilram of Metz?). The addition of *Ordo* 29 was accompanied in the Lorsch manuscript by a theological extract from Alcuin of York's *De fide Trinitate*, the summary 'profession of faith' entitled *Credimus sanctae trinitatis* which would later be recited in a liturgical setting.[77] Was Alcuin also a possible recipient of the letter about Pope Hadrian?

The Lorsch manuscript, today BAV Pal.lat.487, was available to a copyist before the end of the ninth century, and he or she makes it plain that *Ordo* 29 and the note about Pope Hadrian were of highest interest, and, not necessarily, the descriptions of 'pure' Roman liturgical practice, which was reconstructed by Andrieu as Collection A's principal interest. The copy is now in St Petersburg's Russian National Library, and has been dismembered as three physical units: Q. V. I, n° 34, Q. V. I, n° 56 and Q. V. II, n° 5.[78] The original manuscript may have been from Cambrai, although soon after its production it was in Corbie.[79] Even though they had access to BAV Pal.lat.487, the copyists did not simply copy Collection A from the Lorsch exemplar. The

---

[75] At *Ordo* 29, n.46: 'Qua perlecta, dicat sacerdos : *Oremus* ; et diaconus : *Flectamus genua*. Et orent quousque diaconus dicat : *Levate*. Et surgant et sacerdos det orationem *Deus qui mirabiliter creasti hominem*', and at *Ordo* 29, n.47: 'Expletis lectionibus, regrediantur foras, praecedentibus cum duobus notariis cereos tenentes, et induantur sacerdotes et diaconi et ministri et ceteri clerici dalmaticis et stolis et omni ornamento.'

[76] *Les Ordines*, vol. III, p.430.

[77] BAV Pal.lat.487, fol.24r–v; Alcuin of York, *De fide Sanctae Trinitatis et de incarnatione Christi*, in *Quaestiones de Sancta Trinitate*, Erik Knibbs and E. Ann Matter (eds.), CCCM 249 (Turnhout, 2012), p.XIV; the *Credimus* is edited at pp.143–147.

[78] *Les Ordines*, vol. I, pp.348–351; Antonio Staerk, *Les Manuscrits Latins du Ve au xiiie siècle conservés à la Bibliothèque Impériale de Saint-Pétersbourg*, vol. 1 (St Petersburg, 1910; repr. Hildesheim, 1976), pp.174–213; Hubert Mordek, *Bibliotheca capitularium regum Francorum manuscripta* (Munich, 1995), pp.689–702.

[79] Bischoff, *Katalog*, vol. II, p.84: 'wohl Nodostfrankreich, ca.IX Ende'; a Calendar of Corbie was added in the tenth century; Staerk, *Les Manuscrits Latins*, pp.196–200.

36 The 'Roman' Collection of *Ordines*

manuscript they produced began with *Ordo* 11, followed by Theodulf of Orleans' letter to Bishop John (dating from *c*.812), a commentary on a ritual of baptism that describes a somewhat *different* rite of baptism.[80] Three diverse Frankish commentaries on the Mass follow, including the popular *Dominus Uobiscum* on the Canon of the Mass.[81] But there is no sign here of several key texts of Collection A: *Ordo* 1, 27 and 34. A component of Collection A in other manuscripts but not in BAV Pal.lat.487, *Ordo* 13A (the annual cycle of biblical books read in the Night Office), is found in the Corbie manuscript. But the Holy Week *Ordo* unique to the Lorsch manuscript, *Ordo* 29, was inserted into the body of this text at the relevant place in the year, and this copy includes the note about Pope Hadrian.[82] Here it appears as the only narrative of Holy Week available. In this case, it seems the Lorsch manuscript was consulted, and the most interesting element was our *Ordo* 29, a narrative of Holy Week as it unfolded in Lorsch. The 'completing' and filling in of *ordines* with spoken elements was elsewhere used by Andrieu as a sign that a book was intended for liturgical use, and this manuscript is also notable in this regard, having the full texts of the prayers and homilies for *Ordo* 11 taken directly from the Gelasian Sacramentary and inserted into the body of the *ordo*.[83] But this addition also exists here with commentaries and *expositiones* that contrast with and complement the *ordines*, offering different versions of the rites the *ordines* describe.

Our other closely related manuscript, the Regensburg fragments, also acquired another account from Holy Week, specifically about Maundy Thursday, in another hand, celebrated by a mere *presbyter* and lector, and perhaps revealing a hint of the customs of St Emmeram, where the manuscript had probably come by then (note the Old High German term *clocca* also used in *Ordo* 29, n.8, though there the bells did not sound at all).[84]

Ordo Officii in Cena Domini in Nocte

Primo clocca modice sonatur. *Deus in adiutorium meum* non dicatur nec *venite* cantetur. Sed tantum antiphonam *zelus domus tuae*. Ad nullum psalmum *Gloria* non dicatur. Sed psalmo finito finis non trahatur. Pre tertium psalmum omnes pariter dicant versum. Illa nocte lumen non extinguatur. Lector benedictionem petat, sed finem de ipsa lectione facit. homelia de ipso die legantur non lamentationes. Item ad matutinas non dicatur *deus in*

---

[80] Edited in Keefe, *Water and the Word*, vol. II, pp.279–321 with discussion in vol. I, pp.62–65.
[81] *Dominus Uobiscum*, Hanssens (ed.), *Opera omnia*, vol. I, pp.283–336; discussed at pp.110–114.
[82] Staerk, *Les Manuscrits Latins*, pp.201–205.   [83] *Les Ordines*, vol. II, p.370.
[84] *Ordo* 29, n.8: 'Et postea non sonetur clocca usque in sabbato ad missam'; Rudolf Grosse (ed.), *Althochdeutsches Wörterbuch*, vol. IV G–J (Berlin, 1986), p.310.

adiutorium sed antefonas. matutina finita non dicatur *kyrie leyson* nec presbiter orationes. nihilque aliud. nisi tantum inclinant esse. Vadunt.[85]

While agreeing with the preceding *Ordo* 27 in some respects (*Ordo* 27, n.2 reports that the chant *Deus in adiutorium* is not said, nor the Gloria, but only the antiphon), in others it actually contradicts it (*Ordo* 27, n.5: 'Lumen autem ecclesiae ab initio cantus nocturnae incoatur extingui'). The monks of St Emmeram may not have agreed with all the customs presented in the Murbach manuscript that came their way, and indicated here their differences from them. In the same way as the Lorsch text, this *Ordo* therefore provided an alternative to the Collection A ceremonies, and indicated that 'Frankish custom' was not itself uniform between communities like Lorsch and St Emmeram. Readers were apparently not surprised by this, and expected to read these *ordines* with a critical eye, comparing the narratives closely.

The same is clearly true for our first manuscript with the complete Collection A, Montpellier 412, from Tours, in which the Collection is presented only after a first non-Roman *ordo*, *Ordo* 15. This was the original disposition of the manuscript, the 'additional' *ordo* not being an addition, in this case. The new text, *Ordo* 15, is a set of *ordines* and regulations strung through along the liturgical year, and itself contains elements both Roman, including Roman church names, and Frankish, such as baptism at Epiphany, forbidden in Rome.[86] The interest of this text is that it still declares itself to be 'according to how the holy apostolic Roman church celebrates', but it is clearly of Frankish design and manufacture.[87] Andrieu had the text written as a group with the rest of the *ordines* in another early manuscript, the Collection found in St Gallen 349, but that sequence of texts seems rather to have different audiences, and certain details suggest that *Ordo* 15 in fact originated at Tours, where Montpellier 412 was written.[88]

---

[85] Munich Clm 14659, fol.2*r: 'An Order for the Night Office of Maundy Thursday. At first, the bell is rung a little. *Deus in adiutorium meum* is not said nor is *venite* sung, but just the antiphon *zelus domus tuae*. At no psalm should the Gloria be said. But the end of the psalm is not to be drawn out. Before the third psalm everyone should say the verse together. On that night the light is not extinguished. The lector asks for a blessing, but he makes an end from the reading itself [i.e. the usual versicle and response at the end of the reading, "Tu autem domine, miserere nobis", is not said]. The homilies for this day are read, but not lamentions. Then at Matins do not say *deus in adiutorium* but just the antiphons. At the end of Matins, do not say *kyrie eleison*, nor should the priest say prayers and nothing else, just that they are to be inclined. Then they leave.'

[86] *Les Ordines*, vol. III, pp.45–125; Montpellier contains *Ordo* 15, nn.1–85.

[87] *Ordo* 15, tit.: 'QUALITER A SANCTA ATQUE APOSTOLICA ROMANA ECCLESIA CELEBRATUR.'

[88] On the Collection in St Gallen 349, see *Les Ordines*, vol. III, pp.3–21: '*Les Ordines* XV-XVI, XVIII-XIX sont du même auteur'; Arthur Westwell, 'Ordering the Church in the *Ordines Romani*', in Rutger Kramer, Emilie Kurdziel and Graeme Ward (eds.), *Categorising the Church: Monastic Communities and Canonical Clergy in the Carolingian World (780–840)* (Turnhout, 2022), pp.425–445.

38   The 'Roman' Collection of *Ordines*

Another early manuscript to which a partial copy of *Ordo* 15 was added was also in Tours, The Hague, Museum Meermanno-Westreeanium, MS 10. B.4.[89] The *ordo* makes provision for celebration in a community called a *monasterium* in an urban setting, in which a bishop would be also present. Such a setting was the ambiguous position of the Basilica of St Martin at the time Alcuin of York was abbot there (796–804), and when the first copies of *Ordo* 15 begin to appear.[90] This is not to argue for Alcuin's role in the creation of the *ordo* (the level of Latinity is much below him), but the text does probably present something of the liturgy at Tours at the time he arrived there.

Like *Ordo* 29, *Ordo* 15 covered similar ground to the Collection of *ordines* that follow it in the Montpellier manuscript, including an extensive narrative of a pontifical Mass which is clearly a simplified version of *Ordo* 1, and a narrative of baptism which accounts for similar rituals as *Ordo* 11.[91] Alternative versions of the same rituals are also displayed side by side for consultation and comparison.

But Montpellier 412 also has its *ordines* and Collection A following after the text of Augustine of Hippo's *Enchiridion*, and nothing would suggest this was not the original disposition of the manuscript.[92] It was therefore also possible to place this collection in a book along with a resolutely non-liturgical patristic work, as well as the Collection of St Amand, copied on spare leaves of a manuscript of another work of Augustine, the *De gratia et libero arbitrio*, Paris, BnF, MS lat.974.[93] We know of another book that placed a Roman order of the Mass with the same text, one that was in St Gallen in 1446, but which is not today identifiable.[94]

Some later manuscripts hint at other iterations of Collection A. Paris, BnF, MS lat.2399 is also an eleventh-century manuscript, but certain features of the palaeography suggested to Andrieu and Wilmart that it

---

[89] *Les Ordines*, vol. I, pp.140–142; also Wilhelm Levison, 'Handschriften des Museum Meermanno – Westreenianum im Haag', *Neues Archiv der Gesellschaft für ältere deutsche Geschichtskunde*, 38 (1913), pp.513–518; *CLA*, vol. X, p.39.

[90] Jean Chelini, 'Alcuin, Charlemagne et Saint-Martin de Tours', *Revue d'histoire de l'Église de France*, 144 (1961), pp.19–50.

[91] *Ordo* 15, nn.12–65, 85–120.

[92] Augustine of Hippo, *Enchiridion ad Laurentium*, Ernest Evans (ed.), in M. P. J. Van den Hout, E. Evans, J. Bauer, R. Vander Plaetse, S. D. Ruegg, M. V. O'Reilly, R. Vander Plaetse, and C. Beukers (eds.), *De fide rerum invisibilium. Enchiridion ad Laurentium de fide et spe et caritate. De catechizandis rudibus. Sermo ad catechumenos de symbolo. Sermo de disciplina christiana. De utilitate ieiunii. Sermo de excidio urbis Romae. De haeresibus*, CCSL 46 (Turnhout, 1969).

[93] Augustine of Hippo, *De gratia et libero arbitrio ad Valentinum*, A. Goldbacher (ed.), Corpus Scriptorum Eccleisasticorum Latinorum, 57 (Vienna, 1911), pp.380–396.

[94] *Mittelalterliche Bibliothekskataloge Deutschlands und der Schweiz*, Paul Lehmann (ed.), vol. I (Munich, 1918), p.106: 'Epistole Augustini ad Valentinum monachum et e contrario; eciam [*sic*] Ordo ecclesiasticus Romane ecclesiae, quomodo missa celebratur.'

The 'Roman' Collection of Ordines

was copied from a ninth-century exemplar.[95] If so, that exemplar offered only the basic parts of the Collection, *Ordo* I, II and 27, and these texts were here sandwiched between two contrasting Carolingian commentaries which dealt with liturgical matters, Amalarius' *Liber Officiis* and Hrabanus Maurus' *De institutione clericorum*.[96]

Andrieu assumed more consistency in both the function and form of the Collection than these manuscripts would suggest. Clearly, Collection A was accomplished in steps and stages, and a significant proportion of the manuscripts do not display the full set. This was a fluid set of texts that could easily be adapted, and indeed encouraged the contrasting of the components with alternatives, often adapted or entirely non-Roman ones. The *ordines* were not therefore seen as definitive accounts of a ceremony but admitted the possibility of the reader's contrast and comparison. Andrieu's understanding of 'Collection A' as having a single ideological function does not bear the scrutiny of manuscripts. Furthermore, the majority of the *ordines* in the Collection can be identified as significantly interpolated or written by the Franks, not the pure Roman texts they were supposed to be in Andrieu's reconstruction.

The idea that pure Roman texts needed to be preserved and made sense only among others of the utmost purity does not seem to be one that animated Frankish recipients of that tradition. The creation of Collection A already associated Roman and Frankish texts which were allowed to interpret each other. Individual manuscript copyists continued to enrich and deepen this relation by adding new texts.

---

[95] *Les Ordines*, vol. I, p.269, 469.
[96] Hrabanus Maurus, *De institutione clericorum*, D. Zimpel (ed.), 2 vols. (Turnhout, 2006).

CHAPTER 2

The 'Frankish' Collection of Ordines in Verona, Regensburg, Nonantola and Corbie

The second set of *ordines romani* can be identified in more manuscripts. This is the set of texts which Andrieu called Collection B or 'Frankish Collection'. It is not, however, a dramatic break with the priorities or purposes visible in the manuscripts of Collection A, the so-called 'Roman Collection'. Since Collection A expresses Frankish activity and ideological needs just as much as Collection B, the 'Roman' and 'Frankish' designations are not very helpful. Nevertheless, the relation of dependency from A to B means that the letters are still useful to distinguish them. As with Collection A, there is a core of texts broadly shared by the witnesses to Collection B, but every manuscript represents the texts in different ways and alongside additional material at the choice of the compiler. The manuscripts generally all share:

Ordo 1, with some adjustments and additions.[1]
Ordo 13B, where the reading of homilies was added to the cycle of biblical reading of 13A, as well as some Frankish feasts.[2]
Ordo 11, with the concluding narrative of baptism omitted.[3]
Ordo 28, a further adaptation of *Ordo* 27 including a much fuller account of baptism to replace *Ordo* 11.[4]
Ordo 41, the dedication of churches; a developed version of the order in the Gelasian Sacramentary.[5]
Ordo 42, the Roman deposition of relics from Collection A.[6]

---

[1] Summarily dealt with in *Les Ordines*, vol. II, pp.15–21. [2] *Ibid.*, pp.491–506.
[3] *Ibid.*, pp.370–372. [4] *Les Ordines*, vol. III, pp.375–411.
[5] *Les Ordines*, vol. IV pp.311–347. On its origin in the Sacramentary, not dealt with by Andrieu: Bernard Langlois, 'Le manuscrit W de l'*Ordo Romanus* XL (édition M.Andrieu), un *Ordo* de la dédicace des églises, est-il un mauvais manuscrit?', *Studia Patristica*, 26 (1993), pp.47–58. Compare the Sacramentary of Angoulême: *Liber Sacramentorum Engolismensis*, Patrick Saint-Roch (ed.), CCSL 159C (Turnhout, 1987), 2021–2026, pp.301–303.
[6] *Les Ordines*, vol. IV, p.355.

The 'Frankish' Collection of Ordines

Formulae for consecration of vessels from the Gelasian Sacramentary.[7] These should be understood to form part of the church consecration ceremony in the larger sense.[8]

Ordo 37, a Frankish account of the Ember Days, the fasts and Masses taking place four times a year, during which ordination of higher clergy took place.[9]

The Ordination texts, for grades of the church from psalmist to bishop. The rubrics, where each grade is given something representing his office or blessed by a bishop, ultimately go back to the Frankish *Statuta Ecclesiae Antiqua*, a fifth-century collection of laws and canons from Southern France.[10] They came into the Gelasian Sacramentary of the Eighth Century, in which prayers and blessings were provided, and the order of the ranks was reserved, ascending from porter to bishop, not descending from bishop to psalmist (as in the *Statuta*).[11] Collection B offers the form as we find it in the Gelasian of the Eighth Century.[12] Andrieu edited and studied the *Statuta* as the 'original form' of this text, but did not dwell on or edit the intermediary form from the Sacramentary.

Laudes Regiae. A set of ritualised chants invoking aid of the saints for the grades of society, generally including the Pope, the Emperor and family, the local bishop, the clergy and the army, all associated with particular saints whose intercession for them was requested; here the form known as 'Franco-Roman'.[13] *Laudes* were sung during Masses with a bishop, as described in the rubrics in some manuscripts of Collection B.[14]

Ultimate dependence of Collection B on the complete Collection A is clear, but some significant adjustments were made. In the case of ordination, the Roman text, *Ordo 34*, was seemingly discarded entirely in favour of

---

[7] All the manuscripts share the texts of the 'BENEDICTIO CALICEM', 'BENEDICTIO PATENEM' and 'BENEDICTIO CHRISMALE'; the order of prayers is that of the Sacramentary of Gellone: *Liber Sacramentorum Gellonensis*, Antoine Dumas (ed.), CCSL, 159 (Turnholt, 1981), 2430–2435, pp.364–365.

[8] See *Ordo 41*, n.27: 'Deinde tenentes subdiaconi vel acolyti linteamina vel omnia ornamenta ecclesiae, seu vasa sacra quaecumque ad cultum Dei ad ecclesiam pertinere videntur, benedicit pontifex sicut in Sacramentorum continetur.'

[9] This appears in two forms: the earlier *Ordo 37A* (*Les Ordines*, vol. IV, pp.209–238) is adjusted in the manuscript Cologne 138, still an early manuscript, to the later *Ordo 37B*, for which see *Les Ordines*, vol. IV, pp.241–254.

[10] Charles Munier (ed.), *Les statuta ecclesiae antiqua: Édition, études critiques* (Paris, 1960); Andrieu edited the relevant section in his *Les Ordines*, vol. III, pp.615–619 in the form they take in the *Statuta*. On these rituals, see Roger Reynolds, 'The Ordination of Clerics in the Middle Ages', Article XI in *Clerical Orders in the Early Middle Ages* (Aldershot, 1999).

[11] J. D. Thompson, 'The Ordination Masses in Vat. Reg. 316', *Studia Patristica*, 10 (1970), pp.436–440.

[12] *Gellonensis*, Dumas (ed.), p.381.

[13] Ernst Kantorowicz, *Laudes Regiae: A Study in Liturgical Acclamations and Medieval Ruler Worship* (Berkeley and Los Angeles, 1946), pp.85–108.

[14] Cologne 138, fol.44r: 'INCIPIUNT LAUDES FESTIS DIEBUS Quando laudes canendae sunt expleta oratione a pontifice antequam lector ascendat in ambone pronuntiant duo diaconi siue cantores. Responte illis scola hoc modo.'

42   The 'Frankish' Collection of *Ordines*

a Frankish use of considerable antiquity taken from the Sacramentary (as already observed above in the St Petersburg MS). For church dedication, the text for deposition of relics described as Roman (*Ordo* 42) was to be placed alongside another text that gave the rite of church dedication as it was practised in Francia (*Ordo* 41). This second text was extracted from the Frankish Gelasian Sacramentary as well, and had an entirely different conception of that ritual and its meaning.[15] In the latter case, there are some complications that arise from the reconstruction presented by Andrieu, who surmised that the Franks found Collection A too specialised for their use and therefore set out to create a more usable and functional volume that would continue to preserve their own beloved traditions. Yet, as we have seen, manuscripts of Collection A might admit various accounts of the same rituals, which therefore presents some continuity in the processing of *ordines* but which was not noted by Andrieu. As in Collection A, various individual manuscripts of Collection B present distinctive reinterpretations that display an ambiguous and continually changing understanding of the relations between what Andrieu had posed as two entirely separate poles, Roman purity and Frankish adulteration.

Once again, we are fortunate to be able to link some of these manuscripts to places and figures of some importance and significance, and date some of them with precision. This is mostly thanks to the *laudes regiae* that the Collection contained. The earliest manuscript of Collection B, and often the 'best', is Verona Biblioteca Capitolare XCII. This was clearly copied in Verona.[16] The bishop of Verona for the time concerned was the Alemmanian Ratold of Verona (770–840/858), chaplain of the chapel of Pippin of Italy (d.810).[17] Interestingly, this manuscript has no less than three sets of *laudes regiae*, these texts being recopied by different hands and updated over a period of perhaps a few decades (indicating a significant life of liturgical use).[18] The first were copied on fols.70v–71v, at the very end of the manuscript, after a gap of what had originally been five blank folios. We can only speculate why, but the later use of some of these folios probably indicates that the intention was to leave space for potential additions. Unfortunately,

---

[15] Brian Repsher, *The Rite of Church Dedication in the Early Medieval Era* (Lewiston, 1998).

[16] *Les Ordines*, vol. I, pp.367–373; Bischoff, *Katalog*, vol. III, 7067, p.469; I examined this manuscript in person.

[17] Eduard Hlawitschka, 'Ratold, Bischof von Verona und Begründer von Radolfzell', *Hegau. Zeitschrift für Volkskunde und Naturgeschichte des Gebietes zwischen Rhein, Donau und Bodensee*, 42 (1997), pp.5–44.

[18] Giles Gerard Meersseman, E. Adda and Jean Deshusses (eds.), *L'orazionale dell'archidiacono Pacifico e il carpsum del cantore Stefano: Studie e testi sulla liturgica del Duomo di Verona dal' IX all XI sec.* (Freibourg, 1974), pp.188–190.

the second half of this manuscript has suffered from humidity, and many of the names originally present in the *laudes* have thus been obscured. The earliest set of *laudes* can be dated precisely to between 814 and 817, because we have here a single empress Hermingard, wife of Louis the Pious. Louis' second wife, Judith, was added at a later date after their marriage in 820, but then, in a subsequent intervention, her name was erased The next *laudes* in time, on fols.68v–69r, has both Louis and Lothar as emperors. Lothar was crowned emperor in Rome in 823, dating this set between that year and 840, when Louis the Pious died. Judith and Lothar's empress (also named Ermengard) both appear here, though Judith's name was once again later subject to erasure (Figure 2.1). The third and final set of *laudes* (fol.67r–v) is the best preserved, but at this point the scribes no longer chose to name the specific protagonists and simply had anonymous *laudes* (e.g. 'Domno nostro Ill. augusto serenissimo imperatori'), perhaps having grown tired of the need to continually update the texts. This set does however preserve an anonymised set of *laudes* for the bishop of Verona, with three local saints: 'Exaudi Christo (Domno) nostro Illo a Deo electo pontifici uita. III Sancta Firme. RP Tu illum adiuua. Sancte Procule. Tu illum adiuua. Sancte Zeno. Tu illum adiuua.'[19] We can assume that the previous sets of *laudes* had also named the bishop (and Pope), though all have been lost to humidity. Given the dating, in these cases, the bishop named would have been Ratold of Verona.

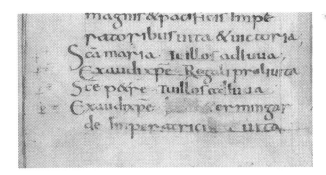

Fig. 2.1 Erasure of the name of Judith in the Second Laudes Regiae of Verona (*c*.823–840). Verona Biblioteca Capitolare XCI fol.62v.

---

[19] Verona XCII, fol.67r.

44   The 'Frankish' Collection of *Ordines*

The striking erasures of Judith's name tell us a particularly vivid story of shifting political allegiances expressed in liturgy. The person who erased them must have been a partisan of Lothar against his father Louis the Pious and stepmother, Judith, and vividly expressed his rejection of the latter by erasing her from the intercession. This reflects what we know of the policy of the Verona clergy. Interestingly, however, it was not the policy of their bishop, Ratold, who was driven from his see for his trenchant support of Louis the Pious and died in exile near Reichenau. He had even rescued Judith from her imprisonment in Tortona.[20] The *laudes* here represented the repudiation of their own bishop's position, in a book that he had likely been closely involved in creating.

A second manuscript of Collection B, Munich Clm 14510, can be precisely dated to 824–827 and located to Regensburg, thanks to its entirely preserved *laudes* on fols.39v–41r, which mention by name Louis the German (as king of Bavaria 826–843), Pope Eugenius (824–827) and Bishop Baturich (817–847) of that city for whom was invoked the local saint, Emmeram.[21]

Another manuscript of Collection B, Rome, Biblioteca Nazionale, MS Sessorianus 52, is from the twelfth century and the monastery of Nonantola, but it was copied directly from a ninth-century exemplar, since the *laudes* preserved here named Emperor Louis and Pope Nicholas, a combination that can only mean Pope Nicholas I (858–867) and Emperor Louis II (844–875), placing it within Nicholas' reign.[22] Nonantola also provides the most likely setting for the copying of the curious ninth-century manuscript, Zurich, Zentralbibliothek, MS Car. C 102, with its unusual orthography and script, towards the end of the ninth century.[23] Zurich Car. C 102 may even have

---

[20] *Annales Bertiniani*, AD 834, G. Waitz (ed.), *MGH Scriptores rerum Germanicarum* 5 (Hanover, 1883), pp.8f.

[21] *Les Ordines*, vol. I, pp.232–238, Bischoff, *Katalog*, vol. II, 3224, p.260; Bischoff, *Schreibschulen*, vol. I, pp.205–206; Friedrich Helmer, Julia Knödler and Günter Glauche, *Katalog der lateinischen Handschriften der Bayerischen Staatsbibliothek München. Die Handschriften aus St. Emmeram in Regensburg*, vol. IV: *Clm 14401–14540* (Wiesbaden, 2015), pp.394–395; digitised at http://daten.digitale-sammlungen.de/~db/0004/bsb00046285/images/;

[22] Jean Morin, 'Notice sur un manuscrit important pour l'histoire du symbole', *RevBen*, 14 (1897), pp.481–488; Kantorowicz, *Laudes*, p.107; Giuseppe Gullotta, *Gli antichi cataloghi e i codici della Abbazia di Nonantola*, Studi e Testi, 182 (Vatican City, 1995), pp.425–437. I examined this manuscript in person.

[23] *Les Ordines*, vol. I, p.458: 'du commencement du Xe siècle, si non de la fin du IXe'; Leo Cunibert Mohlberg, *Katalog der Handschriften der Zentralbibliothek Zürich* vol. I: *Mittelalterliche Handschriften* (Zurich, 1951), p.113; Bischoff, *Katalog*, vol. III, 7591, p.538: '[Schweiz-Oberitalien (?) und eine französische Hand, IX. Jh., 4. Viertel (/Ende)]'; BSB ANA 553, A, I, ZÜRICH: 'Errinert an Ob.It.' According to this, the 'etw. Frz. (etwas französische)' hand wrote fols.31r–32v; I examined this manuscript in person.

The 'Frankish' Collection of Ordines 45

been a source for the *ordines* of Sessorianus 52.[24] Unfortunately this book is now fragmentary (and has no *laudes* surviving), but Collection B was certainly here accompanied by a suite of *expositiones*, including the only complete copies of early works of Amalarius of Metz, which he had shared with the abbot Peter of Nonantola, and provided with their accompanying correspondence.[25] The most likely source for these last was a dossier of the letters held at Nonantola, particularly since Abbot Peter is named repeatedly as 'UENERABILIS ABBAS' in the titles of individual texts.[26] It is pertinent, then, that Nonantola possibly provided a refuge for the exiled archdeacon Pacificus of Verona in 826, who can be attributed a role in the copying of our earliest manuscript of Collection B, Verona XCII itself, or at least some of the notes added to it.[27]

Of the other manuscripts of Collection B, less can be securely said. Cologne, Dombibliothek, MS 138 was most likely copied in the first half of the ninth century, and its place of production has been located to Italy.[28] This version of Collection B has some distinguishing additions, and represents a clear reorganisation of the collection. Unfortunately, the manuscript's *laudes* are fully anonymised, but they show crossovers with Verona XCII, such as naming Theodore as patron of the Frankish army, where Munich Clm 14510 preferred to have Saint Andrew in this role.[29] This army is, in the earliest *laudes*, imagined as Frankish 'exercitui Francorum' (in Verona XCII's first set of *laudes* and Munich Clm 14510), but this, significantly, was changed to a Christian army, 'exercitui christianorum', in Verona XCII's final set of *laudes*.[30] Thus Kantorowicz was mistaken to see the term *'christianorum'*

---

[24] Sessorianus has tidied up the Latin significantly, but, like Zurich Car C 102, contains full prayers for the *ordines*.

[25] Richard Pollard, 'Libri di scuola spirituale: Manuscripts and Marginalia at the Monastery of Nonantola', in Oronzo Pecere and Lucio Del Corso (eds.), *Libri di scuola e pratiche didattiche. Atti del Convegno Internazionale di Studi (Cassino, 7–10 Maggio 2008)* (Cassino, 2010), pp.379–380.

[26] Zurich Car. C 102 fol.76v: 'EPISTOLA UENERABILIS ABBATIS PETRI; fol.77r 'AMALARIUS UENERABILI ABBATI PETRI'; Nonantola or nearby is also suggested by significant commonalities in this manuscript's unusual script with additions of the same period to a liturgical manuscript of Modena, Biblioteca Capitolare, MS O.II.7 (also seen in person); Guido Vigarini, *Inventario dei manoscritti dell'archivio capitolare di Modena* (Modena, 2003), pp.74–75.

[27] Cristina la Rocca, *Pacifico di Verona. Il passato Carolingio nella costruzione dellamemoria urbana, con un nota di Stefano Zamponi* (Rome, 1995), p.180; see below, Chapter 6.

[28] *Les Ordines*, vol. I, pp.101–108; Joachim M. Plotzek, *Glaube und Wissen im Mittelalter die Kölner Dombibliothek* (Munich, 1998), pp.330–332; Bischoff, *Katalog*, vol. I, 1936, pp.401–402: 'Italien, IX Jh., ca.1./2. Viertel'; Digitised at https://digital.dombibliothek-koeln.de/hs/content/zoom/286383; I examined this manuscript in person.

[29] Verona XCI, fol.70v: 'Exaudi christi. Exercitui Francorum uita et uictoria. Sanctae \Theodore/'; Munich BSB Clm 14510 fol.39v: 'Exaudi christe. Exercitui Francorum uita et uictoria. Ter Sancte Andrea. tu illos adiuua.'

[30] Verona, Biblioteca Capitolare XCII, fol.67r.

46 The 'Frankish' Collection of *Ordines*

appear for the 'first and only time' in the Chieti *laudes* of Louis II and Angilberga datable to 865–866, and to link it to 'Christian imperialism'.[31] Saint Theodore invoked for the army in these witnesses is clearly the Greek soldier martyr, venerated in Verona, former patron saint of Venice, as well as of the church of San Teodoro behind the Forum in Rome.[32] Some connection between Cologne 138, Verona XCII, and the chapel of the kings of Italy, often in Verona, is quite plausible.

Paris, BnF MS lat.14008 is related to Cologne 138 but has perhaps the most puzzling provenance and is in the most disordered state.[33] Today it forms part of the manuscript bound with the remnants of other books; the part we are directly concerned with is fols.99r–117v of the current manuscript, which are not bound in the correct order. Other pieces in the same manuscript come from Corbie, and Andrieu located it there, but Bischoff suggested a Breton scribe (though of course, this does not make it impossible that the manuscript was written at Corbie had the scribe travelled there) and the end of the ninth century.[34] This would take us far from the other examples of Collection B, which were found in the closely linked zones of Alemmania, North Italy and Bavaria. Yet Paris 14008 is most closely linked with Italian Cologne 138, and has some of the same additions and peculiarities (namely *Ordo* 37B and *Ordo* 40). Several abbots of Corbie brought manuscripts from Italy to the monastery.[35] A possible direct link to the context already advanced is Adalard, abbot of Corbie from 821, who was advisor to two kings of Italy, Pippin (d.810) and Bernard (d.817).[36] For the former, he served with Waldo of Reichenau and Angilbert of St Riquier.[37]

The final manuscript, St Gallen, Stiftsbibliothek, MS 446 has no *laudes regiae*.[38] Although Andrieu dated this to the tenth century, Bischoff

---

[31] Kantorowicz, *Laudes*, pp.234–235; Gerd Tellenbach, *Römischer und christlicher Reichsgedanke in der Literatur des frühen Mittelalters* (Heidelberg, 1934), pp.24ff.

[32] Meersseman *et al.*, *L'orazionale dell'archidiacono Pacifico*, p.65 suggested a shadowy bishop of the city, Theodore of Verona, but the soldier saint is much more likely for this role. Theodore appears in a Verona martyrology, Verona *Biblioteca Capitolare* CVI, written by a similar hand as Verona XCII, with his feast day of 9 November: Meersseman *et al.*, p.144: '9 id.nou.sci Theodori'.

[33] *Les Ordines*, vol. I, pp.276–279; digitised at http://gallica.bnf.fr/ark:/12148/btv1b9076764f; I examined this manuscript in person.

[34] Bischoff, *Katalog*, vol. III, 4959, p.216: 'Bretagne, IX/X Jh.'

[35] Leslie Webber Jones, 'The Scriptorium at Corbie 1: The Library', *Speculum*, 22 (1947), pp.191–204, at p.202.

[36] Paul Lehmann, 'Adalhard', *Neue Deutsche Biographie*, vol. I (Berlin, 1953), pp.48 f.

[37] Brigitte Kasten, *Adalard von Corbie: Die Biographie eines karolingischen Politikers und Klostervorstehers* (Dusseldorf, 1986), pp.46–47.

[38] Digitised at www.e-codices.unifr.ch/de/csg/0446/bindingE/o/Sequence-551; *Les Ordines*, vol. I, pp.336–343; Vogel, 'La réforme liturgique', pp.223–224; Keefe, *Water and the Word*, vol. II, pp.88–90; Bischoff, *Katalog*, vol. III, p.324: '[St Gallen, IX Jh., 3./4. Viertel].'

The 'Frankish' Collection of Ordines   47

decided instead for a date around the third or final quarter of the ninth, and located its place of origin to St Gallen itself. While a late copy, it accords with early manuscripts, Verona XCII and Munich Clm 14510, in presenting the basic form of Collection B without the additions found in Cologne 138. As in Zurich Car. C 102, we encounter Collection B among *expositiones* for the study of liturgy (a dynamic we shall examine closely in Chapter 4). *Ordo* 1 is on pp.2–18, and the rest of Collection B from p.106, so parts of the Collection are divided from each other. St Gallen 446 was also the exemplar in the eleventh century for the manuscript that is now Einsiedeln, Stiftsbibliothek, MS 110.[39]

No single manuscript confines itself only to the given components of the Collection as Andrieu had them, just as in Collection A. In addition to varied prayers and blessings, which will be discussed in Chapter 4, many added new *ordines* of varied kinds. Cologne, Dombibliothek 138 and Munich, BSB Clm 14510, both of the early ninth century, each possess additional examples of specific *ordines romani* which were edited by Andrieu but also texts which he did not edit. Cologne 138, written in Northern Italy, has the Roman text for the ordination of the Pope, *Ordo* 40A (fol.34r).[40] This very brief text, whose main function is to indicate which bishops ordained the Pope, was demonstrably present in Rome, since it appears in the *Liber Diurnus Romanorum Pontificum*, a collection of papal formulae used in the chancery, probably fully compiled only towards the end of the eighth century. Notably our surviving copies indicate the *Liber Diurnus* was copied in Northern Italy, for example in Nonantola and Bobbio, too. In any case, it is a strange addition indeed to the 'Frankish Collection'.[41] The second addition here is *Ordo* 3 (fols.18r–19r), a Frankish supplement to *Ordo* 1 dealing with some questions that arose in that text, of which more shall be said below.[42]

The Cologne manuscript also offers an *ordo romanus* for the calling of a council (fols.40v–43r), which was not edited by Andrieu despite being entitled here 'ORDO ROMANUS QUALITER CONCILIUM AGATUR'.[43] The last, despite this title, is a Frankish text, and originates

---

[39] *Les Ordines*, vol. II, pp.135–136.   [40] *Les Ordines*, vol. IV, pp.289–297.

[41] Hans Foerster (ed.), *Liber Diurnus Romanorum Pontificum* (Bern 1958), pp.315–316. The Nonantola manuscript is Archivum Apostolicum Vaticanum, Misc., Arm. XI,19.

[42] *Ordo* 3 at *Les Ordines*, vol. II, pp.119–133.

[43] Charles Munier (ed.), 'L'*Ordo Romanus* qualiter concilium agatur d'après le cod. Coloniensis 138', *Revue de theologie ancienne et medievale*, 29 (1962), pp.288–294; *Ordines de celebrando concilio*, Herbert Schneider (ed.), *Die Konzilsordines des Früh- und Hochmittelaters*, MGH (Hanover, 1996), pp.296–315. See also Martin Klöckener, 'Eine liturgische Ordnung für Provinzialkonzilien aus der Karolingerzeit der "Ordo romanus qualiter concilium agatur" des Cod. 138 der

48   The 'Frankish' Collection of *Ordines*

in a tradition from Salzburg. From 798, under Arn of Salzburg, the newly created archdiocese crossed into Northern Italy with the bishopric of Säben, and a similar text was even copied in Chieti (BAV lat.7701). The text described a metropolitan bishop's council, but this does not mean, as has been assumed, that the text would only be of interest to a metropolitan.[44]

The only French manuscript, Paris BnF lat.14008, also has a copy of the papal ordination text, *Ordo* 40, indicating its close kinship with Cologne 138. However, a new *ordo* was written for Holy Week, *Ordo* 32, making use of *Ordo* 28 at certain points but simplifying it significantly, as we have already seen in other monastic copies of Collection B.[45] This *ordo* makes provision for a place where baptism would not take place on Holy Saturday: (*Ordo* 32, n.26) 'Ubi autem babtisma [*sic*] non fit, aqua benedicatur a sacerdote et spargatur in omni domo. Postea, ut ordo est, sicut manifestat in Sacramentorum codice, sic cantent'.[46] However, *Ordo* 28 was originally also present in the manuscript.[47] Theodulf of Orlean's description of baptism was also seemingly preferred in this manuscript to the available narrative of baptismal preparation, *Ordo* 11, of which there is no trace in this manuscript.

The Regensburg manuscript, Munich Clm 14510, shows the same tensions as Cologne 138, distinguishing itself with additions to *Ordo* 1 of Frankish elements of the bishop's Mass never known in Rome (see Chapter 5), but it also offers the only copy of *Ordo* 44 (fols.41r–42v), a description of the Roman *Diligentia* ceremonies at the Vatican when the tomb of St Peter was washed, which was expressly overseen by the *Domnus Papa* and entitled 'ORDO QUALITER DILIGENTIA AGITUR ROMA, ECCLESIA SANCTI PETRI'.[48] This *Ordo* was one of the times

---

Dombibliothek Köln, liturgiegeschichtlich erklärt', *Annuarium Historiae Conciliorum*, 12 (1980) pp.109–182.

[44] Niels Krogh Rasmussen, *Les pontificaux du Haut Moyen Âge, Gènese du Livre de l'évéque* (Leuven, 1998), pp.398–399; see Arthur Westwell, 'The *ordines* of Vat. Lat. 7701 and the Liturgical Culture of Carolingian Chieti', *Papers of the British School at Rome*, 86 (2017), pp.127–152.

[45] *Ordo* 32 at *Les Ordines*, vol. III, pp.513–524.

[46] *Les Ordines*, vol. III, p.522: 'But where baptism is not done, the water is blessed by a priest and sprinkled in the whole dwelling. Afterwards, as the order is, just as it appears in the Sacramentary, thus they sing.'

[47] Paris BnF lat.14008 fol.109r contains the last sentence of *Ordo* 28, nn.85–86, 'omnibus modis celebraetur. It<. . .> diuturnale cursum seperatim ca< . . . >', before it begins the Frankish Vespers, which that text (nn.87–89), shared with *Ordo* 30B, nn.68–69. In his description of the manuscript, Andrieu identifies the text of Paris lat.14008 as *Ordo* 30, but it is much more likely to be the end of *Ordo* 28, given the connections to Cologne 138.

[48] Additions to *Ordo* 1 are listed at *Les Ordines*, vol. II, p.20; *Ordo* 49 at *Les Ordines*, vol. IV, pp.417–433 at n.1: 'Vespera finita, veniens domnus papa in chorum mittit planetam suam'; see also Michel Andrieu, 'La céremonie appelée « Diligentia » à Saint-Pierre de Rome au début du IXe siècle', *Revue des sciences religieuses*, 1 (1921), pp.62–68.

The 'Frankish' Collection of Ordines

when Andrieu was clear about the origin of this text as the observation of a ceremony very poorly attested otherwise, by a Frankish pilgrim present in Rome. This was evident from the vocabulary used, such as *chorus* for the presbytery or *faldo* for the pontifical throne.[49] The *Diligentia* ceremony is otherwise only mentioned in passing for example by the *Liber Pontificalis*, since Pope Paschal I (817–824) apparently received a silver conch 'pro nocturnis diligentiis'.[50] However, the same ceremony apparently took place at Montecassino, at the tomb of Saint Benedict, so the ceremony was comprehensible outside Rome.[51] Could this text have served as a model for the washing of the tomb of Saint Emmeram by a bishop of Regensburg?

As with Collection A, individual manuscripts of Collection B make various adjustments and interventions within their individual *ordines*. While these adjustments will be treated in more depth in the chapters dedicated to baptism, the Mass, and the other rituals which these texts represent, it is helpful to note that they do not always reflect the conception of the Collection as a Frankish endeavour designed for liturgical use. Notably, for *Ordo* 1, the editors of Cologne 138 went back to undo all the adjustments made to this text in Collection B by consulting a second version of it where these adjustments had not been made, something like the recension found in the later manuscript, Albi, BM, MS 42.[52] Thus, some very particular notes about Roman personnel were put back in, but some minor adjustments reflecting Frankish preferences were mostly maintained;[53] most notably, *Ordo* 1, n.98–99, detailing an extensive rite where the names of those invited to the papal table are written down, was removed in other Collection B manuscripts but returned here.[54] Wherever Cologne 138 was written, interest in the personnel of the Roman Church was particularly evident. This is also indicated by the adaptation of Collection B's original *Ordo* 37A, the text concerning the Ember Days, into *Ordo* 37B. A significant addition to the text concerns the cardinals and the ordination of clergy for the parishes by the Pope.[55] In one clear link to Verona, the version of this *Ordo* in Cologne 138 can be found copied in the eleventh-century manuscript, Verona, Biblioteca Capitulare, MS XCIV,

---

[49] *Les Ordines*, vol. IV, p.422; *Ordo* 44, n.1, n.16.
[50] *Liber Pontificalis*, Duchesne (ed.), vol. II, p.53.
[51] Jacques Winandy, 'Un temoignage oublié sur les anciens usages Cassiniens', *RevBen*, 50 (1938), pp.254–291, at p.264, n.20: 'Siue cum die sabbatorum ante completorium apud beati patris confessionem diligentiam facimus.'
[52] *Les Ordines*, vol. II, pp.17–20.
[53] *Les Ordines*, vol. II, p.14; for example the addition of *Ordo* 1, n.68: 'tunc ascendunt ad sede primicerius et secundicerius et primicerius defensorum uni ominibus regionariis et notariis'.
[54] *Les Ordines*, vol. II, p.99.   [55] *Ordo* 37B, nn.6–7.

50 The 'Frankish' Collection of *Ordines*

the so-called 'Carpsum of Stephen the Cantor' (copied from a tenth-century exemplar), including the Roman details.[56]

Cologne 138 is among the earlier manuscripts of Collection B. Already the idea of what the text should do had changed several times as it passed through the hands of scribes. As with the papal ordination in this manuscript, it is difficult to see how these adjustments can be interpreted as a gesture to the usability of the *ordines* in Francia. Clearly various versions of *Ordo* 1 were circulating, and scribes were cognisant of differences between them and the potential to introduce different emphases. Cologne 138 was consulted by a corrector of the earlier manuscript of Collection B, Verona, Biblioteca Capitolare, MS XCII.[57] All the special details that had been added to Cologne 138 to distinguish it from this version in Verona were written into the margins of this manuscript, and *Ordo* 3 was also added at the end of *Ordo* 1, just as it appears in the Cologne manuscript.[58] Some other *ordines* that distinguished Cologne 138 were copied on spare folios, such as the new portion about the cardinals from *Ordo* 37B on fol.66v, now almost entirely erased, but identifiable by the last words 'benedicet. Et hic est ordo' (*Ordo* 37B, nn.6–7).

Similar procedures may be observed to have taken place in St Gallen with *Ordo* 1 where rubrics only found in the 'short recension' were added in the margins to St Gallen Stiftsbibliothek 446, the monastery's copy of Collection B, probably from manuscript St Gallen Stiftsbibliothek 614 which contains the 'short recension'.[59] In both these cases, the marginal notators show awareness of the diversity of the traditions of *Ordo* 1 and encouraged the reader to be aware of them.

Where was this Collection B brought together, and for what purpose? Ratold of Verona provides us with the earliest copy, and we also have the Nonantola manuscripts (Zurich Car C 102 and Rome Biblioteca Nazionale Sessorianus 52), as well as Cologne 138, which speak strongly for Northern Italy. The original incorporation of the 'Franco-Roman' *laudes regiae* to Collection is likely to be linked to Ratold's service in the chapel of King

---

[56] Meersseman, *L'orazionale dell'archidiacono Pacifico*, pp.222–223: 'Dies uero sabbati, quando XII lectiones leguntur, et cum missa et oblationibus ipsa ieiunia consummantur, sacros ordines in ecclesia romana de eis, qui dicuntur cardinalis, tradi consueuerunt. Et in ipsa quattuor superscripta mensuum tempora, qualecumque die domnus apostolicus uoluerit, ad sacros ordines parrochianos clericos per omnes ecclesias, si fuerit necessitas, benedicit. Et hic est ordo.'

[57] For example Verona XCII, fol.16r: 'tunc ascendunt ad sede primicerius et secundicerius et primicerius defensorum uni ominibus regionariis et notariis.'

[58] Verona, Biblioteca Capitolare, MS XCII, fol.21v (presumably an inserted page contained the rest, but this has been lost).

[59] *Les Ordines*, vol. II, p.8, for example at *Ordo* 1, n.123: 'directus ad orientem'.

The 'Frankish' Collection of Ordines 51

Pippin of Italy. Notable is that Baturich of Regensburg also served as chaplain to Louis the German's court in Regensburg.[60] A tangible link between these two bishops is provided, however, by the monastery of Reichenau. Ratold was educated there, and was a great patron of the monastery, providing it with relics of Saint Mark. In return, Reichenau provided his church with liturgical books, as attested by the copies of the Gregorian Sacramentary made in Verona.[61] Baturich of Regensburg's links to the monastery are less known, but he strikingly appears as one of the bishops in the confraternity list of the monastery as the only Bavarian bishop present (and alongside Ratold), which expressly listed those whom the monastery considered friends.[62] The provision of bishops for important Carolingian sees from the great monasteries like Reichenau is a recognisable Carolingian policy. Did Reichenau in its role as a centre for the education of future bishops thus furnish a Collection of *ordines* of Frankish episcopal rites with a strong pro-Carolingian focus? The presence of a copy of the same basic form of the Collection at nearby St Gallen, Stiftsbibliothek, MS 446, may also perhaps derive from a Reichenau archetype.

Whether compiled in Reichenau or in Northern Italy, the 'Frankish Collection' had a strong focus on episcopal rituals, as they could be performed by a bishop, with notably enhanced narratives for church dedication and for ordination, taken from the Gelasian Sacramentary of the Eighth Century (manuscripts of which were available in Alemannia and North Italy). This focus explains why a number of these manuscripts have been described as 'pontificals', as we will see in Chapter 4. Manuscript copies of the collection from monasteries show that Nonantola and St Gallen had a strong interest in texts that are also incorporated in the so-called 'pontifical', indicating that the performance of episcopal ceremonies was not the only conceivable use or interest that this collection had.

---

[60] Eric Goldberg, *Struggle for Empire: Kingship and Conflict under Louis the German* (Cambridge, 2006), p.51.

[61] Meersseman *et al.*, *L'orazionale dell'archidiacono Pacifico*, pp.25–42.

[62] Régine Le Jan, 'Reichenau and its *amici viventes*: Competition and Cooperation?' in Meens *et al.* (eds.), *Religious Franks*, pp.268–269.

CHAPTER 3

Unique Collections of the Ordines *from Worms, Wissembourg, St Amand and St Gallen*

Manuscripts of the two main collections of *ordines romani*, A and B, have demonstrated the potential for individual manuscript compilers to rapidly adapt and edit these groups of texts, seemingly from one copy to the next. The 'meaning' of the collections, and their identity as 'Roman' or 'Frankish' in the terms we find in Andrieu's edition, were not at all fixed, since compilers chose to emphasise one or other liturgical tradition according to what can only be explained as personal preference. Indeed, a shifting between liturgical usages that were very particular to Rome and those which could easily be replicated in Francia or were never done in Rome at all, is characteristic of all the manuscripts, taking place even from one *ordo* to the next, or even within the text of an individual *ordo* (as in *Ordo* 15, or *Ordo* 26). We must integrate this ambiguous relationship to Rome into our understanding of the texts too. The manuscripts of the *ordines* collections were particularly flexible, in a way that other liturgical manuscripts, like the Mass lectionary or Sacramentary were not, or were so only in a less obvious way.

As emphasised in the Introduction, *ordo romanus* collections were something new in the Carolingian Church, and they were designed to serve the needs of the churchmen who wrote them or had them written. The flexibility of the collections thus also expressed the flexible way these churchmen apprehended and made use of the Roman liturgy, and Rome itself. We have also begun to link some of these manuscripts to a network of powerful and influential churchmen, including bishops such as Angilram of Metz, Ratold of Verona and Baturich of Regensburg, but found that copies were also made at the monasteries of Lorsch and Nonantola. We have also already observed hints of other collections, perhaps underlying the two we have studied. The collections which survive only in a single manuscript confirm the picture of the flexibility of the meaning and use of these texts.

One of the most expertly written manuscripts of the *ordines romani* is the collection found in Wolfenbüttel, Herzog August Bibliothek,

Unique Collections of the Ordines   53

Weissenburgenses 91.[1] The manuscript is today the combination of five originally distinct separate units (largely of sermons and catechetical material). Ours is the second unit, comprising fols.25r–88r.[2] It was characterised by Andrieu as a 'timid sketch of the future pontifical', but rather presents us with a fully complete endeavour in its own right in the form of a highly individualised set of *ordines* enriched with many extracts from Sacramentaries and additional ad hoc notes about Roman practice.[3] Bischoff had suggested that the manuscript might have been written in Worms for use at the cathedral of Saint Peter there and, given the date, the bishop would have been Bernharius of Worms (803–826).[4] Bernharius was also abbot of the monastery of Wissembourg in Alsace, where the manuscript came. It is so closely related in script and format to a manuscript of the *Liber Pontificalis*, also written under Bernharius and also later at Wissembourg, Wolfenbüttel, HAB, cod. Guelf. 10. 11 Aug. 4° (at least up until fol.110r, where there is a change of style), that we might see both as part of a single programme of copying undertaken in the city.[5] Although not really given much credit by Andrieu, this manuscript is, in fact, one of the most interesting early testimonies to the conscious deployment of the *ordines romani*. While overlapping with Collections A and B, it presents a unique compilation of texts, which can only be the product of a compiler engaged fully in the currents of what is termed '*correctio*', but in a self-conscious and individualistic way. Andrieu never saw the manuscript in person, and, from microfilm, only considered the content of the *ordines romani* from fol.42v onwards.[6] With access to the digitised version, and new studies of the manuscript, we now know that it had broader content beyond this. It is worth dwelling on a little longer.

---

[1] Digitised at http://diglib.hab.de/mss/91-weiss/start.htm; *Les Ordines*, vol. I, pp.453–458; Bischoff, *Katalog*, vol. III, 7427, p.512.

[2] Hans Butzmann, *Kataloge der Herzog August Bibliothek Wolfenbüttel: Neue Reihe*, vol. X, *Die Weissenburger Handschriften* (Frankfurt am Main, 1964), pp.257–268, p.257: 'B: 25–88r BRIEF des Papsts CLEMENS und *ORDINES*'; more on the manuscript and connections to Worms in Wolfgang Haubrichs, 'Das althochdeutsch-lateinische Textensemble des Cod. Weiss. 91 (Weißenburger Katechismus) und das Bistum Worms im frühen neunten Jahrhundert', in R. Bergmann (ed.), *Volkssprachig-lateinische Mischtexte und Textensembles in der althochdeutschen, altsächsischen und altenglischen Überlieferung: Mediävistisches Kolloquium des Zentrums für Mittelalterstudien der Otto-Friedrich-Universität Bamberg am 16. und 17. November 2001* (Heidelberg, 2003), pp.131–173.

[3] *Les Ordines*, vol. III, p.417: 'une sorte de petit directoire épiscopal, timide ébauche du futur Pontifical'.

[4] Bernhard Bischoff, *Mittelalterliche Studien: ausgewählte Aufsätze zur Schriftkunde und Literaturgeschichte*, vol. III (Stuttgart, 1967), p.93; Arthur Westwell, 'The *Ordines Romani* and the Carolingian Choreography of a Liturgical Route to Rome', *Acta ad archaeologiam et artium historiam pertinentia*, 31 (2019), pp.64–70; on Bernharius: Hans Hummer, *Politics and Power in Early Medieval Europe: Alsace and the Frankish Realm, 600–1000* (Cambridge, 2006), pp.82–83.

[5] Digitised at: http://diglib.hab.de/wdb.php?dir=mss/10-11-aug-4f&pointer=0; Bischoff, *Mittelalterliche Studien*, vol. III, p.93.

[6] *Les Ordines*, vol. I, p.453: 'Je n'ai eu pas le manuscript original entre les mains.'

54   Unique Collections of the *Ordines*

Contents of Wolfenbüttel Weissenburgenses 91

Fols.25v–37r:	Two epistles of Pseudo-Clement to James of Jerusalem. This opens with a full page in capitalis, so is clearly the beginning of the original manuscript.
Fol.37v	The life of Clement from the *Liber Pontificalis*.
Fol.38r	Pseudonymous correspondence of Damasus and Jerome on the hour of Mass.
Fols.38r–42r	The decretal of Pope Gregory's 595 Council of the Roman clergy (including subscriptions).
Fols.42v–52r	*Ordo* 1
Fols.52 r–53r	*Ordo* 3
Fols.53v–60r	*Ordo* 11
Fols.60r–71r	Holy Week (pieces from *Ordines* 24, 28, 28A, 25, 26 and the Roman Easter Week Vespers, which was source for *Ordo* 27)
Fols.71v–72v	*Ordo* 13A
Fols.72v–77r	The decretal *de libris recipiendis et non recipiendis*, attributed to Pope Gelasius.
Fol.77r–v	Some Gelasian *denuntiatii* of the Ember Days.
Fols.77v–83r	Ordination (made up of a Gelasian *ordo de sacris ordinibus* and *Ordo* 34)
Fols.83r–84r	*Ordo* 42
Fols.84v–86v	*Ordo* 41
Fols.86v–88r	Pieces from *Ordo* 15.
Fol.88v	A poem about Pope Gregory, '*Gregorius praesul*'.[7]

It is not difficult to see why Andrieu argued that the compiler of the text knew both Collection A and Collection B. Like Collection B, the scribe of Weissenburgenses 91 copied liturgical texts originally from the Gelasian Sacramentary, which is to say the church dedication rite of *Ordo* 42, and the Gelasian *ordo de sacris ordinibus* (the sequence of grades with rubrics and prayers, here only from porter to bishop). He placed these alongside *ordines* of Collection A. But in fact, in both cases, the compiler has gone directly to the Gelasian Sacramentary and copied the texts, independently of Collection B.[8] This was, then, not unusual action, but a widely shared way of understanding

---

[7] See Bruno Stäblein, '"Gregorius Praesul", der Prolog zum römischen Antiphonale', in *Musik und Geschichte im Mittelalter. Gessamelte Aufsätze* (Göppingen, 1984), pp.117–142, who argued that the text referred originally to Gregory II, and was later misinterpreted to refer to Gregory the Great. Some discussion of the origins in Constant Mews, 'Gregory the Great, the Rule of Benedict and Roman Liturgy: The Evolution of a Legend', *Journal of Medieval History*, 37 (2011), pp.125–144, at p.137.

[8] Langlois, 'Le manuscrit W', demonstrated this with regard to *Ordo* 42, which is closer to the Gelasian in Weissenburgenses 91 than in Collection B. The ordination rites begin not with the psalmist, as in Collection B, but with the ostiarius (porter); and the rubric *et tradit ei diaconus ostium ecclesiae* and the prayer for the subdeacon (fol.79r–v) 'Exhibeatur in conspectus episcopi ...' are both in the Gelasian Sacramentary and the Wolfenbüttel manuscript, but not copied by Collection B, indicating Wolfenbüttel Weissenburgenses 91's direct dependence on the Sacramentary.

Unique Collections of the Ordines   55

and approaching the Roman rites, and placing them in context. We might note that the late Carolingian 'Pontifical of Sens' in Saint-Petersburg Q.v.I, n.35 also has texts of both *Ordo* 42 and *Ordo* 41.[9] On ordination, Weissenburgenses 91 fols.77r–84r proceeds in a similar way and slots *Ordo* 34 from Collection A into the Frankish ordination texts from the Sacramentary (again drawing on these texts independently of Collection B).

The Holy Week narrative from fol.60r is particularly complex. Possessing *Ordines* 24 and 26, it divided up and expanded them, adding its own unique accounts of the blessing of the Paschal Candle taken from the Sacramentary and edited by Andrieu as *Ordo* 25 (fol.65r), and a blessing of the font edited as *Ordo* 28A (fols.63v–66v).[10] These are all Frankish texts. But Weissenburgenses 91 ends the sequence with the special version of the Roman Easter Vespers which was also copied, though there adapted in a maladroit way, in Collection A's *Ordo* 27. This time it is an accurate description of Roman practice, and with Roman Church names and stations on the correct days (fols.69r–71r). The makers of the manuscript thus had access also to underlying sources of Collection A.

Throughout, the manuscript also contains numerous appendices and extracts on varied subjects directly addressing Roman practices set in particular churches of the city, and mentioning the Pope.[11] The uniqueness of these testimonies, and their coherence with matters of Frankish interest such as the stational topography of Rome and the practices of chant, suggests they are eyewitness accounts. It is not unlikely they come from Bernharius of Worms himself, from his visit to Rome in 809 in the company of Adalhard, abbot of Corbie, in order to discuss the Council of Aachen's findings on the Holy Spirit with Pope Leo, so he could easily have observed there some of the Roman peculiarities we have noted, and taken up some Roman texts and customs for his own cathedral.[12] Other

---

[9] Staerk, *Les Manuscrits Latins*, pp.160–163.

[10] *Ordo* 25 at *Les Ordines*, vol. III, pp.301–304; *Ordo* 28A at *Les Ordines*, vol. III, pp.417–425.

[11] Published by Andrieu in various places, for example *Ordo* 24, n.51 var.9: 'Similiter ad vigilias per totam ebdomadam terni psalmi dicendi sunt et per omnes psalmos Alleluia usque octabas pentecosten omnimodis predicenda est. Dominica sancta, **statio ad sanctam Mariam ad prasepio**; qualiter missa celebratur superius habemus conprehensum et per reliquas stationes'; *Ordo* 15, n.83: 'Primum autem ieiunium IIII feria ad **sanctam Savinam** publicae agitur cum cruce et turabulis simul cum laetaniis, id est post Lma et ante XLma, necnon et VI feria similiter faciunt ieiunium publica'; *Ordo* 15, n.84: 'In XLma uero, prima ebdomada, si in mense martio uenerit, IIII et VI feria seu et sabbato, omnes publicas **stationes faciunt ad Sanctum Petrum** in XII lectionibus. Sin autem minime in martio mense prima ebdomada uenerit, in alia uel tertia ebdomada quando pontifex iudicauerit, XII lectiones agenda sunt et ordinantur qui ordinandi sunt'; *Ordo* 42, n.20, var.10 'Sciendum uero est ubi domnus apostolicus dedicat eclesiam, praeter episcopos nulli licitum est infra ipsam ecclesiam missas celebrare.'

[12] Jennifer Davis, *Charlemagne's Practice of Empire* (Cambridge, 2015), p.370, n.132; *Annales Regni Francorum*, Friedrich Kurz (ed.), *MGH* Scriptores Rerum Germanicarum, vol. VI (Hanover, 1895),

56 Unique Collections of the *Ordines*

small appendices deal with minor liturgical matters of genuflection or of the Frankish practice of the episcopal blessings, simply answering what might have been pressing questions.[13] Interpreting the manuscript as merely a timid attempt at the pontifical does not seem fair to the complexity and ambition of its compilation, and this is before we get to the fact that the collection opens with documents of papal history, which will be discussed in Chapter 4 in more depth. Clearly the mind behind this manuscript, whom I suggest was Bernharius, was also plugged into the networks of Carolingian churchmen which shared *ordines romani*, some of which we have already begun to uncover in our examination of the treatment of Collections A and B.

Wolfenbüttel Weissenburgenses 91's collections of personal observations and liturgical regulations, as well as *ordines* of various feasts spread through the liturgical year, addressing both specific Roman practices identified as such and the practical concerns of how Frankish ecclesiastics might place and arrange the festivals, make the manuscript seem less like the Collections of *ordines romani* as Andrieu envisaged them which had singular specific ideological purpose, and more as interactive archives of regulations or noteworthy texts that a community or individual might find significant for various reasons.[14] We saw something very similar in *Ordo* 15, attached to the Tours copy of Collection A, Montpellier 412. This sense is heightened by the other *ordines* of the same tradition as *Ordo* 15, which is also present in St Gallen, Stiftsbibliothek, MS 349, a manuscript of the late eighth century, which nevertheless shows rapid reworking of this family of *ordines*.[15] Here, the first *ordo* is Roman, *Ordo* 14, which was another list of the readings in St Peter's Basilica ('in ecclesia sancti Petri').[16] *Ordo* 16, unique to one manuscript, St Gallen 349, is a reimagining of *Ordo* 15 for a monastic context, coming directly before it in the manuscript.[17] *Ordines*

---

p.129: 'Mense Novembrio concilium habet de processione Spiritu sancti, quam questionem Iohannes quidam monachus Hierosolimis primo commovit; cuius definendae Bernharius episcopus Wormancensis et Adalhardus abbas monasterii Corbeiae.'

[13] *Ordo* 28A, nn.24–25: 'Et sane scientes quod per singulas orationes sabbato sancto et pentecosten et omnem quadragesimam, exceptis diebus dominicis, genua flectere debemus; similiter IIII mensium tempora anni, id est primi, quarti, septimi et decimi mensis, cum feriis ipsarum observandum est; similiter et in dicto ieiunio vel vigiliis festivitatibus sanctorum faciatis. Et quando pontifex benedictiones super populum tradere uoluerit, archidiaconus, vel quem ipse iusserit, aspicit ad pontificem, ut ei annuat, et dicit ad populum: Humilitate uos ad benedictionem. Resp: Deo gratias. Si autem pontifex, ibidem non fuerit, supra scriptum habemus.'

[14] Westwell, 'Ordering the Church'.

[15] *Les Ordines*, vol. I, pp.330–333; digitised at: www.e-codices.unifr.ch/en/csg/0349/4/0/Sequence-494.

[16] *Les Ordines*, vol. III, pp.25–41; Jeffrey, 'The Early Liturgy at Saint Peter's'.

[17] *Les Ordines*, vol. III, pp.129–154.

Unique Collections of the Ordines   57

15 and 16 both together contributed to a third text, *Ordo* 17, found copied into spare folios of early manuscripts both from the Upper Rhine and before the end of the eighth century, BAV Pal.lat.574 (described by Bischoff as 'Oberrhein (alemannisches Gebiet?)' and was later at Lorsch) and Gotha Forschungsbibliothek Membr.I.85 (from Wissembourg).[18] This group of three texts (*Ordines* 15, 16 and 17) are strings of regulations and *ordines* along the liturgical year, sometimes describing ceremonies in greater depth (thus enclosing copies of what we might describe as full *ordines*), and sometimes simply cursorily answering smaller questions of practice, with numerous digressions and appendices, observations and suggestions, including the emotions felt at the ceremonies.[19] In *Ordo* 15, the practices were often described as if they took place in Roman churches; *Ordines* 16 and 17 downplay this somewhat, though maintain the title describing themselves as 'of the Roman church'. Despite Andrieu's comprehensive demonstration that these were actually Frankish documents and described many practices that were never known in Rome, attempts have been made to restate the origin of the whole St Gallen 349 Collection in a Roman monastery.[20] This was also the position of Semmler's edition that divided and positioned these *ordines* artificially in a way no manuscript did, inserting new subtitles and subsections.[21] But these attempts largely failed to deal with the proof that liturgical customs described here (such as baptising at Epiphany) had never been done in Rome.[22] These three rich texts, of Frankish creation, are rather in miniature something like the same undertaking as we saw worked out more ambitiously still in the *ordines* of Weissenburgenses 91, combining pre-existing *ordines* with varied regulations and observations, answering questions that arose about liturgical practice and being full of incidental details.

---

[18] *Ibid.*, pp.157–193; on Palat.lat.574: *Les Ordines*, vol. I, pp.321–322, digitised at https://digi.vatlib.it /view/bav_pal_lat_574; Bischoff, *Katalog*, vol. III, p.414; on Gotha Membr. I. 85: *Les Ordines*, vol. I, pp.138–139; Bischoff, *Katalog*, vol. I, p.297; *CLA*, vol. VIII, p.1209, digitised at: https://dhb .thulb.uni-jena.de/rsc/viewer/ufb_derivate_00015136/Memb-I-00085_00218.tif.

[19] Westwell, 'Ordering the Church'.

[20] Kassius Hallinger, 'Die römischen *ordines* von Lorsch, Murbach und St Gallen', in Ludwig Lenhart (ed.), *Universitas: Dienst an Wahrheit und Leben. Festschrift für Bischof Dr. Albert Stohr*, vol. I (Mainz, 1960), pp.466–477; Stephen J. P. van Dijk, 'Urban and Papal Rites', *Sacris Erudiri*, 12 (1965), pp.450–465.

[21] '*Ordines* aevi regulae mixtae (post seac.VIII. med.)', Josef Semmler (ed.) in Kassius Hallinger (ed.), *Corpus Consuetudinum Monasticarum*, vol. I, *Initia Consuetudinis Benedictinae: Consuetudines Saeculi Octavi e Nonni* (Wiesbaden, 1962), pp.3–76;

[22] Peter Jeffrey, 'Eastern and Western Elements in the Irish Monastic Prayers of the Hours', in Margot Fassler and Rebecca A. Baltzer (eds.), *The Divine Office in the Latin Middle Ages* (Oxford, 2000), pp.128–130, particularly n.85.

58   Unique Collections of the *Ordines*

The compilers of *Ordo* 15, earliest of this particular family of texts and probably redacted at St Martin of Tours before Alcuin arrived there, did have sight of at least one early *ordo romanus*, the 'short recension' of *Ordo* 1, and they used it to make the first Mass *ordo* in the text.[23] The exact difference between short and long recension is also explored in Chapter 5, but, for now, we might note that the 'short recension' has a more informal and ad hoc character.[24] It is likely that the 'short recension' of *Ordo* 1 was therefore one of the very first *ordines romani* to circulate widely in Francia, perhaps from soon after the mid-eighth century. The single manuscript that carries the 'short recension' is therefore of significant interest for us. It can only be found in St Gallen Stiftsbibliothek 614, today a set of gatherings of various ages, including later liturgical literature.[25] The original gathering of the *ordines* is found on pp.183–230.[26] It opens with a blank page, indicating that this was a complete manuscript or booklet at one stage. The copyists of this portion actually combined two distinct and older collections of *ordines romani*, both of which were redacted at different times, and each of which have distinct interests. While Andrieu had the script as from the second half of the ninth century, it is of significance that Bischoff redates this somewhat earlier, to between the first and second quarter.

In the first part of this gathering, we find *Ordo* 1 in the short recension, with its important Supplement *Ordo* 2. This text, which adapts *Ordo* 1 to the potential absence of the Pope and recommends it be followed by all other bishops, is also unique to this manuscript and to a single copy directly taken from it in the same monastery at the end of the century (St Gallen, Stiftsbibliothek, MS 140).[27] These two closely related texts, which form a unit, are followed in St Gallen 614 by two further *ordines* we have already discussed, and which we also have already shown to be among the oldest, *Ordines* 24 and 26, the descriptions of Day and Night Office. *Ordo* 24 has no title, and it is continuous with the text of the preceding *Ordo* 2. It is quite possible that four texts, all among the oldest of our *ordines* (*Ordo* 1 in the 'short recension', *Ordines* 2, 24 and 26), formed a unit that was copied together, compiled by a single person. The case of the final text, *Ordo* 3, is more ambiguous. This is also presented as a supplement to *Ordo* 1, but in St

---

[23] See Chapter 5.

[24] Michel Andrieu, 'Notes sur une ancienne rédaction de l'« Ordo Romanus Primus »', *Revue des sciences religieuses*, 1 (1921), pp.385–401.

[25] *Les Ordines*, vol. I, pp.343–347; digitised at www.e-codices.unifr.ch/en/csg/0614/4.

[26] Bischoff, *Katalog*, no. 5818, p.330: '[St Gallen IX Jh, (1./)2. Viertel]'.

[27] *Les Ordines*, vol. I, pp.326–329; Bischoff, *Katalog*, vol. III, 5596 p.308: '[St Gallen IX/X. Jh]'; digitised at: www.e-codices.unifr.ch/en/csg/0140/bindingA/0/.

Unique Collections of the Ordines 59

Gallen 614 follows on from *Ordo* 26. In two other manuscripts of Collection B which also had the text, Cologne 138 and Weissenburgenses 91, it directly follows *Ordo* 1, which probably was its original setting.

Ordines 24 and 26 appear with *Ordo* 3 in Brussels, Bibliothèque royale, MS lat.10127–10144, another early manuscript that proves the texts are all older than the St Gallen manuscript itself.[28] Attempts to argue that the manuscript was a handbook for a 'local priest' are unsatisfying as regards the presence of these *ordines* here.[29] Before the antiphoner attributed to Pope Gregory (the Great?), we find *Ordines* 13, 26, 3, 24 and 30A. The text edited as *Ordo* 30A is another version of the Frankish Holy Week *ordo*, compared and contrasted with the ostensibly Roman *Ordines* 26 and 24.[30] The manuscript is thus not, in fact, economical in only offering the simplest and most straightforward *ordines*, but admits the same possibility or necessity of comparison as we have seen elsewhere. Further, *Ordo* 3 deals with diverse aspects of the pontifical Mass and includes the celebration of cardinals on great feasts, and the activities of an archdeacon and an archpriest, which are hardly the concerns of our envisaged humble local priest or something that admitted a 'simple use' in that context. The conception of the local priest's abbreviated liturgical book is another modern category which our *ordo romanus* manuscripts challenge. Brussels 10127–10144 is unfortunately largely damaged, but the presence of three of five of the texts also found in St Gallen 614 here does imply the original presence of *Ordo* 1 and *Ordo* 2, as well. After all, *Ordo* 3 is a supplement to *Ordo* 1, and belongs with it. Just like St Gallen 614, *Ordo* 3 would have been separated from *Ordo* 1. Another connection between the French Brussels manuscript and St Gallen 614 is a small note on the practice of chant during the Easter Octave, present in both manuscripts.[31] This little piece was later used in *Ordo* 27, n.66, so it was also available to the Collection A compiler (in Metz?).[32]

Further proof that these texts travelled together is found in another unique collection, that 'of St Amand' found on the spare folios of a manuscript of Augustine's *De gratia et libero arbitrio* from that monastery, Paris, BnF, MS lat.974, probably copied there in the tenth century from a much older source.[33]

---

[28] *Les Ordines*, vol. I, pp.91–96.

[29] Yitzhak Hen, 'The Knowledge of Canon Law among Rural Priests: The Evidence of Two Manuscripts from around 800', *Journal of Theological Studies*, 50 (1999), pp.117–134.

[30] *Les Ordines*, vol. III, pp.449–458.   [31] *Ibid.*, p.298.   [32] *Ibid.*, p.362.

[33] *Les Ordines*, vol. II, pp.137–170; for the manuscript *Les Ordines*, vol. I, pp.255–256; Bischoff, *Katalog*, vol. III, 3999 p.29: 'wurden ca. Xin Bl.1–4 und 115–121 hinzugefügt um einem Meß*Ordo* und andere liturgischen Texte zu kopieren'; I examined this manuscript in person.

60 Unique Collections of the *Ordines*

The compiler of *Ordo* 4 of the 'Collection of St Amand' had access to *Ordo* 1 in the 'short recension', as well as *Ordines* 2 and 3, implying that the three did belong together, and had travelled to France in this form.[34] Wolfenbüttel Weissenburgenses 91 also had access to *Ordines* 24, 26 and 3, which were copied in whole or in part.

The fact that *Ordo* 1 seems to have been disseminated from Metz, and that Chrodegang might have had something to do with the initial conception of the text, leads us to wonder whether this collection of at least four *ordines* (1, 2, 24 and 26), all among the oldest known, were put together and transmitted by Chrodegang himself. This is not so outlandish, when we consider the appearance of a distinct usage from *Ordo* 24 within the stational list of Metz, compiled under Chrodegang.[35] This is found on the final pages of a Gospel Book from Metz, Paris, BnF, MS lat.268, fol.153r–v, and demonstrates Chrodegang's romanising ambitions.[36] It shows how, through Lent and Easter Week, the clergy of Metz celebrated Masses at various churches through the city; this was clearly modelled on the stational system of the Pope, and used conspicuously Roman terminology.[37] The particular usage concerned was the custom of when to say the *orationes sollemnes* or the great intercessions, a list of prayers for the church, monarch, pope, bishops, Jews, heretics and so on.[38] These normally happened on Good Friday, but the Metz stational list has a curious adaptation. They do happen on Good Friday, but they are said first on the Wednesday of Holy Week, by the bishop with all priests of the city present, then again on Good Friday by the priests in their own churches during Vespers.

> f(eria) IIII. Statio mane prima ad sanctum petrum infra episcopio. Tunc caelebrandae sunt orationes sollempnes et tunc conueniunt omnes presbiteri civitatis in eadem ecclesiae aut quomodo tunc pontifex agit orationes sollempnes sic et ipsi presbiteri sexta feria unusquisque ad uesperum in titulo suo – Statio ipsa die ad missas in eadem ecclesia ad nonam.[39]

---

[34] See Chapter 5.

[35] Theodor Klauser, 'Eine stationsliste der Metzer Kirche aus dem 8. Jahrhundert, wahrscheinlich ein Werk Chrodegangs', *EphLit*, 44 (1930), pp.162–193; reprinted in *Gesammelte Arbeiten zur Liturgiegeschichte, Kirchengeschichte und christlichen Archäologie* (Munich, 1924), pp.22–45.

[36] Digitised at: https://gallica.bnf.fr/ark:/12148/btv1b8426041d.

[37] Klauser, 'Eine stationsliste', p.499: 'collecta ad sanctum petrum ... statio ad sanctum stephanum'; p.500 'in titulo suo'.

[38] R. H. Connolly, 'Liturgical Prayers of Intercession', *The Journal of Theological Studies*, 21 (1920), 219–232; on the prayer for the Jews, John Oesterreicher, 'Pro Perfidis Judaeis', *Theological Studies*, 8 (1947), pp.80–96.

[39] Klaussen, 'Eine stationsliste', p.500: 'On Wednesday, the morning station is first at Saint Peter's inside the episcopal complex. Then the orationes sollempnes should be celebrated and then all the priests of the city should gather in the same church, and how the pontiff then performs the orationes

Unique Collections of the Ordines

This is the exact usage described in *Ordo* 24.

> *Ordo* 24, nn.1–3: Feria quarta, quae est pridie caenae domini, hora tertia, pontifex cum clero et ordine suo procedit ad altare in ecclesia maiore et dicit orationes sollemnes hoc ordine: *Oremus*, et dat orationem *Deus a quo et Iudas.* Post *Amen* sequitur et dicit orationes sollemnes sicut in Sacramentorum continetur; tantummodo pro se intermittit. Post imperatorem vero dicit orationem pro rege Francorum, deinde reliquas per ordinem.[40]

And on Good Friday:

> *Ordo* 24, nn.26–28: Hac expleta, venit pontifex ante altare et dicit: *Oremus*; Diaconus: *Flectamus genua. Levate. Oremus, dilectissimi nobis, in primis pro eccesia sancta Dei*, sicut supra in quarta feria diximus ... Presbiteri vero ecclesiarum, sive de urbe seu de suburbanis, vadunt per ecclesias, ut hoc ordine cuncta ad verperum faciant, hoc tantum mutantes, ut, ubi pontifex meminit apostolicum, ipsi nominent episcopum suum.[41]

As Andrieu noted, there is no evidence in the Sacramentary that the Romans held the *orationes sollenelles* twice in Holy Week, in this manner.[42] This does not preclude the possibility that they did so, of course, but the evidence for the usage remains entirely Frankish and, as here, specifically takes place in a non-Roman setting, since the bishop prays for the *apostolicus*. The *orationes sollenelles* are only ever given in the Sacramentary on Good Friday. The source for the *ordines* that prescribe the same usage was always *Ordo* 24, which perhaps saw the invention of the custom.

We have some evidence here that Chrodegang himself either decided to have them said on Wednesday together, or that this was a pre-existing usage in Metz, reflected equally in the station list and in *Ordo* 24, and securing that text's connection to the city. The fact that the same usage had to be promulgated at the Council of Freising, Reisbach and Salzburg in 800 indicates that it was still then a novelty in some places.[43] Did Chrodegang then wish to gather his priests and clergy together on Wednesday to pray together, including the all-important intercession for the monarch, making sure that the Holy Week was more communal, before they had their lonelier intercession on Friday? It would cohere with the goals of his *Regula* and the station list, to promote the communal religious life of his

---

sollemnpes, so all these priests should do the same on Good Friday in their own titular churches. The station for the Mass on this day is the same church at the ninth hour.'

[40] *Les Ordines*, vol. III, p.287–288.   [41] *Ibid.*, p.293.   [42] *Ibid.*, pp.287–288.

[43] *MGH* Conc.II.1, p.212: 'fer.IIII ante cena Domini orationes, quae scriptae sunt ad fer.VI Parasceue, ab episcopis vel presbiteris hora tertia diei supradictae fer.IIII dicuntur in ecclesia cum genuflexione nisi tantum pro Iudaeis, similiter et in Parasceve hora nona, ut Romani faciunt'.

62 Unique Collections of the *Ordines*

clergy. In any case, this unit of St Gallen 614, with its copies of the 'short recension' of *Ordo* 1, two supplements to the text, and *Ordines* 24 and 26, coheres with Chrodegang's stational list, and his other liturgical priorities. It can be evidenced that the same collection was then later available in North-Eastern France in the Brussels manuscript, and in the Collection of St Amand. In St Gallen 614, evidently a manuscript aimed at preserving copies of older versions of the *ordines*, the same collection was copied out.

In the second part of St Gallen 614, what follows this short collection is quite distinct. Almost all the *ordines* are uniquely recorded here or only copied directly from this particular manuscript.

St Gallen, Stiftsbibliothek, MS 614

pp.213–216 *Ordo* 22: On Roman practices in Lent.[44]

pp.216–217 In Andrieu, the 'Appendix' to *Ordo* 28 but actually not related to that text at all: an *Ordo* of readings on Holy Saturday.[45]

pp.217–213 *Ordo* 12: A directory of antiphons and description of saints' feasts.[46]

pp.223–229 *Ordo* 36: An account of ordinations from the deacon to bishops, including the special ceremonies for the Pope himself: '*De gradibus romanae ecclesiae.*'[47]

pp.229–230 *Ordo* 8: Concerning vestments, beginning with the pontiff.[48] In our manuscript, this has lost the end of the text, ending halfway through on p.229, with the end of the quire. The rest of the *ordo* can be found in St Gallen 140, the copy of St Gallen 614.

Andrieu assigned a Frankish origin to each of these *ordines* individually, recognising that they record Roman usages but were of Frankish manufacture and presented for a Frankish audience. *Ordo* 22 has the *collecta* on Ash Wednesday at Santa Anastasia (n.1), according to correct Roman usage and it mentions the *domnus papa* (n.21). The appendix to *Ordo* 28 nn.2, 4, 6, 10 has the readings and chants on Holy Saturday sung in both Greek and Latin, a detail of Roman practice we know from Frankish *ordines*, since, characteristic of the sparseness of the actual Roman sources, there is no mention of the custom in the authentically Roman sources like the Sacramentary.[49] We know that at Metz this was also done, probably learned from Rome.[50]

---

[44] *Les Ordines*, vol. III, pp.254–262.

[45] *Ibid.*, pp.387–388, 412–413; Andrieu's choice to edit it as an appendix and not a separate *ordo* comes from its presentation by Mabillon, who copied it from St Gallen Stiftsbibliothek 140, the later copy, where it appears directly after *Ordo* 28.

[46] *Les Ordines*, vol. II, pp.451–466.   [47] *Les Ordines*, vol. IV, pp.113–205.

[48] *Les Ordines*, vol. II, pp.309–322.   [49] Also described in *Ordo* 32, nn.16–17.

[50] Andrieu, 'Règlement d'Angilramne de Metz', p.353: 'cantica greca quam et latina dixerint'.

Unique Collections of the Ordines

63

In *Ordo* 12 Christmas is noted *sicut agitur ad sanctam mariam* (Maggiore), and ceremonies of the feasts of saints are described, as celebrated *apud Romanos* with eyewitness details.[51] *Ordo* 36 evidences a particularly strong evocation of Rome: on the first of the Ember Days, the people and congregation of Rome's first ecclesiastical region (as described in *Ordo* 1) gather *ad sanctum Adrianum* and process *ad Sanctam Mariam ad presepem* (the traditional name of Maggiore).[52] On the second, the Friday, they travel to *Santi Apostoli*.[53] Then the ordinations of priests and deacons on the Ember Saturday take place *ad sanctum Petrum* and 'all the regions' are there with the pontiff.[54] The episcopal ordinations take place at the oratory of St Martin (in a detail uniquely witnessed here) at St Peter's; the high altar of that basilica is reserved for the papal ordination alone.[55] The new Pope, the *apostolicus*, is chosen *unus ex cardinalibus*.[56] That papal ordination is here described in much greater detail than in *Ordo* 40 (the document we know was actually present in Rome). Yet the texts were not written by a Roman, but by a Frankish liturgist. The *ordines* are marked by their Frankish liturgical vocabulary, with some peculiarities.[57] *Ordo* 36, in particular, has coloured the Roman services of ordination with details of Frankish practices its Frankish author may simply have mistakenly assumed were used in Rome or as part of the papal ordination.[58] The writer was well informed on Roman

---

[51] *Ordo* 12, n.4.

[52] *Ordo* 36, n.5: 'Fit enim conventus populi et congregatio regionum primum ad sanctum Adrianum et inde pergit pontifex una cum populo precedente solito appartu, id est cruces, turibula vel tale, usque ad sanctam Mariam ad presepem.'

[53] *Ordo* 36, n.12: 'Deinde advocantur VI feria ad sanctos Apostolos.'

[54] *Ordo* 36, n.13: 'Sabbato vero egreditur pontifex ad sanctum Petrum.'

[55] *Ordo* 36, n.30: 'egreditur pontifex de ecclesia sancti Petri et ascendit monasterium sancti Martini . . .'.

[56] *Ordo* 36, n.40: 'Summus namque pontifex, quando benedicitur, eligitur unus ex cardinalibus, de qualicumque titulo fuerit.' On the cardinals of Rome, see Michel Andrieu 'L'origine du titre de cardinal dans l'Église Romaine', *Miscellanea Giovanni Mercati*, vol. V (1946), pp.113–144.

[57] The use of *cerei* rather than *cereostata* is one clue: for example *Ordo* 28 Appendix n.1. See also *Ordo* 36, n.37: 'Pontifex vero ponet manum super caput eius et dicit unam orationem in modum collectae, alteram eo modulamine quo solet contestata cantari': 'Contestata' was a Frankish liturgical term for the preface found, for example, in the Gelasian of the Eighth Century. *Ordo* 36, nn.32–33 uses Frankish terms for the clothing of the Pope, such as *brachiale*, *orarium* and *casula Les Ordines*, vol. IV, pp.148–149.

[58] *Ordo* 36, n.3 refers to the 'Sacramentorum codex . . . usque in subdiaconatus officium', a reference to *Ordo de sacris ordinibus*, the Gelasian of the Eighth Century's texts for minor orders, not known in Rome. The papal consecration is mistaken: *Ordo* 36, n.44–45: 'Postea erigitur ab episcopis et statuetur inter sedem et altare et tenent evangelium super caput vel cervicem ipsius. Et accedit unus episcopus, dat orationem super eum et recedit. Et alter similiter. Accedit tertius et conscrat illum'; compare this with the Roman document, *Ordo* 40, n.5: 'Postmodum adducuntur evangelia et aperiuntur et tenentur super caput electi a diaconibus', which takes place only after the first two prayers have been given by the bishops of Albano and Porto.

64 Unique Collections of the *Ordines*

practices, and particularly on Roman topography, but perhaps received his knowledge of the ordinations second-hand, or wrote them after the fact.

By not analysing these *ordines* in depth in their manuscript context, Andrieu did not consider the possibility that this section was, at least substantially, written by the same person, but there are some distinctive clues that they must all stem from the same experience of liturgical ceremonies in Rome. Both *Ordines* 22 and 12 mention liturgical initiatives taken by Pope Hadrian: in *Ordo* 12, it is noted that he allowed that saint's *passiones vel gesta* (hagiographies) could be read at the celebration in St Peter's, not only in the celebration at the saints' particular *titulus* (church dedicated to them).[59] In *Ordo* 22 it is noted that it was not previously the custom to genuflect when praying for the king on the Saturdays of Lent, but Hadrian instituted that they should genuflect '*pro Carolo rege*' (for Charlemagne).[60] It is impossible that this should in either case be other than Hadrian I (772–795), whose liturgical initiatives were within living memory when the manuscript was written. Such liturgical initiatives are recorded nowhere else, not even in the *Liber Pontificalis*. *Ordo* 36, the text for ordinations in St Gallen 614, has another telling detail: at the climax of the ordination of the new Pope, he is acclaimed – 'Domnus Leo papa, quem sanctus Petrus elegit in sua sede multis annis sedere'.[61] This detail confused Andrieu, who had dated the manuscript (and the *ordo* itself), to the late ninth century, when there had been no Pope Leo for decades. But given that St Gallen 614 was dated by Bischoff to the century's second quarter, this must be Leo III (795–816), Hadrian's immediate successor. Therefore, all three *ordines* stand within a relatively narrow timescale. Since Charlemagne is still named as *rex* and not *imperator*, one might be so bold as to propose 795–800 as the possible time when the *ordines* could have been written.

The proposed timing is evidence that these *ordines* can be associated with a particular circle of Rome-focused bishops around Archbishop Arn of Salzburg (r.784–821). I have argued that the unique details of Roman practice, including notes of Roman locations, which are found in the particularly important manuscript Wolfenbüttel Weissenburgenses 91 are

---

[59] *Ordo* 12, n.25: 'Passiones sanctorum vel gesta ipsorum usque Adriani tempora tantummodo ibi legebantur ubi ecclesia ipsius sancti vel titulus erat. Ipse vero tempore suo renovere iussit et in ecclesia sancti Petri legendas esse instituit.'

[60] *Ordo* 22, n.13: 'Nam sabbato tempore Adriani institutum est ut flecteretur pro Carolo rege; antea vero non fuit consuetudo.'

[61] *Ordo* 36, n.54: 'Lord Leo the Pope, whom Saint Peter has chosen for his seat, let him reign many years.'

Unique Collections of the Ordines   65

to be attributed to the personal experience of one of that circle, Bishop Bernharius of Worms.[62] Like Bernharius, Arn of Salzburg made a significant number of visits to Rome, had personal intimacy with Pope Leo III and was, indeed, himself a writer of *ordines*.[63] He was also abbot of the monastery of St Amand, from where another significant collection of *ordines* and observations of Rome had come, that copied on spare folios of Paris BnF lat.974, 'the Collection of St Amand'.[64] This collection has two *ordines* that are closely related to others (*Ordo* 4, which describes a Frankish Pontifical Mass and is a reworking of *ordines* 1, 2 and 3, and *Ordo* 43, which is a reworking of *Ordines* 41 and 42 on church dedication). But it also has unique treatments of particular ceremonies in Rome: *Ordo* 21 for the Great Litany, and *Ordo* 20 for Candlemas, with figures like the *staurofores* and Roman locations like Sant'Adriano al Foro.[65] There is also *Ordo* 30B, its own narrative of Holy Week that includes many Roman details, particularly in the description of Holy Saturday, and *Ordo* 39, a more detailed narrative of the ordination of a priest in Rome.[66] Andrieu detected a connection between *Ordo* 30B and *Ordo* 12 from St Gallen 614, identifying shared language and concerns within these various dossiers of observations about Roman liturgical practice.[67] Was Arn, the frequent visitor to Rome, source for these texts, or did he have them written, as Bernharius might have done for the notes and observations of Weissenburgenses 91?

A possible link to St Gallen among this circle is provided by another intimate, Archbishop Richulf of Mainz.[68] Richulf visited Rome twice as a *missus* of Charlemagne, first in 781 (thus under Pope Hadrian, whose initiatives the *ordines* mention) and again as escort to Pope Leo in 800.

---

[62] Westwell, 'The *Ordines Romani* and the Carolingian Choreography'.
[63] Meta Niederkorn-Bruck and Anton Scharer (eds.), *Erzbischof Arn von Salzburg* (Munich, 2004).
[64] *Les Ordines*, vol. I, pp.492–493.
[65] *Ordo* 20, n.1: 'veniunt in ecclesia sancti Adriani martyris', n.7 'cruces VII, portantur a stauroforo'; *Ordo* 21, n.10: 'Primitus enim paupers de xenodochio, cum cruce lignea picta . . . Et post ipsos egrediantur cruces VII stacionarias, portantes ab stauroferos.'
[66] *Ordo* 30B, n.42: 'egrediuntur de ecclesia quae apellatur Constantiniana', n.64 'presbiteri cardinales', and the Eucharistic rites concerning the *fermentum* (as described in the Saint-Emmeram gloss, for which below, see p.000), a piece of the Host consecrated by the Pope and taken out to the priests of the *tituli*, in *Ordo* 30B, n.65; *Ordo* 39 (at *Les Ordines*, vol. IV, pp.283–285): n.8, 'VI feria veniente, stacio ad sanctos Apostolos'; n.1, 'adstante primicereo et secundicerio et archidiacono et archipres-bitero'; n.12, 'Sabbato autem veniente in XII lectiones, statio ad beatum Petrum apostolum'; n.26, 'Et procedunt de ecclesia beati petri apostoli unusquisque in titulo suo, habens unusquisque paranymfam presbyterum secum.'
[67] *Les Ordines*, vol. II, p.462, at *Ordo* 30B, n.3.
[68] Theodulf Schieffer, 'Erzbischof Richulf (787–813)', *Jahrbuch für das Bistum Mainz*, 5 (1950), pp.329–342; Franz Staab, 'Erzbischof Richulf (787–813)', in Friedhelm Jürgensmeier (ed.), *Handbuch der Mainzer Kirchengeschichte*, vol. I, *Christliche Antike und Mittelalter*, pt.1., Beiträge zur Mainzer Kirchengeschichte, 6 (Würzburg, 2000), pp.102ff, 138, 144–150 and 841–843.

66 Unique Collections of the *Ordines*

In other ways, Richulf was a classic Carolingian enthusiast for Rome, founding St Alban's monastery in Mainz in 805, whose form imitated the Roman basilica, and corresponding with Pope Leo in intimate terms in 809 over the relics he received from Rome for the new church – the head of Saint Caesarius, borne to him by none other than Bernharius of Worms, returning from his own visit to Rome.[69] Richulf hosted the important 813 Council of Mainz, which both Arn and Bernharius attended, and which was conspicuous in enjoining liturgical observance according to Rome.[70] It might therefore be to Richulf or to one his correspondents that we might look for the confection of the 'pilgrim dossier' that only survives in these two copies of St Gallen, and then partially in much later manuscripts from the eleventh century, of which the earliest can be connected to Mainz.[71] Such texts might have been composed in collaboration with Arn and others of his circle, based on their shared enthusiasm and personal experience of liturgical performance in Rome.

This raises the question of how many *ordines* began life as examples of pilgrim or travel literature, and how easily a sharp line can be drawn between these kinds of texts. The difficulty of drawing such a distinction is starkly demonstrated by a single, unique text, *Ordo* 23, because of its manuscript context in the single known copy.[72] The *ordo* is known to survive only in Einsiedeln, Stiftsbibliothek, MS 326 (likely from Fulda), of which the relevant part is fols.67–97. It is a version of the Roman *Triduum*, the three last days of Holy Week, but it also uses Frankish terminology.[73] The *ordo* directly follows the two famous texts designed specifically to effect an imaginative recollection of Rome in readers: the Einsiedeln Itinerary following a pilgrim's route through the city and the *Sylloge* of Einsiedeln describing inscriptions in Rome.[74] These texts present an almost timeless Rome for the imaginative pilgrim to trace his way through,

---

[69] Leo III, Epistle 9: *Riculfo episcopo Moguntino*, *MGH* Epist. 5, Karolini Aevi 3, pp.67–68: 'Cum ad limina beatorum principum apostolorum Bernharius venerabilis episcopus una cum Adalhardo religioso abbate ... De Reliquiis vero sancti Caesarii, sicut petistis, per eundem Bernharium venerabilem episcopum sanctitati vestrae direximus.'

[70] Wilfried Hartmann, *Die Synoden der Karolingerzeit im Frankreich und in Italien* (Schöningh, 1989), pp.128–140; *MGH* Conc.II.1, p.259: 'Hildibaldus, scilicet sacri palatii archiepiscopus, Rinholfus (of Mainz), et Arno (of Salzburg) archiepiscopi seu Bernharius (of Worms).'

[71] Montecassino, Archivio della Badia, MS 451 contains a bishop's ordination with an oath of obedience to Mainz: *Les Ordines*, vol. I, p.191; Vienna ÖNB 701 also comes from Mainz: *ibid.*, pp.373–388; Parkes, *Making of Liturgy*, pp.185–201.

[72] *Les Ordines*, vol. III, pp.265–273.

[73] *Les Ordines*, vol. I, p.13; Bischoff, *Katalog*, vol. I 1132 p.242: 'In Fulda geschulter Schreiber IX Jh., ca.2 Drittel'; digitised at: www.e-codices.unifr.ch/en/sbe/0326/bindingA/0/Sequence-1016.

[74] G. Walser (ed.), *Die Einsiedler Inschriftensammlung und der Pilgerführer durch Rom (Codex Einsidlensis 326). Facsimile, Umschrift, Übersetzung und Kommentar* (Stuttgart, 1987); Franz Alto

Unique Collections of the Ordines   67

one where the city's spiritual past and present were equally accessible. There are many recollections here of what the texts of the *ordines romani* might do for the same readership.

It is hard to call this a liturgical context, in the manner envisaged by Andrieu. Yet *Ordo* 23 still focuses on many of the same details which the *ordines* reveal the Franks were invested in: the topography of the rites in Rome (various processions around the Lateran and, on Good Friday, *ad Hierusalem* – Santa Croce in Gerusalemme), the numbers of clergy performing them and their positions in the churches (*Ordo* 33, n.33: 'respondent IIII accoliti stantes ad rugas'), as well as furnishings and accoutrements (the fabulous reliquary of the cross carried 'post dorsum domni apostolici' is lovingly described at *Ordo* 33, nn.11–12 down to its sweet balsam fragrance). Eucharistic customs remained of interest (and *Ordo* 32 is more faithful to Roman practice than *Ordo* 24).[75] Because it is placed among the Einsiedeln travel writings, it is impossible not to see this text as performing a similar function by allowing the reader to imagine the ritual unfolding on the very topographical framework the pilgrim literature itself discloses. How many other *ordines* might have allowed this kind of imaginative participation? That was not exclusive to their function as disclosing an arrangement that might be followed liturgically, but allowed that function to be properly put in a context of understanding the rituals as a 'paraphrase of Rome'.

Seeing the *ordines* as 'travel literature' helps us to understand the origins of some of these texts, and that the uses made of them went far beyond what we term 'liturgical'. St Gallen 140 (which copied the same set of *ordines* from St Gallen 614 with additions) embraced this ambiguity by having on the first page of the original manuscript (p.255) an extract from the introduction of Amalarius' third edition of his *Liber Officialis*, when the liturgist spoke as a traveller to Rome who had consulted Roman clergy himself from his trip to Rome in 831: 'Haecine sunt quae a Romana sede accepi de his quae hic inserere volo, quamvis iam latius explanatae sint in sequenti volumine.'[76] In St Gallen 140, Amalarius is paraphrased:

> Haec sunt quae a romana sede accepi. Prima salutatio ad populum *pax uobis* pronuntiatur non *pax uobiscum*. Quando uersus de alleluia canitur exuit se

Bauer, 'Das Bild der Stadt Rom in karolingischer Zeit: Der Anonymus Einsidlensis', *Römische Quartalschrift für christlichen Altertumskunde und Kirchengeschichte*, 92 (1997), pp.190–228.

[75] *Ordo* 23, n.22: 'Attamen apostolicus ibi non communicat nec diaconi. Qui vero communicare voluerit, communicat de capsis de sacrificio quod V feria servatum est. Et qui noluerit ibi communcare vadit per alias aecclesias Romae seu per titulos et communicat.'

[76] Hanssens (ed.), *Opera omnia*, vol. II, p.18: 'Of what I received from the Roman see I wish to insert now the following, since they are to be explained in the coming volume . . ..'

Unique Collections of the *Ordines*

planeta diaconus stolamque post tergum ducit, subdis dextram alam una cum planeta et parat se ad ministrandum, ac in eo habitu perseuerat usquedum apostolicus recesserit de altare. Post euangelium non offert incensum super altare. Calix inuolutus sudario porrigitur ad altare. Quod sudarium ponitur in cornu altaris. Calix ad latus oblate in altari componitur non a fronte. Laetaniae ita celebrantur in uigiliis paschae ut noster mos olim obtinuint, id est post baptismum per septernarium et quinarium et ternarum numerum.[77]

Extracted from Amalarius' work, and given without his name, these miscellaneous recommendations resemble nothing more than one of the Supplements and appendices to the *ordines romani* we find in other contexts, for example scattered throughout the manuscript Wolfenbüttel Weissenburgenses 91, and presented as eyewitness records. Thus, the observations of the traveller here incorporated into a commentary and explanation of the liturgy became possible or potential additions to an *ordo* in their new manuscript context.

---

[77] St Gallen 140 p.255: 'These are what I received from the Roman see. First the greeting to the people is given as *pax uobis* not *pax uobiscum*. When the verse of the alleluia is sung, the deacon takes off his chasuble and puts it with his stole behind his back under the right arm, and prepares himself for ministry and he remains in this aspect until the pope has gone back from the altar. After the gospel, the Romans do not offer incense over the altar. When the chalice, which is covered with a maniple, is taken to the altar, that maniple is placed on the side of the altar while the chalice is placed on the altar at the side of the offering, and not behind it. They recite litanies at the Easter Vigil, as we once had the custom, that is after baptism, sevenfold and fivefold and threefold.'

CHAPTER 4

Liturgical 'Usefulness' and Reading the Ordines Romani

A traditional framing by which medieval manuscripts were identified as 'liturgical' has shaped our understanding of how such manuscripts were supposed to have been used. This imposed certain limits that seem not to have been recognised by medieval copyists and users of the manuscripts in question. Indeed, since manuscripts are never specifically identified as 'liturgical' or by an equivalent term in medieval cataloguing practices, the category itself interprets them immediately within a modern point of view. While that does not make the term useless, it becomes more damaging to our understanding when it is assumed that 'liturgical' manuscripts only had certain proper uses, and were only read and understood in a certain way. In the commentary to the editions of the *ordines romani*, Andrieu assumed that a 'liturgical' manuscript was specifically designed only to be used in the ritual context and directly as a guide or aide to ceremonial that was performed. This reflects still widely held assumptions about how liturgical manuscripts should be interpreted. In Andrieu's conception, all of the contents of such a manuscript should be deployed to that end alone. The *ordines* were originally meant to be 'liturgical' in this same, strict sense (at least their hypothetical originals, if not the manuscript witnesses themselves). Andrieu felt confident drawing the line between *ordines* manuscripts that were was really 'liturgical', and those that were not.[1] In his view, some of the manuscripts of the Collections which were originally intended for liturgical use were afterwards copied in other forms for other uses, for example as a 'library piece', to study the liturgy abstractly.[2] For Collection A and Collection B,

---

[1] *Les Ordines*, vol. I, p.473: 'un livret particulier, vrai livre d'église, se présentant comme un directoire pratique pour certaines cérémonies'; p.482: 'Il n'a pas en vue l'exécution pratique des cérémonies, mais bien l'instruction théologique de ses lecteurs. A cette fin, il s'efforce de composer un recueil didactique de pure érudition. Il élimine les textes liturgiques proprement dits, tels que sont *Les Ordines*'; p.487: 'Par les pièces qui accompagnent *Les Ordines*, ce recueil appartient plutôt au genre des compilations didactiques qu'à celui des vrais livres liturgiques'.
[2] *Ibid.*, p.473: 'Aussi devint-il une pièce de bibliotheque.'

69

70   Liturgical 'Usefulness' and Reading the *Ordines Romani*

a number of the manuscripts were identified as library books in this sense. It was generally the presence of 'non-liturgical' content that led to such identification, most notably that of *expositiones*, which were intended to help understand the potential meanings of liturgical acts.[3] But it was never clear that the people writing and using the manuscripts recognised these stark distinctions.

To decide if a manuscript was 'for use', it was generally the judgement of the modern examiner that was decisive. By Rasmussen, for example, the *ordines romani* were termed aides to cult and not cultic documents in themselves.[4] But in general Andrieu identified the creation of manuscripts for 'use' with two trends he identified: the adjustment of Roman rituals to Frankish usages, as well as the replacement of Roman texts with their Frankish equivalents, and the addition of liturgical material from the Sacramentary to complete the *ordines*, so that they give a more complete picture of the ritual in question. Notably, these trends were those that most distinctly differentiated Collection B from Collection A, hence Andrieu's hypothesis that Collection B was a reworking of Collection A to make it more usable by Franks, and his identification of the earliest manuscripts of Collection B as *petits pontificaux*, embryonic forms of a later genre of liturgical book. To Andrieu and Vogel it was self-evident that such books would have exactly the same driving conception as their centuries-later counterpart, which is defined and could be evaluated by its design for use in a liturgical context.[5] Leroquais wrote, describing what we term Collection B in a poetic fashion, and expressing the same mindset of a teleological evolution of book types: 'Ce premier essai fut timide et gauche ... la chrysalide n'est plus chenille et elle n'est pas encore papillon.'[6] Of course, such attempts are only timid and gauche when we measure them against what the modern pontifical would become. We have

---

[3] *Ibid.*, pp.476–485.

[4] Niels Krogh Rasmussen, 'Unité et diversité des Pontificaux latins aux VIIIe, IXe, et Xe siècles', in *Liturgie et l'Église particulière et liturgie de l'Église universelle Conférences Saint-Serge, XXIIe Semaine d'études liturgiques, Paris, 30 juin–3 juillet 1975* (Rome, 1976), p.398.

[5] Vogel, *Medieval Liturgy*, pp.226–229; *Les Ordines*, vol. I, p.475: '(Cologne 138) est même de physionomie plus pur, car, à l'inverse de la vaste compilation du Xe siècle, il n'a admis aucune pièce qui ne fût d'usage liturgique et pût altérer son caractère de véritable livre d'église'; Rasmussen, *Les pontificaux*, p.453: 'Le document liturgique dont il est ici question est un document qui sert exclusivement à l'accomplissement d'un ou du plusiers rites liturgiques réservés d'un évêque'. See also Susan Rankin, 'Carolingian Liturgical Books: Problems of Categorization', *Gazette du Livre Médiéval* 62 (2016) pp.21–33 on the pitfalls of seeing Carolingian books as antecedents of modern genres.

[6] Victor Leroquais, *Les pontificaux manuscrits des bibliothèques publiques de France*, vol. I (Paris, 1938), p.xx: 'This first attempt was timid and inexpert ... the chrysalis was no longer a caterpillar and it was still not yet a butterfly'.

Liturgical 'Usefulness' and Reading the Ordines Romani 71

already seen how manuscripts of Collection B, including those emphatically identified by Andrieu as *pontificaux*, allowed texts that were in fact not easily comprehensible as liturgically useful for the Franks, such as the papal ordination (*Ordo* 40). Clearly, Carolingian manuscripts which have been identified by modern scholars as 'pontificals' were also designed to meet other expectations.[7]

The second trend Andrieu identified as a sign of 'use' also reveals significant individual agency on the part of the compilers, and therefore requires a more in-depth analysis of individual examples. This was the addition of spoken material to the *ordines*, a process identified as critical in the creation of 'pontificals'.[8] However, the rubrics or *ordines* describing actions in a ceremony and the spoken words of the prayers accompanying ceremonies were never as straightforwardly separate as this reconstruction assumed. Certain *ordines* originated in the Sacramentary and had always been accompanied by prayers there. But it is true that Collection B saw the addition of more spoken elements from the Sacramentary to its manuscripts. In all the available manuscripts of this Collection, this process included the insertion of the full homilies and Creeds accompanying *Ordo* II's scrutiny ritual.[9] The manuscripts of Collection B also possess certain blessings of objects following the church dedication ritual of *Ordo* 42.[10] But, in fact, both of these *ordines* had first appeared in the Sacramentary, where they are accompanied by these same spoken elements. Their reinsertion by the Collection B compiler was a somewhat more complex process than Andrieu supposed. In the case of Collection II, rather than being moved away from the original *ordo*, it was returned to looking more like the original.

Even more interesting, however, are a selection of accompanying prayers taken directly from the Sacramentary, which vary according to the manuscripts and reveal the agency of compilers in the selection of material to accompany the *ordines*. In Verona, Biblioteca Capitolare, MS XCI, for example, many of these added prayers concern further ordination rituals (fols.60v–61r *AD CLERICUM FACIENDUM*; fol.63r *AD ABBATEM FACIENDUM UEL ABBATISSAM*), but also prayers for visitations (fol.63r 'ORATIO AD UISITANDOS FRATRES'; fol.63r–v 'ORATIO AD UISITANDAS ANCILLA DEI'). These prayers are taken from both available

---

[7] Hamilton, 'The Early Pontificals'; Westwell, 'Content and the Ideological Construction'.
[8] Leroquais, *Les pontificaux manuscrits*, vol. I, pp.xviii–xx; *Les Ordines*, vol. I, pp.473–476.
[9] *Les Ordines*, vol. II, p.367.
[10] These come (generally) from the Gelasian of the Eighth Century; see *Gellonensis*, Dumas (ed.), 2430–2435, pp.364–365.

72   Liturgical 'Usefulness' and Reading the *Ordines Romani*

Sacramentary traditions, the Gregorian and the Gelasian.[11] The addition of three prayers *IN AGENDA MORTUORUM* on fol.64v reveal that at least one manuscript used was the Gregorian Sacramentary available in Verona, Biblioteca Capitolare, XCI copied around the same time, since these prayers also appear in the Supplement unique to the Verona manuscript.[12] Cologne 138 is obviously closely related to the Verona manuscript and copied many of the same texts, but includes further borrowings from the Gelasian Sacramentary (fol.36r 'BENEDICTIO UESTIMENTORUM UIRGINUM UEL UIDUARUM') on similar themes.[13] From the same source, the manuscript has also added on fol.26v three scrutiny Masses directly following *Ordo* 11.[14] The *Ordo* notes that Masses should be performed, but the Masses are only summarised in that text.[15] Here they appear in full. Ranging more widely for other liturgical sources, Cologne 138 also has a list of antiphons for the procession of relics.[16] Chants for the same occasion can be found in various antiphoners, but the extensive list of eleven antiphons that are found here are identical to none of them.[17] Particularly interesting is the presence on fol.33r of two ritualised announcements for the Ember Days which introduce the *Ordo* for those days *Ordo* 37: 'DENUNTIATIO MENSIS PRIMI QUARTI SEPTIMI DECIMI' and 'ITEM INVITATIO PLEBIS DE IEIUNIO MENSIS QUARTI SEPTIMI ET DECIMI'.[18] Andrieu could not identify their source, but in fact both are present in the Sacramentary *Veronense*, Verona, Biblioteca Capitolare LXXXV (80), the

---

[11] For those from the Gregorian, see for example *Le sacramentaire grégorien*, Deshusses (ed.), vol. I, 991–996, pp.339–342, 996 p.216. For the Gelasian: the Philipps Sacramentary: *Liber Sacramentorum Augustodunensis*, Otto Heiming (ed.), CCSL, 159B (Turnholt, 1984), 1829, 1831, p.226; *Gellonensis*, Dumas (ed.), 2812, 2814, p.442.

[12] These prayers are obscured to a significant degree by damage from humidity but we can identify the words '< . . . >peccata in mundo < . . . >uerissime pietatis absterge. Per dominum' indicating the last of three prayers set out exactly as in Verona XCI; *Le sacramentaire grégorien*, Deshusses (ed.), vol. III, p.162; Meersseman *et al.*, *L'orazionale dell'archidiacono Pacifico*, p.32.

[13] *Gellonensis*, Dumas (ed.), 2604, p.405; Heiming (ed.), *Augustodunensis*, Heiming (ed.) 1617, p.197.

[14] 'INCIPIT MISSA QUA PRO SCRUTINO ELECTORUM CELEBRATUR': *Engolismensis*, Saint-Roch (ed.), 417–423, p.56; *Augustodunensis*, Heiming (ed.), 397–403, pp.46–47; 'ITEM ALIA MISSA PRO SCRUTINIO': *Engolismensis*, Saint-Roch (ed.), 464–467, pp.61–62; *Augustodunensis*, Heiming (ed.), 410–413, p.48; 'ITEM MISSA PRO SCRUTINO DIE IN AURIUM APERTIONEM': *Engolismensis*, Saint-Roch (ed.), 510–513, p.67; *Gellonensis*, Dumas (ed.), 533, p.65.

[15] *Ordo* 11, nn.30–36.

[16] Cologne 138, fol.40r–v: 'ANTIPHONAE PER [VIAM] AD RELIQUIAS DEDUCENDAS.'

[17] *Antiphonale Missarum sextuplex*, René-Jean Hesbert (ed.) (Brussels, 1935), n.212a, pp.218–220.

[18] Cologne 138 fol.33r–v: 'ANNOUNCEMENT OF THE FIRST FOURTH SEVENTH AND TENTH MONTH; THEN THE INVITATION OF THE PEOPLE TO THE FEAST IN THE FOURTH SEVENTH AND TENTH MONTH.'

Liturgical 'Usefulness' and Reading the Ordines Romani   73

oldest surviving book of Roman prayer material.[19] The presence of this ancient, unusual material in Cologne 138 reveals once again the diversity of sources compilers put to use in creating these manuscripts. Here, for example, are represented all three of the Sacramentary traditions identified by modern scholars! Thus, the *ordo romanus* manuscript managed to distil the complex Sacramentary tradition into useful and much less extensive and complex manuscripts.

In the Regensburg example of the same Collection B, Munich Clm 14510, among a number of extra blessings, mostly from the Gelasian (such as those for ordeals and for vessels discovered in antique places), there are several blessings of royalty.[20] Among them is also a series of three prayers under the title 'BENEDICTIO REGALIS' (fol.73r–v), which belong to a rite of coronation.[21] They are highlighted with a signum in the margin, perhaps a form of zeta, indicating scribal attention.[22] We know that Baturich took part in the coronation of Louis the German in Regensburg in 826, along with bishops of Salzburg, Freising, Passau and Eichstätt.[23] Thus we can glimpse here the personalisation of the collection's material to its commissioner, and imagine that this book was used in the royal presence. We can therefore imagine that Baturich himself selected the other blessings in the book, and he also had interest in the *ordo* content, including the curiosities such as *Ordo* 44, describing the Roman *diligentia*.

Finally, Wolfenbüttel Weissenburgenses 91 is another manuscript inter-preted as an attempt at the pontifical, interpreted as meeting the same needs and genre conventions as the later editorial construction of the *Pontifical Romano-Germanique*. However, 'it did not attain the perfection' of the genre.[24] Here, prayers said in the ceremonies described in the *ordines* throughout are generally given in abbreviated form, but with both an incipit and an explicit (and not just an incipit as is usual), which means that the

---

[19] *Sacramentarium Veronense (Cod.Bibl.-Capit. Veron.LXXXV(80))*, Leo Cunibert Mohlberg (ed.) (Rome, 1994), pp.108, 114; on *Veronense*, Vogel, *Medieval Liturgy*, pp.35–46.

[20] Fol.72v: 'BENEDICTIO SUPER PRINCIPEM'; in the Gelasian Sacramentary see *Gellonensis*, Dumas (ed.), 2091, p.296; on the genre, Mary Garrison, 'The *Missa pro principe* in the Bobbio Missal', in Yitzhak Hen and Rob Meens (eds.), *The Bobbio Missal: Liturgy and Religious Culture in Merovingian Gaul* (Cambridge, 2004), pp.206–218.

[21] *Ordines coronationis Franciae: Texts and Ordines for the Coronation of Frankish and French Kings and Queens*, Richard Jackson (ed.), vol. I (Philadelphia, 1995), pp.66–68.

[22] Evina Steinová, *Notam superponere studui. The Use of Annotation Symbols in the Early Middle Ages* (Turnhout, 2019), p.223.

[23] Goldberg, *Struggle for Empire*, pp.51–52.

[24] *Les Ordines*, vol. I, p.490: 'La tentative du moine de Wissembourg n'atteint pas la perfection.'; for the '*pontifical romano-germanique*' as an editorial invention, Henry Parkes, 'Questioning the Authority of Vogel and Elze's PRG', Gittos and Hamilton (eds.), *Understanding Medieval Liturgy*, pp.76–100.

74 Liturgical 'Usefulness' and Reading the *Ordines Romani*

compiler has conscientiously consulted the Sacramentary to find these details, a work that required no small effort and a very deep acquaintance with the Sacramentary.[25] In several cases, the compiler refers directly to the Sacramentary.[26] He also used the same *usque* form to add exact references for several readings and chants, indicating other liturgical sources too.[27] There is one case in *Ordo* 11 where a prayer *post datum salem* is indicated, which can be seen in the Gellone Sacramentary's *ordo* of baptism, but which no other copy of *Ordo* 11 had mentioned.[28] Two of the longest, more important prayers of Holy Week are given similar treatment also unique to this manuscript: the Exultet blessing of the Paschal candle edited by Andrieu as *Ordo* 25, and the blessing of the font, which forms part of *Ordo* 28A, n.4.[29] In the latter case, rubrics accompanying the blessing from the Sacramentary are given in full.[30] Parallel to Cologne 138, but independently, Wolfenbüttel Weissenburgenses 91 has two announcements for the Ember Days to introduce its ordination rituals, but it used the more common forms that were found in the Gelasian Sacramentary, rather than the much rarer texts from the *Veronense* that were used by Cologne 138.[31] Among these four manuscripts, therefore, there is the common excerption of the Sacramentary but in individualised and diverse ways, sometimes seemingly addressing needs that would be directly useful in the localities where the manuscript was used.

---

[25] Many examples but for example *Ordo* 11 n.24 var.10: '*Aeternam ac iustissimam pietatem tuam* **deprecor, domine sancte, pater omnipotens aeterne Deus, usque: ad percipiendum gratiam tuam, per dominum nostrum Iesu Christum Filium tuum qui venturus*'; *Ordo* 28, n.51 var.4: '*Nec te latet Satanas* **usque in nomine domini nostri Iesu Christi qui uenturus est iudicare uiuos et mortuos.*'

[26] *Ordo* 24, n.10, var.4: 'Dicta antiphonam ad introita. **Nobis autem gloriari oportet. Deinde, oratione facta, sicut Sacramentorum continet.**' *Ordo* 34, n.12, var.6: 'Et consecrat eum presbyterum **sicut Sacramentorum continet.**'

[27] *Ordo* 24 n.7, var.3: '*Passio domini nostri iesu Christi secundum Lucam* **cap.CCIX. Adpropinquabat dies festus azymorum, usque in quo nondum quisquam positus fuerat.*'

[28] *Ordo* 11, n.6, var.13: 'Sequitur benedictio post datum salem. *Deus patrem nostrorum, Deus uniuersae conditor ueritatis* et reliqua, usque: *aeterna praemia consequi mereatur*'; *Gellonensis*, Dumas (ed.), 2222, p.313.

[29] *Les Ordines*, vol. III, pp.304, 421–422.

[30] *Ordo* 28a, n.4: '*Deus qui invisibili potentia tua sacramentorum tuorum mirabiliter operaris effectum* usque *indulgentiam consequantur*. Hic signas aquam primam crucem: *hanc aquam*, cum manu tua dividens in modum crucis X: secundam: *Unde benedico X te, creatura aquae*; similiter tertiam: *benedico X te et per Iesum Christum filium eius*, usque *in nomine patris et filii et spiritus sancti*. Hic mutas sensum, quasi lectionem legens: *Haec nobis precepta seruantibus, tu, Deus omnipotens, adesto* usque: *mentibus efficaces*. Hic imponuntur cerei: *Descendat in hanc plenitudinem fontis uirtus spiritus tui*, et insufflas in aquam tribum uicibus.'

[31] 'DENUNTIATIO IEIUNIORUM PRIMI QUARTI SEPTIMI DECIMI MENSES', Old Gelasian in *Liber Sacramentorum Romanae Aeclesiae Ordinis Anni Circuli (Cod. Vat. Reg. lat. 316/ Paris Bibl. Nat. 7193 41/56)*, Leo Eizenhöfer, Leo Cunibert Mohlberg and Petrus Siffrin (eds.), Rerum Ecclesiasticarum Documenta. Series Maior, Fontes 4 (Rome, 1960), 652–653, pp.101–102; *Gellonensis*, Dumas (ed.), 272, 1094, pp.34, 145–146.

Arrangement and Explanation 75

Nevertheless, the *ordines* themselves are among the more ambiguous liturgical texts, and their relation to practice is not at all clear. The distinction between an *ordo romanus* (which offers a potential arrangement of a rite, including the preconditions for its understanding) and an *expositio liturgicae* (a text which in most cases also describes a ritual, step by step, and then offers a commentary on the potential rationale of each individual step) is not very clear cut in most cases. Texts of these kinds seem to have been read in complementary, if not always identical, ways and as part of the same process of working out liturgy, guided by the arrangement of manuscripts. Therefore, *ordines* could rather have been originally designed in many cases to be placed in manuscripts Andrieu would have designated 'non-liturgical', rather than this representing a falling away from their original purpose. It is certainly true that almost every surviving *ordo romanus* manuscript challenges the idea that 'liturgical' (in the sense assumed) was a boundary that medieval compilers confined themselves or their readers within. We have seen the repetition of descriptions of the same ritual in two or more contrasting *ordines*, for example in church dedication (independently in Collection B manuscripts and in Wolfenbüttel Weissenburgenses 91), Holy Week (manuscripts of Collection A from Lorsch and Murbach/Regensburg) and so on. We have also seen the copying of rituals such as the papal ordination (*Ordo* 40) in Cologne 138, which could never be actually performed, in Frankish manuscripts designated as 'pontificals' for use. Liturgical use cannot be conceptualised, then, as mere carrying out of the *ordo*'s instructions. Rather, these arrangements invite, or even demand, the response of the reader to the whole contents of the manuscript, taking in the ideological cues the compiler had set up, comparing distinctive narratives and taking what was useful, integrating and building up a picture of how a rite would be performed and how this arrangement should be understood. The interaction with the reader's own pre-existing knowledge and experience would also come into play, and his or her own priorities for what the rite might mean. Finally, Andrieu's designation of the manuscripts as *petits pontificaux* implied some attention to the physical format of the manuscripts, but he made no systematic study of this, to which we will return in Chapter 5.

Arrangement and Explanation

Where *ordines* stand alongside *expositiones*, the former texts are invited to be read in diverse ways. A particularly good example is the manuscript Zurich, Zentralbibliothek, Car. C 102, probably created at or near Nonantola. Half of the manuscript is a copy of 'Collection B', which

76   Liturgical 'Usefulness' and Reading the *Ordines Romani*

reveals itself to be particularly well developed in taking prayer elements out of the Sacramentary to complement and complete the *Ordo* texts. In *ordines* 11 and 42, for example, all of the spoken prayer texts are written out in full from the Sacramentary.[32] Unique to this manuscript, *Ordo* 28 for Holy Week is provided with the accompanying words for the Mass on the Wednesday of Holy Week the Maundy Thursday Chrism Mass, which includes the rubrics mentioning the *domnus papa* from the Gregorian Sacramentary, and the consecration of the font, where the rubrics from a Gelasian Sacramentary are also inserted in boxes in the margin.[33] These significant interventions run over several pages. At the end of *Ordo* 41, the Mass to be said in the newly dedicated church is given in full, with both the prayers from the Sacramentary and accompanying antiphons. As with the note of an offertory chant *Dextera Domini* with the Chrism Mass, this suggests that, as we more often see in Italy, the Sacramentary used as a source was a local copy which had antiphons added to each Mass.[34] In other manuscripts, not least in the creation of Collection B itself, the addition of spoken material from the Sacramentary to the *ordines* was identified by Andrieu as a sign that the manuscript was intended to be used in a liturgical context, and such manuscripts were represented as *petits pontificaux*. The Zurich manuscript goes significantly further than all other such manuscripts.

But in the case of Zurich Car. C 102, Andrieu presented the manuscript as a classic among his category of non-liturgical *collections didactiques* and

---

[32] For example *Ordo* 11, n.4, var.7: 'Et inponens manum super capita eorum dicit: *Omnipotens sempiterne Deus, pater domini nostri Iesu Christi **respicere digneris super hos famulos tuos quos ad rudimenta fidei** . . . etc.'; *Ordo* 42, n.27 var.12: 'sicut in Sacramentorum continetur. **Prefacio linteaminum. *Domine omnipotens sicut ab inicio hominibus utilia et necessaria creasti* . . . Item benedictio ad omnia in usum basilice. *Dignare, Deus omnipotens* . . . etc.';** Two additional blessings of objects, 'AD TABULAS BENEDICENDAS' and 'BENEDICCIO CRUCIS', also follow *Ordo* 42 on fols.28r–29v.

[33] Only the end of the Mass of Wednesday is found Zurich Car. C 102, fol.14r: *Le sacramentaire grégorien*, Deshusses (ed.), vol. I, p.170–171; *Ordo* 28, n.15, var.4: '**Cantate Offertorio*: Dextera Domini, sequitur super oblata: Ipse tibi quesumus domine sancta pater omnipotens* . . . . Sequitur: *Hanc igitur oblationem* . . . *Qui pridie* . . . .*in sanctas ac venerabiles.* Item in ultimo, antequam dicitur *Per quem hec omnia domine semper bonas creas* levantur de ampullis quas offerunt populi et benedicit tam domnus papa quam quam omnes presbiteri. Benedictio olei pro infirmis: *Emitte* . . .';** see *Le sacramentaire grégorien*, Deshusses (ed.), 329–334, vol. I, pp.171–173.; *Ordo* 28, n.69, var.5: 'et dat oracionem [*sic*] **Benediccio fontis*. Omnipotens sempiterne deus, adesto magne pietatis tuae* . . . Consecratio fontis. *Dominus uobiscum* . . . *Vere Dignum et iustum est, equum et salutare. Deus qui invisibili potenciam* [*sic*] . . . *nova infancia renascatur.* Per',** see *Gellonensis*, Dumas (ed.), 702–704d, pp.98–99.

[34] Andrieu edited it as an appendix to *Ordo* 41, in *Les Ordines*, vol. IV, pp.348–349. The Mass is Gelasian: *Augustodunensis*, Heiming (ed.), 1488–1492, pp.175–176; on Italian Sacramentaries with this feature, see Rankin, 'Carolingian Liturgical Books'.

Arrangement and Explanation

firmly declared that it would not be carried in church (i.e. used liturgically); Susan Keefe followed him by referring to the manuscript as a 'school book'.[35] They were both impressed by the volume of *expositiones* attached to the *ordines* in this case, but the coexistence of dynamics that Andrieu represented as contradictory (the more complete representation of rites by the addition of material from the Sacramentary, and the deeper exploration of the same rites by the addition of *expositiones* addressing the rationale of the individual rituals) should make us question whether copyists felt themselves constrained by such strict understandings of how a manuscript ought to have been used. The *expositiones* appear here in the second part of the manuscript separate from the *ordines*, from fol.33r onwards, and they include the coherent dossier of the rare works by Amalarius of Metz, and his correspondence with Abbot Peter of Nonantola. The content includes two separate expositions of baptism responding to Charlemagne's survey with the accompanying exchange of letters between Emperor and bishop (Amalarius' own on fols.70r–76v and a second, anonymous response on fols.55r–59v).[36] There are also two *expositiones* by Amalarius on the Mass (fols.78r–87r), with differing levels of detail and comprehensiveness.[37] A commentary on the Canon of the Mass known as *Dominus uobiscum* begins on the final folio of this section.[38] This abundance of exposition on the same rites, which approaches the same ritual acts and words from various perspectives and with slightly differing methods, is far from unusual among similar manuscripts. The same tension is visible in the St Petersburg manuscript from Corbie, which also independently excelled in the completion of *ordines* by adding spoken elements from the Sacramentary to *Ordo* 11, yet at the same time offers various *expositiones*, such as Theodulf of Orleans' letter on baptism and the same commentary on the Canon of the Mass, known as *Dominus uobiscum*.[39]

---

[35] *Les Ordines*, vol. I, p.476: 'Un tel volume est fait pour l'étude. On le lit dans une bibliothèque, mais on ne l'emporte pas à l'église'; Keefe, *Water and the Word*, vol. II, pp.17, 29.

[36] On the first text: Hanssens (ed.), *Opera omnia*, vol. I, pp.237–251 and discussed at pp.95–106; Keefe, *Water and the Word*, vol. II, pp.337–351; on the second text (discussed below): Susan Keefe, 'The Claim of Authorship in Carolingian Baptismal Expositiones: The Case of Odilbert of Milan', *Fälschungen im Mittelalter. Internationaler Kongreß der Monumenta Germaniae Historica, München 16–19 September 1986*, vol. V (Hanover, 1988), pp.355–401; Keefe, *Water and the Word*, vol. II, pp.171–183.

[37] Edited as the *Missae expositionis geminus codex*, Hanssens (ed.), *Opera omnia*, vol. I, pp.255–286; see further, and for evidence that the text was by Amalarius and had a specifically epistolary character, Herbert Schneider, 'Roman Liturgy and Frankish Allegory: Editions of Fragments of Amalarius', in Julia M. H. Smith (ed.), *Early Medieval Rome and the Christian West: Essays in Honour of Donald A. Bullough* (Leiden, 2000), pp.358–361.

[38] Hanssens (ed.), *Opera omnia*, vol. I, pp.283–336; discussed at pp.110–114.

[39] *Les Ordines*, vol. II, p.370; Theodulf of Orleans in Keefe, *Water and the Word*, vol. II, pp.279–321.

78   Liturgical 'Usefulness' and Reading the *Ordines Romani*

The association of the *ordines romani* with the works of Amalarius is visible in a number of manuscripts. Particularly interesting is the related group of manuscripts associated with the monasteries of St Gallen and Reichenau. We have already taken note of St Gallen 446 as a manuscript which enclosed the *ordines* of Collection B among a varied set of *expositiones*, some of which were Amalarius' work. It contains the exposition of the Canon known after its first word, *Dominus uobiscum* (pp.85–105), and another, 'A COENOBIO DIONISII UENIT' (pp.50–79), a further *expositio* comprised mostly of extracts from Isidore, described as 'ISTUD A PALATIO AQUISGRANI VENIT' (p.79), as well as two baptismal descriptions, one by Alcuin (pp.145–146) and the one by Amalarius in a letter to Charlemagne (pp.147–159).[40] Directly after *Ordo* 1 in this manuscript appears another detailed Mass exposition, the *Eglogae de Ordine Romano* (St Gallen 446, pp.18–50).[41] This follows the methodology of Amalarius of Metz by interpreting allegorically the gestures and positions as well as the words of the Mass ceremony. Though its attribution to Amalarius has been disputed, it is ascribed to Amalarius in a note: 'SEQUENTIA AMALHERE ABBAS EDIDIT' (p.18), written in the same hand that added context to other expositions in this manuscript. The attribution of the text to Amalarius appears in the other related manuscripts: for example, in St Gallen 614 it is a note in the upper margin: 'Haec amalhere abbas aedidit' (St Gallen 614, p.232), but this hand seems to be a later corrector, maybe working from St Gallen 446 itself. In the case of St Gallen 614, the *Eglogae* was originally separated from the gathering of *ordines romani* I described in the Chapter 3 which ended with the incomplete *Ordo* 8. It also begins with a blank page (p.231), opening a new gathering of texts that was originally distinct. According to Bischoff, this portion was written at Reichenau not long after the *ordines*.[42] Bischoff identified one of the hands at work here with Reginbert, the librarian of Reichenau, hence the *terminus ante quem* of 845, his death, assigned to the manuscript.[43] Another of the hands might be that of Grimald, later abbot of Reichenau and St Gallen.[44] To the *Eglogae* were later added the Frankish episcopal Mass described in *Ordo* 9 (pp.264–269), presented as a continuation to the *Eglogae*, despite having several intermediary blank pages filled in with texts from Isidore on the

---

[40] *Ibid.*, pp.88–90.
[41] Hanssens (ed.), *Opera omnia*, vol. III, pp.229–265; discussed in Hanssens (ed.), *Opera omnia*, vol. I, pp.202–214.
[42] Bischoff, *Katalog*, vol. III, p.330: 'MS 614 (p.231–270) [Reichenau IX.Jh, 2.Viertel (vor AD 846)].'
[43] BSB ANA 553, A, I, ST GALLEN, 8: 'die ll.(Linien?) am 255 und -257 von Reginbert'; Karl Preisendanz, 'Reginbert von der Reichenau. Aus Bibliothek und Skriptorium des Inselklosters', *Neue Heidelberger Jahrbücher* (1952/3), pp.1–49.
[44] BSB ANA 553, A, I, ST GALLEN, 8: '255–263 . . . Grimald?'

Arrangement and Explanation

episcopal office.[45] The portion ends with another blank page, indicating that the *Eglogae* and *Ordo* 9 were the only contents of this portion. The new *Ordo* is laid out in the same way as the *Eglogae*, without a title to differentiate it. As we will see, they are complementary pieces.

The appearance of an attribution to Amalarius in St Gallen 446, probably not long after Amalarius' death, would support his authorship of the *Eglogae*, about which doubts had been raised, probably unnecessarily.[46] The root of these doubts was the understanding that Amalarius as a liturgical 'reformer' would only represent one form of the Mass as definitive, rather than adjusting his depiction of the ceremony according to the needs of his readers and the specificity of the works in question (which he visibly did).[47] This association of the *Eglogae* with the *ordines* is quite revealing about the purpose of the latter. That Amalarius chose to call this work *de ordine romano* is itself an interesting point, since the *Eglogae* does not describe the papal Mass of *Ordo* I involving the Roman clergy, but rather a quite ordinary episcopal Mass. It both influenced and was influenced by the *ordines romani*, but it does not describe the Mass of the *Ordo* I straightforwardly, and adds certain key rituals of its own, such as washing hands, the extinction of candles after the gospel, movements of the candles, a single immixtion before the Pax and so on.[48] The circulation of reworkings of *Ordo* I in *Ordines* 4, and 9 (as well as *Ordines* 5 and 10 which are only known in later manuscripts) suggests that this was the normal way of reading, understanding and 'using' the Roman *ordo*.[49] That is to say, the method Amalarius undertook – where the *ordo* is one source to work out what was meaningful and what the ritual meant, but that many other exigencies and preferences might or might not enter into the repurposing of it – seems to have been a common way of using these texts.

---

[45] The recent catalogue has the same conclusion: Beat Matthias von Scarpatetti, *Die Handschriften der Stiftsbibliothek St. Gallen*, vol. I: pt. IV: *Codices 547–669: Hagiographica, Historica, Geographica, 8.–18. Jahrhundert* (Wiesbaden 2003), pp.198–206. 'Fortsetzung von des (232–258) angefangenen Textes über den 1. Ordo der Papstmesse'; BSB ANA 553, A, I, ST GALLEN, 8: '264–269 . . . IX 3/4?', not, as Bischoff, *Katalog* indicated, at the same time as the rest.

[46] Emmanuel Flicoteux, 'Un Problème de littérature liturgique: Les «Eclogae de officio Missae» d'Amalare', *RevBen*, 25 (1908), pp.304–320; Christopher Jones, *A Lost Work by Amalarius of Metz: Interpolation in Salisbury Cathedral Library MS 154* (London, 2001), p.57.

[47] Wolfgang Steck, *Der Liturgiker Amalarius: Eine quellenkritische Untersuchung zu Leben und Werk eines Theologen der Karolingerzeit* (Munich, 2000), pp.68–74. On Amalarius' methods, see Samuel Collins, *The Carolingian Debate over Sacred Space* (New York, 2012), pp.41–65; Els Rose and Arthur Westwell, 'Correcting the Liturgy and Sacred Language', in Westwell, Rhijn and Rembold (eds.), *Rethinking the Carolingian Reforms*, pp.141–175.

[48] Hanssens (ed.), *Opera omnia*, pp.240–241: 'Candela primo ab acolitis inluminantur extra ecclesiam, et per acolitos portantur in ecclesiae . . .'; p.247: 'Post lectum evangelium candela extinguntur'; p.258: 'Postea namque commixtum corpus Domini cum vino, simulque pace adnuntiata.'

[49] See Chapter 3.

80 Liturgical 'Usefulness' and Reading the *Ordines Romani*

The *Eglogae* are found similarly associated with *ordines romani* in St Gallen, MS 446, and Bamberg, Staatsbibliothek cod.lit.131 (and in a later manuscript, Einsideln *Stiftsbibliothek*, MS 110).[50] In these cases the *Eglogae* either follows *Ordo* 1, dealing with the Mass, or, in the Bamberg example, is immediately followed by *Ordo* 7, which discusses the canon. (*Ordo* 7 also follows the *Eglogae* in St Gallen 446.)[51] This group of three manuscripts represents a related group stemming from St Gallen and Reichenau. After the complex *Eglogae*, these manuscripts share a number of simpler, shorter expositions on various subjects: 'DE VESTIMENTIS SACERDOTALIBUS', 'DE SACRAMENTIS AECCLESIAE', 'DE ORDINE MISSAE', as well as the *Dominus uobiscum*.[52] The connection with Reichenau is implied by a fourth, related book that was once in Reichenau, listed in the book list made by Reginbert of those books acquired between 835 and 846.[53] That book contained: 'expositiones diversae super missam ac Ordo Romanus qualiter missa celebratur, ac walafridi libellus, qualiter Ordo ecclesiasticus . . . et quomodo per temporum augmentationes sit multiplicatus in diuerso'.[54] Therefore, this Reichenau example certainly contained *Ordo* 1, the *Ordo romanus qualiter missae celebratur*, like the St Gallen and Einsiedeln manuscripts do, but which the Bamberg manuscript left out. In the Reichenau example was also found Walahfrid Strabo's *Libellus de exordiis*, another ambitious interpretation of liturgical customs and usages with a different focus to Amalarius, which we see also in St Gallen 446, pp.213–303.[55] In fact St Gallen 446 might represent a direct copy of Reginbert's manuscript, since it contains the same texts (expositions, *ordines* and Walahfrid). If so, Reichenau may have possessed a copy of Collection B.

In the hands of their copyists, the arrangement of this related group of manuscripts was potentially interactive, and could incorporate various additions of *ordines* (including the whole of Collection B in St Gallen 446), as well as the addition or substitution of the *expositiones*. This arrangement of *ordines* and *expositiones* inculcated in St Gallen and Reichenau seems to have reached southern Germany or Italy, judging by the palaeographical verdict on the copy in Bamberg, which was copied by a scribe named Reginpoldo.[56]

---

[50] *Les Ordines*, vol. I, pp.479–482. [51] *Les Ordines*, vol. II, pp.253–305.

[52] *Les Ordines*, vol. I, p.337–338. [53] *Les Ordines*, vol. II., p.88.

[54] *Mittelalterliche Bibliothekskataloge*, Lehmann (ed.), vol. I, p.262.

[55] Strabo, *Libellus de exordiis*, Harting-Correa (ed.).

[56] Bischoff, *Katalog*, vol. I, 222, p.50: 'Wohl Süddeutschland, IX Jh., 2.Drittel'; BSB ANA 553, A, I: BAMBERG: 'IX 4/4, ca IX-X, <ital.>'; digitised at: https://zendsbb.digitale-sammlungen.de/db/0000/sbb00000132/images/.

Arrangement and Explanation 81

There are also a number of cases where one or more *ordines* follow directly after the text of Amalarius' great work, the *Liber Officialis*. For example, the compiler of Bamberg lit.131 added anonymous extracts from the *Liber Officialis* of Amalarius on diverse subjects to his array of *expositiones*: 'DE LETANIA MAIORE', 'DE SEQUENTIBUS SEPTEM DIEBUS PENTECOSTEN', 'DE KYRIEELEISON', 'DE NATIVITATE DOMINI', 'DE NOMINE IESU', 'DE DIE SANCTO PASCHAE'.[57] Paris lat.9421 carries a unique Holy Week *ordo*, *Ordo* 31, presented as an appendix to Amalarius' *Liber Officialis*.[58] A new Holy Week *ordo romanus* which is strongly related to those edited by Andrieu has been discovered in later manuscript in Barcelona in this same configuration.[59] Paris lat.2399 has three *ordines* from Collection A, *Ordo* 1, 11 and 27, between the Amalarius text and *De institutione clericorum* of Hrabanus Maurus.[60]

How these texts might have been read and employed is found in one singular witness, the copy of *Ordo* 27 in Paris BnF lat.12057, from St Germain-des-Prés.[61] It was copied on spare folios in a collection of sermons, copied by the scribe Gundoinus, but was altered by the inclusion of several unique, Frankish additions of particular interest. One concerns the Easter vigil on Holy Saturday, perfunctorily described in *Ordo* 27.[62] Here the author says:

> In vigilia paschae et pentecostes et lectiones et universa officia secundum Librum officialis Amalarii agi debent, quia et in gregorio [*sic*] missali similiter continetur.[63]

There follows a brief description of the vigil with the details that the *Ordo* left out, referring to the Sacramentary: 'sicut in Sacramentorum continetur'. That Amalarius' *Liber Officialis* is recommended here as a guide to the ceremony, in tandem with the Gregorian Sacramentary, again blurs the boundaries between liturgical text per se and *expositio*. But the same text earlier refers to the Gelasian Sacramentary, for the penance rite on Maundy

---

[57] *Les Ordines*, vol. I., pp.87–88.

[58] *Les Ordines*, vol. III, pp.481–509; Bischoff, *Katalog*, vol. III, p.150–151: 'Westdeutschland (?) IX/X Jh. (?).'

[59] Gonzalo Martinez-Diaz, 'Un *Ordo Romanus* in Hebdomada Maiore inédito', *Hispania Sacra*, 15 (1962), pp.192–202.

[60] *Les Ordines*, vol. I, p.469; the manuscript is eleventh-century, but appears to be a direct copy of a Carolingian exemplar.

[61] *Ibid.*, pp.275–276; Bischoff, *Katalog*, vol. III, p.198: 'Wahrscheinlich Saint-Germain-des-Prés, IX Jh., ca.Mitte.'

[62] *Ordo* 27, n. 51, var.1.

[63] *Les Ordines*, vol. III, p.359: 'On the vigil of Easter and of Pentecost the readings as well as the whole office should be done according to the *Liber Officialis* of Amalarius, because the Gregorian Sacramentary does similarly.'

82 Liturgical 'Usefulness' and Reading the *Ordines Romani*

Thursday (which indicates that compilers consulted different kinds of Sacramentaries as well, which presents a contrast to the idea of there being 'official' and 'standard' Mass Books).[64] This single copy of *Ordo* 27 reveals plainly how the authors and users of *ordines* were accustomed to switch between the various sources at their disposal, integrating what they found most useful. Again, the *Ordo* would not be expected to offer everything required, nor would a single Sacramentary contain the sum of all liturgical requirements. The performance (and, indispensable to it, the understanding) of the rite was enhanced by other material available, whether or not that fitted into the strict modern understanding of a 'liturgical' text.

Another manuscript which likewise shows compilers switching between *ordines* and *expositiones* is Paris BnF lat.1248, carrying a portion of texts we recognise from Collection B (*ordines* 41, 42 and 37).[65] But in place of the *ordines* commonly also part of the same Collection, the compiler has selected various texts to replace them. In place of *Ordo* 28, we have here a unique *ordo* of Holy Week, *Ordo* 32, a more simplified version of the rituals, performed only by *presbiteri* and *diaconi* with some personalised elements, and without the Roman setting.[66] In the other cases of the Mass, and baptism, the author compiler offered *expositiones* instead of *ordines*; once again the manuscript carries the *Eglogae de ordine romano*, as well as three other anonymous *expositiones* of the Mass, in place of *Ordo* 1, and the letter of Theodulf of Orleans on baptism in place of *Ordo* 11. The compiler made very selective use of the remaining *ordines* when he wished, quoting from *Ordo* 28, nn.71–75 the description of the moment of baptism itself.[67] But the second half of the manuscript (fol.88r ff) contains a selection of personal and penitential spiritual exercises which suggests a very personal

---

[64] *Ordo* 27, n.21, var.4: 'diligenter reconciliation poenitentum **sicut in sacramentario Gelasii** habetur et eorum missa peracta'.

[65] *Les Ordines.*, vol. I, pp.265–269; Keefe, *Water and the Word*, vol. II, pp.70–71; Bischoff, *Katalog*, vol. III, 4008, p.32: 'Frankreich, IX Jh., ca. 3. Drittel.'

[66] *Les Ordines*, vol. III, pp.525–532, for example the mention of a church of Saint Gregory: *Ordo* 32, n.2: 'Lumen ad Sanctum gregorium vadunt petere ad missam'; n.9: 'in sabbato sancto primitus letania. Postea diaconus vadit ad sanctum Gregorium cereo petere inluminato.'

[67] Paris, BnF lat.1248, fol.82r: 'Haec omnia expleta, fundit chrisma de vasculo in fonte super ipsam aquam in modum crucis et cum manu sua miscitat ipsum chrisma cum aqua. Et spargit per omnem fontem vel super omnem populum., Hoc facto omnis populus qui uoluerit accipit benediccionem in vasis suis de ipsa aqua antequam ibi baptizentur parvuli ad spargendum in domibus eorum et vinies et campis et fructibus eorum. Deinde presbiteri aut diaconi etiam si necesse fuerit et accoliti discalciati [blank line – text missing] -diuntur in fontes intro aquam et baptizantur primo masculi deinde feminae sub ac interrogacione. Credis in deum patrem omnipotentem? et reliqua. Et acceptos infantes de parentibus, baptizant eos sub trina.'

Arrangement and Explanation

use for the manuscript.[68] In Albi BM 42, we see the same contrasting of commentary and *ordo*. Here, the unique copy of a letter of Almannus of Hautvilliers to Sigebord of Narbonne encloses an accompanying commentary on the church dedication rite.[69] Almannus explained the Frankish ritual of church dedication, with its lustrations, processions, hymns and writing of the alphabet, the same rite described by *Ordo* 41. Thus, the explanation differs strikingly from the *Ordo* in the same manuscript, *Ordo* 42, the much briefer Roman ritual where the focus is on the deposition of relics. The Albi manuscript also contains Theodulf of Orlean's letter on baptism, in addition to the *ordo* of baptism, *Ordo* 11.

The fact that *ordines* and *expositiones* seem here to have been almost interchangeable in the eyes of compilers is surely significant, as is once again the abundance of *expositiones*, offering many differing perspectives. Among the *collections didactiques*, such abundance is commonplace: for example Bamberg 131 has three separate expositions of the Creed and four of baptism, while St Gallen 446 has six different glosses on the Mass, in addition to *Ordo* 1. These varied accounts of the same ceremony can differ quite strikingly in the order of how the rituals were envisaged to have unfolded, and in the emphasis placed on individual components; an element that is key to the ritual in one such text might go entirely unmentioned in another.[70] As with the *ordines*, there is no sense that any single text represented in such manuscripts the 'official' or 'authorised' understanding by which compilers wished to 'reform' understanding of the rite to a single, uniform standard, but rather the manuscripts are designed to offer such diverse perspectives side by side. Since manuscript compilers presented these various texts on an equal footing, readers had to have been able to compare, sift and decide for themselves what was the most cogent and useful for their own understanding of the rite.

These manuscripts suggest that *ordines* were commonly read and understood in the same way and as part of the same processes, alongside *expositiones*.

---

[68] These include the *Confessio Peccatorum pura* (*PL* 101, 524D–526A) and the *De Psalmorum Usu* (*PL* 101, 466B–C) by Alcuin, two litanies, and a set of long-form penitential and intercessory prayers including the 'DEPRECATIO QUAM PAPA GELASIUS PRO UNIVERSALI ECCLESIA CONSTITUIT CANENDAM ESSE' (*PL* CI, 560–561); for such texts and manuscripts like this, see Jonathan Black, 'Psalm Uses in Carolingian Prayerbooks: Alcuin and the Preface to De psalmorum Usu', *Mediaeval Studies*, 64 (2002), pp.1–60; Black, 'Psalm Uses in Carolingian Prayerbooks: Alcuin's Confessio Peccatorum Pura and the Seven Penitential Psalms', *Mediaeval Studies*, 65 (2003), pp.1–56.

[69] André Wilmart, 'La lettre philosophique d'Almanne et son context littéraire', *Archives d'histoire doctrinale et littéraire du Moyen-Age*, 3 (1928), pp.285–320.

[70] Keefe, *Water and the Word*, vol. I, pp.52–69, 151–152.

84   Liturgical 'Usefulness' and Reading the *Ordines Romani*

Within such practices of reading, the *ordo* could certainly contribute to the physical arrangement of a rite as performed. However, such arrangement clearly involved the choice and perspective of the reader and user of the *ordo* in question much more than Andrieu admitted, in his strict understanding of how a liturgical text properly would have been used. The manuscripts certainly admit the possibility that texts we now describe as 'liturgical' and 'non-liturgical' equally contributed to how a reader might understand the ritual in question, and so how he or she might choose to perform it. A distinction of this kind clearly dissolves on the level of the manuscript. Studying and thinking about liturgy was the indispensable precursor to performing it correctly, and that was the very heart of the incredible efflorescence of texts explaining the liturgy in the Carolingian period.

Canon Law and Roman History

Beyond the *expositiones*, it is also relatively common for *ordo romanus* manuscripts to offer various forms of texts that similarly trouble the understanding of a sharp distinction between a 'liturgical' manuscript and a library book. In the case of Munich Clm 14510, Bischoff identified that the opening material from fols.1–30 – four sermons of Candidus Wizo, Book 1 and most of Book 2 of Alcuin's *De Trinitate* – was in fact part of the same manuscript as the *ordines*, which Andrieu had not recognised. This led Bischoff to assert that the manuscript could not be considered liturgical 'in the strictest sense'.[71] BAV Pal.lat.487 also has an extract from Alcuin added in the same slightly later intervention that gave us the new *Ordo* 29, a text orientated towards Frankish use. The same work of Alcuin also appeared in Paris BnF lat.1248, suggesting a repeated association of this theological tract with liturgical texts and the *ordines* which would be difficult to account for in our current methods of categorisation. In a similar vein, Montpellier 412 had Collection A added after the *Enchiridion* of Augustine, while Albi 42 contains Augustine's *De agone christiano* just before its *ordines*.[72] The distinction Bischoff made – 'liturgical in the strictest sense' – does not seem a wholly satisfactory characterisation for these manuscripts. Instead, Carolingian writers did not seem to regard the presence of what we see as non-liturgical texts as absolutely disqualifying from a manuscript from being considered as a guide to the liturgy.

---

[71] Bischoff, *Mittelalterliche Studien*, vol. III, p.187, n.2: 'ist er nicht im strengen Sinn eine liturgische Hs'.

[72] Augustine of Hippo, *De Agone Christiano*, J. Zycha (ed.), Corpus Scriptorum Ecclesiasticorum Latinorum, 41 (Vienna 1900), pp.99–138.

Canon Law and Roman History   85

In many cases, 'additional' or 'non-liturgical' content is critical to understanding what the *ordines romani* meant to their readers, and how compilers wished them to be understood. This is the case particularly when the *ordines romani* are presented alongside and in continuity with documents of Roman history. This can be seen from some of the earliest manuscripts. In St Gallen 349, the collection of *ordines romani* opens with a copy of Pope Innocent's letter to Decentius of Gubbio, an important early document of a pope intervening and explaining liturgical matters.[73] Interest in Innocent's letter was also the catalyst for an important *ordo romanus* gloss written in Regensburg.[74] In St Gallen 349, historical arguments for Rome's faithfulness through heresies, and the interventions of the historic popes and otherwise unknown abbots of the Basilica of Saint Peter in the liturgy are used to support the promulgation of certain Roman usages in Francia.[75] The fact that this argument follows a visibly interpolated and composite set of documents of Frankish manufacture that contradict elements of papal practice should caution us not to assume that such arguments were simply understood to support uniformity according to the Roman model. In an earlier part of the same manuscript, as part of *Ordo 15*, obedience to the Roman See is implored but is limited to single adjustment in the Mass *ordo*, the saying of the *Gloria Patri* twice. Striking, too, is the insistence on the rationality (*racionabiliter*) of the usage, as opposed to the arbitrariness of one's own preference.

> Hoc iterum aque [*sic*] iterum super omnia admonemus ut omnis sacerdos qui desiderat racionabiliter [*sic*] sacrificium Deo offerre ut et conplaciat, secundum sanctae institutionis orthodoxorum patrum, beati atque gloriosa sedis sancti Petri apostoli, isto more, cum omni devotione retinere atque celebrare stodit (sic. studeat), ut semper quando intrat missas celebrare, primitus enim psalmum cum *Gloria patri* vel antephona, adiungentes *Kyriaeleison*; ita ad communionem antephona psalmum antephona, psalmum, adiugentes adiungentes semper *Gloria patri* quod est laus sanctae trinitatis. Sic est tenendum et super omnia gratia Dei conplendum. Qui enim isto modo not offert, postquam cogonverit, non recto ordine offert sed barbarico et suo arbitrio sequitur, vel eorum qui ad voluntatem suam sacras scripturas convertere nituntur.[76]

---

[73] Innocent I, 'Epistle 25', Robert Cabie (ed.), *La lettre du Pape Innocent Ier à Decentius de Gubbio* (Louvain, 1973); Martin Connell, *Church and Worship in Fifth-Century Rome. The Letter of Pope Innocent I to Decentius of Gubbio* (Cambridge, 2010).

[74] See Chapter 5.   [75] *Ordo 19*, nn.33–49; *Les Ordines*, vol. III, pp.9–15.

[76] *Ordo 15*, nn.155–156: 'But we have stressed this again and again, that every priest who wishes to offer sacrifice to God in a rational matter, according to the holy institution of the orthodox fathers and of the blessed and glorious see of Saint Peter, should keep this custom with all devotion and study to celebrate it; that, every time when they enter to celebrate mass, first they sing a psalm with the *Gloria patri* and antiphon, adding the *Kyrie eleison*; then at the antiphon during communion sing a psalm, adding the *Gloria Patri*. which is the praise of the Holy Trinity. This is to be held and above all else

86   Liturgical 'Usefulness' and Reading the *Ordines Romani*

Matters, then, may be more complex than the fraudulence Andrieu detected here.[77]

A particularly cogent example of such use of Roman history for Frankish purposes is the manuscript Wolfenbüttel Weissenburgenses 91. This was characterised as one of the *pontificaux embryonique* by Andrieu, and Vogel further described it as a particularly 'pure' example of an early pontifical since its contents were exclusively orientated for liturgical use.[78] The composite and individualised set of *ordines romani* in fact went far beyond such use in representing the ceremonies in question on the stage of Rome, with many additional topographic and temporal details added in various appendices, stemming, I suggest, from personal acquaintance with Roman usages.[79] To make it even clearer that the liturgical 'use' of the manuscript cannot be extricated from the placement of its contents in Rome, the manuscript's original form opened with a dossier of texts represented from the early day of the papacy to the time of Gregory the Great. Andrieu did not see this part of the manuscript, and was not aware that it was part of the same original book as the *ordines*.[80] The introductory material includes: the Pseudo-Clementine letters and Clement's life from the *Liber Pontificalis*, the letter of Pseudo-Damasus to Jerome on the timing of the Mass, and the full decrees of Pope Gregory's 595 Council in Rome, including the subscriptions of the clergy with their churches.[81] The Pseudo-Clementine epistles describe Clement's ordination by Peter, the foundation of apostolic succession, and Peter's long discourse on the duties and responsibilities of a bishop. The second letter concerns itself with the grades of the church, sacred vessels and the responsibility of the clergy.

Even more intimately associated with the *ordines* is the Pseudo-Gelasian decretal *De libris recipiendis et non recipiendis* (fols.72v–77r), directly following the text that deals with the annual cycle of reading the books

---

fulfils the grace of God. But he who does not offer in this fashion, after he has thought about it, does not offer according to a correct order, but a barbaric one and follows his own will, and contends to turn the holy scriptures to his own will.'

[77] *Les Ordines*, vol. I, p.92.

[78] Vogel, *Medieval Liturgy*, p.277: 'In its manner of composition the *Guelferbytanus* 4175 is even purer than the RGP.'

[79] See above.   [80] *Les Ordines*, vol. I, p.453.

[81] Pseudo-Clement's first Epistle in *PL* 130, cols.19–27B; Pseudo Clement's second epistle in *PL* 130, cols.37–44; 'The Life of Clement' as in *Liber Pontificalis*, Duchesne (ed.), vol. I, p.53; English translation, Raymond Davis, *The Book of Pontiffs* (Liverpool, 1989), p.3; Pseudo-Damasus in Roger Reynolds, 'A South Italian Mass Commentary', *Mediaeval History*, 50 (1988), pp.626–670; Gregory the Great, *Decretum ad Clerum in Basilica Petri Apostoli*, Paul Ewald and Ludwig Hartmann (eds.), *MGH* Epp. I (Berlin, 1891), pp.362–367.

of the Bible, *Ordo* 13A (fols.71v–72v).[82] The same arrangement with the Pseudo-Gelasian decretal can also be seen in the eleventh-century example of Collection A, British Library Add.MS 15222, probably copied directly from an early Carolingian exemplar from Metz. While the contents of Collection A are not changed, this manuscript was described as a 'pontifical', because it has explicit signs of use as a prop in liturgical ceremonies (in the oaths of obedience by bishops and abbots added over some decades to the spare folios), and it also clearly embodied and reflected the claims and status of the archbishopric (including historical texts which confirmed the rights of Besançon to ordain the bishops).[83]

The association of Pseudo-Gelasius with *ordines* is further illustrated by manuscript Gotha Membr.I.85, also made at Wissembourg, though somewhat earlier. This was a copy of the canon law collection, BAV Pal.lat.574, including *Ordo* 17 at the end, as that book does. The Gotha manuscript has the Pseudo-Gelasian decretal on the first pages, fols.1v–5r, before the collection of canons begins. Here, it presents itself as a mirror text to *Ordo* 17 (which deals with readings for most of its middle section), that comes at the end.[84] The exemplar manuscript, BAV Pal.lat.574, originally had the Pseudo-Gelasian decretal in the same position. That text, now a detached part of the original manuscript and found in BAV Pal.lat.493, Faszikel III, fols.100r–106v, was written in the same style as *Ordo* 17 and had almost certainly been added to BAV Pal.lat.574 at the same time as *Ordo* 17, proving a lasting connection of Pseudo-Gelasius and these kinds of *ordines*.[85]

In manuscripts such as Weissenburgenses 91, most of these Roman texts incorporated with the *ordines* discuss liturgical matters that were current concerns in Carolingian times. The evocation of the apostolic succession direct from Peter (in the Pseudo-Clementine Epistles) and the care of the popes for the liturgical usages of Rome probably lay behind their selection, as well as the topography of the city, evoked clearly in the subscriptions of the attendees to Gregory's council which give a list of the *tituli* churches. The contents of this introductory dossier raise the question of the applicability to MS Wissenbourg 91 of the term 'pontifical' in the generic sense

---

[82] Pseudo-Gelasius in Ernst von Dobschütz (ed.), *Das Decretum Gelasianum de libris recipiendis et non recipiendis* (Leipzig, 1912).

[83] Westwell, 'Content and Ideological Construction', pp.234–241.

[84] Ludwig Traube and Rudolf Ehwald, *Jean-Baptiste Maugérard: ein Beitrag zur Bibliotheksgeschichte.* Palaeographische Forschungen 23.4 (Munich, 1904), p.357.

[85] Bernhard Bischoff (ed.), 'Panorama der Handschriftenüberlieferung aus der Zeit Karls des Großen', in *Karl der Große*, pp.233–254, at p.243 (reprinted. Bischoff, *Mittelalterliche Studien*, vol. III, pp.5–38, at p.20f); BAV Pal.lat.493 digitzed at: https://digi.vatlib.it/view/bav_pal_lat_493.

88   Liturgical 'Usefulness' and Reading the *Ordines Romani*

understood by Vogel and Andrieu. The presence of such material makes it clear that the manuscript (and the *ordines* that interact with the same Roman topography) had important ideological functions directed to the Carolingian readership, which in turn would have deeply affected the 'use' of the book as a liturgical guide.

Weissenburgenses 91 is far from alone in engaging with the historical dimensions of the Roman liturgy even as it describes their arrangement. Another manuscript described as a *petit pontifical*, Cologne 138, records amid its *ordines* the speech that Gregory the Great gave to the people of Rome on 25 April 603, for the institution of a sevenfold litany in Rome, here DENUNTIATIO SEU INVITATIO SANCTI PAPAE GREGORII PRO SEPTIFORMIS LAETANIA.[86] The presence of this document in our manuscript allows no simplistic interpretation. The Franks associated Gregory's institution with the custom of the Great Litany they themselves adopted from Rome, which was inextricably linked to specific locations in Rome in the manuscript tradition of the Sacramentaries.[87]

The presence of a papal decretal in St Gallen 349 and a papal council in Weissenburgenses 91 also speaks to a common interaction of *ordines* with canonical texts. The Corbie manuscript with *Ordo* 29, St Petersburg Q.V.ii. no.5, has a whole host of admonishments and laws from diverse sources addressing matters of the church, including liturgy, with references to both the councils and decretals of popes, including, once again, Innocent's letter to Decentius. This collection was copied from an earlier Cambrai manuscript, Laon BM 201, and it was likely compiled there.[88]

The appropriation by the Franks of the body of papal and conciliar legislation thus mirrored their appropriation of liturgical texts describing papal rites, and we are safe to assume that they made the same creative use of the latter as they did the former. It is, for example, common for a number of *Ordo* manuscripts to extract and copy select canons to present

---

[86] Gregory the Great, *Denuntiatio pro septiformi letania*, Ludwig Hartmann (ed.), *MGH* Epp. II (Berlin, 1890), pp.365–367.

[87] Jacob Latham, 'Inventing Gregory the Great: Memory, Authority and the Afterlives of the Laetenia Septiformis', *Church History*, 84 (2015), pp.1–31, mentions Cologne 138 briefly at p.13, n.47.

[88] Staerk, *Les Manuscrits Latins*, pp.193–201 for example: 'De eo quod secundum ordinem Romanum debemus facere. Innocentius Decentio episcopo Egubino salute. Si instituta ecclesia . . . De scrutiniis. Ut presbiteri per loca congrua ea celebrare non neglegant et infantes ienitores uel genitrices eorum ad ecclesias hora constituta deferant . . . Antioceni Concil. Ut nullus ad episcopatum pro se constitutit promouendum . . . etc.'; Mordek, *Bibliotheca capitularium regum Francorum*, pp.698–702; Lotte Kéry, *Canonical Collections of the Early Middle Ages (ca. 400–1140). A Bibliographical Guide to the Manuscripts and Literature* (Washington, DC, 1999), pp.166–167; Bischoff, *Katalog*, vol. II, p.209, mentions an *Ordo Romanus* among the contents of the Laon manuscript, but this does not seem to be present, and may have been a confusion with its copy, in St Petersburg.

Canon Law and Roman History 89

alongside their ordination rites. This is witnessed almost universally across the Frankish world in the copying of Gregory the Great's *Capitulum* (and the possible liturgical recitation of it, which is prescribed in one witness, the Sacramentary of Drogo, Paris, BnF, MS lat.9428) before the subdeacon's ordination, and the quite common addition of an extract from Pope Zosimus, often given without his name, to the *Ordo de sacris ordinibus* concerning the time each should spend in the grades concerned.[89] In Collection B, this extract is accompanied by another from a decretal of Pope Leo I.[90] Other manuscripts go further, revealing individual initiatives which compilers might take if they chose. This is the case in St Gallen 140, which is a copy of St Gallen 614, and thus includes the 'pilgrim dossier' described above, along with most of Collection B (*Ordo* 28 at pp.282–301, *Ordo* 37 at pp.319–326 and the *ordo de sacris ordinibus* on pp.334–335, with psalmist) but gives them a new context. After *Ordo* 36 (the text discussing Roman ordinations) and the added text from Collection B, *Ordo* 37 (discussing Frankish Ember Days), the new manuscript also added plentiful extracts from the decretals of Gelasius, Zosimus and the Council of Neocaesarea discussing the timing of ordination.[91] The section on vestments (pp.340–345) is particularly cogent, offering one after the other an anonymous Frankish exposition, DE VESTIMENTIS SACERDOTALIBUS, an extract from an apocryphal letter of Pope Stephen and then *Ordo* 8, all of which address the same subject.[92]

---

[89] The extract from Gregory can be found in *Gregorius Syagrio, Etherio, Vergilio et Desiderio Episcopis a Paribus Galliarum*, *MGH* Epp. II, p.206; Pope Zosimus' decretal *Haec autem singulis gradibus*, *PL* 84 col.673–676 is transmitted in the Sacramentary as well, for example *Gellonensis*, Dumas (ed.), p.181; Paris BnF lat.9428, fol.5v: 'QUANDO ORDINANDI SUNT SUBDIACONI DIACONI PRESBITERI DICIT EPISCOPUS.'

[90] Pope Leo the Great, *Ad Episcopos Africanos Provinciae Mauritaniae Caesariensis* in *PL*, LIV, col.647, 658: 'PAULUS APOSTOLUS PRAECEPIT TIMOTHEO Manus cito nemini inposueris, neque communicaueris peccatis alienis. Quid est nemini manum inposueris nisi ante aetatem maturitatis ante tempus examines ante meritum laboris ante experientiam disciplinae. Sicut beni operis conportat fructus, qui rectum seruator ineligendo sacerdotem iudicium. Ita graue semetipsum efficit damnum qui in sue dignitatis collegium sublimat indignum.'

[91] 'DE DECRETIS GELASII PAPAE CAP. XI. PRESBITERORUM ET DIACONORUM ORDINATIONES CERTIS CELEBRARE TEMPORIBUS' from *PL* 59, 52; 'ITEM EIUSDEM CAP. XVI. UT NEMO LITTERAS NESCIENS VEL ALIQUA PARTE CORPORIS IMMINUTUS PROMOVEATUR AD CLERUM' from *ibid.*, col.53; 'ITEM UNDE SUPRA. DE DECRETO ZOSIMI PAPAE, CAP. I' from *PL* 20, 671; 'ITEM UNDE SUPRA CAP. III. QUAE IN SINGULIS CLERI GRADIBUS TEMPORA SINT PRAEFIXA' from *ibid.*, col.672–673; 'QUO TEMPORE PRESBITERUM CONVENIAT ORDINARI' is (unattributed) the Council of Neocaeserea Canon 2; Joseph Hefele-Leclercq (ed.), *Histoire des Conciles d'après les documents originaux*, trans. Henri Leclerq, vol. I, 2 (Paris, 1907), p.332.

[92] The exposition edited by Gerbert, *Monumenta*, vol. II, p.290 from Einsiedeln 110; the letter of Pseudo-Stephen in *PL* 3, 1036–1037.

90   Liturgical 'Usefulness' and Reading the *Ordines Romani*

In a related phenomenon, we have significant evidence of *ordines* transcribed onto the spare folios of legal manuscripts. Since canon law was made up of a Roman historical inheritance, applied and arranged in quite diverse ways, an analogy which occurs here with the *ordines romani* was equally obvious to the Frankish compilers themselves.[93] A significant part of *Ordo* 15, which was created in Tours, is copied into a set of manuscripts of a legal collection known as the Collection of Saint-Maur, but also, crucially, possessing an abridged copy of the *Liber Pontificalis* from Peter to Pelagius II (the Felician Epitome).[94] The two ninth-century manuscripts are: the Hague, Meermanno-Westreeanium cod. 10.B.4 (of the late eighth century, with the only copy of the canons of the 858 Council of Archbishop Herardus of Tours added, so probably kept in Tours, later in Clermont), which was then copied for Vatican Library Reg.lat.1127 (copied in the vicinity of Tours, later in Angoulême).[95] In the Hague manuscript, *Ordo* 15 is found at fols.47r–50r; in Reg.lat.1127, it is at fols.52r–56v. The *ordo* was added to the canonical collection in the Hague manuscript just after the text from the Council of Nicaea in a slightly later supplementation and repair made to the manuscript (probably undertaken at Tours), with an extra added quire (fols.47–53) that also contained the 595 synodal letter of Gregory the Great (which is thus placed out of historical sequence).[96] The text of the *ordo* was not here fully finished in this manuscript.

The same fate preserved a descendant of *Ordo* 15, *Ordo* 17, only found copied onto spare folios at the end of another pair of manuscripts of canons. The two manuscripts are BAV Palat.lat. 574, fols.152r–165r and Gotha Forschungsbibliothek Membr.I.85, fols.107v–112v.[97] Both manuscripts contain the same canonical collection, including extracts from the *Dionysiana-Hadriana* with the decrees of councils and letters of popes, known as the *Collectio Laureshamensis*.[98] But most interesting is that *Ordo*

---

[93] Schieffer, 'Redeamus ad fontem', pp.62–63.

[94] On the Collection of Saint-Maur, Kéry, *Canonical Collections*, pp.45–46; the Felician Epitome in Matthias Simperl, 'Ein gallischer Liber Pontificalis? Bemerkung zur Text- und Überlieferungsgeschichte des sogenannten Catalogus Felicianus', *Römische Quartalschrift für christliche Altertumskunde und Kirchengeschichte*, 111, 3.4 (2016), pp.272–287.

[95] For the Hague MS, *Les Ordines*, vol. I, pp.140–142; also Levison, 'Handschriften des Museum Meermanno'; *CLA*, vol. X, p.39; for the Vatican MS, *Les Ordines*, vol. I, pp.322–323, digitised at https://digi.vatlib.it/view/MSS_Reg.lat.1127.

[96] *CLA*, vol. X, p.1527b: text of Gregory the Great, *Decretum ad Clerum*.

[97] On Palat.lat.574, *Les Ordines*, vol. I, pp.321–322, digitised at https://digi.vatlib.it/view/bav_pal_lat_574; Bischoff, *Katalog*, vol. III (2014), p.414. On Gotha, *Les Ordines*, vol. I, pp.138–139; Bischoff, *Katalog*, vol. I, p.297, digitised at: https://dhb.thulb.uni-jena.de/rsc/viewer/ufb_derivate_00015136/Memb-I-00085_00218.tif.

[98] Kéry, *Canonical Collections*, pp.49–50.

Canon Law and Roman History 91

17 is directly preceded in both manuscripts by the correspondence of Pope Gregory the Great and Augustine of Canterbury in which Gregory accepted and validated divergence from Roman practice, a 'proof text' for liturgical diversity used by authors such as Amalarius.[99] In the first manuscript, BAV Palat.lat.574, both texts are in the same hand, an appendix to the original collection (fols.147v–165r) by a single scribe who intended to associate *Ordo* 17 with Gregory's allowance of deviation from Rome, since *Ordo* 17 itself engages creatively with Roman models.[100] Rather than hiding their divergence from Roman models, which Andrieu represented as reluctant or disguised, this compiler made his workings plain and justified them with reference to a papal pronouncement which supported it! Within the text, *Ordo* 17 also appeals to one of Gregory's homilies to support the performance of three (stational) Masses at Christmas.[101] Therefore, like other liturgical miscellanea, the *ordines* were seen as suitable additions to canonical collections which contained the letters of popes (often added slightly after the original manuscript was finished).[102] The tradition of *Ordines* 15, 16 and 17, which were themselves a disparate collection of rulings and guidelines strung along the overarching structure of the liturgical year, seems to have found a natural home there.

The more brief *ordines* of reading, similarly arranged according to the liturgical year, were particularly suited to this use. Several canonical collections acquired the variants of *Ordines* 13 or 14 on their originally blank pages, including some very early witnesses, but it is particularly interesting to note the texts selected to join them. For example, *Ordo* 14 appeared in four eighth-century manuscripts, as well as St Gallen 349: St Gallen Stiftsbibliothek 11, Metz BM 134 (destroyed in 1944), Paris BnF lat.3836 and BAV Pal.lat.277. The last, in uncial, placed *Ordo* 14 as a second half to Pope Leo's *sententia* on apocryphal scriptures.[103] The Metz and St Gall

---

[99] Gregory the Great, *Gregorius Augustino Episcopo*, *MGH* Epp. II, pp.332–343, emphasised at pp.334, 342f; Paul Meyvaert, 'Diversity within Unity: A Gregorian Theme', *The Heythrop Journal* 4 (1963), pp.141–162; Hanssens (ed.), *Amalarii Episcopi Opera omnia*, pp.233–234.

[100] See the most updated description of the MS by Michael Kautz: www.ub.uni-heidelberg.de/digi-pdf -katalogisate/sammlung51/werk/pdf/bav_pal_lat_574.pdf.

[101] *Ordo* 17, nn.15–16: 'celebrant missas sacre nauitatis domini unam postquam gallus cantauerit, aliam mane prima, tertiam in die, sicut mos est in honore sanctae trinitatis sicut sanctus Gregorius in umiliis suis loquitur dicens'.

[102] Roger Reynolds, 'Pseudonymous Liturgica in Early Medieval Canon Law Collections', in *Fälschungen im Mittelalter. Internationaler Kongreß der Monumenta Germaniae Historica München, 16.–19. September 1986*, vol. II (Hanover, 1988), pp.67–77 reprinted in *Law and Liturgy in the Latin Church, 5th–12th centuries* (Aldershot, 1994), pp.67–76.

[103] *Les Ordines*, vol. III, p.25; *CLA*, vol. I, p.91: 'VIII med'; Bischoff, *Katalog*, vol. III, p.455, digitised at: https://digi.vatlib.it/view/bav_pal_lat_277; Carlo Silva-Tarouca, 'Giovanni « archicantor » di S. Pietro a Roma et l'« Ordo romanus » da lui composta (anno 680)', *Atti della Pontificia*

92   Liturgical 'Usefulness' and Reading the *Ordines Romani*

manuscripts transmit *Ordo* 14 between the Pseudo-Gelasian decretal, on 'books to be received and not to be received', and an anonymous list of books of the Old and New Testament (also transmitted in Pal.lat.277).[104] One Italian manuscript, BAV lat.6018 (Italian, mid-ninth century), transmits the Collection A version of the order of readings, *Ordo* 13, also with Pseudo-Gelasius, as they also appeared in the Wolfenbüttel Weissenburgenses manuscript and in the British Library Pontifical from Besançon.[105] Finally, in Paris lat.3836, *Ordo* 14 appears with the authentic letter of Pope Innocent to Decentius of Gubbio on liturgical matters, added on the final folios of a canonical collection 'of Saint-Blaise' (which itself ends with Pseudo-Gelasius).[106] In St Gallen 349, Innocent's letter opens the series of *ordines*, beginning with *Ordo* 14. These *ordines* – which dealt, in brief, with the reading of Old Testament, non-Gospel and apocryphal New Testament books through the liturgical year – thus consistently travelled with papal or pseudo-papal material about readings. In the hands of Frankish compilers they became more complex than simple and dry lists.

In one case, the ideological relation of a Roman *ordo* to the legal content is obvious. Roger Reynolds discovered a particular recension of part of *Ordo* 34 (nn.14–45) in the manuscript Paris BnF lat.2449 fols.135v–136r, dated to the ninth/tenth century boundary, and probably from Lyons, which was edited for the use of that city.[107] Rather than the *domnus apostolicus*, the *domnus archiepiscopus* undertakes the ceremonies.[108] As a whole it discusses the position, prestige and responsibility of the bishop, in dialogue with several of the Pseudo-Isidorian decretals, and reflecting Lyonnais discourse surrounding the problem of chorbishops. The narrative of the *Ordo* for the ordination of a bishop here plays a role in illustrating the unique ordination of bishops, their ultimate dependence on the metropolitan.

Accademia Romana di Archeologia (Serie III) . *Memorie* 1 (Roma, 1923), pp.159–213, at 173–178; Leo the Great, *Epistola XV: Leo Episcopus Turribio episcopo*, cols.678–692 at col.688.

[104] Metz 134 (destroyed in 1944) *Les Ordines*, vol. I, p.166; *CLA*, vol. VI, p.788; *Katalog*, vol. II, pp.186–187; *Les Ordines*, vol. 1, pp.325–326 on St Gallen 11; *CLA*, vol. 7, p.896: '781 vel ante', digitised at: www.e-codices.unifr.ch/en/searchresult/list/one/csg/0011; Anonymous 'LIBRI VETERIS AC NOVI TESTAMENTI IUXTA PRIORUM TRADITIONEM' in *PL* 83, col.155–160; or printed by Gerbert, *Monumenta*, vol. II, p.181; Pseudo-Gelasius, as above, in von Dobschütz (ed.), *Das Decretum Gelasianum*.

[105] BAV lat.6018, described in *Les Ordines*, vol. I, p.304; Bischoff, *Katalog*, vol. III, p.455.

[106] *Les Ordines*, vol. I, pp.271–272; *CLA*, vol. V, p.554.

[107] Roger Reynolds, 'A Ninth-Century Treatise on the Origins, Office and Ordination of a Bishop', *RevBen*, 85 (1975), pp.321–332; reprinted as Article V in Reynolds, *Clerical Orders*, p.327, n.8, 328; Bischoff, *Katalog*, vol. III, 4196, p.75: '[(Etwa) Lyon, IX./X. Jh.]'; The manuscript is digitised at: http://gallica.bnf.fr/ark:/12148/btv1b8572241g.r=2449?rk=193134;0.

[108] Paris BnF lat.2449, fol.135v: 'et ueniunt ad archiepiscopum'.

Canon Law and Roman History 93

Surviving early medieval booklists offer some clues as to how the Franks framed and conceived the *ordines* as not strictly 'liturgical' in the way modern scholars have assumed, but rather having varied potential uses and often interacting with texts of more diverse genres. In 822 Reichenau possessed a manuscript *Ordo romanus de divinis officiis in cod.* I, which was recorded in the catalogue immediately after the monastery's copy of the *Liber Pontificalis*, in the section 'De Vita Patrum' and not in the section with other liturgical books.[109] Another particularly interesting entry comes from the same abbey's later catalogue of 835–842:

> In XVII libro continentur leges diversae, id est lex Alemannorum, lex Ripuaria, lex Salica, lex Theodosiana et diversi capitularares Pippini, Karoli et Hludovici regum et ordo ecclesiasticus romanae aecclesia et qualiter missa celebratur et de officiis divinis in noctibus a caena domini usque in pascha et qualiter in sancta romana ecclesia reliquiae conduuntur et quomodo in sancta romana ecclesiae ordinationes fiant. Et capitula in omnibus laborandi cura.[110]

These titles of the *ordines* are clearly identifiable as *ordines* 1, 27, 42 and 34, together comprising a substantial portion of Collection A, in fact what I have reconstructed as the original form of that collection as seen in Pal. lat.487, before 13A and 42 were later added to it. We know Reichenau had this form at its disposal. The Reichenau manuscript has not survived. But here Collection A was associated with capitularies from the Frankish monarchs! Documents concerning ecclesiastical discipline are, in fact, not uncommon accompaniments to the *ordines*. St Gallen 446 and Bamberg 131 contain the *capitula* of Haito of Basel which deal with matters of church discipline and liturgical matters, while the former has the *capitula* of Theodulf of Orleans as well.[111] Albi 42 opened with synodal chapters of Hincmar of Reims from 852.[112]

In all these manuscripts, therefore, there is a clear invitation to read the *ordines* more expansively. The constantly rewritten adaptations of *ordines*, and the presentation of the developments or alternatives side by side, show that the Franks were clearly not reading *ordines* as straightforward scripts to

---

[109] *Mittelalterliche Bibliothekskataloge*, Lehmann (ed.), vol. I, p.247.

[110] *Ibid.*, p.260: 'In the seventeenth book are found diverse laws, that is the Lex Alemannorum, the Lex Ripuaria, the Lex Salica, the Lex Theodosiana and capitularies of kings Pippin, Charles and Louis. There is also an ecclesiastical order of the roman church and also how the Mass is celebrated and how the divine offices of the night from Maundy Thursday to Easter and how in the Roman church relics are carried and how in the holy Roman church ordinations are done. And capitula for the care of all which is produced.'

[111] Haito of Basel, *Capitulary*, P. Brommer (ed.), *MGH* Capitula Episcoporum I (Hanover, 1984), pp.203–219; Theodulf of Orleans, *Capitulary, ibid.*, pp.73–184.

[112] Wolf-Dieter Runge (ed.), *MGH Capitula Episcoporum* II (Hanover, 1995), pp.8–90.

94   Liturgical 'Usefulness' and Reading the *Ordines Romani*

perform by rote, but as invitations to rework and revise – sometimes in writing, but more often in a rich architecture of unwritten adaptations which are less easy to access. Commentaries on these same rites, even the ones that directly refer to a written *Ordo* (in the case of Amalarius) or are clearly parsing one, show these exact processes in action. They never slavishly followed a single text but drew out the nuances that made the ritual reasonable and meaningful in their eyes. Without apology they adapted the rite to their own needs, by adding additional practices they felt would be meaningful, removing those that are less so and reordering the way in which the ritual unfolded where necessary in the service of their own vision of what a reasonable and coherent version of the ritual would look like. In the very rare cases that we have access to the independent narrative of the actual performance of rituals, the differences from available written *ordines* are just as striking.

Ordines in Other Liturgical Manuscripts

A form of manuscript in which the *ordines romani* can appear which we almost entirely miss in Andrieu is the other 'types' or 'genres' of liturgical manuscript, which in Andrieu were solid categories that admitted little interaction in his editorial vision. This means that his reconstruction of the history of several texts is quite partial. In some cases, the copying of an *ordo* into a liturgical book follows the same patterns we have already seen, of using extra space to record an individual *ordo* for posterity. Among others, a Gospel Book, BAV Pal.lat.47 fol.156v, on the blank final page, has an *ordo* of Holy Week, incorporating a portion of *Ordo* 27, nn.35–45 with idiosyncratic narratives of Maundy Thursday and Holy Saturday, describing simpler, perhaps monastic usages.[113]

The *ordines* remained, however, particularly closely related to the Sacramentary. Sometimes *ordines* were reinserted into the Sacramentary: the *ordo* for readings structured on the liturgical year, *Ordo* 13A, is found in a witness not known to Andrieu, the Sacramentary used at Essen Abbey (Dusseldorf UB MS D1).[114] Moving from the Gelasian of the Eighth

---

[113] *Les Ordines*, vol. I, p.318; BAV Pal.lat.47, fol.156v: 'omnes gloggas sonant. Subdiaconi cum subtilibus se parent.III. Similiter et diaconi cum dacmatio [dalmaticis] et non dicunt Flectamus genua. Candelas portant et incensum et benedicamus domino ... QUA FACIENDA SINT IN SABBATO SANCTO Primitus legantur XII lectiones cum singulis collectis et cantentur tractus. Post novissimum tractum, sequuntur collectae II. Deinde letania, deinde Gloria in excelsis deus, deinde collecta ad missam, deinde epistola. Post epistolam Alleluia. Confitemini. Deinde tractus Laudate. Deinde evangelium et presbiter alta voce.'

[114] Dusseldorf UB MS D1 fols.39v–40r.

Ordines *in Other Liturgical Manuscripts*   95

Century, new forms of the Sacramentary imagined by Frankish compilers continued to incorporate its *ordo* elements: for example the Gregorian *Paduensis* manuscript copied by the court school of Lothar (Padua Biblioteca Capitolare D 47) of *c.*850 contains, among its Frankish additions, another copy of *Ordo* 41, as do a number of other Mass Books of Frankish design.[115] The so-called Sacramentary of St Eloi from Corbie of around the same date, Paris BnF lat.12501, actually incorporated *Ordo* 24 into the narrative of Holy Week, the inverse of the process of extraction of prayers into *ordo romanus* manuscripts.[116] The complex tenth-century Sacramentary of Fulda in Göttingen has a version of the baptismal order.[117] This was not a trend that was ended by the creation of the collections of *ordines romani* as the supposed 'counterpart' to the Sacramentary, but rather compilers of Sacramentaries continued to have the freedom to incorporate *ordines* as they wished.

The Gelasian Sacramentary manuscripts notably predate the available examples of the *ordines romani* manuscripts which contain the same *ordines*. Andrieu did not seriously consider the interaction of the edited *ordines* with the Sacramentary, but examination reveals the Gelasian to be the earlier state of some of these texts. This is a very different pattern of textual relationship from that which Andrieu had presented, and is clearly demonstrable for at least one such text, *Ordo* 7, which is the rubrication of the Canon of the Mass, taken directly out of a *Paduensis* Gregorian Sacramentary.[118] But I argue in Chapter 6 that the baptismal *ordo*, *Ordo* 11, which Andrieu had presented as a Roman accomplishment and which is a key part of Collection A, was similarly first inculcated by Frankish writers within the Gelasian Sacramentary, with at least three stages of development from simple rubrics to the complex *ordo* evident in the Sacramentary before we even reach the *ordo romanus* manuscripts and the text that Andrieu edited.[119] Even as the *ordines romani* were copied through the ninth century, the same *ordines* were still being contemporaneously reproduced in Sacramentaries just as they were in the pontifical manuscripts, and they were also added to the new versions of the Sacramentary which the Franks created. The limitations of Andrieu's editions were based on the boundaries envisaged by the modern liturgist. According to these

---

[115] *Liber Sacramentorum Paduensis*, Alcestis Catella, Ferdinandus dell'Oro and Aldus Martini (eds.), Monumenta Italiae Liturgica, vol. III (Rome, 2005), pp.403–405; Also the St Eloi Sacramentary, *Divi Gregorii Papae Huius Nominis Primi Cogonomento Magno Liber Sacramentorum*, Hugh Mènard (ed.) (Paris, 1642), pp.147–157.

[116] *Ibid.*, pp.61–75.

[117] *Sacramentarium Fuldense seaculi x*, Gregor Richter and Albert Schönfelder (eds.), repr. HBS 101 (London, 1980), pp.329–353.

[118] *Les Ordines*, vol. II, pp.253–305.   [119] See Chapter 6.

96   Liturgical 'Usefulness' and Reading the *Ordines Romani*

assumptions, ultimately each *ordo* had to go back to a self-contained text purely addressing the gestures and actions, without the speech, and which was plainly intended for liturgical imitation. In fact, *ordines* have shown themselves to be a particularly versatile type of text. They demonstrate particularly plainly the potential adaptability of all kinds of liturgical texts. The *ordines* were not conceived of as wholly independent texts at any point in their history, but part of a common inheritance of texts that compilers saw no problem with mixing and reinterpreting.

There are other significant witnesses where the *ordines* are intrinsic to the original structure of the liturgical manuscript itself. We have already seen the relation which Leroquais and Andrieu hypothesised between the 'Collection B' manuscripts (presented as the preliminary first attempt) and the true 'pontifical'. The latter was envisaged as the bishop's book for use. Generally it should contain texts for the rites peculiar to the bishop and emblematic of his authority: church dedication, ordination, the Chrism Mass on Maundy Thursday and the episcopal blessings.[120] Manuscripts which we today class as 'pontificals' do begin to appear from the turn of the eighth to ninth centuries, around the same time as the first *ordo romanus* manuscripts. The earliest example to which we have any access would appear to be the lost 'Pontifical of Turpin', once found in the library of St Remi Abbey in Rheims. It was partially excerpted by Edmond Martène: 'antiquum pontificale ante annos 900 litteris Longobardicis exaratum, Tirpini archiepiscopi Remensis nomine vulgo appellatum'.[121] The same book had been earlier seen by Jean Morin:

> Antiquissimus est codex in Abbatis S.Remigii litteris Gothicis sive Longobardicis scriptus, ut videtur, in Gallia Belgica; sit enim in eo mentio festorum S. Vedasti, Remigii, Germani, Martini. Continent potissimum varias Benedictiones episcopales.[122]

---

[120]   Rasmussen, *Les pontificaux*, pp.503–512; Vogel, *Medieval Liturgy*, pp.225–230. Typical for the ninth century are the two MSS edited by Max Metzger, *Zwei karolingische Pontifikalien vom Oberrhein* (Freiburg, 1914).

[121]   Edmond Martène, *De Antiquis Ecclesiae Ritibus Libri*, vol. I (Antwerp, 1736) in the Syllabus librorum, p.[XV]: 'an ancient pontifical from 900 years ago written in Lombard script, popularly known as that of Turpin archbishop of Reims'; Rasmussen, *Les pontificaux*, pp.418–419; Aimé-Georges Martimort, *La documentation liturgique de dom Edmond Martène. Étude codicologique* (Vatican City, 1978), p.181 mistakenly attributes to this MS some of Martène's excerpts from another great lost treasure of St Remi, the Sacramentary of Godelgaudus (a Gelasian of the Eighth Century). Where Martène refers simply to an 'MS codice S. Remigii Remensis ante annos 900 exarato', he meant the Sacramentary.

[122]   Jean Morin, *Commentarius Historicus de Sacramento Poenitentiae* (Antwerp, 1682), p.593: 'There is a very old codex in the Abbey of St Remi of Reims, written in Gothic or Lombard letters, as it seems, in North-Eastern France. For in it there is mention made of the feasts of Saints Vaast, Remi, Germain and Martin. It contains chiefly various Episcopal Blessings.'

Ordines *in Other Liturgical Manuscripts*   97

Undoubtedly this perished, with other treasures, in the 1774 fire at the abbey. The *litteris longobardicis* would have been a Merovingian minuscule, likely the Corbie ab script (as in the fragments of another liturgical book still in Reims, the Index of St Thierry).[123] Nothing here forbids a date for the lost manuscript before 800. From Turpin's Pontifical, Martène reproduced one extraordinary text: an *ordo romanus* of Maundy Thursday containing the Chrism Mass (called *Ordo* 51 by Chavasse), set specifically at the Lateran Basilica (later also found in several English manuscripts termed pontificals).[124] The association of what seems to have been a Frankish collection of episcopal blessings and the Chrism Mass with penitential rites that contain a unique formula of absolution said by 'ego . . . immeritus et peccator episcopus' suggest that this was indeed a bishop's liturgical book, whether or not it can be said to have really belonged to Archbishop Tilpin of Reims (749–795).[125] In that case, the copying of an *ordo romanus* associated with the Lateran in such a context was from the beginning something bishops were interested to do. Chrodegang of Metz would thus be operating within a wider context.

Church dedication and ordination are two rituals contained in many surviving identified ninth-century pontificals, and were also addressed among edited *ordines romani*. In almost all of these cases, the church dedication rite is an earlier version of *Ordo* 41, the Frankish rite, which was the source for Collection B, in which some alterations were made.[126] There, and in most other cases, the ordination sequence offered is the Frankish 'ORDO DE SACRIS ORDINIBUS' (sequence of seven or eight grades) which was present in Collection B as well. Sometimes the sequence goes all the way up to the bishop (who would only be ordained by a metropolitan), but sometimes the bishop is removed.[127] The variance in the content of the pontificals is remarkable, and some contain additional

---

[123] The erroneous title comes from Mabillon, who believed Corbie ab script to be Italian; André Wilmart, 'L'index liturgique de Saint-Thierry', *RevBen* 30 (1913), pp.437–450.

[124] Martène, *De Antiquis*, vol. III, cols.283–284; Antoine Chavasse, 'A Rome, le Jeudi-saint au VIIe siècle d'après un vieil *Ordo*', *Revue d'histoire ecclésiastique* 50 (1955), pp.21–35: 'celebratur missa ad Lateranis'; Anscharius Mundó, 'Adnotationes in antiquissimum ordinem romanum feriae V in cena domini noviter editum', *Liturgica*, 2 (1958), pp.181–216 noted that the monastic vespers took place after the ceremony '*in Sancto Petro*' and not at the Lateran, which suggests the time that the Lateran's monasteries were inactive from the end of the seventh century until they began to be restored by Pope Gregory III (731–743).

[125] Morin, *Commentarius*, p.150: 'I, an unworthy bishop and sinner, absolve you . . . .'

[126] *Zwei Pontifikalien*, Metzger (ed.), pp.25*–36*, as in Collection B accompanied by blessings of objects varying depending on manuscripts; the differences are identified by Bernard Langlois, 'Le manuscrit W'.

[127] In Donaueschingen 192 the bishop's ordination is present, but in Freiburg UB 363 it is not; *Zwei Pontifikalien*, Metzger (ed.), pp.16*–18*.

98   Liturgical 'Usefulness' and Reading the *Ordines Romani*

rites similar to the edited *ordines romani*. The manuscript once Donauschingen cod.192, now in private hands, contained a version of the scrutiny and baptismal *ordo*, taken directly from a Sacramentary and including the full text of the Creeds in Greek and Latin.[128] Vienna ÖNB ser.n.2762, of Regensburg, has the earliest copy of Andrieu's *Ordo 38*, addressing the Ember Saturday.[129] Andrieu thought this *ordo* was only created *c*.950, in line with later manuscripts, but the Vienna manuscript is at least a century earlier.

It is also true, nevertheless, that many of the pontificals do not contain the full set of texts the modern pontifical 'should' have, and a significant proportion have additional or extra material, in many cases what 'should not be there' if we analyse these books as merely antecedents of the modern pontifical with the same use as that kind of text. BAV lat.7701, for example, contains a conciliar *ordo* which Schneider argued to be the work of Archbishop Arn of Salzburg, a more developed version of the text preserved in Cologne 138, also called 'ORDO ROMANUS QUALITER CONCILIUM AGATUR'.[130] Rasmussen found this confusing, because he identified the manuscript as originating in a minor Italian see; it is in fact from Chieti, but the conciliar *ordo* was specifically led by a metropolitan bishop.[131] It would not be 'performed' from our manuscript in a simple way in the see in which the manuscript was written. Likewise, the presence of the coronation *ordo* in the Pontifical of Sens in St Petersburg need not be linked to a specific performance of a coronation in Sens itself but appears to reflect the aspirations and interests of the see.[132] In time, coronation and conciliar *ordines* would appear in various 'pontificals' from all kinds of churches, most of which would never see the ritual performed there. The same can be said of the presence of the episcopal ordination, which was only performed by the metropolitan, when it appears in a manuscript linked only to a normal bishop (of Constance), for example in the once Donaueschingen 192, or the papal ordination in a manuscript like Cologne 138.

---

[128] *Ibid.*, pp.82*–104*. The Donaueschingen manuscript was sold at auction to an unknown private collection; see Vogel, *Medieval Liturgy*, p.241, n.214 (Sotheby's, Auction date, June 21 1982, lot 5).

[129] *Das Kollektar-Pontifikale des Bischofs Baturich von Regensburg (817–848) (Cod.Vindob.ser.n.2762)*, Franz Unterkircher (ed.), Spicilegium Friburgense, 8 (Freiburg, 1962), pp.91–92; *Ordo 38* in *Les Ordines*, vol. IV, pp.257–269.

[130] *Ordo 7*B in *Die Konzilsordines des Früh- und Hochmittelaters, MGH*, H. Schneider (ed.) (Hanover, 1996), pp.55–57, 331–342.

[131] Rasmussen, *Les pontificaux*, pp.398–399; Westwell, 'The *ordines* of Vat.lat.7701', pp.127–152.

[132] Shane Bobrycki, 'The Royal Consecration *ordines* of the Pontifical of Sens from a New Perspective', *Bulletin du centre d'études médiévales d'Auxerre*, 13 (2009), pp.131–142.

Ordines *in Other Liturgical Manuscripts*   99

This is particularly illuminated by one extraordinary example, Paris Bibliothèque de l'Arsenal 227, once known as the 'Pontifical of Poitiers', but actually from the Paris region.[133] With 279 folios, it is an exceptionally long and comprehensive book of this kind. The core is the narrative of Lent and Holy Week, stuffed with details and beginning with the *ordo* of public penance on Ash Wednesday. Available *ordines romani* for the Lenten scrutinies (*Ordo* 11) and Holy Week (*Ordines* 24/26) were clearly employed, but also 'supercharged' by the addition of various Frankish customs, some attested here for the first time, including alternatives when a bishop was or was not present, developed stational notices from Rome, notes and commentary describing Roman practices, full chants and prayers, as well as complete Gospel readings, going far beyond what almost any other pontifical offers.[134] It includes papal sanction for one of the details of its rites, by mentioning the text of the letter of Pope Nicholas I (858–867) to Radulf of Bourges (842–864), from 864.[135] The St Petersburg 'Pontifical of Sens', Vatican BAV say lat.7701 and the Vienna Pontifical from Regensburg themselves all carry various *ordines* of Holy Week of Frankish manufacture, but only a few pages at most.[136] The Paris manuscript opens with a copy of the *Ordo de sacris ordinibus* (undeveloped in comparison to the Holy Week portion). It has an extraordinarily developed description of Holy Week, including many episcopal and papal ceremonies, but lacks other key elements of the pontifical such as church dedication. The authorial voice often intervenes, interpreting a number of rites for the reader.

> Sane observandum est, ut cum lecta fuerint evangelica lectio, sive in hac missa sive in praecedenti, praesbiter consenso pulpito tractet, exponendo tam historiae seriem quam inaestimabilem clementissimi dei misericordiam.[137]
>
> Numerus vero laetaniarum iuxta numerum personarum vivificae trinitatis in mysterio ea nocte agitur.[138]

---

[133] *Il cosiddetto pontificale di Poitiers: (Paris, Bibliothèque de l'Arsenal, cod. 227)*, Aldo Martini (ed.) (Rome, 1979); Leroquais, *Les pontificaux manuscrits*, vol. I, pp.263–270; digitised at: https://gallica.bnf.fr/ark:/12148/btv1b55005681f.

[134] Westwell, 'Content and Ideological Construction', pp.242–248.

[135] *Il cosiddetto pontificale*, Martini (ed.), p.139: 'Gloria etiam in excelsis Deo secundum decretum Nicolai pape, si episcopus adest, canitur; Nam ipse sanctus pontifex, sciscitante Rodulfo, Bituricensi archiepiscopo, utrum hoc fieri conveniret, apostolica beati Petri auctoritate et sua inrefragabili sanctione, metropolitis tantum episcopis hoc agree.'

[136] Staerk, *Les Manuscrits Latins*, pp.156–158; *Kollektar-Pontifikale*, Unterkircher (ed.), pp.122–126 is a baptismal rite; p.130 preserves scanty fragments of what was clearly a developed Holy Week *Ordo*; Rasmussen, *Les pontificaux*, p.396.

[137] *Il cosiddetto pontificale*, Martini (ed.), p.153: 'It is wisely held, that when the gospel reading has been read, both in this mass and the preceding one, the priest, having climbed the pulpit should teach, expounding the series of history and the inestimable compassion of most merciful God.'

[138] *Ibid.*, p.219: 'But the number of litanies that are done during this celebration of this night are the same as the number of persons of the living Trinity.'

100   Liturgical 'Usefulness' and Reading the *Ordines Romani*

A Roman rite is described, of the blessing of the Candle, itself a unique *ordo romanus*, and there is even a brief pilgrim report from Jerusalem on liturgical practices there.[139] It has now been settled that the book was made for (and probably by) the community of the monastery of St Maur-des-Fossés outside Paris, who are addressed at several points.[140] These monks could not have used the episcopal rituals here contained, but they still copied them, and in overwhelming depth and detail. As Henry Parkes wrote, 'liturgy emphatically did not need to be used to be of value'.[141]

This important insight should be applied more broadly to all manuscripts that contain *ordines*. The idea that monks could never be interested in episcopal rituals, or bishops in those that were performed by a metropolitan, or that the Franks saw Roman texts as useful only to the extent they might actually imitate them, does serious disservice to the compilers and readers of such manuscripts. We limit our access to the imagination applied in the compilation of books when we use such a stringent and restrictive criterion for what a liturgical book is and how it must have been used. Just as with Andrieu's Collections, compilers were quite capable of selecting what they intended for use from a broader set of texts, while surrounding material might be read just for intellectual interest, or help to give context and rationale. Since 'pontifical' is not a title ever used until the thirteenth century, it becomes difficult to see the extent to which these kinds of books were perceived as a distinct genre of book always compiled for the same ends, in the way modern scholars have viewed them.

---

[139] *Ibid.*, p.218: 'Mane autem benedicendi cerei romana ecclesia frequentat . . .'; p.219: 'Enim uero sicut veracium personarum relatione traditur, qui nostro tempore de Hierusalem aduenerunt . . .'

[140] Michel Huglo, 'Notes sur l'origine du "Pontifical de Poitiers" (Paris Bibliotheque de l'Arsenal MS 227)', in A. Andrée and E. Kihlman (eds.), *Hortus Troparium: Florilegium in Honorem Gunillae Iversen* (Stockholm, 2008), pp.176–188.

[141] Parkes, *Making of Liturgy*, p.182.

PART II

The Arrangement of Rites

CHAPTER 5

Orders for the Stational Mass in Frankish Cities and Monasteries

As we have now seen, liturgical texts of this nature do not easily yield a single explanation. *Ordines romani* appear in various contexts, mostly in deliberate configurations, but sometimes added to complete manuscripts as a device to preserve (or perhaps to reinterpret) them. The *ordines* thus offer us a particularly illuminating case study in the particular fluidity of liturgical texts. They reveal the extent to which Carolingian engagement with liturgical texts was dynamic, creative and thoughtful, offering lessons for our broader understanding of how early medieval scribes constructed and used authoritative models. We have also begun to uncover the personal input of those having the texts written.

A further key point is that the same manuscript might allow or invite the *ordo* to be read in multiple ways. Intimately involving as they did the complex perception and appropriation of Rome by the Carolingians, the *ordines romani* certainly challenge the prevailing notion of a 'merely' liturgical text, showing that liturgical texts engaged the historical and analytical mindset of their writers and readers. When *ordines* were 'acted out', and the evidence suggests that participants did not assume any simple translation of written text to performance, the manuscript might function as a way of understanding that process, and what it meant on multiple levels. The increased focus on the understanding of liturgy at all levels in the Carolingian period is undoubtedly the important driving force in the creation and the circulation of the *ordines romani*, and the manuscripts suggest that the attempt to understand precluded and was intrinsic to performance rather than a function that had to be diametrically separated from it, as in Andrieu. The *ordines romani* are certainly key to understanding the thirst of the Frankish Church for the 'confrontation with the specific conditions of the (Roman) city liturgy', as Häußling put it, rather than the imitation of this or that specific usage perfectly.[1] It was one key

---

[1] Häußling, *Mönchskonvent und Eucharistiefeier*, p.181: 'die Auseinandersetzung mit den besonderen Bedingungen der (römischen) Stadliturgie'.

103

element of a broader movement that was more wide-ranging, more consequential and more diverse in both its goals and effects, the drive of the Church at every level to create a liturgy that was (in the words of those most involved) rational and concordant, and to find new ways of recording, replicating and explaining it. With this understanding, we can place the *ordines romani* within a vast collective initiative of cultural improvement that encompasses all fields of knowledge and within which liturgy is intrinsically and centrally involved.

If an *ordo* is a record of liturgical 'arrangement', our first assumption would be that this is presented in order to be carried out in exactly the same way. Many *ordines romani* give such instructions as set in Rome and carried out by the officials of the Roman Church. Therefore, this replication is not at all straightforward, but it required the active engagement of the user, including activating his own understanding of what 'Roman' meant, and the history and special place of the Roman Church. Which aspects of the text were replicable outside Rome? How did they need to be altered to fit their new context? What would he like to add to the ceremony, and why? What did it mean to his own understanding of his office and liturgical role to be acting in the person of the Pope, for example, or the Roman archdeacon, or the *diaconi regionarii*? Likewise, what did it mean for his understanding of his own church (both the corporate body and the physical space) that these topographies played the role of Rome in these ceremonies? Depictions of Frankish ceremonies in both art and epistolary writing do not suggest that the use of the *ordines* was a straightforward proposition that one acquiesced to by simple assent.

Ordo i was clearly highly valued and widely copied.[2] It records the papal stational Mass and the centrepiece is the papal cortege, with a hierarchy of exotic dignitaries; for example *Ordo* i, nn.9–10: 'diacones, primicerius et duo notarii regionarii, defensores regionarii, subdiaconi regionarii . . . vicedomnus, vesterarius, nomincolator atque sacellarius'.[3] The 'short recension' found in one manuscript (St Gallen 614) appears to be an original attempt to record the event, with a narrower and more informal narrative, recording a generic stational Mass which could be on any day.[4] This was built on and enhanced to become the full text much more widely found but only among other *ordines romani*, the 'long recension', which records further details of the Roman Mass.[5] Although Romano argued that the

---

[2] *Les Ordines*, vol. II, pp.3–108.   [3] *Les Ordines*, vol. II, p.70.
[4] *Ibid.*, pp.5–6; it begins with the title n.24: '*Ordo* Romanae Ecclesiae denuntiatione statuis diebus festis' and the setting is 'ecclesiam ubi statio antea fuerit denuntata'; also Michel Andrieu, 'Notes sur une ancienne rédaction'.
[5] *Les Ordines*, vol. II, pp.55–58.

Orders for the Stational Mass

'long recension' is the truly Roman original, and the 'short recension' a Frankish adaptation, I will present here additional evidence based on a key liturgical rite (immixtion) that there is no reason to overturn Andrieu's assessment.[6] Accurate representation of Roman details or use of Roman terminology do not suffice to prove Roman origin. The main difference in the 'long recension' is the increased attention to the technical outworking of the stational Mass as it actually took place in Rome on a particular day, Easter, including its topographical framework there. Notably, the 'long recension' also begins with a key introduction on the seven ecclesiastical regions of Rome, how *diaconi regionarii* were selected for them and how each served at the stational Mass on each day of the week.[7] This text serves as the opening sequence for the more significant Collections, A and B among them, where *Ordo* 1 is often the first text. The 'long recension' then goes on to describe the stational Mass as taking place on Easter Day itself, including specifications of the places in Rome that would be specifically involved on that day: 'ecclesia Salvatoris', 'partiarchium Lateranensis', 'Sanctam Mariam', 'loco qui dicitur Merolanus'.[8] From the rare 'short recension' to the much more common 'long recension', we therefore see an increase in the specificity of what the text addresses. But the more specific 'long recension' is much more widely copied in surviving manuscripts, the 'short recension' in only one. The Franks appear to have valued the specific details of the latter.

In a number of cases, *Ordo* 1 is also accompanied by one of what Andrieu edits as two Supplements, although they are not fully separated from the former text in the manuscripts themselves but follow it without a clear break. Both Supplements are present in the only manuscript of the 'short recension', St Gallen Stiftsbibliothek 614. The first, *Ordo* 2, purports to address what would happen if the *apostolicus* was not present to undertake the stational Mass, adding specifications to certain places in *Ordo* 1 where

---

[6] Romano, 'The Fates of Liturgies' discusses the missing opening, dismissing this as from a mutilated exemplar, but does not discuss other variations in the text of the 'short recension'. Nor does he take account of the fact that the earlier extant *ordines* (*Ordines* 7, 15, 4) are rather based on the 'short recension', not the long, nor the fact that the 'short recension' appears in a unit with other early *ordines romani* (24, 26 and 2). See also Romano, *Liturgy and Society in Early Medieval Rome* (Abingdon, 2014).

[7] *Ordo* 1, nn.1–23, beginning 'Primum omnium observandum est septem esse regions eccleiastici ordinis Urbis Romae et unaquaeque regione singulos habere diaconos regionarios'; in the 'Collection A' manuscripts, this is acknowledged as a differing section of the text by the twofold title: 'Incipit *Ordo* ecclesiastici ministerii romanae ecclesiae (referring to the new introduction) **vel** qualiter missa celebratur' (referring to the narrative of the Mass); for analysis see *Les Ordines*, vol. II, pp.55–56.

[8] *Ordo* 1, nn.7, 15, 18.

106　　　　　　　Orders for the Stational Mass

adjustments would have to be made.[9] This text is only found with the 'short recension', in St Gallen 614 and its copy St Gallen 140, and has left no imprint on the 'long recension'. The majority of *Ordo* 2 assumes an *episcopus* to be standing in for the Pope (presumably one of the junior bishops of the suburban dioceses Rome who appear in *Ordo* 1). But it also notes (n.9) that a priest would do almost the same, should he be standing in instead, except that he is forbidden to say the *Gloria*: 'Similiter etiam et a presbitero agitur, quando in statione facit missas preter *Gloria in excelsis Deo* quia a presbitero non dicitur nisi in Pascha.'[10] Given the lengthy absences of popes in Rome, as well as the demands of the stational schedule, we can imagine either contingency being the real case fairly often. By the twelfth century, the Pope would celebrate stations on only the highest feasts, and it is not difficult to imagine delegation was a normal part of the affair in the ninth as well.[11] *Ordo* 2 closes with a key phrase:

> Episcopi, qui civitatibus praesedent, ut summus pontifex ita omnia peragunt.[12]

This is obviously a suggestion that bishops outside Rome undertake their own stational Masses, using *Ordo* 1 as the model to do so, and may be key to unlocking the text's purpose. Since the 'short recension' narrates a 'generic' stational Mass, its suitability for this purpose is more obvious than the 'long'. It would not be untoward, in fact, to argue that the configuration of the 'short recension' and *Ordo* 2 accompanying it could have been specifically designed in order to propagate stational usages outside Rome. It is possible that some Frankish cities had an uninterrupted tradition of stational Masses, in whatever form, so, in that case, the Roman stations might provide a new layer of interpretation and understanding of these pre-standing uses.[13]

---

[9] *Les Ordines*, vol. II, pp.111–116; *Ordo* 2 tit.: 'Si autem summum pontificem ubi statio fuerit contigerit non adesse, haec sunt que ab alio episcopio dissimiliter fiunt.'

[10] 'But this is done in the same way by a priest, when he says mass at the station except for the *Gloria in excelsis Deo* because this is not said by a priest except on Easter Day.'

[11] Joseph Dyer, 'City Streets as Sacred Space: The Topography of Processions in Medieval Rome', in Harald Buchinger and David Hiley (eds.), *Prozessionen und ihre Gesänge in der mittelalterlichen Stadt – Gestalt, Hermeneutik, Repräsentation* (Regensburg, 2017), p.29: 'during Lent, the most intensive period, the Pope was not a regular participant'; Sible de Blaauw, 'Contrasts in Processional Liturgy: A Typology of Outdoor Processions in Twelfth-Century Rome', in Nicolas Bock, Peter Kurmann, Serena Romano and Jean-Michel Spieser (eds.), *Art, cérémonial et liturgie au Moyen Âge: actes du Colloque de 3e Cycle Romand de Lettres, Lausanne-Fribourg, 24–25 mars, 14–15 avril, 12–13 mai 2000* (Rome 2002), p.360.

[12] *Ordo* 2, n.10: 'Bishops, who preside over cities, should do everything just as the Supreme Pontiff does.'

[13] Häußling, *Mönchskonvent und Eucharistiefeier*, p.198.

Orders for the Stational Mass 107

Evidence for the setting up or reinvigoration of stational Mass systems in Carolingian Francia is widely present across episcopal sees of the Empire.[14] It is hard to overstate just how ubiquitous the Roman stational system was in the liturgical manuscripts copied by the Franks and thus as part of the Frankish experience of reading liturgy. The notices of the church in which the Pope would celebrate on the relevant days were recorded in Sacramentaries, antiphoners, evangelieries and the many *comes* coming at the end of Gospel Books or recorded on their own.[15] Carolingian clergymen must have understood their own liturgical year by reference to this Roman schedule. But the Franks also intimately understood the schedule as a historical phenomenon that had been deliberately changed and augmented over the years by several famous popes.[16] There was an intimate connection between the Roman liturgy as it was received and understood in Francia, and the historic narrative of papal intervention in liturgy as recorded in the *Liber Pontificalis*. This is witnessed not only by the framing in the varied writings of liturgical commentators, from sophisticates such as Amalarius and Walahfrid Strabo to the large stock of varied anonymous tracts, but also by the deliberate presentation of the *ordines romani* alongside the real or pseudonymous documents of that history.[17] This meant that liturgists were very aware of the contingent and historical phenomenon of the Roman liturgy, that it had changed by the will of the popes at several instances, and was thus an adaptable source of inspiration and not a straightjacket to which to conform. In the case of the stational liturgy, the *Liber Pontificalis* recorded several interventions by the popes of recent centuries: notably Pope Sergius' (687–701) introduction of collectae and procession to three Marian feasts, and Pope Gregory III's (731–747) addition of stational Masses to the Thursdays in Lent.[18] Because of the constant movement of material out of Rome, the Franks continued to have

---

[14] Johann Dorn, 'Stationsgottesdienste in frühmittelalterlichen Bischofsstädten', in Heinrich M. Gietl (ed.), *Festgabe für A. Knöpfler* (Freiburg, 1917), pp.43–55; Rolf Zerfaß, 'Die Idee der römischen Stationsfeier und ihr Fortleben', *Liturgisches Jahrbuch*, 8 (1958), pp.218–229; Carol Heitz, *Recherches sur les rapports entre architecture et liturgie à l'époque carolingienne* (Paris, 1963), pp.82–87; Häußling, *Mönchskonvent und Eucharistiefeier*, pp.189–212; Baldovin, *Urban Character of Christian Worship*, p.249; Donald Bullough, 'The Carolingian Liturgical Experience', in R.N. Swanson (ed.), *Continuity and Change in Christian Worship*, Studies in Church History, 36 (1999), pp.41–42.

[15] Éamonn Ó Carragáin and Carol Neumann de Vegvar (eds.), 'Introduction', in *Roma Felix: Formations and Reflections of Medieval Rome* (Farnham, 2007), p.8.

[16] In the Supplement to the Gregorian *Hucusque*, see *Le sacramentaire grégorien*, Deshusses (ed.), vol. I, p.351: 'Nam sicut quorundum relatu didicimus, domnus apostolicus in eisdem diebus a stationibus paenitus uacat, eo quod ceteris septimanae feriis stationibus uacando fatigatus, eisdem requiescat diebus. Ob id scilicet ut tumultuatione populari carens, et aelemosinas pauperibus distribuere . . . .'

[17] See Chapter 2.   [18] *Liber Pontificalis*, Duchesne (ed.), vol. I, p.376 and vol. II, p.402.

108   Orders for the Stational Mass

access to numerous sources, both Sacramentaries and *comes*, that originated
before these interventions and therefore had significant gaps. Rather than
copying these old texts simply and reverently, the Franks engaged their
own creative liturgical mindsets to update them according to what they
understood to be the latest trends in Rome. This did not happen only once,
but independently in many cases: Frankish copies of early Gregorian
Sacramentaries, Padua, Biblioteca Capitolare, MS D 47, Trent, Museo
Provinciale d'arte del Castello del buonconsiglio, MS 1590 and the
Sacramentaries of Tours all witness independent attempts to add Masses
for the Thursdays of Lent which each proceed in slightly different ways, as
does the *Comes* of Alcuin, among other lectionaries.[19] We have already seen
one attempt in *Ordo* 27, to add a stational Vespers celebration for the
Thursday after Easter. These interventions show that the Franks were
engaged consumers of the stational information in their books, checking
the record against what they knew of Roman liturgical history, supplied by
the *Liber Pontificalis*, or by their own experience or understanding of what
happened in Rome. They did not simply copy the stational notices
automatically and skim over them when reading. While the Frankish
adjustment of these sources has previously mostly been used to recover
the 'original' and archaic forms they now disguise, the Frankish motivation
for such adjustments has not been widely considered (as is the case with the
ordines romani themselves). It must be argued from this fact that the Franks
were invested in a 'complete' stational record. They wished to be able to
follow the Pope in his current journey through Rome, even if Masses and
readings for such ceremonies had to be created anew to fill in the gaps. The
important matter was the stational system allowed the daily celebration to
follow the Pope's own schedule: it was celebrating at the same time as the
Pope, and knowing that they were doing so, and in which church the Pope
celebrated, that the Franks seem to have prized, rather than the utmost
accuracy to what was actually said in Rome.

   The copying of *Ordo* 1 might be taken as one piece of indirect evidence
of such interest in the stational phenomenon, as would other *ordines* (*Ordo*
15 is a clearly stational narrative of the liturgical year). Carolingian Metz
presents itself as a model for how this was done. I have mentioned the
stational list found in the Gospel Book, Paris BnF lat.938, from the time of

---

[19] Andrieu, 'Les messes des jeudis'; Jean Deshusses, 'Le sacramentaire gregorien du Trente', *RevBen*, 78
    (1968), pp.264–266; Deshusses, 'Les anciens sacramentaires de Tours', *RevBen*, 89 (1979), p.301;
    André Wilmart, 'Le lectionnaire d'Alcuin', *EphLit*, 51 (1937), pp.136–197; Arthur Westwell, 'The
    Lost Missal of Alcuin and the Carolingian Sacramentaries of Tours', *Early Medieval Europe*, 30
    (2022), pp.350–383, at pp.359–360.

Orders for the Stational Mass

Chrodegang of Metz.[20] Indeed, Chrodegang's Rule for his secular clergy makes it clear that he envisaged that the performance of 'public' stations should be a normal feature of liturgical life in Metz.[21] At one point the same text even refers to the *ordo romanus*, indicating that the clergy should come to chapter on Sundays: 'parati cum planetis vel vestimentis officialibus sicut habet ordo romanus'.[22] The 'planeta' is the Roman term for the chasuble, used repeatedly in the text of *Ordo* 1, which indicates that all kinds of clergy wore the *planeta* and not just priests (a similar situation to the one Chrodegang assumed), but which also gives a detailed description of the pontiff's vestments at *Ordo* 1, n.34.[23] A more detailed description of the clothing of all Roman clergy was found in another text, *Ordo* 8 (found in St Gallen 614) and it may be to that text that Chrodegang's Rule referred.[24]

Chrodegang's interest in inculcating Roman liturgical norms in Metz is well known from Paul the Deacon's testimony. According to Paul, he undertook a complex but cohesive programme involving architectural adjustments, the translation of relics, the improvement of chant practices and various liturgical initiatives that shared a Rome-orientated focus.[25] The performance of stations (which may have been an older tradition in Metz repurposed by Chrodegang) could be understood as 'Roman' through the use of a text like *Ordo* 1 to model and interpret it, but also because the initiatives of Chrodegang made the space of the city itself sacred by analogy with Rome.

Under Chrodegang's successor, Bishop Angilram (768–791), the performance of stations in Metz continued, as we know from the Register carried in a late manuscript of Collection A, British Library Add. MS 15222, which records the salaries of those who performed various liturgical functions.[26] The manuscript is an eleventh-century one, and from the archbishopric of Besançon, but the copy must have been made from a ninth-century exemplar of Collection A from Metz itself, for there is

---

[20] Klauser, 'Eine stationsliste'; Claussen, *Reform of the Frankish Church*, pp.276–289; also Carol Heitz, 'La groupe cathedral du Metz au temps du Saint Chrodegang', *Saint Chrodegang: communications présentées au Colloque tenu à Metz à l'occasion du douzième centenaire de sa mort* (Metz, 1967), pp.123–131.

[21] Bertram (ed.), *Chrodegang Rules*, p.80: 'Si autem statio publica fuerit per illas ecclesias forenses . . .'; p.61: 'et ipsius diebus stationibus suis parati custodiant.'

[22] *Ibid.*, p.74: 'prepared with chasubles and the official vestments as the *ordo romanus* describes'.

[23] *Ordo* 1, n.47: 'Diaconi vero, priusquem venaiant ante altare, infra presbiterio exuunt se planetis; n.92: Tunc subdiaconus sequens suscipit eam super planetam.'

[24] *Les Ordines*, vol. I, pp.309–322.   [25] Claussen, *Reform of the Frankish Church*, pp.227–280.

[26] Andrieu, 'Règlement d'Angilramne de Metz'; on the MS, *Les Ordines*, vol. I, pp.142–144, for the use in eleventh-century Besançon, Westwell, 'Content and Ideological Construction'.

110   Orders for the Stational Mass

otherwise little to explain why the very specific Angilram text, entirely outdated in the eleventh century and practically irrelevant, should have been available to the copyists of the Besançon manuscript. Angilram's text assumes a stational Lent and Easter, as already set out in the list by Chrodegang. He paid a modest sum to fifteen clergy who took a special duty as '*stationarii*': two priests, two deacons, two subdeacons, two cantors, one acolyte and the rest being miscellaneous clergy. According to Angilram, these people were entrusted:

> per totam quadragesimam stationes suas iuxta consuetudinem sedis apostolice custodiunt.[27]

Again, this links stations directly to the desire to perform Masses as the Pope himself did. The appointment of the *stationarii* clergy, however, suggests that Angilram himself rarely performed the demanding schedule found in the Metz stational list for Lent. Given he was chancellor to Charlemagne, this is unsurprising. Andrieu suggested that the performance of stations by delegates rather than the bishop himself would be an imperfect solution according to the aspirations of 'Romanising' bishops such as Chrodegang – he viewed this reform in terms of a subjugation imposed by higher clergy without any real understanding of the system in Rome.[28] Outside Rome, it lost any real 'reason to be'. But *Ordo* 2 suggests that delegation of the stations was a normal and expected circumstance even in Rome. We might assume that the pageantry narrated by *Ordo* 1 was the ideal in written form, but circumstances would often have intervened.

Notably, Angilram's *stationarii* also appear in a curious text, which we only know from George Cassander's 1561 record of it, edited as *Ordo* 6.[29] Here, at n.3 the *diaconii stationarii* process with the bishop, at n.10 *notarius ipsius stationis* remains with the pontiff as he is dressed and at n.29 *proximae stationis subdiaconum* carries the thurible. It is impossible not to see in these figures the *stationarii* of Angilram's list.[30] Since there is

---

[27] Andrieu, 'Règlement d'Angilramne de Metz', p.356: 'keep the stations through the whole of Lent according to the custom of the apostolic see'.

[28] *Les Ordines*, p.236: 'Malgré le zèle des évêque romanisants, l'institution si localement romaine des stations ne s'acclimata que fort imparfaitement dans nos regions'; Andrieu, 'Règlement d'Angilramne de Metz', p.361: 'Quelques évêques romanisants essayèrent de l'y implanter. Mais, le premier enthousiasme passé, elle apparut comme un élément de surérogation. Très tôt confiée à des ecclésiastiques subalternes, sans la participation effective du chef religieux de la cité, elle perdit ainsi son sens primitif et toute raison d'être.'

[29] *Les Ordines*, vol. II, pp.231–250; from *Ordo Romanus de officio Missae*, Georges Cassander (ed.) (Cologne, 1561); reprinted in *Georgii Cassandri Belgae Theologi impp. Ferdinando I et Maximiliano II a consiliis, Opera quae reperiri potuerunt Omnia* (Paris, 1616), pp.87–145.

[30] *Les Ordines*, vol. II, p.238.

Orders for the Stational Mass

no surviving ninth-century manuscript, this will not be discussed at length, but it indicates some afterlife of Angilram's arrangements and may have been copied in Metz. It has another significant passage:

> *Ordo* 6, n.69: Cum autem communicaverit archidiaconus calicem interea tenet primus Episcopus. Sicut enim in Romana ecclesia summo pontifici ministrant episcopi, sic in caeteris ecclesiis debent episcopis facere presbyteri.[31]

Ordo 1 could be copied with various adjustments to Frankish taste while maintaining the prized connection to Rome. In Collection B, a series of interpolations address the movement of the candles and acolytes.[32] In *ordines* of Frankish design, attention to such details is evident.[33] Wolfenbüttel Weissenburgenses 91, independently of Collection B, suggests the movement of candles at the same time in the Mass.[34] Light and sound were objects of particular attention in these Frankish adjustments, indicating the increasing attention paid to symbolic and theatrical dimensions of the Mass, reflected in the writings of Amalarius.

Collection B also removes one of the most overtly 'Roman' sections of the text: the entirety of *Ordo* 1, nn.98–99 (also missing in the 'short recension').[35] This section details that the Roman dignitaries such as the *nomenculator, sacellarius* and *notarius videcomini* stand before the Pope to hear and record the names of those invited to the Pope's table for a meal after the Mass. From Collection B, the *nomincolator* and *sacellarius* are also removed in *Ordo* 1, nn.119–122. However, tracing the reception of this portion is not entirely straightforward, since one manuscript of the Collection, Cologne 138 (which is also supposed to be a 'pontifical' for Frankish use) returns this portion to the proper place in the *ordo*.

---

[31] *Ibid.*, pp.249–250: 'But while the archdeacon communicates, the first bishop holds the chalice. Just as in the Roman church the bishops minister to the High Pontiff, so in other churches the priests should do the same for their bishops.'

[32] First, at *Ordo* I, n.52, the acolytes put the candles in a horizontal line across the church. At *Ordo* I, n.54, the acolytes move the candles again, now into a vertical line. At *Ordo* I, n.66, the acolytes now put the candles behind the altar.

[33] For example *Ordo* 4, nn.19: 'Deinde ponunt acholithi cereostata quas tenant in terram'; n.23: 'Leventur acolithi cereostata et ponunt ea ante altare sicut ordinem habent'; n.34: 'et ponunt ea retro altare, seu et reliqua cereostata.'

[34] *Ordo* 1, n.55: 'Tamen septem cereostata mutandae sunt iuxta ipsarum ordinem et tempus.'

[35] *Les Ordines*, vol. II, p.99: 'Et redit ad sedem. Mox primicerius et secundicerius et primicerius defensorum cum omnibus regionariis et notariis ascendant ad altare et stant ad dextris et sinistris. Nomincolator uero et sacellarius et notarius uicedomini, cum dixerint: *Agnus Dei*, tunc ascendant adstare ante faciem pontificis, ut annuat eis scribere nomina eorum qui invitandi sunt sive ad mensam pontificis per nomincolatorem, sive ad vicemdomini per notarium ipsius; quorum nomina ut conpleverint, descendunt ad invitandum.'

112 Orders for the Stational Mass

Adaptation of the *ordo* did not run one way, from Roman specificity to Frankish elasticity, but different compilers had different ideas about what exactly to do with details such as these, and how they might be read and 'used'.

Other individual manuscripts make their own adjustments, including adding dialogue which the original *ordo* left unclear. Of particular significance, Weissenburgenses 91 adds the speech of the archdeacon who announces the next station:

> *Ordo* I n.108: Deinde venit archidiaconus cum calice ad cornu altaris et adnuntiat stationem **ita: Illo die veniente, statio erit ad sanctum Illum, foras aut intus civitate. Resp. Deo Gratias.**[36]

Such an addition suggests the performance of stations at Worms, from where Weissenburgenses 91 likely comes. In these cases, the desire seems to have been for a more complete representation of the ritual in question, going beyond the *ordo*'s 'proper' function to represent only actions and gestures. It is possible that such dialogues were said in the Roman Mass, if observed by a sufficiently well-informed person, but Franks were also entirely capable of adding dialogue from their own established practice, or inventing it for the occasion.

For example, another manuscript of Collection B, Munich Clm 14510, the 'pontifical' from Regensburg, inserts into the narrative of the Roman Mass the instructions for various Frankish customs that were not, at this stage, performed in Rome at all.[37] These include:

> The chanting of the *laudes*:
> *Ordo* I, n.54: Et tunc si tempus fuerit, sicut pascha vel aliis festis, faciunt laudes maiores, id est Exaudi Christe et cetera, sicut continentur. Nam cereosta, cum dictum fuerit Amen ad primam orationem, statim tollantur . . ..[38]
> Saying the Creed during Mass:
> *Ordo* I, n.63: Et imponit symbolum si tempus fuerit, id est *Credo in unum Deum.* Finito symbolo, dicit: *Dominus uobiscum.*[39]

---

[36] *Les Ordines*, vol. II, p.102: 'Then the archdeacon comes with the chalice to the side of the altar and he announces the station thus: On the coming day, the station will be at such and such church, within or without the city. They respond: *Deo gratias*.'

[37] *Les Ordines*, vol. II, p.20.

[38] *Ibid.*, p.85: 'And then, if it should be the time of year, that is on Easter and the other feasts, they sing the great *laudes*, that is *Exaudi Christi* and the rest, as is here contained. But the candles are moved at once, when the *Amen* is said at the first prayer . . ..'

[39] *Ibid.*, p.89: 'And he chants the symbol if it should be that time, that is the *Credo in unum Deum*. When the symbol is finished, he says *Dominus uobiscum*.'

Orders for the Stational Mass

Another particularly extensive addition is the Frankish episcopal blessing, again a non-Roman custom:

> *Ordo* 1, n.94, var.7: Finitam ipsam orationem, tunc uertit se pontifex ad populum et unus ex diaconibus excelsa uoce clamat *Humiliatae capita uestra ad benedictionem*, et alter diaconus uel presbiter tenet benedictionarium librum super caput suum apertum et flectit se ad pontificem et benedicit pontifex omnes benedictionem ad ipsam diem pertinentem sicut in sacramentorum continetur.[40]

The explicit writing of these customs into the narrative of *Ordo* 1 is extraordinary in the Regensburg book. An interesting smaller addition is one where the *subdiaconus regionarius* must address the schola 'alto' 'in a raised voice', an addition found only in this manuscript, another testament to the preoccupation of the Franks with the modalities of how liturgical speech was used, something also visible in Frankish adaptation of the Mass *ordo*.[41] Baturich's adaptations shows how the written 'Roman' Mass could assimilate necessary or beloved elements of Frankish custom, and the possibility was thus open to anyone reading *Ordo* 1. Again, in Weissenburgenses 91 the same custom of the episcopal blessing (as well as the possibility that the bishop should not be present) appears as one of the many notes, comments and appendices through the manuscript, given here as Andrieu's *Ordo* 28A:

> *Ordo* 28A, n.25: Et quando pontifex benedictiones super populum tradere uoluerit, archidiaconus, vel quem ipse iusserit, aspicit ad pontificem, ut ei annuat, et dicit ad populum: Humilitate uos ad benedictionem. Resp: Deo gratias. Si autem pontifex, ibidem non fuerit, supra scriptum habemus.[42]

---

[40] *Ibid.*, p.97: 'When this prayer is finished, then the pontiff turns himself to the people and one of the deacons in a raised voice exclaims: *Humiliate capita uestra ad benedictionem*, and another deacon or a priest holds the book of blessings open above his head, and turns himself to the pontiff and the pontiff blesses them all with the blessing pertaining to this day as is contained in the Sacramentary'; on the episcopal blessings, actually forbidden by Pope Zacharias, see Eligius Dekkers, '"Benedictiones quas faciunt Galli": Qu'a voulu demander saint Boniface?', in Albert Lehner and Walter Berschin (eds.), *Lateinische Kultur im VIII. Jahrhundert. Traube-Gedenkschrift* (St Ottilien, 1989), pp.41–46; an example of a Bavarian 'benedictionarium librum' is *The Benedictionals of Freising (Munich, Bayerische Staatsbibliothek Cod.lat.6430)*, Christopher Hohler, B. J. Wigan and Robert Amiet (eds.), HBS 88 (London, 1974).

[41] *Ordo* 1, n.37, var.7: 'subdiaconus regionarius . . . dicit <alto>: Scola'.

[42] *Les Ordines*, vol. III, pp.424–425; 'And when the pontiff wishes to give blessings over the people, the archdeacon, or whom he will have chosen, waits for the pontiff to signal to him, and then says to the people: *Humilitate uos ad benedictionem*. And they respond: *Deo gratias*. But if the pontiff should not be there, we have written above' (referring to *Ordo* 3).

Orders for the Stational Mass

These adjustments already clearly show the elasticity of the *ordo romanus*. Such a text becomes a venue for experimentation in the syncretism we can imagine occurring in every case a 'Roman' rite was received, surveyed and assimilated on Frankish soil. Frankish clergy desired (or felt they needed) to perform such functions too, so when they read *Ordo* 1 they would consider where to place such rites in the Mass as performed. Ultimately, the actual performance of the stational Mass might well end up looking quite different from the Mass narrated in *Ordo* 1, because various needs, desires and principles might enter into the translation of the written to the performed. Thus, for example, the almost singular occasion when we have an episcopal Mass depicted in art in any detail from this period, the set of ivories on the cover of the Drogo Sacramentary (Paris BnF lat.9430), the images have similarly adjusted and added to the narrative of *Ordo* 1, to the extent that no *ordo* can be fully identified to be the exact script of the Mass here depicted.[43] This is indicated by Angilram's provision of *stationarii*, one of the few texts that directly addresses the tension, if indirectly, by acknowledging the need for a specialised staff to take over the stations in his place. But to Angilram, the stations were still being performed 'according to the custom of the apostolic see'. In the same way as architecture, liturgy outside Rome could adjust to such circumstance and still be understood as *more romano* because the essential idea of its connection to Rome was maintained.[44]

We see these dynamics explicitly at play when *Ordo* 1 is reworked into entirely new versions of the text in Frankish hands. Broadly, we possess four main such rewritings which are either in ninth-century manuscripts, or probably were originally. These are: *Ordo* 4 (part of the 'Collection of St Amand'), *Ordo* 6, *Ordo* 9 and the Mass *ordo* enclosed in *Ordo* 15.

Ordo 4 opens the 'Collection of St Amand', copied onto folios added at the beginning and end of a manuscript of Augustine probably at the monastery of St Amand, perhaps at the beginning of the tenth century.[45] Duchesne believed *Ordo* 4 to be authentically Roman, but it is not so.[46] While presented with other *ordines* in the collection which do speak more accurately to Roman rites and include Roman

---

[43] Detailed in Roger Reynolds, 'Image and Text: A Carolingian Illustration of Modifications in the early Roman Eucharistic *ordines*', *Viator: Medieval and Renaissance Studies*, 14 (1983), pp.59–75, reprinted as Article VII in Reynolds, *Clerical Orders*.

[44] Emerick, 'Building *more romano* in Francia'.   [45] *Les Ordines*, vol. II, pp.137–170.

[46] Duchesne, *Origines du culte chrétien*, p.157: 'strictement romain, romain de Rome'; the texts are edited at pp.476–500; disproven already by Bishop, *Liturgica Historica*, pp.151–160.

Orders for the Stational Mass

place names, *Ordo* 4 is the work of a Frankish adaptor, working from *Ordo* 1 and both its Supplements. Access to these three texts suggests a manuscript that was similar to one part of St Gallen 614 as the source text. Given the sources, *Ordo* 4 is a stational Mass, and begins with a procession to the church in question, but one much simplified and summarised; it is likely that *Ordo* 4 derives from the 'short recension' where the papal cortege was not described and no church was singled out as the particular station of the day, both being still true here.[47] The station to come is announced:

> *Ordo* 4, n.68: . . . vadit archidiaconus in dextra parte altaris, stans ante eum acolitus cum sciffo priore et adnunciat stacione et respondent omnes: Deo Gratias.[48]

And again, in closing section, where the author adds details about how the celebration might proceed if played out by other clergy without the presence of the bishop *pontifex*, the deacon is shown playing this role:

> *Ordo* 4, n.114: Et dum confractum habuerint, adnunciat diaconus stacione [*sic*] sicut mos est.[49]

Using *Ordo* 2, *Ordo* 4 also maintains the option for the performance of the stational Mass by the priest, if the bishop was not present.[50] But the text goes further in addressing the possibility of a stational Mass *sans* bishop, including the detail that if the pontiff should not process, the deacons did so in his place.[51] That was a Frankish solution, continuing Frankish probing of potential ways to have stational Masses without all the Roman accoutrements. The text addresses the movement of candles with much greater attention than even Collection B did.[52] A number of the

---

[47] *Ordo* 4, n.1: 'Primitus enim procedit omnis clerus ad ecclesiam vel omnis populus . . . .'; *Les Ordines*, vol. II, pp.140–141.

[48] *Ibid.*, p.165: 'the archdeacon comes to the right side of the altar, the acolyte standing before him with the first chalice and he announces the station and everyone responds: *Deo Gratias*'; in Rome, there would be only one chalice on the altar so the idea of a '*primo sciffo*' is nonsensical there, as in Gregory II's letter to Boniface: 'Congruum non est, duas uel tres calices in altare ponere cum missarum sollempnia celebraturi' in *MGH* Epp. III, Merowingici et Karolini aevi 1, pp.275–277 at p.276.

[49] *Les Ordines*, vol. II, p.170: 'And when the fraction has happened, the deacon announces the station as is custom.'

[50] *Ordo* 4, n.102: 'Et si presbiter missa debet celebrare, non dicit Gloria in excelsis Deo sed tantum psallit et dicit oracione . . .' and n.110: 'Et episcopus aut presbiter qui fecit missa . . . .'

[51] *Ordo* 4, n.98: 'si pontifex non processerit, diaconi sic procedant superius dictum est'.

[52] *Ordo* 4, n.7: 'Deinde oblationarius inlumint duos cereos ante secretario pro luminaria pontificis, quod est consuetudo omni tempore, et antecedit ante pontifex et ponit eos retro altare, in duo candelabra, dextra levaque'; n.19: 'Deinde ponunt acolithi cereostata quas tenant in terrum'; *Ordo* 4, n.23: 'Leventur acolithi cereostata et ponunt ea ante altare sicut ordinem habent'; *Ordo* 4, n.34: 'Et

116 Orders for the Stational Mass

Roman staff are still recorded, including the *subdiaconii regionarii* (nn.40, 45, 61). Notable in *Ordo* 4 is the increased attention to the modalities of volume and tone in prayer.[53] *Ordo* 4 also assumes the orientation and layout of the Frankish cathedral, which meant that the positioning of the bishop's throne and how he would face the people differed from the Roman basilica.[54]

Another text, *Ordo* 9, only appears in St Gallen 614 and in the direct copy, St Gallen 140.[55] In the former, it was part of the unit with the *Eglogae de ordine romano*, attributed to Amalarius and located to Reichenau. Since St Gallen 140 is to be dated to the third quarter of the ninth century, it must have travelled to St Gallen by that point. Of the related St Gallen manuscripts using this same corpus, both of which also assimilated the full Collection B, St Gallen 140 copied *Ordo* 9, but not the *Eglogae*, while St Gallen 446 took the *Eglogae* but not *Ordo* 9 (placing the *Eglogae* after *Ordo* 1 instead). Like Amalarius' text, *Ordo* 9 describes the episcopal Mass, and makes no specific claims to be Roman or set in Rome.[56] As *Ordo* 4 had done, it rewrote *Ordo* 1 in more accessible language including the German 'kanna' for the chalice (nn.22, 27, 30). The Mass is not explicitly stational here, but the text clearly draws an analogy between the papal cortege and the introit procession through the church, described precisely and, as in *Ordo* 4, with increased attention to the number and arrangement of the minor clergy.[57] Frankish rites, such as the washing of hands before Mass, appear, as they did in the preceding *Eglogae*.[58] It shows the attention to the modalities of speech.[59] While Andrieu saw *Ordo* 9 as dependent on a third text, *Ordo* 5, it is in fact far more likely that *Ordo* 5, which also draws on the *Eglogae*, was the later text, and employed *Ordo* 9, along with works of Amalarius.[60] *Ordo* 5 appears in

---

ponunt ea retro altare seu et reliqua cereostata'; n.86: 'et revertuntur cereostat post ipsum'; n.92: 'Et venientes acolithi ante pontificum cum cereostata stant ante ostium, usquedum ingreditur pontifex sacrarium et extinguunt cerea.'

[53] Aubert, 'When the Roman Liturgy Became Frankish', pp.99–102.

[54] *Les Ordines*, vol. II, pp.143–146.   [55] Ed. in *Les Ordines*, vol. II, pp.325–336.

[56] *Les Ordines*, vol. II, pp.325–336.

[57] *Ordo* 9, n.1: 'et septem aut quinque vel tres diaconi et tot numero subdiaconi et acoliti quot fuerint diaconi'; n.3: 'post quos sequantur septem aut quinque sive tres acoliti cum candelabris, iuxta numerum scilicet, ut pediximus diaconorum seu subdiaconorum. Deinde subsequantur subdiaconi bini procedentes, quos similiter bini sequantur diaconi ....'; n.4: 'dividantur ex utraque parte pontificis, id est si septem fuerint; IIII stent ad dexteram et III ad sinistram'.

[58] *Ordo* 9, n.21: '*Credo in unum* itaque decantando'; n.32: 'Infra accione *Te igitur* detur aqua presbiteris, ut lavent manus sua ....'

[59] *Ordo* 9, n.11: 'Ipse vero pontifex cantori annuat, quando excelsiori voce *Kirieleison* sive *Christeleyon* dici debeat'; n.57: 'tota scola alta dicat voce: *Amen*.'

[60] *Les Ordines*, vol. II, pp.325–326; *Ordo* 5, ed. in *Les Ordines*, vol. II, pp.173–227.

Orders for the Stational Mass 117

manuscripts only from the eleventh century, a part of the family of manuscripts which Andrieu incorporated into his '*Pontifical Romano-Germanique*'.

As we saw, *Ordo* 15 was copied particularly early, in St Gallen 349, though it probably originated in Tours.[61] It has an adapted Mass *ordo* at nn.12–65. This is another abridgement and simplification of *Ordo* 1. It is not true, as Van Dijk claims, that this simplicity and the absence of the many exotic personnel means that the text is an early version of *Ordo* 1, preceding that text historically.[62] Instead, we have another early adaptation of *Ordo* 1 by a Frankish reader. In *Ordo* 15's runthrough of the liturgical year, this *ordo* appears as the third Mass of Christmas, the one that takes place in St Peter's Basilica, while the 'long recension' had specifically applied it to Easter instead. It was the 'short recension' that our text worked from, and thus the Mass is represented as the generic stational Mass. Indeed, its subtitle makes clear that it would be applied much more broadly than at Christmas alone.

> *Ordo* 15, n.12: Modus autem vel consuetudo tam ipsius diei quam omnium dominicorum diem vel paschalium seu natalicia sanctorum, talis est.[63]

Drawing from *Ordo* 1, the Mass is certainly stational, as announced by the archdeacon, again with a speech given to him by the Frankish compiler:

> n.12: et veniunt ad ecclesiam ubi stacio denunciata ...[64]

This phrasing is copied from the 'short recension', and is not part of the 'long recension' of *Ordo* 1.[65]

> n.56: Tunc arcidiaconus accepto ipso calice, vadit iuxta altare in dexteram partem et tenens calicem in manibus suis pronuntiat venturam stationem dicendo: Illa feria veniente, natalis est illius sancti, sive martyrum sive confessorum statio in basilica illius in illo et illo loco. Respondent omnes: Deo gratias.[66]

While the Mass is still celebrated by the *domnus apostolicus/pontifex*, the accompanying clergy are simplified, except in a mention of the *subdiaconibus regionariis* at n.58. Again, a greater attention is paid to the sonic

---

[61] Ed. in *Les Ordines*, vol. III., pp.45–125.   [62] Van Dijk, 'Urban and Papal Rites', p.458.

[63] *Les Ordines*, vol. III, p.97: 'But the custom and form is thus, both on this day of Christmas and on all Sundays, and Easter and the days of saints.'

[64] *Ibid.*, p.97: 'And they come to the church where the station was announced.'   [65] *Ordo* 1, n.24.

[66] *Les Ordines*, vol. III, p.107: 'Then the archdeacon having taken the chalice, he goes before the altar on the right side and holding the chalice in his hands, pronounces the coming station, saying: *Illa feria veniente, natalis est illius sancti, sive martyrum sive confessorum statio in basilica illius in illo et illo loco*. And they all respond: *Deo gratias*.'

118   Orders for the Stational Mass

elements, with different parts of the Canon audible to 'God alone', to 'everyone' and 'only to those around the altar'.[67]

Andrieu's dismissal of one *Ordo* as 'more of a literary exercise than the work of a liturgist attentive to concrete realities' again shows how his strict understanding of genre failed to capture the ways it is necessary to see these *ordines* working in the hands of Frankish compilers.[68] There was a 'literary' element to every *Ordo*, in the sense that it could not entirely capture liturgical ceremonies from every perspective. The recounting of even the most strictly Roman rites went beyond 'concrete realities' in suggesting how rituals were to be understood in ideological and intellectual terms. Here the idea of *Ordo* as 'arrangement' rather than as 'script' of a ritual remains helpful. *Expositiones missae* work in much the same way, which explains the constant affinity and ample exchange between them and the *ordines*, crossing barriers that historians of the liturgy have subsequently erected. As with the *Eglogae de ordine romano*, the Mass which is explained and expounded by Amalarius' *Liber de Officialis* and other works does not cohere with any given *ordo romanus*, but takes elements from them, reframes them and adds new elements, according to what made the most sense to Amalarius and what he thought his readers should understand.[69] Like him, his colleagues creating *ordo romanus* manuscripts who often read and used his work, and who presented his work alongside their own *ordines*, did not take *Ordo* I as a wholesale script, but allowed it to inspire the possibility of rearrangement to their own purposes.

Stations in Francia and the Papal Eucharist

The canon of the 876 Council of Pavia under Louis II enjoining that laypeople and '*saeculares*' were required to attend 'public stations' on feast days assumes that stations were still a normal feature of urban liturgical life among the clergy, at least.[70] An even more explicit document of Carolingian stational observances was the monastic 'Pontifical' in Paris Bibliothèque de l'Arsenal MS 227. The text's complex and detailed Holy Week narrative, based on several *ordines romani*, also records the Roman

---

[67] *Ordo* 15, n.35: 'Tunc pontifex inclinator vulto in terra, dicit orationem super oblationes ita ut nullus preter Deum et ipsum audiat, nisi tantum Per omnia secula seculorum'; n.37: 'Inde vero pontifex, elevans voce et dicit ipsa prefationem, ita ut ab omnibus audiatur', n.38: 'Et incipit pontifex canone dissimili voce et melodia, ita ut a circumstantibus altare tantum audiatur.'

[68] *Les Ordines*, vol. II, pp.237–238: 'Son travail est plutôt un exercice littéraire que l'ouevre d'un liturgiste soucieux des réalités.'

[69] Rose and Westwell, 'Correcting the Liturgy and Sacred Language'.

[70] *MGH* Conc.V, p.22: 'Et ut saeculares et fideles laici diebus festis qui in civitatibus sunt, ad publicas stationes occurant.'

Stations in Francia and the Papal Eucharist 119

stations for the Triduum and for Easter week, doubtless copied from a *comes* or Sacramentary.[71] But in much greater depth, the same manuscript explicitly assumes a complex stational observance for Holy Week, and particularly for Maundy Thursday.[72] This is to take place over three stations, with the bishop and clergy processing from one to another. For the final station, properly at St John in the Lateran, the manuscript explicitly notes:

> AD ECCLESIAM MAIOREM STATIONIS EIUSDEM CELEBRITATIS QUE IN SEDE QUIDEM APOSTOLICA AD SANCTAM IOHANNEM IN LATERANIS AGITUR. IN CAETERIS UERO URBIS SEU MONASTERIIS PRO OPORTUNITATE ET CONGRUENTIA UNIUSCUIUSQUE LOCII.[73]

This remains one of our best indications that the Roman stations, recorded in manuscripts, were used as an opportunity to layer onto a given ecclesiastical space the map of Rome. Here the episcopal church, the *ecclesiam maiorem*, is the equivalent for the Lateran, Rome's Cathedral.

As *Ordines* 2 and 6 both explicitly indicate, the bishop would stand in for the Pope, as his church would stand in for the Lateran, or any number of the other stational churches of Rome, depending on congruency. This meant that many of the rubrics applied to the Pope would be taken to apply to the bishop himself. There are some *ordines* which indicate the function more explicitly, and among them the *Ordo* edited by Chavasse as *Ordo* 51, also dealing with the Chrism Mass, is a case in point. This appeared fully in the lost 'Pontifical of Turpin' once in Reims, and Martène recorded that the *Ordo*, whose title sets it 'AD LATERANIS', integrally contained the prayer texts of the Chrism Mass, another key component of the bishop's office and one which many later 'pontificals' would likewise offer.[74] A *diaconus cardinalis* also makes an appearance (nn.6, 16). The *ordo* was later copied in several English pontificals of the tenth and eleventh century.[75] The text of the Chrism

---

[71] *Il cosiddetto pontificale de Poitiers*, Martini (ed.), pp.190, 258, 264, 307; Westwell, 'Content and the Ideological Construction'.

[72] *Ibid.*, p.161: 'Qua expleta, pontifex cum eclesiastico ordine pergit ad ecclesiam, ad quam secundum morem convenient populi ad stationem celebrandae missae'; p.163: '-Hac missa expleta, pergunt ad stationem secundam, ubi missa chrismalis a pontifice ordine suo celebranda est'; p.166: 'Sane observandum est, ut in his tribus stationibus, quae hac die peragendae sunt, taliter processiones ordinentur, ut in prima tres quidem dyaconi cum suibecto sibi ordine et numero induti dalmaticis cum episcopo procedant; in secunda autem quinque; in tertia autem septem.'

[73] *Ibid.*, p.165: 'At the great church where the same station is celebrated which in the apostolic see is done at St John in the Lateran. But in other cities or in monasteries (it can be done) in whichever place presents itself for opportunity and congruency.'

[74] Martène, *De Antiquis*, vol. III, cols.283–284.

[75] For example, Rouen BM 369, edited in *The Benedictional of Archbishop Robert*, Henry Wilson (ed.), HBS 24 (London, 1903), pp.13–15.

120   Orders for the Stational Mass

Mass which is given as part of the *Ordo* is taken from the Gregorian *Hadrianum*. Chavasse supposed that the prayers of the Mass were added by the Franks to the pre-existing Roman rubrics, but equally likely they were integral to a Frankish composition of the text, giving a setting and context to the words as the Franks found them in the Sacramentary.[76] The presentation of the text of the Chrism Mass in the *Ordo* allowed the bishop to perform this important ritual, but enclosed it in the framing device of the ceremony *in Lateranis*, while offering gestures and changes in tonality he could perforce himself imitate:

> n.4: Stante ante altare pontifice, et elevata dicente voce: *Sursum corda.*[77]

> n.6: At ille paululum divertens se ab altare, stans in suo gradu, signans oleum in manu diaconi et orationem institutam supra tacite dicens . . .[78]

> n.9: Et pontifex tacite signat calicem cum oblata sanctificata nemine respondente . . .[79]

> n.13: Et ille pontifex tribus vicibus sufflans in ampulam, tangens sua manu dicit magna voce: Sursum corda . . .[80]

> n.14: Et pontifex signat in modum crucis tribus vicibus cum police, et insufflat iterum tribus vicibus, cum halitu signat in crucis modum . . .[81]

> n.17: Et ille oleum signans, oratione consecrationis, nullo respondente, submissa quasi tacita magis voce benedicens . . .[82]

In this *ordo*, the framing of such instructions as taking place in the Lateran would add an extra resonance to the sorts of instructions Frankish bishops would be interested in. Evident here, the Frankish interest in the tonalities and volume of prayer, and their significance, is well attested in the *ordines romani* they themselves developed.[83]

---

[76] Chavasse, 'A Rome, le Jeudi-saint', p.25, n.6.

[77] *Ibid.*, p.26: 'While the pontiff stands before the altar, he says with a raised voice: *Sursum corda* . . ..'

[78] *Ibid.*, p.26: 'And he, turning himself a little from the altar, stands in his place, signing the oil which is in the hand of the deacon, and says the instituted prayer . . ..'

[79] *Ibid.*, p.26: 'And the pontiff silently touches the chalice with the consecrated Host, responding nothing.'

[80] *Ibid.*, p.27: 'And the pontiff blows three times in the ampulla, touching it with his hand. He then says in a great voice: *Sursum Corda* . . ..'

[81] *Ibid.*, p.27: 'And the pontiff signs it with a cross three times with his finger. He blows again three times, signing it with his breath in the shape of a cross . . ..'

[82] *Ibid.*, p.28: 'And he signs the oil and then puts forth the prayer of consecration almost silently, to which no one responds, then with a great voice, he blesses . . ..'

[83] Aubert, 'When the Roman Liturgy Became Frankish'.

Stations in Francia and the Papal Eucharist

A Gregorian rubric for the Chrism Mass was noticeably incorporated in the Carolingian *ROMANUS ORDO IN EBDOMADA MAIORE* discovered by Martinez-Diaz in Barcelona Biblioteca Central de la Diputación MS 944 (unknown to Andrieu), here appearing between what would be, in Andrieu's edition, *Ordo* 24, nn.13–14.[84] While the manuscript is an eleventh-century one, its content includes both Amalarius' *Liber Officialis* and this *ordo*, suggesting a Carolingian exemplar. In two other places the *domnus papa* makes an appearance in this *ordo* only, and not in *Ordo* 24 otherwise: 'Et intrant tam domnus Papa quam omnes presbiteri in consecratione chrismatis excelsa voce. Sed antequam benedicatur domnus Papa halat in ampullam' and, on Holy Saturday, 'unus ex ministris sumpta ampulla cum oleo precedit pontificem in loco ubi sunt a domno Papa infantes exorcizandi sicut mos est'.[85] While Martinez Diaz interpreted these additions to mean that the text was '*más genuinemente romano y papal*' than *Ordo* 24 as edited by Andrieu, in fact such additions are plainly Frankish insertions based on the Gregorian Sacramentary. After all, the principal actor of the rest of this *ordo* is still a *pontifex* or *episcopus* (the latter a title not used for the Pope) and everyone communicates on Good Friday, in the Mass of the Presanctified (as in *Ordo* 24), which contradicts what Amalarius tells us was the practice at the papal station on this day.[86] Thus the appearance of the Pope is to be interpreted here similarly to the *ordo* of 'Turpin's Pontifical': the Frankish bishop is to imitate the actions given to the Pope himself, and thus identify himself with him. This *ordo* even more explicitly blurs boundaries between the actions of the *pontifex/episcopus* and the *domnus papa*.

To return to the more standard formulation of the Mass, another important *ordo* presents with particular clarity the same function. This is *Ordo* 7.[87] It is built fundamentally around a rubrication of the Roman Canon of the Mass, as it is found in the Sacramentary; thus the bulk of the text are the words of that singularly important prayer, but with multiple additional rubrics whose protagonist is the *domnus papa*. This text appears in a number of volumes, of which three are ninth-century: St

---

[84] Martinez-Diez, 'Un *Ordo Romanus* inedito', p.200: 'Qua expleta communicat solus episcopus. Ipso die conficitur chrisma. Antequam dicatur: Per quem haec omnia, domine, semper bona creas levantur de ampullis quas offerunt populi et benedicit tam domnus Papa quam omnes presbiteri'; *Le sacramentaire gregorien*, Deshusses (ed.), p.172.

[85] *Ibid.*, pp.200, 201.

[86] *Ibid.*, p.199: 'Qua expleta communicat solus episcopus ....'; p.201: 'et communicant omnes cum silentio'.

[87] *Les Ordines*, vol. II, pp.253–305.

122   Orders for the Stational Mass

Gallen Stiftsbibliothek 150, St Gallen 446 and Bamberg cod.lit.131. In the South German manuscript, Bamberg lit.131, *Ordo* 7 appears between the *Eglogae de ordine romano*, attributed to Amalarius (the attribution ultimately stemming, perhaps, from St Gallen 446), and the other *expositio missae* also attributed as in St Gallen 446: 'a coenobio Dionisii' (Saint-Denis).[88] St Gallen 446 has the same texts, but opens the sequence with *Ordo* 1.[89] In these books, the *ordines romani* present themselves as one such kind of text, among the *expositiones*. *Ordo* 7 is here entitled: 'QUALITER QUAEDAM ORATIONES ET CRUCES IN *TE IGITUR* AGENDAE SUNT.'[90] It follows directly after the *Eglogae* as a kind of epilogue, not really distinguished from it.

The earliest manuscript, St Gallen 150, presents the *ordo* quite differently, however.[91] This manuscript is from the same monastery, and earlier than the first two; it gives us our best impression of how the *ordo* would have originally appeared (though the end is missing). This time, it appears among penitential material, in a unit dated by Bischoff to the second quarter of the ninth century (around the time St Gallen was also copying its other great *ordo romanus* manuscript, St Gallen 614).[92] In St Gallen 150 the *ordo* is simply entitled *Item alia missa*, and it takes the place of the canon in the format of a daily Mass from the Sacramentary, with the collect and the *super oblata* preceding it, as they would in the Sacramentary. As Andrieu identified, the text of this Mass with the Canon of the Mass inside it is lifted from the same format in the last of the *missae cotidianae* in the *Paduensis* Gregorian (part of the many Frankish adaptations of what was originally a very early type of Gregorian, earlier than *Hadrianum*).[93] The Canon is thus a variant form with the special *memento* for the dead transmitted in that type of Sacramentary. St Gallen 150 makes it clear that the *ordo* began life as rubrics added to the Canon attached to this 'daily' Mass, in a copy of a Gregorian Sacramentary like that which today only survives in complete form in *Paduensis*, another example therefore of the breadth of liturgical sources used to create *ordines romani*. The appearance of Saint Stephen protomartyr in the *Libera nos* prayer (alongside saints who appear in other Frankish Sacramentaries, Hilary, Martin and

---

[88] Andrieu, *Les Ordines*, vol. I, pp.84–86; Bischoff, *Katalog*, vol. I, 222, p.50: 'Wohl Süddeutschland, IX Jh., 2.Drittel.'

[89] *Les Ordines*, vol. I, pp.336–34.

[90] *Ordo* 7. Title: 'How certain prayers and signs of the cross in the Te Igitur should be done.'

[91] *Les Ordines*, vol. II, p.253–255; digitised at: www.e-codices.unifr.ch/en/csg/0150/3.

[92] Bischoff, *Katalog*, vol. III, p.309, n.5608: 'St Gallen IX Jh. 2 Viertel (1./2. Viertel).'

[93] *Les Ordines*, vol. II, pp.258–262; *Liber Sacramentorum Paduensis*, Catella *et al.* (eds.), pp.375–383.

Stations in Francia and the Papal Eucharist 123

Benedict), not to be seen in the surviving *Paduensis* manuscript, suggests that this might have been undertaken in a place where he was patron of the cathedral, indicating Metz as the most likely origin.[94] The full Mass with the added rubrics was lifted from the Sacramentary into St Gallen 150. In the later books with *expositiones* (St Gallen 446, being the likely source of Bamberg lit.131), the introducing Mass prayers were removed and the *ordo* specifically retitled as a guide to the canon, and particularly the signs of the cross made during it. Thus, an *ordo* moved from a Sacramentary to a self-contained text, to an *expositio missae*. This is a clear demonstration of the multiple meanings and uses readers might take to these texts, and how the texts moved between what modern editors present as genres. Like the words of the Gregorian Chrism Mass enclosed in the rubrics of Chavasse's *Ordo* 51, the canon in *Ordo* 7 is presented to Franks who would say it within a framework of actions undertaken by the *domnus papa*. This compiler also knew the 'short recension' of *Ordo* I.[95] This text seems to have had a broad influence at an initial stage of the transmission of the *ordines*, despite the lack of surviving copies.

These gestures are attributed initially to a *sacerdos* but in the second half of the *ordo* to the *domnus papa*. Again, the focus is on the modalities of tone and gesture which could be imitated by the Frankish reader:

> *Ordo* 7, n.18: Hic levat domnus papa oblationes duas usque ad oram calicis et tangens eum de oblationibus, tenente illum archidiacono: *Per ipsum et cum ipso et in ipso est tibi Deo patri omnipotenti in unitate spiritus sancti omnis honor et gloria.* Tunc dicit in altum: *Per omnia saecula saeculorum.* Resp. *Amen.* Tunc reponit oblationes in altare et dicit in altum: *Oremus.*[96]
>
> *Ordo* 7, n.20: Tunc dicit domnus papa interveniente nullo sono hanc orationem: *Libera nos . . .*[97]

Ordo 3 implied that the Pope normally celebrated with three Hosts, not two, but the Frankish custom was to use two, and this was reflected here.[98]

---

[94] *Ordo* 7, n.20: 'et intercedente beata et gloriosa semper virgine Dei genetrice Maria et sanctis apostolis tuis Petro et Paulo atque Andrea et sancto Stephano protomartyre tuo et beatis confessoribus tuis Hylario, Martino atque Benedictio'; also n.17 in the *Nobis quoque*: 'cum Iohanne, Stephano, Mathia, Barnaba, Ignatio . . ..'

[95] *Les Ordines*, vol. II, p.286.

[96] *Ibid.*, p.302: 'Here the Lord Pope raises two Hosts to the lip of chalice, which the archdeacon is holding, and touches it with the Hosts: *Per ipsum et cum ipso et in ipso tibi Deo patri omnipotenti in unitate spiritus sancti omnis honor et gloria.* Then he says in a raised voice: *Per omnia saecula saeculorum.* The response: *Amen.* Then he returns the offerings onto the altar and says in a raised voice: *Oremus.*'

[97] *Ibid.*, p.303: 'Then the Lord Pope, with no sound coming between, says this prayer: *Libera nos . . ..*'

[98] *Ordo* 3, n.1: '*unicuique eorum oblatas tres . . ..*'

124 Orders for the Stational Mass

Related to such differences, the text shows specific concern with a more complex confrontation with Roman liturgical norms:

> *Ordo* 7, n.22: Dum uero domnus papa dicit: *Pax domini sit semper uobiscum*, non mittit partem de Sancta in calicem, sicut caeteris sacerdotibus mos est. Dum confringunt et *Agnus Dei* dicit.[99]

Here, by contrast, the figure of the Pope is supposed to have done something different during communion from others who would celebrate it in imitation of him. We recognise again the same concern as the text of *Ordo* 6. Here, the Franks identified that they celebrated as the Pope did, but there were certain actions of the Pope that no other bishop or priest was properly permitted. How to identify and explain them?

Fascination with the particular Eucharistic privileges of the Pope can be widely demonstrated. There is a particularly interesting gloss on the mention of the Roman custom of *fermentum* in the important letter of Pope Innocent to Decentius in a manuscript from St Emmeram in Regensburg, today Munich BSB Clm 14747, fol.78r, probably to be dated in the second half of the ninth century.[100]

> De fermento quod dicit mos est Romanis, ut de missa quae cantatur in caena domini et in sabbato sancto et in die sancto paschae et in pentecosten et in natalis domini die sancto, per totum anno servatur, et ubicumque per stationes, si ipse papa ad missam praesens non fuerit, de ipsa missa mittitur in calicem, cum dicit: *Pax domini sit semper uobiscum*. Et hoc dicitur fermentum. Tamen sabbato sancto paschae nullus presbyter per ecclesias baptismales neminem communicat antequam mittatur ei de ipsa Sancta quam obtulit domnus papa.[101]

We can recognise in this gloss the germ of an *ordo romanus*, probably the observation of someone who had been to Rome and wanted to know exactly

---

[99] *Ibid.*, p.304: 'Then when the Lord Pope says: *Pax domini sit semper uobiscum*, he does not place a part of the Host in the chalice as is the custom of other priests and bishops. Then they break it and say the Agnus Dei.'

[100] Recorded by Jean Mabillon, *Iter Germanicum* (Hamburg, 1717), pp.60–61 from a manuscript *Glossis MSS super canones apostolorum et decretales pontificum* in St-Emmeram, quoted from Mabillon in *Les Ordines*, vol. II, p.62; MS identified by Arthur Bauckner, *Mabillons Reise durch Bayern* (Munich, 1910), pp.44–45; on the manuscript, Bischoff, *Schreibschulen*, vol. II, p.245; digitised at: www.digitale-sammlungen.de/de/view/bsb00096536?page=157.

[101] 'Concerning the *fermentum* he mentions, the custom of the Romans is that from the Masses which are said on Maundy Thursday, Holy Saturday, Easter, Pentecost and Christmas, they save a bit of the Host for the whole year, and whenever at the stations the Pope is not present, a piece of that Host is placed in the chalice, when they say: *Pax domini sit semper uobiscum*. And this is called the *fermentum*. However on Holy Saturday of Easter no priest at any of the baptismal churches should communicate at all before a piece of this Host obtained from the Lord Pope is placed in it.'

Stations in Francia and the Papal Eucharist

what the *fermentum* mentioned in Innocent's letter was (though the rite had changed substantially since Innocent's day, of course).[102] The sending of the Host out to the priests on Holy Saturday recurs in *Ordo* 30B, from the Collection of St Amand, indicating Frankish interest in these customs.[103] Research into the meaning of obscure terminology and the special Eucharistic privileges of the popes to better understand both contemporary practice and the history of rites might give rise to such texts, themselves then becoming notes added to descriptions of practices that distinguish from the papal ones. *Ordo* 2 prescribes an entirely similar ritual at a stational celebration in the Pope's absence and indicates that this is the *fermentum*.[104]

Although Andrieu suggested that lost Roman documents underlay many of such indications, Frankish observance of Roman custom can probably explain them, as in the case of a portion recorded in *Ordo* 3, the second Supplement to *Ordo* 1.[105] *Ordo* 3 is also found in St Gallen 614, with 24 and 26 (on Holy Week), but it is also significantly more widely witnessed than the other Supplement, *Ordo* 2. In Brussels 10124–10177 it appears between *Ordines* 26 and 24 (in the current state of the manuscript, without *Ordo* 1, the text it supplements which might have been lost). But in two of the 'pontificals', Cologne 138, carrying Collection B, and Wolfenbuettel Weissenburgenses 91, with its unique collection, it follows directly after *Ordo* 1. It was added to Verona XCII fol.21v (another indication of an adaptation of this manuscript which was made on the basis of a source close to Cologne 138) but only the opening has survived (a spare leaf was probably inserted with the rest, but this is lost). *Ordo* 3 deals with additions and clarifications to *Ordo* 1. The first part describes a ceremony of concelebration by the pontiff with the *presbyteri cardinales*, which takes place on four high feasts. The cardinals recite the canon with the pontiff, who alone does the gestures of the cross. Munich Clm 14510, which otherwise tends to fill *Ordo* 1 with native Frankish usages, had also inserted this same portion into the narrative, so its compilers knew *Ordo* 3 in full or in part, but chose only to

---

[102] On the fermentum generally, *Les Ordines*, vol. II, pp.59–64.

[103] *Ordo* 30B, n.65: 'Et transmittit unusquisque presiter mansionarium de titulo suo ad ecclesiam Salvatoris et expectant ibi usquedum frangitur Sancta, habentes secum corporalis. Et venit oblationarius subdiaconus et dat eis de Sancta, quod pontifex consecravit, et recipient ea in corporalis et revertitur unusquisque ad titulum suum et tradit Sancto presbitero. Et de ipsa facit crucem super calicem et ponit in eo et dicit: *Dominus uobiscum*. Et communicant omnes sicut superius.'

[104] *Ordo* 2, n.6: 'Sexto loco, quando dici debet *Pax domini sit semper uobiscum*, deportatur a subdiacono oblationario particula fermenti, quod ab apostolico consecratum est datur archidiacono. Ille vero porrigit episcopo. At ille, consignando tribus vicibus et dicendo: *Pax domini sit semper uobsicum*, mittit in calice.'

[105] Ed. *Les Ordines*, vol. II, pp.119–133.

126   Orders for the Stational Mass

copy the segment on concelebration in particular.[106] Likewise, *Ordo* 4 inserted and expanded the rubric to eight feasts, removing the mention of *cardinales*, and three Roman Hosts becoming two Frankish ones.[107] The use by both these witnesses of the text does seem to imply that the Roman configuration for concelebration was studied, imitated and adapted on Frankish soil. We do have significant later evidence for *cardinales presbyteri*, the 'liturgical cardinals' in many of the great cathedrals of France, whose prerogative was to concelebrate with the bishop on a number of great feasts.[108] This configuration even appears in ivory in the late ninth-century depiction of an archepiscopal Mass now covering the manuscript Frankfurt Staatsbibliothek MS Bart.181, where five concelebrating clergy stand behind the bishop each holding a corporal, exactly as the *Ordo* suggested.[109] Andrieu divides the sections of *Ordo* 3 between those 'of Roman provenance' (nn.1–2) and those of Frankish origin (nn.3–6), but the use of concelebration by the Frankish clergy demonstrated in the Frankfurt ivory proves that both parts of this Supplement appealed to and were used by Franks to adjust the ceremonial of *Ordo* 1, with their own input.

Ordo 3, nn.2–3 goes on to address the fraction and then immixtion of the Host in the wine, moments of particularly intense interest for the Franks. In the 'long recension' of *Ordo* 1, there was an inexplicable double immixtion, in the course of the single Mass, meaning the celebrant appears to dip the Host in the chalice twice. First, at n.95 (the last phrase is absent in the 'short recension'):

> Cum vero dixerit: *Pax domini sit semper uobiscum*, **mittit in calicem de Sancta**.[110]

This rubric seems to accord with the indications of the St Emmeram gloss for when the Pope was not present, where the Host in question was the

---

[106] *Ordo* 1, n.84, var.13: 'et stat post pontificem. Nam diebus festis id est pascha pentecosten sancti Petri, nat. domini, per has quattuor sollemnitates habent colligendas presbiteri cardinales unusquisque tenens corporalem in manum sua . . . .'

[107] *Ordo* 4, n.52: 'In natale domini sive in aepyphania et in sabbato sancto seu in dominica sancta et in feria secunda, in ascensa domini et in pentecosten vel in natale sancti Petri et sancti Pauli, stant episcopi post pontificem inclinato capite, presbiteri vero dextra levaque et tenet unusquisque corporale in manu sua et dantur eis ab archidiacono oblatas duas ad unumquemque et discit pontifex canon ut audiatur ab eis, et sanctificantur oblaciones quas tenent sicut et pontifex . . . .'

[108] Stephen Kuttner, 'Cardinalis: The History of a Canonical Concept', *Traditio*, 3 (1945), pp.165–173.

[109] Pierre de Puniet, 'Concelebration Liturgique', in *Dictionnaire d'archéologie chrétienne et de liturgie*, vol. III (Paris, 1913/14), col.2476–2477.

[110] *Les Ordines*, vol. II, p.98: 'But when he will have said: *Pax domini sit semper uobiscum*, he puts some of the Host in the chalice.'

Stations in Francia and the Papal Eucharist

fermentum consecrated on a previous occasion by him. Then again, at n.107, the Pope dips the Host in the chalice.

> Qui dum communicaverit de ipsa Sancta quam mormorderat ponit in calice in manus archidiaconi dicendo: *Fiat commixtio et consecratio corporis et sanguinis domini nostri Iesu Christ accipientibus nobis in uitam aeternam.* Amen.[111]

The various reinterpretations of *Ordo* 1 made matters somewhat clearer. In *Ordo* 7, as noted above, the first immixtion was not done by the Pope, but only by *ceteris sacerdotibus* (all other bishops and priests), and the second would only be done when the *domnus apostolicus* is present (*Ordo* 7, nn.22–23: 'Et expleta confractione, quando communicat domnus apostolicus partem sibi mordet et reliquam in calicem mittit faciens crucem de ea tribus vicibus super calicem nihil dicens.').[112] All the Frankish adaptations of *Ordo* 1 in fact agree with *Ordo* 7 here, maintaining a single immixtion at the *Pax domini*, sometimes adding to it the formula from the second, *Fiat commixtio*, sometimes not.[113] Amalarius indicated that the Franks practised a single immixtion, but some did it before the Pax and some afterwards; he personally preferred to do it during the Pax, as the *libelli romani* told him.[114]

In Andrieu, these descriptions are 'errors' arising from ignorance of real Roman usage.[115] But, as *Ordines* 7, 2 and the St Emmeram gloss all indicate, the Franks seem to have understood that the first immixtion was performed during the stational Mass when the Pope was absent, and so was appropriate to them in their own stational Masses, while the unique privilege of the second immixtion was not, because that seems to have been reserved for the Pope alone. Particularly telling is the Mass *ordo* in *Ordo* 15, which only knew the 'short

---

[111] *Ibid.*, pp.101–102: 'But when he has communicated, he puts the Host he had bitten into the chalice, which is in the hands of the archdeacon, saying: *Fiat commixtio et consecratio corporis et sanguinis domini nostri Iesu Christi accipientibus in uitam aeternam. Amen.*'

[112] *Ibid.*, p.305: 'And when the fraction is finished, then the Domnus Apostolicus communicates from the part he has bitten, and places the rest in the chalices, making a cross with it thrice over the chalice, saying nothing.'

[113] *Ordo* 3, n.3; *Ordo* 4, n.206: 'Et dum dixerit *Pax domini sit semper uobiscum*, tenent subdiaconus de Sancta cum corporale ad cornu altaris, quod pontifex consecravit et accipit eam diaconus et tradit eam episcopo aut presbitero. Et exinde facit crucem super calicem, dicendo: *Pax domini sit semper uobiscum* (the immixtion here implied)'; *Ordo* 6, n.59: 'Cum dixerit: *Pax domini sit semper uobiscum* mittit in calicem de sancta, subingens haec verba: *Fiat commixtio et consecration corporis . . . .*'; *Ordo* 9, n.36: 'Rumpatque unam oblatam et ex ea particulam unam in corporale et aliam in calicem dicendo: *Pax domini sit semper uobiscum . . . .*'

[114] Hanssens (ed.), *Opera omnia*, vol. II, p.361: 'Immissionem panis in vinum cerno apud quosdam varie actitari, ita ut aliqui primo mittant de sancta in calicem et postea dicant *Pax Domini* ; e contra aliqui reservent immissionem usquedum pax celebrata sit et fractio panis.' Andrieu collected testimony about this in *Immixtio et Consecratio. La consecration par contact dan les documents liturgiques du moyen-âge* (Paris, 1924).

[115] *Les Ordines*, vol. II, pp.151, 237.

128   Orders for the Stational Mass

recension' of *Ordo* 1, but nevertheless does the same as the other adaptations of
the 'long recension' in having just one immixtion during the *Pax Domini*.[116]

It is unclear why the 'long recension' of *Ordo* 1 has two immixtions, but
Amalarius suggested he was somewhat sceptical that it was actually done in
Rome.[117] It is more likely that there has been a mistake in the conception of
the text, confusing the papal Mass with the one that was done properly by his
surrogate (perhaps a critical rubric was lost very early). The 'short recension'
agrees with what we have said by only having one immixtion done by the
Pope, the second, and making no mention of the first, which was only
mentioned in the Supplement *Ordo* 2, as appropriate to the celebration by
a bishop other than the Pope. If the text of the 'long recension' is here
mistaken (as Capelle believed, and the Frankish evidence beyond this text
stands in bulk against it), it adds to the argument that *Ordo* 1 is not absolutely
infallible in representing the Roman Mass.[118] This notably suggests that *Ordo*
1 is the work of a Frankish observer, and not a Roman instruction booklet. In
their adaptations of the text of *Ordo* 1, the Franks seem to have been aware of
the problem, and tried to make clearer what happened here. In certain places
outside Rome, as in St Emmeram in Regensburg, a deeper understanding of
the role of the *fermentum* in the ceremony was attained, by reading and
pondering sources such as Innocent's letter, and adding additional knowledge probably from direct experience of Rome. Thus, imitation of the Pope
was not done in the thoughtless and artless way Andrieu seems to have
envisaged, but rather was deeply considered, taking account of the particular
privileges the Pope would reserve to himself. The presentation of *ordines*
alongside documents of the Roman liturgy such as Innocent's letter to
Decentius is thus important for interpreting this process, and should not
be left aside when we evaluate the copying and use of the *ordines romani*.[119]

The Monastic Experience of the Stational Mass

A remarkable element in the 'Pontifical of Paris' is the indication that the
Maundy Thursday Mass with its three stations might also proceed in the
monastery. In fact, we know the Pontifical was certainly copied in

---

[116] *Ordo* 15, n.47: 'Et pontifex duas oblationes proprias, quas diximus ponet in ipsa patena et frangit
modicum de ipsa oblatione et mittit in calice ter faciendo crucem et dicit: *Pax domini sit semper
uobiscum.*'

[117] See Hanssens (ed.), *Opera omnia*, vol. II, p.363: 'Si hoc ita agitur in Romana ecclesia, ab illis potest
addisci quid significet bis positus panis calicem. Non enim vacat a mysterio quicquid in eo officio
agitur iuxta constitutionem patrum.'

[118] Bernard Capelle, 'Le rite de la fraction dans la messe romaine', *RevBen*, 53 (1941), pp.5–40.

[119] See Chapter 2.

The Monastic Experience of the Stational Mass

a monastery, probably St Maur-des-Fossés, near Paris.[120] As in the cathedral city, the rubric quoted above indicated that the monastery should also select a place for opportunity and congruency that would suit for the 'station', standing in for the Lateran on Maundy Thursday. Since a monastery would not in normal circumstances host the Chrism Mass at all, as that was an episcopal duty, the rubric here questions our assumption of the 'use' of *ordines* when copied in such contexts. Episcopal 'use' was, of course central to Andrieu's idea of what a pontifical was, as well, and the Paris manuscript is an important clue that such manuscripts were far more wide-ranging in application and audience than the modern taxonomy has allowed.[121] But most significantly, this rubric supplies a key piece of evidence that confirms Häußling's thesis that different altars in monasteries would stand in for the stations in Rome, meaning that monasteries, too, performed their own stational Masses.[122] The plan of St Gallen, St Gallen 1092, with its dedications of various altars to saints including dedicatees of Roman churches, provides a vision of a potential layout.[123] Since we know that monasteries such as Lorsch and St Gallen were copying and producing manuscripts of the *ordines romani*, including *Ordo* 1, the indication of the Paris book opens up a quite different vision of how the text could conceivably be employed. Similarly this is probably the only way we can explain an element found in the St Gallen version of *Ordo* 15, a second Mass *ordo* (nn.133–151), beginning with the sentence:

> In die dominica vel in aliis precipuis solemnitatibus sanctorum, quando publice missas celebrant ad sanctam Mariam maiore sive ad Presepe vel in monastiria monachorum p[re] antephona uel kyrieleison p[re] lectionem apostoli aut profete siue actus apostolorum vel apocalipsi, secundum tempus et responsurio [*sic*] vel Alleluia atque evangelium, cum debent offerre, habent in sacrario preparatus oblationes.[124]

---

[120] *Il cosiddetto pontificale de Poitiers*, Martini (ed.), pp.46*–54*; Huglo, 'Notes sur l'origine du "Pontifical de Poitiers"'.

[121] Rasmussen, *Les pontificaux*; Helen Gittos, 'Researching the History of Rites', in Gittos and Hamilton (eds.), *Understanding Medieval Liturgy*, p.35.

[122] Häußling, *Mönchskonvent und Eucharistiefeier*, pp.315–322.

[123] *The Plan of St. Gall: A Study of the Architecture & Economy of, & Life in a Paradigmatic Carolingian Monastery*, Walter Horn and Ernest Born (eds.), 3 vols. (Berkeley, CA, 1979); also the St Gallen plan website: www.stgallplan.org/en/index_plan.html; altars include an *altare sancti salvatoris ad crucem* (the Lateran and Sta Croce); *SS Phillippi et Iacobi, Sancti Stephani martyris, sancti Laurentii, sancti Sebastiani, SS Luciae et Ceciliae, SS Agathae & Agnetis*, as well as *hic petrus ecclesiae pastor sortitur honorem* and *Hic pauli dignos magni celebramus honores*, equivalences to the basilical churches of Peter and Paul.

[124] *Les Ordines*, vol. III, p.122: 'On Sunday and in other solemnities of the saints, when they celebrate public masses at Santa Maria Maggiore (also known as at the crib) or in the monasteries of monks,

130   Orders for the Stational Mass

This Mass *ordo* refers several times back to the first one earlier in the same text here (directly at nn.146, 147, 148), but it stands at a further distance removed from *Ordo* 1 and the Roman Mass as it would have actually taken place in Santa Maria Maggiore, as described in that text. The mention of Maria Maggiore remains mysterious, but it seems to assimilate the setting of a Frankish monastery with the Roman basilica. It is celebrated simply by a *sacerdos*, and is obviously orientated to a monastic use:

> *Ordo* 15 n.145: Et tunc si in monasterio fuerit, offert abba oblatione, sive secundus seu presbiter vel arciclavius in loco suo pro ipso abbate et pre(sic. post) ipsis devoti vel boni christiani.[125]

The archiclavius was a treasurer, and we know such a figure was at the monastery of St Martin in Tours.[126] Some minor Frankish customs including the washing of hands are included here, but the centrepiece is an introit procession of the offerings, in the Eucharistic 'towers' also mentioned in the letters of Pseudo-Germanus and, in passing, by Gregory of Tours.[127] Pseudo-Germanus' letters have long been the most important source of the 'Gallican' Mass, a tradition and a Rite held in distinction from that of Rome, which the 'Carolingian Reforms' were supposed to have opposed, and even swept away entirely.[128] Yet this exposition survives only in one Carolingian manuscript, Autun, BM, MS 184, probably also from somewhere near Tours, and according to the *ex libris* certainly in the possession

---

before the antiphon and *Kyrieleison*, before the reading of the apostle, prophets, Acts of the Apostles or Revelations, according to the season, and the responsary and Alleluia and Gospel, when they must offer, they have the offerings ready and prepared.'

[125] *Ibid.*, p.123: 'And then if this is in a monastery, the abbot offers the offering, and the second or the priest and the *archiclavius* (treasurer) in his place for the abbot and after them the devoted and good Christians.'

[126] *Ordo* 18, n.6: 'Si est consuetudo apud ipsos ut ille archeclavius qui clavis ecclesiae sive ministerium sacrum sub cura sua ipse costodit et oras canonicas ad cursum celebrandum, quando signum pulsare debeat, ut reddantur'; Pierre Gerard, 'Le Cartulaire de Saint-Sernin de Toulouse et ses problèmes: l'église de Martres-Tolosane, le culte de saint Vidian et la légende de Vivien d'Aliscans', in Ellis Roger, René Tixier and Bernd Weitemeier (eds.), *The Medieval Translator. Traduire au Moyen Age: Proceedings of the International Conference of Göttingen (22–25 July 1996). Actes du Colloque international de Göttingen (22–25 juillet 1996)* (Turnhout, 1998), pp.118–119.

[127] *Ordo* 15, nn.133–136: 'turres': also n.144: 'et post hoc statim clerus canit offerenda, quod Franci dicit sonum'; Pseudo-Germanus, *Expositio Antiquae Liturgiae Gallicanae*, Edward Craddock Ratcliff (ed.), HBS 98 (London, 1971) 14: 'Sonum autem, quod canitur, quando procedit oblatio . . . .'; 17: Corpus vero domini ideo defertur in turribus, quia monumentum domini in similitudinem turris fuit excisum in petra . . . .'; commentary and translated into French in Philippe Bernard (ed.), *Transitions liturgiques en Gaule carolingienne* (Paris, 2008), pp.166, 180–185; Gregory of Tours, *Liber in gloria martyrum*, B. Krusch (ed.), *MGH* Scriptores Rerum Merovingicarum, vol. I, pt.2 (Hanover, 1885), pp.96–97: 'Accepta quoque turra diaconus, in qua mysterium dominici corporis habebatur.'

[128] Angenendt, 'Keine Romanisierung', p.163; Smyth, *La liturgie oubliée*.

The Monastic Experience of the Stational Mass 131

of the Basilica of St Martin, whose clergy were most likely composers of *Ordo* 15, as well.[129] The author of the exposition knew Isidore and probably wrote only around 800, presenting a ritual already much 'romanised', that is, a similar mix as we see in *Ordo* 15.[130] Since mass expositions of this allegorical nature begin to appear only in the Carolingian era, it is more likely that Pseudo-Germanus is of that time than earlier.[131] In fact, Pseudo-Germanus and *Ordo* 15's Mass *ordo* together comprise our only detailed surviving descriptions of the 'Gallican Mass *ordo*', sometimes assumed to represent the practice of all of Gaul before 'contamination' by the 'Roman rite'. Since both originate from Tours, probably written at around the same time, we might be better speaking of some traditions that might be peculiar to Tours.

Tours seems to have held on to some archaic or unusual liturgical practices, probably reflecting a long local tradition, since we know from Amalarius that the Basilica of St Martin in Tours continued some divergent practices which have been identified as 'Gallican', into his day.[132] Indeed, the writing of Pseudo-Germanus' expositions might have constituted a defence of those traditions. Interestingly, Germanus' name is invoked in the diatribe that follows in St Gallen 349, as among the fathers whose names were used to defend traditions the author saw as in variance with Rome.[133] I cannot see the justification for the claim made by Mews: 'The criticism of those who appealed to Gallican saints makes little sense if formulated by a Frankish monk in the later eighth century, when Charlemagne was enforcing his authority. It is more likely to reflect anxiety in Rome in the late seventh century about the liturgical independence of the church in Gaul.'[134] This reflects the dangers of assuming the framework of imperial reform and using that to interpret evidence. Why should anyone have hesitated to invoke the names of Gallic saints under Charlemagne, and how ever should he have enforced his authority sufficiently to put an end to it? Additionally, was Rome ever anxious about the liturgical independence of Gaul? The popes seemingly did not put much

---

[129] Bischoff, *Katalog*, vol. I, p.39: 'Umkreis von Tours, IX Jh., ca. (2. bis) 3. Viertel'; in Bischoff's the Nachlass BSB ANA 553 A, I: AUTUN indicates he thought the part with Pseudo-Germanus to be '825–840'.

[130] Bernard, *Transitions liturgiques*. [131] McKitterick, *The Frankish Church*, p.216.

[132] Hanssens (ed.), *Opera omnia*, vol. II, p.464: 'Propter hoc sacramentum, ut opinor, audivi cantare in vigilia Paschae in ecclesia Turonensi post lectiones: *Benedici.*'

[133] *Ordo* 19, n.39: 'Nescio qua fronte vel temeritate presumptuoso spiritu ausi sunt beatum Hilarium atque Martinum sive Germano vel Ambrosio seu plures sanctos Die, quos scimus de sancta sede Romano a beato Petro apostolum et soccessoribus [*sic*] suis.'

[134] Mews, 'Gregory the Great', p.139.

132   Orders for the Stational Mass

effort into spreading their liturgical usages. Mews does not advance any other evidence to support his argument against Andrieu that *Ordo* 19, and the rest of the St Gallen Stiftsbibliothek 348 collection, was really Roman and written 'soon after 687', against which stands for example the Epiphany baptism based on the Sacramentary of Gellone's text, whose manuscript is dated around 800.

In incorporating a description of their own Mass to *Ordo* 15, the canons of St Martin's Basilica seem to have made use of the *ordo romanus* format to describe and codify characteristic and local practices which diverged from Rome.[135] Andrieu surmised that this Mass description represented a compromise between Roman usages and the traditions of Francia, on account of the monasteries being full of the elderly, naturally attached to the past and little inclined to novelty.[136] As we have seen, elsewhere Frankish usages were entering the Roman Mass *ordo* whether written or unwritten as part of the normal process of reception of these texts, whereby reasonable arrangement of the liturgy would demand them. Such negotiation was not always against the will of those who Andrieu straightforwardly identified as 'reformers' or 'zealous romanisers'.

The stations allowed bishop and clergy to see their own city as the simulacrum of Rome, and the liturgy they practised as according to a Roman pattern (even where there were significant differences in putting it into practice). This connected them to the history of the Roman Church which the *ordines* manuscripts also often described. But Carolingian monasteries were particularly precocious in aspiring to the assimilation of Roman sanctity by the means most often laid out, in taking on Roman relics, in the architecture and in the ceremonies practised there. Fulda distinguishes itself in many of these respects. The basilica was originally dedicated like the Lateran *in honorem sanctis salvatoris*. Its consecration by the archbishop of Mainz was viewed by contemporaries as having proceeded '*more Romano*' with the deposition of the relics of St Boniface, perhaps meaning according to the ceremony described in *Ordo* 42.[137] Einsiedeln, Stiftsbibliothek, MS 326, with the copy of the observation of the Roman Holy Week and the Itinerary and Sylloge, laying out Rome's topography and some of the exotic rites that took place over that topography, also comes from Fulda. We have one particularly rare source concerning the same monastery that sheds light on the practice there.

---

[135] Further discussed in Westwell, 'Ordering the Church'.   [136] *Les Ordines*, vol. III, p.79, n.3.
[137] Janneke Raaijmakers, *The Making of the Monastic Community of Fulda c.744–c.900* (Cambridge, 2012), pp.109–110.

The Monastic Experience of the Stational Mass   133

The source is the letter of the deacon Theotroch, to a priest Ootbert.[138] The letter is half preserved on the front flyleaf of a manuscript from Lorsch, BAV Pal.lat.1341, apparently written there in the last quarter of the ninth century. Originally it continued on the rear flyleaf, but that page was unfortunately lost. It is not certain where the letter was written, but Theotroch might be the monk of the same name who was abbot of Lorsch from 864 to 876. Theotroch tells Ootbert that it was clear that the exact role and office of deacons during the Mass diverged in many places, not only in monasteries but also in cities. He proposed to write to Ootbert the document of how the deacons acted in Fulda so that it might remain in their own monastery as a good example.[139] What Theotroch goes on to narrate is in fact an *ordo* for the Mass whose genre and terminology could not be easily distinguished from the *ordines romani* edited by Andrieu. How many *ordines* began life in such variant contexts as this, as letters or personal recommendations? We recall the snippet of the letter with Hadrian's recommendations attached to *Ordo* 29, in another Lorsch manuscript, and the 'pilgrim dossier' in St Gallen 614, both seeming to be markedly personal initiatives. Does it change our understanding of the texts to acknowledge this potential fluidity, which the stricter understanding of 'liturgical' text does not address? Theotroch stated that the *ordo* could help Fulda not to stray from the 'right arrangement'.[140] But he also explicitly acknowledged that Fulda had many more deacons that they did, and that the *ordo* would have to be filtered and adjusted by the circumstances of the monastery before they might put it to use. While Theotroch's *ordo* is likely to be 'literary' (in Andrieu's term) to a certain extent, as it is presented as an exemplar and a prescriptive text, this is one Mass *ordo* that at least purports to be an eyewitness account of a Mass as actually performed in a Frankish church, in this case in a monastery.

What is more, the reason Theotroch gives that Fulda should be emulated is because the Mass there 'ordinabiliter et cum sufficentia rituque Romano eadem officia peraguntur'.[141] Theotroch understood that Fulda's Mass ritual was according to the Roman rite. He also, equally as important,

---

[138] Albert Schönfelder (ed.), 'Bruchstück eines Fuldaer *Ordo* missae aus dem frühen Mittelalter. Mit einer Einleitung', *Quellen und Abhandlungen zur Geschichte der Abtei und der Diözese Fulda* 5 (1910), pp.97–105; and with French translation in Eric Palazzo, 'Les fastes de la liturgie. Lettre du diacre Theotrochus sur la messe à Fulda', in Olivier Guyot-Jeannin (ed.), *Autour de Gerbert d'Aurillac, le pape de l'an mil. Album de documents commentés* (Paris, 1996), pp.216–223.

[139] Schönfelder (ed.), 'Bruchstück eines Fuldaer *Ordo* missae', p.102.

[140] *Ibid.*, p.102: 'ordinem rectum'.

[141] *Ibid.*: 'in an orderly way and with sufficiency and according to the Roman rite the same office is done'.

134   Orders for the Stational Mass

understood it as an ordered and appropriate celebration. His description is therefore a particularly valuable testimony for understanding what is going on with the *ordines romani* of the Mass. Theotroch focused on the role of the deacons, as indicated, and the Mass *ordo* is only half complete, ending with the offertory. We therefore sadly have no description of the immixtion and communion itself. Nevertheless, Theotroch's description accords with a number of the adaptations of *Ordo* 1 in ways that show that these adaptations were meeting the common understanding of how to perform the rites *Ordo* 1 described in Francia, without this compromising the ability to identify the rite as a whole as 'Roman' and worthy of emulation, just as Amalarius' *Eglogae* described a similar episcopal Mass as '*de Ordine Romano*'. On the one hand, the Mass is celebrated here by a *presbiter*, as it would likely be in a monastery, and the language is that of the Frankish adaptations, with a *chorus* for the sanctuary and the *fano* for the maniple. Furthermore, Fulda clearly enacted a significant number of adaptations we see elsewhere applied to the text of *Ordo* 1 in its Frankish adaptations, and most reflected in the *Eglogae* as well:

1)   There should be either seven, five or three deacons.[142]
2)   There should be the same number of subdeacons and the same number of candles.[143]
3)   The introit procession comes in two by two.[144]
4)   The *diaconus regionarius* gives the kiss of peace first, and also signals the cantors to end the Introit with the *Gloria patri*.[145]
5)   The candles change position at the *Kyrie*.[146]

---

[142] *Ibid.*, p.102: 'Septem namque quinque triumve diaconorum par officium ministrationis forte videtur'; *Ordo* 9, n.1: 'septem aut quinque vel tres diaconi'.

[143] *Ibid.*, p.102: 'Subdiaconi vero eodem numero . . . . Primo portatur incensum ab uno vel duobus, et tunc caerei aequali numero diaconorum sic ordinate . . . .'; also, *Ordo* 9, n.1: 'tot numero subdiaconi et acoliti quot fuerint diaconi'; See Amalarius' *Eglogae de ordine romano*, Hanssens (ed.), *Opera omnia*, vol. III, p.232: 'non amplius quam septem diaconi, totidem subdiaconi, totidem acoliti'.

[144] *Ibid.*, p.103: 'Ut bini et bini pariter incedant et post eos unus solus. Tunc subdiaconi etiam ipsi bini et bini, solus ille propius diaconis qui evangelia portat. Tum demum diaconi secuntur similiter bini, sic tamen, ut regionarium duo novissime cingant et sint illi tres pariter incendentes'; *Ordo* 9, n.3: 'Deinde subsequantur subdiaconi bini procedantes, quos simliter bini sequantur diaconi.'

[145] *Ibid.*, p.103: 'Paululum superius diaconis progressis tunc quoque et illi orant usque dum finiatur versus, et iterum coepto introitu post dictum versum erigentes se dat osculum pacis regionarius diacono ad dexteram sui stanti, inde ad sinistram, et sic omnibus hic alternatim, et tunc annuit cantori, ut dicat *Gloria Patri*, et procedunt ad altare ibique diu orantes bini et bini accedunt et osculantur altare'; the pontiff does so in *Ordo* 4, n.14.

[146] *Ibid.*, p.103: 'Qui vero caereos tenent, stant ab utraque regione in choro et iuxta eos incensaria tenentur et cum dicitur *Kyrie eleison* statuunt candelas hinc et inde tres, mediam autem unam et iterum cum subdiaconus accredit ad legendum, veniet unus eorum et sistit omnes in ordinem orientem versus'; *Ordo* 4, n.19: 'Deinde ponunt acolithi cereostata quas tenant in terram.'

The Monastic Experience of the Stational Mass 135

6) The subdeacon who reads the epistle climbs to the 'first level' of the pulpit.[147]

7) The priest says the *Gloria in excelsis deo* 'the *angelicum carmen*'.[148] It was technically only allowed for a mere priest to chant this on Easter Day, according to the Gregorian Sacramentary, but there is no mention of such a ban here.[149]

8) The candles and thurible face the deacon as he reads the Gospel.[150]

9) The priest washes his hands after saying *Oremus* at the canon.[151]

10) Offerings are given by the *patriarchae*.[152]

Like the other texts, Theotroch's *ordo* also has its own peculiarities. The lowliest grade among the Franks, the *ostiarius* (doorkeeper) played an expanded role in Theotroch's Mass, where normally he very rarely appears in the *ordines*.[153] He carries the offerings and the ampoule with water, and carries off the Gospel Book when the reading is done.[154] The minor orders were not necessarily, then, 'dead letters' as a literal reading of the edited *ordines romani* might suggest.[155] It is possible that they played many otherwise unrecorded roles in practice, acting in the place of others written in the *ordines*.

Theotroch's presentation of this rite as 'rituque Romano' is further proof that a Mass could vary quite significantly from the Roman Mass as narrated in *Ordo* I, incorporating the kind of adaptations which the Franks seem to have widely viewed as necessary, or rational interpolations, without

---

[147] *Ibid.*, p.103: 'Sane subdiaconus cum leget ascendet primum gradum ambonis, cantor vero alleluia vel gradalis minime, sed iuxta stantes psallunt'; Amalarius' *Eglogae* in Hanssens (ed.), *Opera omnia*, vol. III, p.244.

[148] *Ibid.*, p.103: 'Et dum presbiter Angelicum carmen hoc est *Gloria in excelsis deo* incipit, subdiaconi non se vertunt ad orientem nequem quando dicit *Dominus Uobiscum* donec audiunt *Oremus*.'

[149] *Le sacramentaire grégorien*, Deshusses (ed.), p.85: 'A presbyteris autem minime dicitur nisi solo in pascha.'

[150] Schönfelder (ed.), 'Bruchstück eines Fuldaer *Ordo* missae', p.104: 'Et obviam habent duos caereos et incensum quod presbiter adhuc sedens imposuit et pergunt ad ambonem scanditque diaconus ad sinistram ambonis, subdiaconus ad dextram, et iterum perlecto evangelio, descendit diaconus ad dextram; stabunt quoque caeroferarii versi ad diaconum et medium inter eos subdiaconum maiorem et ex utraque parte incensario.'

[151] *Ibid.*, p.104: 'Presbiter subit ad altare et dicit *Dominus Uobiscum*, deinde *Oremus*, et allatur ei aqua et manus lavat'; *Ordo* 9, n.32: 'Infra accione Te Igitur detur aqua presbiteris, ut lavent manus suas.'

[152] *Ibid.*: 'Interea sumit presbiter oblationes a clero et post hoc accipit oblationes patriarcharum'; Häußling, *Mönchskonvent und Eucharistiefeier*, pp.315–323, interprets these *patriarchae* as standing in place for the Roman nobility in *Ordo* I.

[153] One exception: *Ordo* I, n.78: 'defert ea plicata ... accepta a manibus ostiarii'.

[154] Schönfelder (ed.), 'Bruchstück eines Fuldaer *Ordo* missae', pp.103–104: 'Cumque canitur alleluia veniet ostiarius portans oblatas et dat omni scolae ad offerendum qui sunt in inferiore gradu diaconatus; et iterum veniet ostiarius afferens ampullam cum aqua et dat cantori ... et sic exiens de choro dat ostiarius ad reponendum.'

[155] Julia Barrow, *The Clergy in the Medieval World* (Cambridge, 2015), pp.43–45.

136   Orders for the Stational Mass

them feeling that it lost touch with the essence of what made the rite 'Roman'. This is a very different picture from the one assumed by Andrieu. A significant curiosity for this question is the place of the *diaconus regionarius* in Fulda's Mass, as narrated by Theotroch. He carries the *maiorem fanonem* and comes in the final row of deacons in the introit procession, then he is first to give the kiss of peace, and first to kiss the altar.[156] In *Ordo* 1, the *diaconus regionarius* would have to be one of the seven deacons from the seven regions of Rome (there is normally no need to distinguish him as such in Rome, because these were the only seven deacons there).[157] In Theotroch there is one *diaconus regionarius*, singled out among the deacons present for particular honour. Amalarius of Metz used the same terminology to divide the subdeacons: the *subdiaconus regionarius* had different tasks from the *subdiaconus sequens* (using these as normal and expected terminology with no specific mention of their special place in Rome).[158]

As we seem to have already witnessed with the *presbiteri cardinales*, Franks appear to have applied the Roman terminology which had a very specific meaning in the liturgical zones of influence in Rome to their own clergy as a way of sorting and arranging those clergy during the performance of Masses described as Roman. Seven deacons appear in Chrodegang's *Regula*, obviously recalling the Roman system.[159] For the cardinals, this honour seems to have meant they could concelebrate with the bishop on high feasts, according to *Ordo* 3. We have already seen the maintenance of the related title for a subdeacon *subdiaconus regionarius*, including both by Amalarius and extensive use by the lost *Ordo* 6.[160] Again, it seemed to be a title of honour and a way of distinguishing and arranging the types of clergy and their various duties (something the *ordines* continually strive to do and with which Theotroch was especially concerned). But, on the other

---

[156] Schönfelder (ed.), 'Bruchstück eines Fuldaer *Ordo* missae', pp.102–104: 'Ibi sumit regionarius maiorem fanonem ... ut regionarium duo novissimi cingant ... erigentes se dat osculum pacis regionarius diacono ad dexteram sui ... ut regionarius et qui sibi ad dexteram stat primum accedant et salutent pariter in sinistra plaga altaris ....'

[157] *Ordo* 1, n.1: 'et unaquaque regio singulos habere diacones regionarios'.

[158] Hanssens (ed.), *Opera omnia*, vol. II, p.220: 'Subdiaconi sequentes, qui accipiunt ab archiacono orciolum ad ministrandum uinum in eucharistiam corporis Christi, ipsi etiam accipiunt sciffum aquae et aquae manile cum manutergio. Merito ab archidiacono suscipiunt, quia in eius adiutiori consecrati sunt. Subdiaconus regionarius tempore sacrificii stat in facie pontificis; ideo necesse est ut subsequentes necessaria a foris ministrant.'

[159] Bertram, *Chrodegang Rules*, p.74.

[160] *Ordo* 6, n.20: 'Reliqui gradus procedunt in *Ordo* suo, excepto quod unus de regionariis subdiaconibus, debet praecedere cum thymiaterio quem sequuntur septem acoliti illius regionis ...'; n.65: 'ac deinde vadit ad patenam quam tenent duo subdiaconi regionarii ...'; in *Ordo* 1, n.105 it is not specified that the *subdiaconii regionarii* hold the paten; the *subdicaonus sequens* still appears for example in *Ordo* 6, n.46: 'Postea autem subdiaconus sequens descendit in scholam ....'

The Monastic Experience of the Stational Mass

hand, the link between the *diaconus regionarius* and the 'regions' of Rome was the subject of the much copied and preserved introduction to *Ordo* 1. Theotroch refers to the *regione* of the church immediately after the second mention of the *regionarius*.[161] Häußling argued that we see in this terminology the 'quotation', or perhaps better a 'paraphrase', of Rome by the monastery of Fulda. It is a deacon playing the part of a *regionarius* of Rome, so implicitly the monastery itself becoming the plan of Rome on which the Mass would proceed. Thus, the Mass was still *rituque Romano* because the essential idea of connection was maintained without it being a quotation exact in every detail. More evidence for the Fulda monastery 'paraphrasing' Rome by employing the stational Mass is found in a marginal note in manuscript Kassel UB 2° Ms. astron. 2, fol.83v, next to the conclusion of the text by Bede's *De Temporum ratione*.[162] The marginal note reads:

> Feria II veniente statio erit in basilica sanctae maria in monte omnes conveniente.[163]

This seems to be a version of the stational announcement made by the archdeacon in several narratives of the Mass, like *Ordo* 1, here indicating the liturgical celebration on a Monday at a given basilica, today the Frauenberg in Fulda, made to be a 'station'.[164]

We are supplied with further evidence of this process for another monastery, Angilbert's *Institutio* for his monastery at Centula of St-Riquier.[165] Copied incomplete in a single eleventh-century manuscript, BAV, MS Reg.lat.235, within a history of the monastery by Hariulf of Saint-Riquier, it presents itself rather like *Ordo* 15 and that text's descendants, being a series of various *ordines* strung together basically along the course of the liturgical year with rulings and recommendations on antiphons and readings, but principally concerned with the arrangement and use of the ecclesiastical space, and the clergy within it. While he did not use the terminology in the surviving pieces, it is clear that Angilbert's

---

[161] Schönfelder (ed.), 'Bruchstück eines Fuldaer *Ordo* missae', p.103: 'Venientes in chorum subdiaconi ab utraque regione stant . . . .'

[162] Digitised at: https://orka.bibliothek.uni-kassel.de/viewer/image/1327910656180/176/; Bischoff, *Katalog*, vol. I, p.372: 'Fulda, IX Jh., 1. Drittel und Mitte'; it also contains the *Annales Breves Fuldenses*, Georg Pertz (ed.), *MGH* Scriptores II, Scriptores rerum Sangallensium. Annales, chronica et historiae aevi Carolini (Hanover, 1829), p.237.

[163] Kassel UB 2° Ms. astron. 2, fol.83v: 'On the coming Monday, the station will be in the basilica of Saint Mary on the Mount with everyone gathering'; Maximilian Diesenberger drew this text to my attention during a conference in Oxford in 2022.

[164] Hadrian W. Koch, *Kloster Frauenberg in Fulda* (Fulda, 2009).

[165] Edited in Bishop, *Liturgica Historica*, pp.322–332.

138 Orders for the Stational Mass

arrangement is a stational one. Different churches and chapels in the complex, but also different altars, were the setting for the individual celebrations of the days, or constituent parts of them. Among them, St-Riquier had its main church *sancti salvatoris*, another obvious analogue to the Lateran Basilica: there was a round chapel of St Mary perhaps modelled on the Pantheon (Sta Maria ad Martyres) or Aachen, and an altar of the Holy Cross to stand in for Santa Croce on Good Friday, while the main church had a *paradisum* (like St Peter's Basilica in Rome and the plan of St Gallen).[166] We unfortunately lack the description of the Christmas office, but it seems that Angilbert originally described there a procession and pontifical Mass that was likely in the vein of *Ordo* 1, as is also found in the text of *Ordo* 15.[167] Likewise, Candlemas probably also had a full procession so described, as it does in *Ordo* 15, where that procession was set in Rome (or the text of *Ordo* 20).[168] The most complex of the surviving elements is the description of the Rogations. Here, seven villages surrounding St Riquier send seven processions and seven crosses, and the clergy and laity seven by seven. There are a number of influences here: Angilbert himself suggests that it recalls 'in nostro opera gratiam septiformem Sancti Spiritus' (the same justification used for the seven scrutinies in *Ordo* 11), but obvious too is the influence of Gregory the Great's septiform litany, and the annual Great Litany of Rome as described in *Ordo* 21, which had seven stational crosses. The other influence is of course the seven regions of Rome.[169] Like the city, the monastic countryside could also be envisaged as the simulacrum or 'paraphrase' of Rome, but its church with thirty altars was the real heart of the ecclesiastical map, and saw processions to and fro on the model of the stational programme. As in architecture, Angilbert certainly innovated in putting this ideal into practice in Francia. As Rabe argued, much of his liturgical programme was also orientated towards teaching and representing Trinitarian orthodoxy.[170] His *Institutio* is remarkable as having survived as a witness to the configuration of liturgy

[166] Jean Hubert, 'Rome et la Renaissance carolingienne', in *Roma e l'etá carolingia. Atti della gioranle di studio 3–8 Maggio 1976 a cura dello Istituto di Storia dell'arte dell'università di Roma* (Rome 1976), pp.10–11; Jean-Charles Picard, 'Les origins du mot paradisus-parvus', *Melanges de l'école française de Rome* 83 (1971), pp.159–186.

[167] Bishop, *Liturgica Historica*, p.313: 'In die autem sanctissimo Paschae tam de processione et reliquo officio quem et de missa ita **ut in Nativitata Domini** omnia peragantur.'

[168] *Ibid.*, p.327: 'In Nativitate (the Nativity of Mary) autem illius tam de officia quamque de processione ita ut in Purificatione ipsius, exceptis candelis, omnia perficiantur.'

[169] Hendrik Dey, *The Afterlife of the Roman City: Architecture and Ceremony in Late Antiquity and the Early Middle Ages* (Cambridge, 2015), pp.221–243.

[170] Susan A. Rabe, *Faith, Art, and Politics at Saint-Riquier: The Symbolic Vision of Angilbert* (Pennsylvania, 1995).

The Monastic Experience of the Stational Mass

as (at least in ideal) it might have been realised in a particularly wealthy and vast Carolingian monastery. But it also shows that celebration in the minds of even those closest to Charlemagne, whom we would expect to fully buy into any 'reform programme' that monarch had proposed, allowed for significant individual contribution into the putting into practice of the kind of arrangements the *ordines* describe.

More indirectly, even manuscripts themselves suggest this in presenting the *ordines* not as the final word for the performance of a liturgical ceremony, but as the first proposal, allowing the building up of a full picture of what would 'actually' happen and how it was supposed to be understood. Allowing that Angilbert's text represents a high point in the intensity of his preoccupation with management of space and the resources at his command, and represented a height of intensely personalised and institutional interpretation, we can still envisage a whole array of different possibilities for the stational celebrations of Masses in various contexts. Basing ourselves on the manuscripts, it was clearly important that such arrangements were perceived and understood as being connected to Rome.

CHAPTER 6

The Ordo Romanus *of the Baptismal Scrutinies*

Baptismal texts have perhaps undergone more extensive historical analysis than most accounts of liturgical ritual during the Carolingian period.[1] This is due, in part, to baptism's role in the formation of community, and, thus, in the liturgical definition of a people. The Carolingian period also yielded a huge wealth of texts surrounding the interpretation and meaning of baptism, only rivalled by the texts that interpret the Mass, which permit a greater perception of the stakes around baptism for contemporaries, and the more tangible outworking of the period's intense preoccupation with 'getting liturgy right'.[2] Carolingian laws and councils mention baptism somewhat more often than they do other specific rituals, and sometimes do so by reference to Rome, noticeably in the Council of Mainz led by Arn of Salzburg, Richulf of Mainz and Bernharius of Worms: 'Sacramenta itaque baptismatis uolumus, ut, sicut sancta vestra fuit ammonitio, ita concorditer atque uniformiter in singulis parrochiis secundum Romanum ordinem inter nos celebetur iugiter atque conservetur, id est scrutinium ad ordinem baptismatis.'[3] Such mentions are still very sporadic and without any programmatic terminology, but these laws were once taken as the starting point to understand the reception of a Roman *ordo* of baptism in Francia, which was seen as the replacement of many diverse rituals with a single,

---

[1] J. D. C. Fisher, *Christian Initiation: Baptism in the Medieval West* (London, 1965); Peter Cramer, *Baptism and Change in the Early Middle Ages (c.200–1150)* (Cambridge, 1993); Felice Lifschitz, 'A Cyborg Initiation? Liturgy and Gender in Carolingian East Francia', in Celia Chazelle and Felice Lifshitz (eds.), *Paradigms and Methods in Early Medieval Studies* (New York, 2007), pp.101–117; Owen Phelan, *The Formation of Christian Europe: The Carolingians, Baptism and the Imperium Christianum* (Oxford, 2014).

[2] Most examples edited in Keefe, *Water and the Word*, vol. II.

[3] *MGH* Conc.II, p.261; Keefe, *Water and the Word*, p.52, n.1: 'Therefore we wish the sacrament of baptism shall be, according to your holy admonition, thus concordantly and in a uniform fashion in each parish according the Roman order celebrated, ordered and kept, that is with a scrutiny to the baptismal order': other texts refer to a 'morem romanum', 'traditionem Romanum', 'ordinem traditionis Romanae', 'ritum Romanorum'.

140

The Ordo Romanus *of the Baptismal Scrutinies*   141

uniform and standard performance and text.[4] They were interpreted to suggest that there was a single official version of the 'Roman Rite' of baptism, taken to be 'pure'; that is, without alteration and as close to actual Roman practice as possible. By the personal decree of Charlemagne this would have been imposed upon his realms and was directly to be received in exclusion to *any* alternative ritual of baptism. Generally, it was assumed on these grounds that the Carolingian efforts to 'reform' baptism failed. The liturgical evidence is undeniable that diversity in the practice of baptism was not eliminated.

As was most fruitfully pointed out by Susan Keefe, it is not self-evident what these laws meant as regards the baptismal rite itself, and they most likely did not mean by 'Roman' what modern scholars read into this.[5] The terminology is rather vague. Description of the desired rite in the Council of Mainz as 'concorditer atque uniformiter' is, in that text, at least as significant as the reference to the Roman order. There is certainly no mention of a Roman text, nor even the *Hadrianum*, though the ambiguity of the Latin term *ordo* could suggest a type of text (as in Andrieu's *Ordo*) or simply an ordering of a ritual. Manuscript evidence stands firmly against any sense that the Carolingian scribes and celebrants could possibly have understood 'Roman' to mean one uniform procedure. If we begin from the liturgical manuscripts, our perspective is different.

What the 'Roman' rite of baptism meant to Carolingian liturgists was considered with some noticeable success by Keefe, but her evidence was the expositions on baptism, which she edited in bulk, and not the evidence of liturgical manuscripts themselves. Keefe focused on the many responses and after-effects of the letter Charlemagne sent out to his metropolitans in 812. Only one of the attested responses, that of Amalarius, then bishop of Trier, mentions the 'Roman *ordo*'. In Keefe's examination, the rite of scrutiny foregrounds itself. Amalarius, she noticed, referred three times to a Roman *ordo*, and on each of these occasions the context was during the ritual of

---

[4] Adrian Nocent, 'Un Fragment de sacramentaire de Sens au Xe siècle. La liturgie baptismale de la province ecclésiastique de Sens dans les manuscrits du IXe au XVIe siècles', in *Miscellanea liturgica in onore di S.E. il cardinale Giacomo Lercaro*, vol. 2. (Rome, 1967), pp.658–659: 'Le capitulaire de 23 mars 789 insistait pour que soitsuivi pour le baptême le ritual de l'Hadrianum; Charlemagne tenait beaucoup à voir adopter sans plus le pur rite romain. Une prescription semblable fut reprise au concile de Mayence en 813. Mais, on le voit, ces rappels et ces exigences ne purent supplanter facilement les usages du Gélasien et de l'*Ordo* XI.'; Cramer, *Baptism and Change*, p.115: 'The Roman rite of baptism (Hadrianum) provided the basis of Carolingian liturgical reform.'

[5] Keefe, *Water and the Word*, vol. I, pp.52–69; Peter Jeffrey, 'Rome and Jerusalem: From Oral Tradition to Written Repertory in Two Ancient Liturgical Centers', in Graeme A. Boone (ed.), *Essays on Medieval Music in Honor of David G. Hughes* (Cambridge, MA, 1995), pp.207–248, particularly n.108.

142 The *Ordo Romanus* of the Baptismal Scrutinies

scrutinies prior to baptism.[6] In conjunction with the Council of Mainz, which seems to conflate the Roman *ordo* with the performance of the scrutiny, this led Keefe to propose that the Roman *ordo* was, for the Franks, any performance of baptism with a system of preparatory scrutinies.

Andrieu's *Ordo Romanus* 11: Is It Actually a 'Roman Text'?

The central text most often viewed as the source of the Roman liturgy in Francia was edited by Andrieu as *Ordo* 11. Before Andrieu, a version based on only one manuscript had been edited by Mabillon as *Ordo* VII, and it can show up in earlier treatments under this number. The Roman origin of *Ordo* 11 had been assumed by Mabillon and was corroborated firmly by Andrieu. Even so, de Puniet had already given significant reason to doubt the Roman origin of Mabillon's text, which Andrieu hastily dismissed.[7] Klaus Gamber subsequently presented doubts about Andrieu's conclusions, but did not develop them.[8] As it is given in the edition of Andrieu, the text made no explicit internal claims to be Roman, unlike other *ordines romani* he edited. Its title related simply to the dating and timing of the scrutiny rite, and describes the text simply as an *ordo*, not a Roman one.[9] There are some curiosities to the structure which suggest it is a compilation of various texts, not a wholesale accomplishment. At *Ordo* 11, n.83, a subtitle indicates what is presented as a different 'Ordo vero qualiter catecizantur est' and which seems to open a text from another source, taking place on Holy Saturday; it is indeed at this point where Wolfenbüttel Weissenburgenses 91, for example, breaks off (the manuscript often preserving ancient versions of *ordines romani*).[10] Another break occurs at *Ordo* 11 nn.89–90, where the whole setting and protagonists change. This is where the Collection B manuscripts end the text. Prior to this point, the celebrant is only a *presbiter*, with the archdeacon.[11] Now suddenly (at *Ordo*

---

[6] Keefe, *Water and the Word*, pp.59–62.

[7] Pierre de Puniet, 'Les trois homélies catéchétiques du Sacramentaire Gélasien' *Revue d'histoire écclesiastique*, 5 (1904), pp.503–529, 755–786 and 6 (1905), pp.15–32, 304–318, p.318: 'Ceci de montre une fois de plus que le VIIe Ordo Romain a beaucoup d'éléments gallicans : il est moins romains que l'*Ordo* de Sacramentaire Gélasien'; *Les Ordines*, vol. II, p.367, n.1.

[8] Klaus Gamber, 'Fragmenta Liturgica IV', *Sacris Erudiri* 19 (1969/70), pp.207–209; Gamber, 'Fragmenta Liturgica III', *Sacris Erudiri*, 18 (198), p.325; also Alois Stenzel, *Die Taufe: eine genetische Erklärung der Taufliturgie* (Innsbruck, 1958), pp.201ff.

[9] *Ordo* 11, Tit.: 'Incipit Ordo vel denuntiatio scrutinii ad electos quod tertia ebdomada in Quadragesima, secunda feria initiatur' with some manuscript variance. This awkward title is another sign of the Frankish compilation of the text from older sources.

[10] Andrieu, *Les Ordines*, vol. II, p.243.

[11] *Ibid.*, pp.243–244: 'tangit eos presbiter singulorum nares de sputo oris sui . . . Postea dicitur eis ab archidiacono.'

Andrieu's Ordo Romanus II

143

II, n.90) the pontiff proceeds out of the church with 'all the priests' and two notaries, to the baptistery.

In general, *Ordo* II lacks the specific details of an unambiguously Roman *ordo*. No Roman church names are given since the announcements of churches to meet in give no specifications, although in Rome this would have been simple and fixed according to the stational system.[12] The celebrant is either a *sacerdos* (during the scrutinies) or a *pontifex* (on Holy Saturday). None of the elaborate and exotic personnel seen in *Ordo* I make an appearance. The *ordo* presupposes the performance of the ritual by several priests, an archdeacon, at least two acolytes, at least four deacons and at least one subdeacon, while, most significantly, the choir are described as *clerus* and not even the Roman *schola cantorum*.[13] At the grandest point in the ceremony, a procession takes place from the church to the baptistery:

> Hoc expleto, procedit pontifex de ecclesia cum omni ordine sacerdotum laetania canentes, hoc est *Kyrieleison*, usquedum veniunt ad fontes, praecedentibus ante eum notariis, cum duobus cereis ardentibus, statura hominis habentes, in altum, cum turabulis et timiateribus et incipunt laetania quae subsequitur: *Christe audi nos*, et reliqua.[14]

Andrieu was clear how he interpreted this detail: 'C'est le ceremonial suivi au baptistere du Latran qui a fourni les elements de la description ... La pontife qui s'avance processionellement ... est le pape lui-meme.'[15] Is this actually the case however? Grand though it is described, it does not have the pomp and circumstance of the similar stational procession described in *Ordo* I, and it lacks any specifically Roman detail. The *notarii* are not described as the *notarii regionarii* of *Ordo* I, and nor are they accompanied, as there, by any of the Roman personnel like the *defensores regionarii*, the *primicerius*, the *secundicerius* or the *primicerius defensorum regionarii*.[16] Nothing here was beyond the staff of a standard cathedral clergy. Even the vocabulary has a few characteristics entirely different from *Ordo* I: generally it

---

[12] For example *Ordo* II, n.37: 'Deinde adnuntiat presbiter ut ipsa ebdomada revertantur ad scrutinium, ita dicendo : *Die sabbato venite, colligete vos temporius ad ecclesiam illam vel illam.*'

[13] For example *Ordo* II, n.8: 'Tunc primum incipiat clerus ant[iphonam] ad introitum . . . .'

[14] *Les Ordines*, vol. II, p.444: 'When this is finished, the pontiff proceeds with all the orders of clergy, singing a litany, that is the *Kyrie eleison*, until they come to the fonts, and there proceed before him notaries with two burning candles, each one having the height of a man, with thuribles and incense boats and they begin the litany which follows: *Christe audi* nos, and the rest.'

[15] *Les Ordines*, vol. II, p..413: 'It is the ceremonial followed at the baptistery of the Lateran which furnished the elements of this description ... the pontiff who advances processionally is the Pope himself.'

[16] Seen in *Ordo* I, n.32, n.81. Simple *notarii* appear in *ordines* Andrieu specifically designated as non-Roman, *Ordo* 4, n.81, p.167. 'Deinde stant notarii ante eum, tenentes calamario et tomum in manu ... et descendunt notarii a sede . . . .'

144   The *Ordo Romanus* of the Baptismal Scrutinies

used the Latin-derived terminology of Frankish liturgical texts 'turabula' not
the Greek 'thimiamaterium' of the *Ordo* I (with the exception of the procession above where 'timiateribus' (probably incense boats) are distinguished
from 'turabulis' in a way foreign to the vocabulary of *Ordo* I), and 'candelabra' is given exclusively, instead of *Ordo* I's 'cereostata'.[17] In other *ordines*,
Andrieu used just such clues to distinguish a Frankish origin and redaction.
But in this case, Andrieu had already concluded that *Ordo* II was of Roman
origin, and that it was, in fact, among the earliest of the surviving *ordines
romani*, indeed perhaps from the end of the sixth century![18] This has generally
been accepted and followed in accounts of baptism in Rome.[19]

Apart from Andrieu's ideological assumptions, the text's Roman origin
was to rest on two elements:

1) The *ordo* assumes a structure of seven scrutinies in Lent. These
    scrutinies were a Roman custom of preparation prior to baptism
    (though one that was shared widely across Western churches including
    Gaul and Northern Italy from as early as the fourth century).[20] The
    Roman sources suggest a structure of three scrutinies with each having
    a Mass performed at the end of the ceremony. These are John the
    Deacon's Letter to Senarius (from the end of the fifth century) and the
    Old Gelasian Sacramentary (the manuscript, BAV Reg.lat.316, is from
    c.750; the text is older).[21] *Ordo* II has been taken as the proof that
    Rome would subsequently develop a system of seven scrutinies.
2) The Greek Creed. In its earliest form (Pal.lat.487 and directly related
    MSS), *Ordo* II describes a custom where the acolyte takes a child of
    either sex and the priest asks the baptised infant (or presumably the
    godparents) which language they confess in.[22] This forms part of the

---

[17] For example *Ordo* II, n.44: 'Inde vero procedunt quattuor diaconi de sacrario . . . praecedentibus eis
duo candelabra cum turabula et incensum . . . .'
[18] *Les Ordines*, vol. II, pp.409–413.
[19] Fisher, *Christian Initiation*, p.22–26; John Romano, 'Baptizing the Romans', *Acta ad archaeologiam
et artium historiam pertinentia*, 31 (2019), pp.43–62.
[20] Albert Dondeyne, 'La discipline des scrutins dans l'église latine avant Charlemagne', *Revue d'histoire
écclesiastique*, 28 (1932), pp.5–33, 751–787; Antoine Chavasse, 'La discipline romaine des sept scrutins
prébaptismaux', *Recherches de science religieuses*, 48 (1960), pp.227–240.
[21] John the Deacon edited by André Wilmart, 'Un florilège carolingien sur le symbolisme des
cérémonies du baptême', in *Analecta Reginensia*, Studi e Testi 59 (Vatican City, 1933), pp.170–179;
Old Gelasian in *Liber Sacramentorum*, Eizenhöfer *et al.* (eds.).
[22] *Ordo* II, nn.62–65: 'Ipsa expleta, tenens acolitus unum ex ipsis infantibus masculum in sinistro
brachio et interrogat eum presbiter, dicens: *Qua lingua confitentur dominum nostrum Iesum
Christum?* Resp.: Graece. Adnuntiat fidem ipsorum qualiter credant. Et dicit acolitus symbolum
graece, cantando in his verbis: *Pisteuo his enatheon.* Hoc expleto, vertit se ad feminas et facit similiter.
Iterum acolitus alter accipiens ex latinis infantibus unum in sinistro brachio, ponens manum
dextram super caput ipsius et interrogat eum presbiter: *Qua lingua confitentur sicut prius.* Et

Andrieu's Ordo Romanus II 145

custom of the *Traditio Symbolum*, where the catechumens received the truth of the Faith, and took place in the most solemn of the scrutinies, the third, which was called IN AURIUM APERTIONEM. The godparents could respond, according to the *ordo*, with either Greek or Latin, and the priest would then recite the Creed to them in the chosen language. Most versions of *Ordo* II do not give either Creed in full, but only the *incipit*. This question and response made sense in the context of Rome, and most likely of seventh-century Rome, which had an established Greek community and several popes of Greek extraction; Andrieu was prepared to place the initial redaction of the rite to just after the invasion of Justianian on this basis.[23]

So, are these convergences sufficient to interpret the text of *Ordo* II as given by Andrieu as a record of the Roman rite of baptism, in every detail and stemming from the pen of a Roman author to describe rites performed in Rome itself? These crucial elements (the performance of scrutinies and the text of a Greek Creed in Latin letters) were already given in another source that had demonstrably passed into Francia decades before the creation of *Ordo* II, the Old Gelasian Sacramentary, now BAV Reg.lat.316.[24] The Gelasian Sacramentaries of the Eighth Century, in the immediate run-up to the creation of the first *ordo romanus* manuscripts used by Andrieu, drew on the same source and developed more extensive scrutiny and baptismal rituals that are clearly very closely related to *Ordo* II, yet give all indications of being earlier versions than it. Andrieu's conception of the *ordines romani* as a genre that was created in Rome and spread from there to Francia necessitated that he understood all of these Gelasian texts as Frankish adaptations of the Roman original (*Ordo* II) that he reconstructed and presented in his edition.[25] Chavasse argued that the Old Gelasian Sacramentary had to have primacy, with the *Ordo* II being the later adaptation of that text – in his view, both being Roman versions of the rite of baptism.[26] Despite this relationship, and the substantial identity between the Gelasian texts (particularly the Sacramentary of Gellone, Paris BnF lat.12048) and the published *Ordo* II, Andrieu did not take account of the Sacramentaries in a comprehensive way.

---

respondit: *Latina*. Dicit ei presbiter. *Adnuntia fidem ipsorum qualiter credant.* Et ille cantatur symbolum. *Credo in unum Deum patrem omnipotentem (factorem caeli et terrae) visibilium.*'

[23] *Les Ordines*, vol. II, p.394; Bernice M.Kaczynski, *Greek in the Carolingian Age: The St Gall Manuscripts* (Cambridge, MA, 1988), p.100.

[24] *Liber Sacramentorum*, Leo Eizenhöfer *et al.* (eds.), pp.42–53.

[25] *Les Ordines*, vol. II, pp.380–408.

[26] Chavasse, *Le Sacramentaire gélasien*, pp.166–168; Vogel, *Medieval Liturgy*, p.165: 'the more probable hypothesis'.

146 The *Ordo Romanus* of the Baptismal Scrutinies

Andrieu's proposition was always odd, given the antiquity and comparative simplicity of the Old Gelasian, as well as the obviously convergent adaptations of it in the Gelasians of the Eighth Century (with *Ordo* 11 as simply one path taken among many), but his conception of *Ordo* 11 as a Roman original demanded that he make the evidence into a fitting *stemma* where his *Ordo* 11 stood at the crown. What Chavasse did not say, but will be argued here, is that that *Ordo* 11, as edited by Andrieu, is not a Roman text in any but the most basic details, including some of the prayers and the homilies. The *ordo* itself, that part most prized by Andrieu, represents a heavily adapted Frankish text. That text was continually reworked into various forms, all of equal relevance and value in discerning Frankish priorities. For this purpose, the initial reconstruction of 'three families' by de Puniet forms a practical structure.[27] De Puniet considered, exclusively, the three homilies said in the third scrutiny 'DE AURIUM APERTIONE', but he did discuss the Sacramentaries as intimately related to *ordines*. He showed that the manuscripts of the Old Gelasian, the first *ordo* in the Sacramentary of Gellone and the *ordo* in the Sacramentary of Angoulême, Paris, BnF, MS lat.816, gave one version of these homilies that he identified as the primitive version from Rome (his demonstration that one of the homilies actually goes back to the time of Pope Leo the Great, and even perhaps his own hand, is compelling), while every other witness showed a form of these homilies that had already been adjusted in Francia by reference to the versions found in Gallican Missals.[28] The 'adjusted' form itself clearly divided into two further subgroups: the earlier, lost Sacramentary of Godelgaudus and the later Pontifical of Poitiers (actually of Paris) forming a second family, and the *ordines* forming a third. For the *ordines*, de Puniet used Hittorp's edited version of *Ordo Romanus* VII (our *Ordo* 11), with two manuscripts he could access which each displayed some differences from it: Rome *Biblioteca Nazionale* Sessorianus 52 (twelfth-century, Nonantola) and Zurich Car. C 102 (which each represent Collection B), and the Sacramentary of Gellone's second *ordo*, as well as the probably ninth-century *Ordo Scrutiniorum* published by de Rubeis from the later manuscript in Friuli, Museo archeologico nazionale MS LXXXV.[29]

[27] De Puniet, 'Les trois homélies catéchétiques'.
[28] The Bobbio Missal, for example, carries scrutiny homilies; *The Bobbio Missal: A Gallican Mass-Book*, E. A. Lowe (ed.), 2 vols., HBS 58 and 61 (London, 1920–24), repr. in one volume (Woodbridge, 1991), pp.54–59.
[29] On Sessorianus 52 (copied from a ninth-century manuscript), *Les Ordines*, vol. I, pp.287–294; Melchior Hittorp (ed.), *De divinis catholicae ecclesiae officiis et mysteriis varii vetustorum aliquot Ecclesiae Patrum ac scriptorium ecclesiasticarum libri* (Paris, 1610), pp.39–42; Bernard de Rubeis (ed.), *Duae Disserationes de Rufino et ritibus Foroiuliensis provinciae* (Venice, 1754), pp.228–246; *CLLA*, vol. 1, p.189.

De Puniet's investigation was more comprehensive in the genre of manuscript considered, and he took full account of the intimate relationship between Sacramentary and *ordo*. In doing so, he made it clear that he considered what we know as *Ordo* 11 to be a Frankish adaptation. Further, his findings are confirmed by an investigation of the *ordo* in its entirety, beyond the three homilies to which his analysis is confined.

Roman Custom, the First Gelasians and the Station List of Chrodegang of Metz

The scrutinies were clearly central to the Carolingian reception of the Roman rite of baptism. Charlemagne's circular letter, Amalarius' response and the Council of Mainz all disclose that the scrutiny was understood to be an intrinsic part of the act of baptism; the various preparatory rituals here were part of one ritual performed over several ceremonies. Rome itself had clearly practised three scrutinies in Lent, leading up to baptism on Holy Saturday. The scrutinies took place, originally, on the three Sundays of Lent prior to Easter.[30] By the time they were codified in forms that have survived, such as *Ordo* 11, it seems the scrutinies were highly ritualised, and largely consisted of various exorcisms, blessings and the placing of salt in the mouth of the child. Each of the three Roman scrutinies also had its own Mass that followed the ceremony.[31] These three Masses were marked out by special interjections in the Canon of the Mass where the priest was to recite the names of the catechumens ('et recitantur nomina electorum') and their godparents ('et dicit reliqua que secuntur usque infractione ubi dicit *Memento domine famulorum famularumque tuarum: qui electus tuus suscepturi sunt ad sanctam gratiam baptismi tui. Et tacit . Et recitantur nomina uirorum hac mulierum qui ipsius infants suscepturi sunt, ab eo a quibus scripti sunt*'), and where these latter were to be blessed.[32]

The third scrutiny was the most important. In Rome it acquired a venerable name that endured in Carolingian testimonies, 'IN AURIUM APERTIONE'.[33] This was a solemn ceremony of ritualised

---

[30] Chavasse, 'La discipline romaine des septs scrutins'.

[31] *Liber Sacramentorum*, Eizenhöfer *et al.* (eds.), pp.32, 36, 39.

[32] *Ibid.*, p.32: 'and the names of the elected are recited'; 'and he says the rest which follows until the fraction, when he says "*Memento domine . . .*" and then he is silent. And there are recited the names of the men and women who are to receive these children by he who has written them'.

[33] The title originally referred to the *Effeta*, the opening of the ears of the catechumen with spittle, but that practice was later moved to Holy Saturday, though the name remained. In *Ordo* 11, n.42, the two prophetic and epistle readings of the day are introduced in these terms: 'et tunc leguntur duae lectiones in aurium apertione', but this is a much later (and Frankish) interpretation.

148   The *Ordo Romanus* of the Baptismal Scrutinies

teaching by homily. After two readings (Isaiah 55:2–7 and extracts from Colossians 3:9 and Romans 10:18), books of the four gospels were processed to the altar and placed on the four corners. The priest addressed himself directly to all present, telling them he would explain the four gospels and the figures that represented them in the vision of Ezechiel.[34] In turn, the openings of the four gospels were read and, after each, a homily on the Evangelist and the meaning of his figure was addressed to the people.[35] Then the priest introduced the Creed, that was given over each of the infants in turn by the acolyte. Here the Greek or Latin Creed might be offered. The priest explained the Creed, clause by clause (only in Latin). Then the same was done with the Lord's Prayer. Finally, the third scrutiny Mass, as given in the Sacramentary, was performed, with the catechumens again invited to absent themselves. 'IN AURIUM APERTIONEM' gave a perfectly adequate 'crash-course' in the fundamentals of Christian doctrine, and could, one imagines, refresh the knowledge of godparents and attending laypeople, as well as building community in a common Christian faith. The programme cohered with Charlemagne's own priorities for the education of the laity in doctrine.[36]

Out of Rome, we can certainly say that there came the material for three scrutinies, several rubrics and full prayers, plus the long homilies and creeds in both Greek and Latin given for 'IN AURIUM APERTIONEM', and there was also a Mass for each of the three. This accords with what is implied in the structural presentation of these rituals in the Sacramentaries, particularly the more restrained Sacramentary of Angoulême, Paris, BnF, MS lat.816 and the oldest witness, the Vatican Old Gelasian.[37] Integral to the structure of the Old Gelasian Lent, these Masses appear in each Sunday from the third, and they are entitled as such: 'TERTIA DOMINICA QUAE PRO SCRUTINIIS ELECTORUM CELEBRATUR', 'QUARTA DOMINICA PRO SCRUTINIO II', 'QUINTA DOMINICA QUAE PRO SCRUTINIUM CELEBRATUR'.[38]

Modification of this basic form was, however, immediate, and it went through several discernible stages. This can be seen even in our oldest

---

[34] *Ordo* II, n.45; *Liber Sacramentorum*, Eizenhöfer *et al.* (eds.), p.46.   [35] *Ordo* II, nn.46–60.

[36] To Gerbald of Liège Charlemagne instructed that every sponsor should be able to recite the Lord's Prayer and Apostle's Creed. Charlemagne, *Ad Ghaerbaldum Episcopum Leodiensem Epistola*, Alfred Boretius (ed.), *MGH* Cap. Regum Francorum I (Hanover, 1883), p.241.

[37] *Engolismensis*, Saint-Roch (ed.), pp.56, 61–62, 67–68, 95–107.

[38] *Liber Sacramentorum*, Eizenhöfer *et al.* (eds.), p.32: 'Third Sunday for the scrutinies of the elected is celebrated' (note that the title of *Ordo* II obviously goes back to this); p.36: 'Fourth Sunday for the Second Scrutiny'; p.39: 'The Fifth Sunday which for the Scrutiny is celebrated.'

Witness, in the Old Gelasian Sacramentary itself, in the addition of an announcement to the *Ordo* of scrutinies, in the form of an introduction just before the *Ordo* began: DENUNTIATIO PRO SCRUTINIO QUOD TERTIA HEBDOMADA IN QUADRAGESIMA SECUNDA FERIA INITIARUM.[39] This is a brief announcement to the people of when the scrutiny would begin (in the speech, the day is simply unspecified *illa*, but the timing is specified as to the sixth hour) and the purpose of the scrutiny. The scrutinies were each on the Sunday, but this announcement's title now moves the first scrutiny from the third Sunday of Lent to the Monday immediately after that. Chavasse explained that the Old Gelasian here replicated two distinct traditions, one with scrutinies on Sundays, and one when the scrutinies were moved to weekdays.[40] Almost every other witness to the scrutiny *ordo* (including *Ordo* 11) reproduced this announcement, or bears marks of this initial change.[41] The announcement itself would obviously take place before the first scrutiny, though it is not given when this would be exactly. One witness of the *ordo*, the Pontifical of Paris of *c.*870, did modify the announcement's title to add SED IPSA ADNUNCIATIO IN HESTERNA DOMINICA PERFICITUR, thus placing the announcement on the Sunday, the day before the first scrutiny, and this would seem to be the usual setting.[42]

Compared to later developments of the scrutiny *ordo*, the Old Gelasian is extremely terse. Rubrics are not more than three or four lines, the bulk of the text is taken up with spoken elements, prayers and homilies, and much is left unwritten.[43] Further evidence that this was a basic form of the scrutinies and it was initially received in Francia *in this exact form* is supplied by the stational list of churches in use in Metz, most likely from the time of Bishop Chrodegang (d.766).[44] The list echoes completely the indications of the Old Gelasian. The first scrutiny is given here on the Monday of the third week of Lent, with the announcement and scrutiny itself being, just as in the Sacramentary, somewhat blurred

---

[39] *Liber Sacramentorum*, Eizenhöfer *et al.* (eds.), p.42: 'AN ANNOUNCEMENT FOR THE SCRUTINY BEGINNING IN THE THIRD WEEK OF LENT ON MONDAY.'

[40] Chavasse, *Le sacramentaire gélasien*, pp.155–71.   [41] *Ordo* 11, n.1.

[42] *Il cosiddetto pontificale di Poitiers*, Martini (ed.), p.50: 'BUT THIS ANNOUNCEMENT IS CARRIED OUT ON THE PRECEDING SUNDAY.'

[43] The two most extensive are *Liber Sacramentorum*, Eizenhöfer *et al.* (eds.), p.42: 'Ut autem venerint ad ecclesiam, scribuntur nomina infantum ab acolyte et uocantur in ecclesia per nomina, sicut scripti sunt. Et statuuntur masculi in dexteram partem, feminae in sinistram. Et dat orationem presbiter super eos'; p.46: 'Primitus enim procedunt de sacrario IIII diaconi cum quattuor evangelia, praecedentibus duo candilabra cum turabulis, et ponuntur super III angulos altaris. Et tractet praesbiter, antequam aliquis eorum legat, his uerbis.' Both feed directly into *Ordo* 11, nn.2, 44 and 49.

[44] Klauser, 'Eine stationsliste'; the manuscript is Paris BnF lat.268, fol.153r–v.

150   The *Ordo Romanus* of the Baptismal Scrutinies

together.[45] The second takes place on the fourth Sunday, and the third on the fifth Sunday.[46] In all three cases a 'libro sacramentorum' (clearly, something like the Old Gelasian) is pointed to as the guide for the performance of the ceremony. It did not use *Ordo* II, even though Andrieu suggested that this text was supposed to have already crossed into Francia by Chrodegang's time (around 750), as part of the Romanising initiatives Chrodegang was involved in. Thus, Chrodegang is unlikely to have known or accepted *Ordo* II, but stuck to the Roman form, seemingly as it is carried in the Old Gelasian.

The Old Gelasian was taken up and adapted by the family known as the 'Gelasians of the Eighth Century'.[47] Copyists of these Sacramentaries intervened in the scrutiny *ordo* in some key ways. An initial attempt can be seen in the Sacramentary of Angoulême, also in the lost Sacramentary of Noyon, which was very close to it.[48] Here, just as in the Old Gelasian, the *ordo* for the scrutiny introduces itself with the DENUNTIATIO, identifying the first scrutiny to take place on the Monday of Lent's third week. The *ordo* follows. It is placed here between Good Friday and Holy Saturday, as a kind of run-up to the baptism ritual itself (which happened on Holy Saturday) and it is again entirely separate from the three Masses that are still on three Sundays in Lent. Angoulême presents some additions to the very terse rubrics of the Old Gelasian. In particular, 'IN AURIUM APERTIONEM' now has an extensive rubric introducing it, making it plain that the third scrutiny also involved the repetition of much of what had been done in the previous texts.[49] This rubric is not related to the practice of 'IN AURIUM APERTIONEM' as given in *Ordo* II or the Sacramentary of Gellone, but is not replicated in them, and the rest of the ceremony is much less detailed than we see there.

---

[45] Klauser, 'Eine stationsliste', p.30: 'Feria II hedomada III quae pro scrutiniis electorum celebratur – tunc denuntiandum est scrutinium ad incoandum sicut in sacramentorum libro continetur – statio ad sanctam crucem iuxta columnas.'

[46] *Ibid.*, p.33: 'Dominica IIII. In xlmo statio ad sanctum petrum infra episcopio – tunc caelebrandum est scrutinium sed sicut in sacramentorum libro continetur . . .'; p.34: 'Dominica V in Xlmo statio ad sanctum petrum infra episcopio – eadem celebatur scrutinio tertium sicut in sacramentorum libro continetur.'

[47] Antoine Chavasse, *Le sacramentaire dans le groupe dit 'Gélasiens du VIIIe siècle. Une compilation raisonnée, Études des procédés de confection et Synoptiques nouveau modèle*, vol. II (The Hague, 1984), pp.51–55.

[48] For the lost manuscript: Aimé-Georges Martimort, 'Un Gélasien du VIIIe siècle: Le Sacramentaire de Noyon', in *Miscellanea Pietro Frutaz* (Rome, 1978), pp.183–206.

[49] *Engolismensis*, Saint-Roch (ed.), p.99: 'Primitus enim canunt antephonam ad introitum: dum sanctificatus fuero in uobis, sicut mos est . . . deinde adnuntiat diaconus ut orent electi sicut in superior scrutinio scriptum est . . . Novissime sacerdos dans orationem super capita infantum his uerbis: Aeternam ac iustissimam pietatem . . . .'

Rome, Metz and the Gelasians in Francia   151

In the Sacramentaries of Angoulême and Noyon, the Lent section has the three Masses for the first three scrutinies which are still placed at the three Sundays in Lent, and the first scrutiny is identified by the DENUNTIATIO to fall on the Monday of Lent's third week. However, in both the Sacramentaries of Angoulême and Noyon, place was still made for a seventh scrutiny in the title for the Wednesday of Holy Week: 'ORATIONES AD MISSAM IN FERIA IIII. EBDOMADA VI. HIC COMPLES SEPTIMUM SCRUTINIUM.'[50] This title assumes there to be seven scrutinies, but there is no indication in the *ordo* how these would fall. Since Gellone, which is more specific on exactly that question, has this same title as well, it seems it may be an initial intervention, early in the Gelasian of the Eighth Century's transmission.[51] At that point, seven scrutinies was an assumed use, but the Sacramentary had not caught up yet. It assumed that the *ordo* of the Gelasian could be used to perform more than the three such meetings. The first was said to be on the Monday of the third week of Lent, and the seventh on the Wednesday of the sixth week: the silence of the Sacramentary of Angoulême probably implies that the others could be placed within Lent between them, wherever the celebrant decided and announced them.

In the first scrutiny *ordo* of the Sacramentary of Gellone, this feature becomes ever more explicit. At the end of the scrutiny *ordo*, at the point where both Old Gelasian and Angoulême end rather suddenly, this Sacramentary offers a crucial and significant coda:

> Ita tamen pensandum est, ut, a primo scrutinio qui incipit III ebdomada II feria Quadragesima usque in sabbato sancto vigilia paschae, septem scrutinii esse debeant, secundum furma[*sic*] VII donis spiritus sancti.[52]

This is the early form of the justification given for the shift from three to seven scrutinies. It can be found, in this basic form, in the lost Sacramentary of Godelgaudus from Reims, as well as in the two Pontificals of Paris and Constance. These texts still do not make it absolutely clear where all seven of the scrutinies would fit. Commentators have remarked on the strange artificiality of the change, but have accepted Andrieu's assumption that the change from three to seven scrutinies was made in Rome, based purely on his assumption of the primacy of his *Ordo*

---

[50] *Engolismensis*, Saint-Roch (ed.), p.76: 'Prayers for the Mass on the Wednesday of the 6th Week. Here you complete the seventh scrutiny'; Martimort, 'Un Gélasien du VIIIe siècle'.

[51] *Gellonensis*, Dumas (ed.), p.101: 'LXIV HIC CONPLES SEPTIMO SCRUTINIO. EBD VI FER IIII. AD SANCTAM MARIAM.'

[52] *Gellonensis*, Dumas (ed.), p.73: 'However it is thought that from the first scrutiny which begins on Monday of the 3rd week of Lent until Holy Saturday there should be seven scrutinies according to the form of the gifts of the Holy Spirit.'

152   The *Ordo Romanus* of the Baptismal Scrutinies

11.[53] This is the only place in the *ordo* of baptism where a justification for a usage is given in terms we might call allegorical, most likely because some justification was needed for what was a novelty, rather than the simple rubrical description of the ceremony. The sevenfold gifts of the Holy Spirit were conferred at confirmation, and did not have much to do with the scrutinies, so the justification might even be called a little strained.

The first baptismal *ordo* of the Sacramentary of Gellone shows some new attempts to navigate, place and define the exact structure of the scrutinies, and how to fit them in the Sacramentary structure. Only in this manuscript is the DENUTIATIO placed before the third Sunday in Lent 'STATIO AD SANCTUM LAURENTIUM', with the addition to its text: 'sequente illam feria circa horam diei sextam convenire dignamini' in red.[54] This places the DENUNTIATIO explicitly on that Sunday, the day before the first scrutiny on the following Monday. Unlike in the Sacramentary of Angoulême, the *Ordo* for the first scrutiny follows here, within the Lent section: 'HIC INITIANTUR PRIMUM SCRUTINIUM.'[55] Masses for the second and third scrutinies can be found in Lent itself, still next to the fourth and fifth Sundays.[56] The scribe made some errors in entering the *ordo*, and had to direct his reader to turn back, at one point: 'Sequitur ad caticuminum faciendum : in retro sicut scriptum est infra Quadragesima.'[57] This makes it clear he was innovating by adding the full *ordo* within Lent itself. The archetype which the scribe was copying had the entire *ordo* for all the scrutinies placed just before Palm Sunday, but the Masses for the three scrutinies on the Sundays of Lent. This is exactly the configuration we see in the Old Gelasian. The scribe attempted to move the scrutiny *ordo* itself back into Lent, to allow both Mass and *ordo* to be together in their proper places in Lent, but, on his first attempt, ended it where the Old Gelasian had. When he came to the end of Lent, he, or a new scribe taking over, then began to copy the *ordo* once again from his model, but realised his mistake halfway through. Nevertheless, he still wished to have some additional descriptions of the Masses and the end of the scrutiny (these not being in the Old Gelasian), and he continued the rest of the *ordo* here, this text now being cut in half and divided between the middle of Lent and its end.

---

[53] Cramer, *Baptism and Change*, pp.142–143.
[54] *Gellonensis*, Dumas (ed.), p.47: 'on the following day around the sixth hour'.
[55] *Ibid.*, pp.48–51: 'Here begins the first scrutiny.'
[56] *Ibid.*, p.56: 'LXXV MISSA QUAE PRO SCRUTINIO II CELEBRATUR'; this even refers 'ut supra in I scrutinio', though the Mass in question is missing; p.60: 'LXXXIII MISSA QUAE PRO SCRUTINIO III CELEBRATUR. EBDOMADA V.'
[57] *Ibid.*, p.64: 'What follows for the making of a catechumen, is written above back in the middle of Lent.'

Rome, Metz and the Gelasians in Francia 153

In the Sacramentary of Angoulême, the text of the *ordo* for the first scrutiny ended simply with the rubric: 'ANTEQUAM acolitus manum inponat, adnunciat diaconus ut supra: *Orate electi flectite ienua*: postquam orauerint dicit diaconus: *leuate, omplete orationem uestram in unum* et dicite *amen*: et respondent omnes: *Amen.*'[58] In the Old Gelasian, even this rubric is missing there, so it is itself a step in the gradual filling in of the *ordo* by Frankish hands.[59] Given the set-up of the scrutinies, it can be assumed that the Mass would follow and presumably a reading from the Gospel, but this is not explicitly indicated. We see this same rubric in the Sacramentary of Gellone's first *Ordo*.[60] However, in that text, the reading of a non-Gospel text from the *capitulare* (the book which indicated the readings for liturgical feasts), a responsary, the dismissal of the catechumens, and the reading of a gospel *ad ipsam diem pertinente* and the offertory for Mass, are then described.[61] The special rubrics about the announcements of the name of godparents and the children from the Mass were also moved here, becoming part of the *ordo*.[62] All are communicated, and then, something key happens, the priest announces the next scrutiny to the assembled people:

> Finita uero missarum solemnia, communicant omnes. Deinde adnunciat presbyter qualem diem uoluerit ipsa ebdomada ut reuertantur, ita dicendo: *Illa feria ueniendo, collegiate uos temporius ad ecclesiam illam uel illam.* Et cum reuenerint, facit scrutinium secundum eo que et primum; tanto alio missa que in II scrutinio titolata est.[63]

No hint of this announcement was given in the Sacramentary of Angoulême or in the Old Gelasian. It should also be noted that the rubric states that the second scrutiny, as it was announced, would take place in the *same* week,

---

[58] *Engolismensis*, Saint-Roch (ed.), p.99: 'Before the acolyte lays on his hand, the deacon announces as above: "*Orate electi, flectite ienua*"; after they have prayed, the deacon says: "*Levate, complete orationem uestram in unum et dicite amen*" and they all respond: *Amen.*'

[59] *Liber Sacramentorum*, Eizenhöfer *et al.* (eds.), p.53 ends with the homily on the Lord's Prayer: 'Audistis dilectissimi . . . .'

[60] *Gellonensis*, Dumas (ed.), p.64.

[61] *Ibid.*, p.64–65: 'Inde reuertitur sacerdos ad sedem suam et legitur lectio quae in capitulari continetur. Inde sequitur responsuriam et adnuntiat diaconus ita: Catecuminus recedant. Si quis catecuminus est, recedat. Omnes catecumini exiant foras. Et egrediantur omnes, expectantes pro foribus usquedum conpleta fuerint missarum solemnia. Deinde legitur euangelium ad ipsam diem pertinente et offeruntur oblationis a parentibus uel qui eos suscepturi sunt . . . .'

[62] *Ibid.*, p.65: 'Et dicit sacerdos orationem super oblata. Infra actionem uero, recitantur nomina uirorum et mulierum qui ipsus infantes sunt suscepturi. Item infra actionem, recitantur nomina electorum.'

[63] *Ibid.*, p.65: 'When the solemn mass is finished, everyone communicates. Then the priest announces that they should return on whatever day he chooses in the same week, saying this, "On this day coming together, gather yourself in a timely fashion at this or that church". And when they will have returned, he does the second scrutiny as he did the first ; except that the Mass which is entitled "in the second scrutiny" is celebrated instead.'

154   The *Ordo Romanus* of the Baptismal Scrutinies

the third in Lent. A similar announcement preceded 'IN AURIUM APERTIONEM'.[64] By this token, 'IN AURIUM APERTIONEM' was to take place in the following week, on a day of the priest's choosing. Clearly, these mark the necessary adjustments to the timing of the scrutinies to fit seven of them into Lent. The first and second both take place in the third week in Lent, the third takes place in the fourth week, and the seventh takes place on the Wednesday of Holy Week.

Subsequent testimonies to the scrutiny *ordo* all follow the first *ordo* of the Sacramentary of Gellone in displaying seven scrutinies, and giving the key 'allegorical' justification. A Sacramentary from Neustadt near Würzburg in Anglo-Saxon minuscule, now fragmentary, belongs to a similar stage, since its scrutiny *ordo* is placed in Holy Week without exact specification of where the scrutinies would themselves fall in the preceding Lent.[65] Nevertheless, it represents yet another branch of the Frankish experiment with fitting the seven scrutinies into Lent since the *ordo* is placed seemingly not, as in the first *ordo* of Gellone, just before Palm Sunday, but instead just after it. We see in one of the surviving fragments in Saint Petersburg the end of 'IN AURIUM APERTIONEM' largely as in Gellone, and the justification for seven scrutinies as above, then immediately the 'FERIA II AD SANCTOS NERUEM ET ACHILLEUM', which is the Monday of Holy Week, and the rest of Holy Week follows on the *verso*. This means Palm Sunday must have proceeded the *ordo*. This placement necessitated an addition which the scribe himself added, unique to this manuscript:

> ET ITERUM ADNUNTIAT presbiter qualem diem uoluerit (quod) reuertantur ad scrutinium . Ita tamen pensandum est ut primo scrutinio qui incipit tertia ebdomada in Quadragesima usque in sabbato sancto septem scrutinia esse debeant secundum formam VII dona spiritus sancti .**et require retro in ebdomada V in quadragesima et cane illa missa in palmas de passione domini et require retro in illo tertio quaternione a finiente et hic est ille missa.**[66]

---

[64] *Ibid.*, p.65: 'Sequente uero ebdomada, iterum unum qualem sacerdos uoluerit, adnuntiat ut faciat aurem apertionem hoc modo. Ueniunt ad ecclesiam die qua eis fuerit adnuntiandum, et clamat diaconus dicens: *Caticumini procedant* ...'; the Sacramentary of Angouleme's rubric for 'IN AURIUM APERTIONEM' also lacks any suggestion of this announcement.

[65] Josef Hofmann, 'Verstreute Blätter eines deutsch-insularen Sakramentars aus Neustadt am Main', *Mainfränkisches Jahrbuch*, 9 (1957), pp.133–141.

[66] St Petersburg, Rossijskaja Akademija Nauk, Institut Istorii West-European Section 3/625: 'AND AGAIN the priest announces on which day he should wish them to return to the scrutiny. However it is thought that from the first scrutiny which begins in the third week of Lent, until Holy Saturday, there ought to be seven scrutinies, according to the form of the seven gifts of the Holy Spirit; and return back to the fifth week in Lent and sing this mass on Palm Saturday "*de passione domini*" and then come back to this third quaternion at the end and here is the next mass.'

Baptism in the Frankish Gelasians and Pontificals

This directs the reader to go back in the Sacramentary to find the Mass for the Palm Sunday, then to come back to this exact spot, in the third quire, once they were done to get to the Mass that was needed for the Monday that follows. No other Sacramentary of which I am currently aware navigates, in this way, by quaternions. Like the Sacramentary of Gellone's first *ordo*, the Neustadt Sacramentary still demanded the reader flick back and forth. The fragment makes plain the complexities and difficulties of adapting the Sacramentary (initially intended to have only three scrutinies) to seven scrutinies that the *ordo* now demanded, and shows how that was undertaken in several stages and in various ways by experimentation within the Gelasian format. The Sacramentary fragment from Sens from the end of the ninth century or beginning of the tenth (BAV Reg.lat.567), where the scrutiny *ordo* is divided up in Lent, is also in this 'first family', indicating old forms continued to be copied.[67]

Some of the Gelasians of the Eighth Century lack the baptismal *ordo* entirely. One of the examples, the Sacramentary of Rheinau in St Gallen Stiftsbibliothek 348 (Rhaetia, *c*.800), nevertheless has a hint of a usage that differs from the forms discussed thus far. Among the many marginal notes that pepper it, most addressed seemingly directly to the celebrant, is one: 'hic facis scrutinium primum'.[68] This stands next to the Mass of the day: 'SABBATO AD SANCTOS MARCELLINUM ET PETRUM', that is, the Saturday of the second week of Lent, much earlier in Lent than we see in other manuscripts. This is actually in line with the Ambrosian placement of the scrutinies, perhaps by coincidence or attenuated influence.[69] The Rheinau Sacramentary does not give any further information on the scrutinies. We may assume here the use of an *ordo* copied separately, or memorised practice. Where Sacramentaries are entirely silent on the scrutinies, this may also apply.

The Sacramentary of Godelgaudus, the Fragments in Bruges and Two Pontificals

De Puniet noticed that the text of the now lost Sacramentary of Reims written for Godelgaudus (copied at Reims between 798 and 800) made one important adjustment to the witness of the other Gelasian

---

[67] Nocent, 'Un fragment de Sacramentaire de Sens'.

[68] *Das fränkische Sacramentarium Gelasianum in alamannischer Überlieferung*, Leo Cunibert Mohlberg (ed.) (Münster, 1971), p.109: 'here you do the first scrutiny'.

[69] They took place on three Saturdays of Lent in Milan: Pietro Borella, 'I sacramenti nella liturgia ambrosiana', in Mario Righetti (ed.), *Manuale di storia liturgica* 4 (Milan, 1959), pp.555–610, at p.579; *Manuale Ambrosianum ex codice saec. XI olim in usum canonicae vallis Travaliae*, Marco Magistretti (ed.), vol. 2, Monumenta veteris liturgiae Ambrosianae, 3 (Milan, 1905), pp.123, 142–143.

156   The *Ordo Romanus* of the Baptismal Scrutinies

Sacramentaries.[70] For the homilies 'IN AURIUM APERTIONEM', this text discarded the primitive Roman versions in favour of a set of the same homilies in a different redaction de Puniet characterised as 'Gallican', that is, they had some adjustments which mirror texts like the Bobbio Missal, rather than the pure Roman originals.[71] But de Puniet did not discuss manuscript structure, and did not note explicitly that the same manuscript displayed a significant structural innovation, stemming from the complexities that Gellone and Würzburg Sacramentaries both ran into. It removed the scrutiny *ordo* and the Masses for the scrutinies entirely from their position in Lent and Holy Week.[72] With the trouble the scribe of Gellone got himself into while trying to fit the increasingly developed *ordo* of the scrutinies into Lent, and the more or less explicit contradiction of the structure of the Masses inherited from the Old Gelasian with the new seven scrutinies suggested in the *ordo* itself, this was an obvious move for a scribe to make. It is, nevertheless, an important step in the removal of the *ordo* from the Sacramentary format, into what Andrieu characterised as *Ordo* 11, a text that has an existence entirely independent from the Sacramentary. Instead of being scattered within Lent and slotted awkwardly between the normal Masses of the year, now the whole structure of the scrutiny *ordo* – Masses, rubrics, prayers and homilies – falls with the ceremony of baptism, under an overarching title 'INCIPIT ORDO BAPTISTERII', in a new section of the Sacramentary outside the narrative of the liturgical year. In the Godelgaudus Sacramentary, the *ordo* for the scrutinies fell after the Canon of the Mass and before the dedications of objects for the church, in the second 'book' of the Gelasian concerned principally with *ordines* and pontifical matter.[73] Two scrutiny Masses are given in the form of an introduction before the 'DENUNTIATIO' opens the *ordo*, simply entitled 'MISSA QUAE PRO SCRUTINIO CELEBRATUR' and 'MISSA PRO SCRUTINIO IN AURIUM APERTIONE'.[74] The Old Gelasian structure of three scrutinies on three Sundays of Lent had now been entirely abandoned without trace.

[70] Florentine Mütherich, 'Das Godelgaudus-Sakramentar ein verlorenes Denkmal aus der Zeit Karls des Großen', in Piel Friedrich and Jorg Traeger (eds.), *Festschrift Wolfgang Braunfels* (Tübingen, 1977), pp.267–274.

[71] De Puniet, 'Les trois homélies catéchétiques'.

[72] *Sacramentaire et martyrologie de l'Abbaye de Saint-Remy*, Ulysse Chevalier (ed.) (Paris, 1900), pp.345–353.

[73] Bernard Moreton, 'The Liber Secundus of the Eighth Century Gelasian Sacramentaries: A Reassessment', *Studia Patristica*, 13 (1975), pp.382–86.

[74] *Sacramentaire et martyrologie*, Chevalier (ed.), p.345.

Baptism in the Frankish Gelasians and Pontificals 157

Even after *Ordo* 11 appeared, as an updated version that was much more explicit, texts from the Gelasian 'families' persisted and were copied for at least two centuries. The detailed scrutiny *ordo* in the tenth-century Sacramentary of Fulda in Göttingen is also independent of *Ordo* 11, as is an eleventh-century missal from Abruzzo, BAV lat.4770.[75] Later ninth-century 'pontificals' of Paris and Constance each offer a narrative of the scrutinies in the same vein. In both cases, they clearly depend on what is transmitted in the Gelasian Sacramentary of Godelgaudus, and owe nothing to the separate *Ordo* 11. The continued and mutual interdependence of pontifical and Sacramentary shows how the two 'genres' were still viewed as common stock. In Paris and Constance, the Gelasian *ordo* persisted as the first choice. Under the heading 'INCIPIT ORDO BAPTISTERII', the Constance Pontifical gives the three scrutiny Masses first, then the DENUNTIATIO, and then follows the *ordo*, all just as in the Sacramentary of Godelgaudus. At the end of the third scrutiny, the same form of the allegorical justification appears.[76] We can even say that the Constance Pontifical copied its *ordo* directly from a Gelasian that was similar to that of the Godelgaudus Sacramentary. We might note that another way the Gelasians of the Eighth Century had a lasting influence was through the pontifical format, again questioning verdicts on their obsolence or replacement by the Gregorian. In one important commonality, both Godelgaudus and Constance add, at the very end of the *ordo*, another separate description of catechesis on Holy Saturday, all in the second person and with some differences from the narrative of the same events in the full *ordo*.[77] In fact, this alternative version presents the same order as the Supplemented Gregorian's version

---

[75] *Sacramentarium Fuldense*, Richter and Schönfelder (eds.), pp.329–353; de Puniet employed BAV 4770 (*CLLA*, vol. 2, p.531 (1413)). It is digitised at: https://digi.vatlib.it/view/MSS_Vat.lat.4770.

[76] *Zwei karolingische Pontifikalien*, Metzger (ed.), pp.95*–96*: 'Et iterum adnuntiat presbiter qualem diem uoluerit et reuertantur ad scrutinium: ita tamen pensandum est ut a primum scrutinium qui incipit tertia ebdomada in Quadragesima, usque in sabbato sancto septem scrutinia esse debeant secundum formam septem dona spiritus sancti.'

[77] *Ibid.*, p.100*: 'Sabbato sancto, qui veniunt ad baptizandum, facies eos catecuminos: Prius dices orationem: *Omnipotens sempiterne deus pater domini nostri iesu christi*. Et reliqua. Completa autem oratione intinges policem in sale benedicto et mittes ei in os; et inpones ei nomen; et dicis illi taliter: *Accipe salem sapientiae in vitam propitiatus eternam. Pax tibi*. Deinde dicit: *Eternam ac iustissimam pietatem*. Et reliqua. Completa ista oratione cat(h)ecisas his verbis: *Nec te lateat satanas*. Et reliqua. Postea intingis policem in saliva moris tui, tangis ei nares et aures et dices secreto ad aurem: *Effeta*. Deinde ad abrenuntiandum dicis illi: *Abrenuntias satane?* RP. *abrenuntiat*. *Et omnibus operibus eius?* RP. *abrenuntiat*. *Et omnibus pompis eius?* RP. *Abrenuntiat*. Et intingis policem in oleo benedicto et signas ei in pectus et inter scapolas et dicis: *Et ego te lineo oleo salutis in christo jesu domino nostro*. Deinde interrogat simbolum, ut mos est, et baptizas cum sicut alios'; Godelgaudus in *Sacramentaire et martyrologie*, Chevalier (ed.), p.353.

158   The *Ordo Romanus* of the Baptismal Scrutinies

of this ritual on Holy Saturday morning, distinguishing itself from the Gelasian by the use of salt with the formula *Accipe* and the use of the prayer *aeternam ac iustissimam*.[78] Again, compilers did not shy away from repeating various versions of the same rituals. Presumably the celebrant might choose which version to follow or take elements from each, depending on taste and circumstance.

The Pontifical of Paris is a more complex witness. The base was certainly de Puniet's second family as represented by the Sacramentary of Godelgaudus. Yet here full readings are given, as well as the chants, including the openings of the gospels before they are explained during 'IN AURIUM APERTIONEM'.[79] This is in line with the usual practice of the Pontifical of Paris, which gives full readings for every other rite it narrates. At the end of 'IN AURIUM APERTIONEM', the scrutiny ends as usual and we have the same justification as Godelgaudus.[80]

Then the three scrutiny Masses are given, but here there is much that is new. The compiler stuffs them with details otherwise not found within them, including the full chants of the introit and full readings from Ezechiel and Matthew.[81] With rubrication, he made sure his reader knew exactly how every detail would fall even though one had to flick back and forth; the scrutiny he had narrated above should come, he says, between the *oratio* (collect) of the Mass and the prophetic reading.[82]

The compiler of the Pontifical begins to exert himself even more fully in the second scrutiny's Mass. This opens with a unique rubric:

> Ad introitum et reliqua sequentis officii sume de superiori missa, similiter et in reliquis quinque scrutiniis. Solum modo autem in tertio scrutinio, quod fit in aurium apertione, dimittitur responsorium superius adnotatum et canuntur alia duo, quae ordo ipsius diei commemorat.[83]

Here the compiler assumed clearly the reality of seven scrutinies and makes it plain that chants and prayers of the second Mass would suit for five of them.

---

[78] *Le sacramentaire gregorien*, Deshusses (ed.), vol. I, pp.371–378.

[79] *Il cosiddetto pontificale di Poitiers*, Martini (ed.), pp.57, 59, 61, 62.

[80] *Ibid.*, pp.70–71: 'Et iterum adnuntiat presbiter qualem diem uoluerit ut revertantur ad scrutinium. Ita tamen pensandum est ut a primo scrutinio quod incipit tertia ebdomada in Quadragesima, usque sabbatum sanctum septem scrutinia peragantur, secundum formam septem donorum spiritus sancti.'

[81] *Ibid.*, pp.71–72.

[82] *Ibid.*, p.71: 'Finita ista oratio complentur omnia erga electorum institutionem, quae ordo scrutinii continent, usque ad lectionem propheticam.'

[83] *Ibid.*, p.74: 'At the introit and the rest of the following offices do these exactly as in the above mass, and do similarly in the other five scrutinies. But only in the third scrutiny, which is done *in aurium apertione*, do not use the responsories noted above and sing another two, which are recalled in the *ordo* of this day.'

Baptism in the Frankish Gelasians and Pontificals 159

In the third Mass DE TERTIO SCRUTINIO IN APERTIONE AURIUM, he went beyond the *ordines* even more extensively. Two readings from Isaiah are given, 49:8–15 and 55:1–7, and two epistle readings, Corinthians 6:14–7:1 and Colossians 3:9–17; each of these has its given responsory and verse.[84] In *Ordo* 11, readings were noted, but only one prophetic (Isaiah 55) and an epistle reading from extracts of two letters of Paul (Colossians 3:9 and Romans 10:18) each. In one unique rubric, the compiler gave a detailed explanation:

> Istae duae lectiones apostolicae, quae subsequuntur cum subiectis sibi respon-soriis, de quodam tomulo ordinis romani sumptae sunt, quae et legi in hac eadem missa de apertione aurium iubentur. Ut quoniam quattuor lectiones initiorum sanctorum evangeliorum a quattuor dyaconibus in hac missa recitantur, quattuor quoque lectiones, duae scilicet propheticae et duae apostolicae a quattuor nihil hominus subdyaconibus legantur, totidemque responsorio hic inserta ab eiusdem numeri cantoribus modulentur, sumptis orationum precibus per unamquamque lectionem de missis priorium scrutiniorum:[85]

This short extract indicates that the compiler consulted a copy of what he described as an *ordo romanus*, but one in which Corinthians was also read, which we do not see in our extant manuscripts. Elsewhere, the use of readings familiar from *Ordo* 11 suggests the compiler employed this *ordo* as a reference for a final portion of the text.[86] There is a familiar liturgical logic of the Carolingians in this comment, matching numbers to numbers (and the compiler had read Amalarius). In a sense we have a rare glimpse here of how practitioners of liturgy might respond to gaps in the written record, with the logic of how they were trained to read liturgy and think about it. Thus, four deacons meant four subdeacons, and two apostolic readings demanded two prophetic ones. Whether this was ever actually put into practice is another question, but it certainly reflected the ideal of what Carolingians expected from their liturgy.

---

[84] *Ibid.*, pp.77–79.

[85] *Ibid.*, p.78: 'These two apostolic readings which follow with their own suitable responsories, are taken from a certain little book of the Roman order, where also it is ordered that these are read in the same Mass *de apertione aurium*. Now since the four readings of the beginnings of the holy gospels are recited in this mass by four deacons, therefore four readings, two clearly prophetic and two apostolic by four subdeacons likewise are read, and each with a response here inserted, which by the same number of cantors are sung, with the addition of the prayers for each reading from the Masses of the previous scrutinies.'

[86] *Ibid.*, p.72: 'Deinde legitur evangelium secundum Matthew: *In illo tempore, respondens Iesus, dixit: Confiteor tibi pater caeli usque Iugum meum suave est et onum meum leve.*'

160   The *Ordo Romanus* of the Baptismal Scrutinies

At the end of the section, the compiler gave further descriptions of the ceremonies of 'IN AURIUM APERTIONEM', noting that for the reading one should go back ('invenies retro in ordine pleni scrutinii') and finally the Mass is finished there.[87] Here we find rubrics from *Ordo* 11, indicating the consultation of the 'tomulus ordinis romani', given as distinct from the pieces that lined up with the Gelasian, and rounding up the picture of the ceremony with the details that *Ordo* 11 used. Thus, our compiler knew the scrutiny *ordo* at two stages of its development (Gelasian and *Ordo* 11), and employed both. As with the rest of the book, the scrutiny *ordo* is exhaustive in its detail and fixes every point of confusion. One telling addition to *Ordo* 11's text in the Pontifical of Paris is as follows: 'Et adnunciat dyaconus, non de illis qui quattuor lectiones evangeliorum isto die recitant, sed ill cui adnunciationis officio eo die deputatum est, quae observatio et in caterorum diebus scrutiniorum custoditur.'[88] The responsibilities and numbers of clerics involved here were absolutely fixed by the book, and the Pontifical of Paris is singular in the intensity of this preoccupation. Elsewhere in the same book numbers are given important symbolic value, and it is expected that, for example, the number of deacons be matched by the number of candles.[89] But in general this preoccupation, reflected by the writings of Amalarius, is a good way to explain the initial attempt to raise the number of scrutinies to seven for symbolic aptness.

Scrutinies in the *Ordines Romani*

The important witness of the Sacramentary of Godelgaudus may be closely dated to between 798 and 800, according to the detailed colophon. Around that time, the first manuscripts of the *ordines romani* also appeared. *Ordo* 11 is the most widely copied, and ultimately the most influential text, but the baptismal narrative in Andrieu's *Ordo* 15 does represent an important Frankish offshoot of the tradition.[90] This early *ordo romanus* stems independently from the Gelasian and bears no sign of being influenced by *Ordo* 11 (since it knew *Ordo* 1 in the 'short recension', this indicates the independent influence of that earlier tradition of *Ordo* 1 before forms of

---

[87] *Ibid.*, pp.80–81: 'Hic explicitis, procedunt quattuor dyaconi de sacrario cum quattuor libris evangeliorum . . . peraguntur omnia quae in ordine apertionis aurium et scrutinii continetur.'

[88] *Ibid.*, p.80: 'and one of the deacons, not any of the four who recite the four readings of the gospel on this day, but another, the same one to whom the announcement of this day was assigned, who keeps this observance also in other days of the scrutinies, recites this'.

[89] *Ibid.*, pp.220–221.   [90] *Les Ordines*, vol. III, pp.45–125.

Scrutinies in the Ordines Romani 161

Collection A were first achieved, in which *Ordo* 11 was also present). The full *ordo* for the scrutinies appears in one, the manuscript St Gallen Stiftsbibliothek 349, the others remove or reduce it.[91] The St Gallen manuscript is likely earlier than any witness to *Ordo* 11 and the milieu in which it was copied clearly knew the Gelasian of the Eighth Century and the scrutiny *ordo* in de Puniet's 'second family'. The narrative of the scrutinies is simplified extensively. The full prayers given there are given only in *incipit* form, while the homilies 'IN AURIUM APERTIONE' and the performance of the Masses are noted, but the texts for them are not given, nor is the DENUNTIATIO.[92] However, the dependence on the Gelasian is clear: for example, the announcement of the scrutiny is noted, without the words of the announcement being given.[93] At the end of 'IN AURIUM APERTIONEM', the tell-tale demand for seven scrutiny begins but then abruptly shifts into one of the author's interpolations:

> Ita tamen pensandum est ut, a primo scrutinio usque in sabbato sancto, septem **vicibus, hoc fiat, id est, in prima ebdomada duobus vicibus, in secunda unam, inde in tercia duabus, in quinta vero, qui est ultima, iterum duabus.**[94]

The numbering is a little confusing, because the text counts from the first scrutiny ('a primo scrutinio') and not actually from the beginning of Lent, so what it calls the fifth week is here Holy Week ('qui est ultima'), actually the sixth week of Lent itself. However, if that timing still seems off, that is because the compiler has indeed decided to alter the order of the scrutinies in Lent. The scrutiny *ordo* itself opens with: 'Quarta vero ebdomata ante pascha incipiunt scrutinium facere ad infantis qui in sabbato sancto baptizandi erunt', then the first scrutiny begins: 'Secunda vero feria in ipsa ebdomada veniunt ora tercia ad ecclesiam matris cum infantibus eorum.'[95] Again, the scrutiny is on Monday, but four weeks before Easter specified would properly place this scrutiny not in the third

---

[91] Montpellier 412 ends abruptly at *Ordo* 15, n.85: 'Quarta uero ebdomata ante pascha incipient scrutinium facere ad infantis qui in sabbato sancto baptizandi erunt.'

[92] *Ordo* 15, nn.91, 94, 96, 105, 108, for example n.105: 'Inde lecuntur initia evangeliorum cum expositionibus suis.'

[93] *Ordo* 15, n.99: 'Et adnuntiat presbiter qualem diem voluerit in ipsa ebdomada et revertuntur et facit similiter.'

[94] *Ordo* 15, n.112: 'However it is thought that from the first scrutiny until Holy Saturday seven times this is done, that is in the first week twice, once in the second, in the third twice, but in the fifth, that is the last, again twice.'

[95] *Ordo* 15, nn.85–86: 'But the fourth week before Easter they begin to do the scrutiny to the infants who will be baptized on Holy Saturday. But on Monday of this week they come at the third hour to the mother church, with their children.'

162   The *Ordo Romanus* of the Baptismal Scrutinies

week of Lent, but the second. This would be the only way to fit the timetable laid out by the compiler for the seven scrutinies. One may also note the unique mention of an 'ecclesia matris' (perhaps Tours cathedral?), implying a system of locating the scrutinies among the pre-existing geography of a Frankish liturgical space.

The text records (without providing the wording to be uttered) the need to announce the coming scrutinies: 'Et adnuntiat presbiter qualem diem voluerit in ipsa (ebdomada) ut revertantur et facit similiter. Sequente vero ebdomada, iterum una die quale presbiter adnuntiaverit, similiter facit. Tercia vero ebdomada, similiter die qua elegeret presbiter facit aures apertionum.'[96] This makes 'IN AURIUM APERTIONEM' the fourth, and not the third, scrutiny. It seems the scribe prized keeping the scrutiny 'IN AURIUM APERTIONEM' in the fourth week of Lent over its position as third in the numbering. *Ordo* 15 is an odd offshoot, suggesting a lasting period of experimentation and lack of certitude about the placement of the scrutinies. Here, two scrutinies would take place in Lent's second week (of which one was on Monday), one would take place in the third, two in the fourth week (of which the first was 'IN AURIUM APERTIONEM'), none in the fifth week of Lent, and in Holy Week itself, the sixth week of Lent, two more would take place. The importance of *Ordo* 15, in addition, is that it proves that the Franks were taking the rubrics from the Gelasian Sacramentary and presenting them as a complete narrative, abbreviating the prayers to *incipits*. It is not necessary, therefore, to hypothesise that *Ordo* 11 left Rome in its current state just because it is a distinct kind of text from the Sacramentary but Frankish creativity was sufficient to give rise to this text too.

While Andrieu reconstructed Pal.lat.487 as the 'best' testimony to the 'Roman' *Ordo* 11, as he edited it, there had already been fifty years of attested Frankish intervention in the text before the writing of this manuscript. Analysis of the number and timing of the scrutinies above bears some fruit here. Andrieu supposed that Rome raised the scrutinies from three to seven, and the result was *Ordo* 11, a text that, he said, had left Rome around 750. Because Andrieu gave *Ordo* 11 primacy even over the Old Gelasian, he was compelled to push this passage (and thus that of Collection A as a whole) to before the Old Gelasian manuscript (BAV Reg.lat.316). The analysis of the various stages of experimentation in the

---

[96] *Ordo* 15, nn.99–101: 'And the priest announces whatever day he wishes in this week that they should return and do similarly. But in the following week, again one day which the priest will have announced, he does similarly. But in the third week, similarly on a day of the priest's choosing, he does *aures apertionem*.'

Scrutinies in the Ordines Romani 163

Gelasian Sacramentaries before we even reach *Ordo* 11 has shown how impossible this was. *Ordo* 11 can actually be seen to descend from something like the Sacramentary of Godelgaudus, a Sacramentary of the Gelasian of the Eighth Century family. The idea that a text that was very clear about where the scrutinies fell, *Ordo* 11, could be adapted to one which was entirely unclear, the Gelasian Sacramentary, is not realistically arguable.

Once the Gelasians had removed the scrutiny *ordo* from Lent and made it into a separate section under the title 'ORDO BAPTISTERII', it would be much simpler to extract the text into an *ordo* entirely independent of the Sacramentary, and this is the form we encounter it in *Ordo* 11. The full title given in Andrieu's edition is: 'INCIPIT ORDO VEL DENUNTIATIO SCRUTINII AD ELECTOS, QUOD TERTIA EBDOMADA IN QUADRAGESIMA, SECUNDA FERIA INITIATUR.'[97] In general, BAV Palat.lat.487 gives us the same shape of the scrutinies that de Puniet's second family did; its dependence on a text like Godelgaudus is very clear, but so is the editorial hand.[98] As was attempted in the first *ordo* of Gellone, the rubrics that are special to the Masses of the scrutinies and go back to the Old Gelasian are placed in seamless sequence as part of the *ordo*, at *Ordo* 11, nn.33–35, but the Mass prayers themselves are only given in *incipit*.[99] The most obvious difference in this manuscript is that the prayers, homilies and Creeds for 'IN AURIUM APERTIONEM' are all abbreviated to *incipits*. Another obvious intervention is to specify the readings and chants, generally left unspecified in the Godelgaudus and Gellone texts. Here, the readings are given with their extent marked, for the first scrutiny at *Ordo* 11, n.28: 'Et legitur lectio Hiezechielis propheta; *Haec dicit dominus: Effundam super vos aquam mundam*, usque *et salvabo vos ex universis inquinamentis vestris*. Sequitur responsorium: *Aspiciam vos et crescere faciam*'; and at *Ordo* 11, n.31: 'Deinde legitur evangelium secundum Matheum: *In illo tempore, respondens Iesus dixit: Confiteor tibi, pater aeli* usque: *iugum enim meum suave est et onus meum leve.*'[100] As Gamber mentioned, however, the reading of Matthew 11:25–30 does not at all agree

---

[97] *Ordo* 11, Tit.: 'Here begins the order and announcement of the scrutiny to the elected, which starts on the Monday, in the third week of Lent.'

[98] *Ordo* 11, n.7 has the rubric added in the Sacramentary of Godelgaudus: 'Inde vero exeant foras ecclesiam, expectantes horam quando revocentur.'

[99] *Ordo* 11, nn.33–35: 'Et ponat ipsas sacerdos super altare et dicit orationem secreto: Miseratio tua, Deus, ad haec percipienda mysteria. Ubi dicit: Memento, domine, famulorum famularumque tuarum, recitantur nomina virorum ac mulierum qui Ipsos infantes suscepturi sunt. Item infra actionem *Hanc igitur*. hac expleta recitantur nomina electorum . . . .'

[100] Also 'IN AURIUM APERTIONEM', *Ordo* 11, nn.43–45.

164 The *Ordo Romanus* of the Baptismal Scrutinies

with the Roman Gospel lists for this day.[101] In the Roman *Capitulare Evangeliorum*, for example, the gospel reading for the first scrutiny is actually Matthew 19:13–14, where Jesus speaks of the little children (the same reading is given here in the gospel list from Metz, that directly precedes Chrodegang's station list), and in the other two scrutinies the same story from Mark (10:13–16) and Luke (18:15–16) was repeated.[102] Gamber pointed instead to rare North Italian witnesses, of which an important one, because it is likely earlier than *Ordo* 11, is the palimpsest from the eighth century overwritten in the tenth or eleventh century for the book today under the shelfmark Monza Biblioteca Capitolare b-23/141, in which the same reading is certainly part of a catechetical rite.[103] Gamber identified the book as substantially 'Ambrosian'; however, as he noted, this reading of Matthew is not known in complete Ambrosian books, nor does *Ordo* 11 agree with the Ambrosian liturgy in its setting of the scrutinies.[104]

Did a compiler of Collection A therefore find *Ordo* 11 in a North Italian manuscript? If they did, it was probably in the setting of a plenary missal, including full readings and chants, which helps to show why *Ordo* 11 indicates these explicitly with the *usque* form, in contrast to earlier versions of the same text, which do not indicate texts explicitly. Such texts are not uncommon even this early in Northern Italy.[105] Expansion of the number of scrutinies is witnessed in at least one North Italian source from the same period, the *ordo* from the eighth century copied into the eleventh-century Milan, Biblioteca Ambrosiana, MS T. 27. Sup. (independent of *Ordo* 11), which seems extraordinarily to foresee some kind of scrutiny on every day of Lent.[106] It was thus part of practice in this region, and expanding to seven was perhaps less unlikely there. Curious contacts of Metz with the Ambrosian liturgy are, in fact, known from the Sacramentary of Drogo (Paris, BnF, lat.9428), created *c*.855, including the Mass for Saint Arnulf of

---

[101] Gamber, 'Fragmenta Liturgica IV', p.208.

[102] Theodor Klauser, *Das Römische Capitulare Evangeliorum: Texte und Untersuchungen zu seiner ältesten Geschichte*, vol. I, 2nd ed. (Münster, 1972), p.46; Paris BnF lat.268, fol.193r.

[103] Klaus Gamber, 'Teile eines ambrosianischen Messbuches im Palimpsest von Monza aus dem 8. Jh.', *Scriptorium* 16 (1962), pp.3–15, at p.13; *CLA*, vol. III, p.384; Gamber also indicated a fragment today Clm 29300(29, taken out of a Tegernsee book; he identified it as a North Italian plenary missal from the ninth or tenth century, although the catalogue has it, instead, as eleventh-century and from Tegernsee itself, and I would agree: Hermann Hauke, *Katalog der lateinischen Fragmente der Bayerischen Staatsbibliothek München*, vol. I (Wiesbaden, 1994), pp.142–143.

[104] Borella, 'I sacramentari nella liturgia ambrosiana', p.579.

[105] Rankin, 'Carolingian liturgical books'; Andrew Irving, 'Mass By Design: Design Elements in Early Italian Mass Book', in Barbara A. Shailor and Consuelo W. Dutschke (eds.), *Scribes and the Presentation of Texts (from Antiquity to c. 1550). Proceedings of the 20th Colloquium of the Comité international de paléographie latine* (Turnhout, 2021), pp.251–274.

[106] *North Italian Services of the Eleventh Century*, Cyrille Lambot (ed.), HBS, 67 (London, 1931).

Scrutinies in the Ordines Romani   165

Metz, adapted simply from that of Saint Ambrose in the Ambrosian liturgy, and the other local patron, Saint Stephen, of whom four prayers are of Ambrosian origin.[107] Perhaps the same plenary missal source was employed here too and Angilram's involvement might be detected in both cases. A North Italian presence in Angilram's vicinity was, of course, Paul the Deacon (died *c.*796), from Friuli, who spent time in Benevento, Montecassino and Pavia, and who wrote for Angilram the *Liber de episcopis mettensibus*, on the model of Rome's *Liber pontificalis*.

The text of *Ordo* II made some final and significant advances on the specification and ordering of seven scrutinies in a way that finally clarified them to satisfaction of the author. The DENUNTIATIO, as we saw, originally took place on Sunday to announce the scrutiny on Monday: but *Ordo* II presents a version of the DENUNTIATIO where the *illa feria* when the scrutiny took place, assumed to be the Monday, is now given as Wednesday, *quarta feria*.[108] The title that referred to the Monday in Lent was taken to apply to the *Denuntiatio* itself, so the *Denuntiatio* was said on the Monday, now announcing the first scrutiny to take place on the following Wednesday, of the third week in Lent. This is entirely explicable as an interpretation from the copying and adjustment of the Gelasian, but not the other way round. In the same vein, numerous additions made now show the priest at every scrutiny, with his exact words, announcing to the people when and where they should reconvene for each of the seven scrutinies.[109] These announcements fix the days of the scrutinies: the first scrutiny took place on the Wednesday of the third week of Lent, the second on that same week's Saturday, the third, 'IN AURIUM APERTIONEM',

---

[107] Leo Cunibert Mohlberg, 'Milano e Metz nella redazione del Sacramentario di Drogone', *Rediconti della Pontifica Accademia Romana di Archeologia*, 16 (1940), pp.151–155; Franz Unterkircher, *Zur Ikonographie und Liturgie des Drogo-Sakramentars: Paris, BnF, Ms. Lat. 9428* (Graz, 1977), pp.33, 78–79; Corey Nason, 'The Mass Pericopes for Saint Arnulf's Day from the Drogo Sacramentary', *RevBen*, 124 (2014), pp.298–324.

[108] *Ordo* II, n.1: 'succedente sequenti **quarta feria,** circa horam tertiam convenire dignemini'.

[109] *Ordo* II, n.37: 'Deinde adnuntiat presbiter ut ipsa ebdomada revertantur ad scrutinium, ita dicendo: Die sabbato venite, colligite vos temporius ad ecclesiam illam vel illam'; *Ordo* II, n.39: 'Iterum adnuntiat presbiter qualem die voluerit in sequenti ebdomada, quod ab initio Quadragesimae est quarta, ita dicendo: Illa feria venite, colligite vos temporius ad ecclesiam illam, qualem eis denuntiaverit'; *Ordo* II, n.76: 'Iterum adnuntiat presbiter qualem diem voluerit in sequenti ebdomada, quod est quinta ab initio quadragesimae, ut revertantur ad scrutinium. Et ut venerint celebraturi ipsum scrutinum faciunt per omnem ordinem sicut illi duo priores ante aurium apertionem fuerunt'; *Ordo* II, n.78: 'Et postea adnuntiat presbiter ut ipsa ebdomada, qualem diem vel ad qualem ecclesiam voluerit, ut revertantur ad scrutinium quintum. Et ut venerint, faciunt ipsum scrutinum per omnem modum sicut anterius fecerunt'; *Ordo* II, n.80: 'Hoc expleto, iterum adnuntiat ei, sicut superius, ut revertantur ad scrutinium sextum, in sequenti ebdomada, ultima ante pascha, qualem diem vel ad qualem ecclesiam voluerit. Et complent ipsum scrutinum vel missam per omnia sicut anterius fecerunt.'

166   The *Ordo Romanus* of the Baptismal Scrutinies

was in the following week, the fourth and fifth both had to happen in the
following week, the fifth in Lent. The sixth took place in the following
week, the sixth in Lent; that is, it was in Holy Week itself.

After the above specifications, the Sacramentary's demand for seven
scrutinies appears, and it was also updated:

> *Ordo* 11, n.81: lta tamen **agendum** est, ut, a primo scrutinio qui incipit tertia
> ebdomada in quadragesima, usque in sabbato sancto **vigilia paschae**, sep-
> tem scrutinii esse debeant, secundum formam septem donis spiritus sancti,
> **ut, dum septenario numero inplebuntur, detur illis gratia septiformi
> spiritu sancti.**[110]

The original justification, as it was transmitted through all the Gelasians of
the Eighth Century, was not satisfying. The creator of *Ordo* 11 has recap-
itulated the justification a second time here, with a new clause adding that
the seven scrutinies all built up to the giving of the grace of the sevenfold
Holy Spirit, the confirmation by the bishop here assumed, as it is presented
in the *ordo*, to take place on the same day as baptism itself; that is, Holy
Saturday.[111] The grace of the sevenfold spirit is referred to in the Gelasian
confirmation prayer itself whence our compiler looked for inspiration:
'immite in eos septi formem spiritum sanctum tuum paraclitum'.[112]
While the other adjustments (e.g. *agendum* instead of *pensandum*) make
the Latin simpler and the text more definitive, they are important in clearly
marking out this new development of the justification of seven scrutinies
from the stages given in the Sacramentaries and pontificals. Again, it is not
likely that one would move from a more suitable justification like this to
the simpler and less suitable one in the Gelasians (first seen in Gellone).
The *ordo* has, up until this point, actually only given six scrutinies. In the
next sentence the author makes it plain that the meeting on Holy Saturday
itself is to be counted as the seventh and final scrutiny.[113] In the process, the
seven scrutinies are identified with *septem oblationes*, that is, seven offerings
made for seven Masses.

---

[110] *Les Ordines*, vol. II, p.442: 'But this is to be done so that, from the first scrutiny which begins in the
third week in Lent until Holy Saturday, the Vigil of Easter, there should be seven scrutinies,
according to the seven gifts of the Holy Spirit, so that when this entire sevenfold number will be
fulfilled, the grace of the sevenfold Holy Spirit shall be given to them.'

[111] Fisher, *Christian Initiation*.

[112] *Liber sacramentorum*, Eizenhöfer *et al.* (eds.), p.74: 'send into them your sevenfold Holy Spirit, the
Paraclete'.

[113] *Ordo* 11, n.82: 'Item adnuntiat presbiterut in ipso sancto sabbato hora tertia revertantur ad ecclesiam
et tunc catecizantur et reddunt symbolum et baptizantur et complebuntur septemo oblationes
eorum.'

Scrutinies in the Ordines Romani 167

The second baptismal *ordo* of the Sacramentary of Gellone knew these adjustments.[114]As above, the first baptismal *ordo* in this Sacramentary was at an earlier stage in the development of the text, stretched over Lent and Holy Week which led the compiler to some difficulties. The second *ordo* was a new attempt by the same compilers to represent the full *ordo* on its own. It is a separate *ordo* placed as what Dumas calls a 'pure interpolation de notre sacramentaire' and it stands after the *orationes cottidianes* at the head of a number of other *ordines* for baptism in other circumstances, when the child was sick or a pagan, or to reconcile a heretic.[115]This is a clear witness to the difficulties posed by using the Sacramentary as a source of liturgical practice. It was quite possible here, as in many other cases, for such a manuscript to represent the same rite several times, which certainly implies diverse and self-conscious practices of reading.

There is one puzzle here: the DENUNTIATIO's title. Instead of saying it is on Monday, as in *Ordo* 11, it is 'PRO SCRUTINIO QUOD III EBD. IN XLMA III FER INICIANTUR'; that is, it suggests the first scrutiny would take place on the Tuesday, and not the Monday, of Lent's third week.[116] This is a unique placement for the first scrutiny, demonstrating the exceptionality of this *ordo* in trying to frame and fix various difficulties. Otherwise, the text narrates the seven scrutinies, each with the announcement by the priest, as *Ordo* 11 did. It has the same enhanced version of the justification for seven scrutinies as *Ordo* 11.[117] But unlike that text in the form of Pal.lat.487, the prayers (including homilies and the Creed) are here given in full, and so are the readings (Ezechiel, Matthew, Isaiah and Colossians) and the chants that that text had specified. This was also true in the much later Paris Pontifical – such levels of complexity could be achieved at various points in the century and in various genres; there seem to be no constraints apart from the particular desire of the compiler, and Gellone also shows the same concern for fixing details and numbers.[118] The first Mass is given in the body of the first scrutiny, the second and third Mass follow at the very end of the whole baptismal *ordo* (after confirmation): 'MISSA IN SECUNDA SCRUTINIO' and 'ITEM MISSA IN

---

[114] *Gellonensis*, Dumas (ed.), pp.312–339.

[115] *Ibid.*, pp.xxxi–xxxii: 'a pure interpolation into our sacramentary', p.312.

[116] *Ibid.*, p.312: 'FOR THE SCRUTINY THAT BEGINS ON THE TUESDAY IN THE THIRD WEEK.'

[117] *Ibid.*, p.331: 'Ita tamen agendum est ut ad primum scrutinio qui incepit tercia ebdomada in quadragisima, usque in sabbatum sanctum uigilia pascha VII scrutinia debeant secundum formam VII dona spiritus sancti ut dum septenarium numerum implebantur dabitur illis gratia septeformis spiritus sancti.'

[118] *Ibid.*, pp.319–330. For example p.321: 'Inde Kyrieleison repetitis nouem uitibus.'

168   The *Ordo Romanus* of the Baptismal Scrutinies

TERTIO SCRUTINO Quod de aurium apertionem uel in aliis scrutiniis que secuntur'.[119] This text therefore tries to solve the issue of there being only three Gelasian Masses to seven scrutinies by suggesting the scrutinies four, five and six all repeated the same Mass which originally applied to 'IN AURIUM APERTIONEM'. This is one of the unique adjustments only in the second baptismal *ordo* of Gellone, stemming from the pen of the Sacramentary's active and sometimes overambitious compiler. He would not be the only example of such an attempt: the 'Collection B' manuscripts also went back to the Gelasian to add the homilies and a Creed back into *Ordo* 11.

The *ordo* of Lupus of Aquileia edited by de Rubeis is another such odd and unique offshoot, but it demonstrates the persistence of strikingly local deployments of the scrutinies in Aquileia. The text mentions, in the first person, a *Pontifex* of the Church of Aquileia named Lupus.[120] The mention comes in a ritual that is known only in North Italy when the priest and the deacon ritually dismiss representatives of ten heresies.[121] As De Rubeis noted, there are two contenders for Lupus of Aquileia. The first was a ninth-century bishop, reigning from 855, the second in the tenth century around 932 to 944. The text given clearly depends on *Ordo* 11, but is a unique deployment of the seven Lenten scrutinies of that text. The Aquileia *ordo*, in the Friuli manuscript, keeps the elements of *Ordo* 11 that mark out seven scrutinies with their preceding announcements.[122] It maintains, in a significantly adapted form, the justification based on both the gifts and the sevenfold grace of the Holy Spirit:

> Quoniam ita agendum est a primo scrutinio, quod incipit tertia ebdomada in Quadragesima, usque in Sabbato ante Palmas, ut septem dona Spiritus sancti in eis compleantur, et septenario numero impleantur : dabiturque illis gratia septiformis Spiritus sancti.[123]

---

[119] *Ibid.*, p.338: 'for *Aurium apertionem* and in the other scrutinies that follow'.

[120] De Rubeis (ed.), *Duae Dissertationes*, pp.229–230, 246: 'Et huic mysterio Pontifex interesse debet, sicut mihi LUPONI uisum est, ecclesiae sanctae AQUILEGENSIS Pontifici.'

[121] *Ibid.*, p.245.

[122] *Ibid.*, p.234: 'Finita missa, communicant qui uolunt. Deinde annunciant Presbyter ut ipsa hebdomada reuertantur ad Scrutinium, dicendo: Die Ill., venite temporius, colligate vos ad Ecclesiam'; p.236: 'Venientes autem omnes ad illum diem, sicut eis denunciatum fuit; faciunt ipsum scrutinium per ordinem, sicut superius est scriptum ... Iterum annunciat Presbyter, qua die uoluerit, ita dicendo: Feria ill.venite, colligete vos ad ecclesiam. Venientes autem ad Ecclesiam die, quo eis fuerit annunciatum, faciant ipsum scrutinium, sicut superius habetur. Hoc expleto, iterum annunciat Presbyter diem in sequenti hebdomada, ut revertantur ad scrutinium quartum. Et postea annunciat Presbyter, sicut superius, et faciunt sicut superius habetur, et veniunt ad scrutinium quintum. Hoc expleto, annunciat Presbyter, sicut supra, ut revertantur ad scrutinium sextum.'

[123] *Ibid.*, p.236: 'However this is to be done from the first scrutiny, which begins in the third week of Lent until the Saturday before Palm Sunday, so that the seven gifts of the Holy Spirit are filled in them, and the sevenfold number is fulfilled. And then they are given the grace of the sevenfold Holy Spirit.'

Evidence from the Expositiones   169

As this text makes clear, the seven scrutinies of *Ordo* II were all present but redeployed through Lent in the *ordo* of Aquileia. The first was apparently located more specifically to *Feria sexta ante Laetare Ierusalem*, the Friday before the fourth Sunday of Lent; that is, in the third week of Lent but not the Monday or Wednesday.[124] The seventh scrutiny is the Saturday before Palm Sunday, thus all seven are to be done during Lent and even before Holy Week. Further, it is this last, seventh scrutiny that is 'IN AURIUM APERTIONEM' in the *ordo* of Aquileia.[125] This therefore scrupulously maintains the Roman progression towards 'IN AURIUM APERTIONEM' as the climax of the scrutinies, and it is also an adaptation to a legacy of a local tradition. In Northern Italy, the Saturday before Palm Sunday, 'SABBATO IN SYMBOLO', was the day for the tradition of the Symbol; the Aquileia *ordo* fits *Ordo* II to this tradition by presenting the entire 'IN AURIUM APERTIONEM', including the tradition of the Symbol, within this long-established session. The adaptations the Franks had applied to the Gelasian to create *Ordo* II made it suitable to be redeployed in still local configurations as represented in the *ordo* of Aquileia. It is far from impossible that many other adaptations might have been applied but remained unwritten, except in the hints we receive from commentaries.

Evidence from the *Expositiones*

Decades earlier, Maxentius of Aquileia's response to Charlemagne in 812 made no mention of many of these peculiarities of the Lupus *ordo*.[126] Even if the *ordo* of Lupus can be taken as a straightforward description of Aquileia's practices in the ninth century, Maxentius' letter, it must be noted, is simply not the same kind of text. We are not certain of the exact intentions of every one of the respondents to Charlemagne, and therefore attempts to track the development of practice in Aquileia in particular based on comparing Maxentius to Lupus may lead to a misunderstanding of what exactly is represented in either. Some of the letters on baptism provide a useful case study in the relation of commentary to practice: there are four available that address the placement of the scrutinies directly. A number of the texts relate to *Ordo* II. Some, however, had different ideas.[127]

---

[124] *Ibid.*, p.230.
[125] *Ibid.*, p.236: 'Iterum annunciat Presbyter, ut in Sabbato illo ante Dominicam Palmarum veniant ad scrutinium septimum, in Aurium Apertione.'
[126] Maxentius' text edited in Keefe, *Water and the Word*, vol. I, pp.107–111; vol. II, pp.462–466.
[127] One exposition from the province of Sens, perhaps marshalled by Magnus of Sens as part of his response to Charlemagne, has a distinctive curiosity of only two scrutinies: one on the second

170 The *Ordo Romanus* of the Baptismal Scrutinies

One Carolingian exposition on baptism, a florilegium of patristic citations once attributed to Odilbert of Milan (*c*.803–814), which has little otherwise creative to say, curiously employed the characteristic justification for seven scrutinies also used by *Ordo* 11 explicitly – 'In his fiunt scrutinia secundum formam septem donorum spiritus sancti' – without distinguishing this from the Isidore quotation preceding it.[128] This text was perhaps used by Odilbert in his response to Charlemagne's request, probably predating him.[129] Indeed, a similar citation of the scrutiny explanation under Isidore's name appears in another scrutiny explanation in another North Italian manuscript Monza, Bibl. Capitolare e. 14/127, fols.30v–36v.[130] These sources suggest that *Ordo* 11 was available first of all in Italy, and the 'allegorical justification' was found there. Indeed, Odilbert's introduction of ferial Masses in Lent, an innovation in Milan's Ambrosian liturgy, probably indicated that he intended to use Lent more intensively as an urban (and stational) liturgical event, in line with other Carolingian bishops like Chrodegang or Angilram.[131] A later archbishop of Milan, Angilbert II (archbishop 824–859) specifically imitated Chrodegang in founding canonical life at the cathedral.[132] However, it does not seem that *Ordo* 11 reflects Milanese practice. Scrutinies in church across Northern Italy had varied placements into the eleventh, twelfth and even thirteenth century, and the use of seven Lenten scrutinies was lasting in North Italian and Tuscan cities in a way that it was not north of the Alps.[133] This suggests that the custom had deeper roots in such places.

Saturday in Lent (just like the note added in the Rheinau Gelasian now in St Gallen) and one on the Monday *after* Easter; Keefe, *Water and the Word*, vol. II, p.322.

[128] Friedrich Ludwig Leonhard Wiegand, *Erzbischof Odilbert von Mailand über die Taufe ein Beitrag zur Geschichte der Taufliturgie im Zeitalter Karls des Großen* (Leipzig, 1899), p.31; Keefe, 'The Claim of Authorship'; Keefe, *Water and the Word*, vol. I, p.74, vol. II, pp.171–183. Another ninth-century text written down in Novara, which used this exposition, presents the same text as part of Isidore's own, Ambrosius Amelli, *Spicilegium Casinense: Analecta sacra et profana*, vol. I (Monte Cassino, 1888), pp.337–41 at 383: 'YSIDORUS: In his fiunt scrutinia secundum formam septem dona spiritus sancti'; Lucy Donkin, 'Suo loco: The Traditio evangeliorum and the Four Evangelist Symbols in the Presbytery Pavement of Novara Cathedral', *Speculum*, 88 (2013), pp.92–143.

[129] Although Keefe indicated that it appeared in manuscripts of the eighth century, in the earliest manuscript, St Gallen 236, it is an addition from the beginning of the ninth century: St Gallen Stiftsbibliothek 236, pp.294–296, digitised at: www.e-codices.unifr.ch/en/csg/0235/294/0/; Bischoff, *Katalog*, vol. III, p.316, n.5672.

[130] Jean-Paul Bouhot, 'Un florilège sur le symbolisme du baptême de la seconde moitié du VIIIe siècle', *Recherches augustinniennes*, 18 (1983), pp.154, 167.

[131] Klaus Gamber, 'Frammento Ratisbonense di un messale Ambrosiano', *Ambrosius*, 35 (1949), pp.51–54.

[132] Pietro Borella, 'Influssi carolingi e monastici sul Messale Ambrosiano', *Miscellanea L. Cuniberti Mohlberg*, vol. I (Rome, 1948), p.99.

[133] Donkin, 'Suo loco', pp.113–117; Ferdinando dell'Oro, 'L'Iniziazione cristiana a Novara da V al XI Secolo', *Rivista Liturgica* 1 (1978), pp.678–718.

Evidence from the Expositiones

Jesse of Amiens wrote a letter to the priests of his diocese perhaps around 802, with a detailed *ordo* of the scrutiny within it, and it appears he drew on a text like *Ordo* 11 but chose to make some changes.[134] The first scrutiny takes place, as in the Gelasian, in the Monday of the third week of Lent.[135] The second scrutiny was also in the third week, the third and fourth took place sometime between then and the Wednesday of the fifth week of Lent, the fifth was on that Wednesday, and the sixth and last was on the Friday of the fifth week in Lent (before Palm Sunday).[136] Thus, Jesse only has six scrutinies. The last scrutiny, according to Jesse, was the ceremony 'IN AURIUM APERTIONEM'. This maintained the final climax of the scrutinies just before Holy Week, as Lupus of Aquileia also had it.

Amalarius of Metz explicitly refers to the Roman *ordo*, in the context of describing the scrutinies that form the first part of that *ordo*.[137] However, instead of using the justification of the sevenfold grace of the spirit, Amalarius gives seven as a universal number representing the entire Church, as John wrote to seven churches in Asia.[138] Keefe wrote: 'It seems likely that Amalarius would have used the explanation of OR XI had he known it. Since he did not use it, it may be that his *ordo* was a variation of OR XI without the explanation.'[139] However, this reasoning does not do justice to Amalarius' methodology. His new explanation is much more sophisticated than the basic allegory of *Ordo* 11. As Keefe herself noted, he referred to the Roman *ordo* only in a few places but he did not use its instructions as the entire basis for his explanation. As the

---

[134] Edited in Keefe, *Water and the Word*, vol. II pp.405–428.

[135] *Ibid.*, p.406: 'tertia ebdomada in Quadragesima, II feria, hora tertia, veniant ad ecclesiam et antequam in aecclesiam introeant scribantur nomina infantum et eorum qui eos suscepturi sunt ab acolito'; the scrutiny Jesse describes is identical to *Ordo* 11, despite Keefe's attempt on p.55 to see *Ordo* 15 as the parallel.

[136] *Ibid.*, p.409–410: 'iterum denuntiet presbyter ut in ipsa ebdomada, feria quale voluerit, veniant omnes ad ecclesiam qualem eis denuntiaverit. Venientes autem ad ecclesiam condictam, faciant scrutinium alterum per ordinem, sicut prius fecerunt. Similiter faciendum est de scrutinio tertio, quartio, vel quinto in ills tribus edomadis usque in quarta feria ante palmas. In eadem autem quarta feria adnunciet presbyter ut sexta feria sequente veniant ad ecclesiam, qualecumque dixerit, et tunc faciant scrutinium per omnem ordinem, sicut illa quinque fecerunt usque ad locum ubi dicit: signate illos state cum disciplina et silentio, et legatur in aurium apertione lectio esaie prophetae . . . .'

[137] *Ibid.*, pp.339: 'In scrutinio quippe facimus signum crucis super pueros, sicut invenimus scriptum in romano ordine'; p.344 'Ipso die facimus scrutinium septimum, sicut in romano ordine invenimus scriptum'; p.346: 'Deinde per scrutamur patrinos vel matrinas si possint cantare orationem - dominicam et symbolum, sicut praemonuimus ac postea per ordinem, sicut in romano ordine scriptum est.'

[138] *Ibid.*, pp.340–341: 'cur septies scrutinium agatur. Scrutinium fit ante pascha septies. Septenario enim numero saepe universitas designator, sicut iohannes scribit septem ecclesiis quae sunt in asia, per has enim septem ecclesia omni ecclesiae scribit'.

[139] Keefe, *Water and the Word*, vol. I, pp.59–60.

172   The *Ordo Romanus* of the Baptismal Scrutinies

Roman *ordo* was also cited in his later *Liber Officialis*, it was demonstrably a useful source to him, and gave recommendations he found useful and pertinent. But it was not the definite and final shape of the ritual. Layered on top of the diverse texts we have, it is crucial to remember there were even more diverse ways of interpreting them and actually putting them into practice. The persistent assumption that Carolingian *expositiones* stick very closely to a given, written *ordo* does not really cohere with the actual way these authors employed sources. Rather, liturgical *ordines* were marshalled as authorities when they were needed, much like a helpful reference to a patristic authority, but the agenda of the compiler of the *expositio* was the shaping force of the text. This agenda might be to describe and explain a living but unwritten performance of a rite, or to give an 'ideal' ritual that fitted the compiler's sense of how a liturgical ceremony ought to proceed.

It is not always necessary to assume that the authors were parsing lost or unknown texts. This assumption privileges the codified written text as the exact record of what occurred in liturgical practice in a way that is clearly unsustainable in this period. As we will see, it would be quite possible to put the available texts of baptism to use in various arrangements, with adjustments and interpolations where these were required. The 'record' of liturgy in a liturgical manuscript, it bears repeating, is not entirely or simply prescriptive.[140] In this period, it immediately and constantly invited dialogue from the reader. This might mean deploying the rituals in various configurations or different orders, or interpreting ambiguous or absent elements of the ritual in various ways, and it might also mean finding 'rational' explanations for the elements, individually and within the broader meaning of the entire ritual. Every manuscript to a greater or lesser extent left space for, or specifically encouraged, these diverse practices of reading and performance.

Decades after Charlemagne's questionnaire, the exposition by Engilmodus, bishop of Soissons, clearly shows the survival of the sevenfold scrutiny structure as the symbolically ideal and most rational preliminary to baptism. This text was written as a letter to Bishop Odo of Beauvais, probably around 861, and it survives only in an eleventh-century manuscript now in Barcelona, Archivio y Biblioteca Capitular de la Catedral de Barcelona, MS 64.[141] Engilmodus' analysis is shaped by his assumption of

---

[140] Carol Symes, 'Liturgical Texts and Performance Practices', in Gittos and Hamilton (eds.), *Understanding Medieval Liturgy*, pp.241–244.

[141] F. Stegmüller, 'Bischof Angilmodus über die Taufe. Ein Beitrag zur spätkarolingischen Tauftheologie', *Römische Quartalschrift für christlichen Altertumskunde und Kirchengeschichte*, 52 (1957), pp.15–32; Keefe reproduced the edition of Stegmüller in *Water and the Word*, vol. II, pp.438–461.

Evidence from the Expositiones

the underlying *ratio* of ritual, just like Amalarius.[142] Though he does not refer explicitly to a Roman order, Engilmodus clearly knew the placement of the scrutinies described above: seven scrutinies beginning in the third week of Lent, the second to be fixed on that Saturday and the last on Holy Saturday (the first in the third hour, the others on the second hour).[143] Engilmodus did not give an exact day to the other scrutinies but clearly knew *Ordo* 11's developed justification of the septiform numbering, though he gives it some further development, using the key phrase of its 'type' of the grace given.

> Non vero sufficiens iudicata est semel acta catechumenorum instructio. Verum septies, cum ea, quae die baptismi sit repetenda, more tenetur ecclesiastico, quoniam dignum est proposito caelestis disciplinae diligentius praeexerciti stadium praerogare, radiante quoque in hoc regeneratricis typo septiformis gratiae ... Ipse etiam praestructiones consuetudine ecclesiastica scrutinia dictitantur.[144]

He described the special ceremony of 'IN AURIUM APERTIONEM', but he focused exclusively on the procession of the Gospels out of the Sacristy and the homilies of the Evangelists, because these suited his overall allegorical framework and not necessarily because he did not know that the Lord's Prayer and Creed were also explained.[145] Engilmodus' exposition reveals the persistence of the sevenfold scrutiny prior to baptism into the 860s as an ideal for its symbolic aptness.

The diversity of the baptismal ritual in other testimonies (both adaptations of the *Ordo* and commentary) are important for showing that

---

[142] Stegmüller, 'Bischof Angilmodus', p.16: 'Ea, quae in ecclesiasticis officiis, antique religiosorum tradita decreto, vel private serventur more vel publico, licet nostrum scientiam eorum fugiat ratio, non pie sentimus sine certae observationis instituta merito ....'

[143] *Ibid.*, p.18: 'Admittantur autem hebdomada tertia paschalis quadragesimae, ut ipso hebdomadarum numero attestentur, quem expetunt libertatem gratiae, tertio mundi tempore caelitus nobis indultae ... Admitte inde vero catechumeni secunda sabbati prescriptae hebdomadis ad ecclesiam vocantur, quoniam de fide et operibus informandi sumuntur. Quod fit hora diei tertia, vel secundum aliquos sexto; hoc ut diximus numero radiante, propter quam expetunt gratia, tertio saeculi tempore sive sexta mundi aetate datum ... quae die baptismi sit repetenda.'

[144] *Ibid.*, p.23: 'But it is not judged sufficient to perform the act of the instruction of the catechumens only once. But rather ecclesiastical custom holds this seven times, including one which on the day of baptism itself should be repeated, since it is rightly proposed to repeat more carefully the study of celestial discipline, by shining in this type of the regenerating sevenfold grace .... So this custom of instruction is called the ecclesiastical scrutinies.'

[145] *Ibid.*, pp.23–25: 'Quod autem in aurium apertionem, quando et nomen merentur competentium, inter missarum sollemnia quattuor de sacrario diaconi cum quattuor codicibus evangeliorum quid usa docendi sunt, egrediantur ... Lumine quoque duum praecedentium candelabrorum ostenduntur ipsa evangelii dicta supernae virtutus ... Porro thymiamaterium praecedentia atque nectare vaporis optimi nidorum corruptiaeris propellentia ... Delatorum etiam evangeliorum in quattuor angulis altaris ordinate positione significant evangelium ....'

174   The *Ordo Romanus* of the Baptismal Scrutinies

reading an *Ordo* did not mean following its every prescription literally, but rather one came to it as a source whose particularities might meet the required needs in full, in part or not much at all. Modern liturgists were so invested in the utility of the liturgical manuscript as intrinsic that it was assumed the *Ordo* had to straightforwardly reflect performance, accomplished by robotic imitation of the steps given in their order. With the mindset of the Frankish copyists in mind, it is not necessary to hypothesise the circulation of dozens more variants than we possess, but remember that these copyists were quite able to fill in gaps, follow the logic of their own liturgical speculations, or shift and shape the ritual around competing priorities of symbolic representation or utility. We already know that they consulted various versions of these books. The increase from three to seven scrutinies is a particularly clear instance of something universally meaningful in this period, the importance of a liturgy that made intellectual, symbolic or aesthetic sense to the copyist and the commentator.[146]

It should be again reiterated that *Ordo* 11, the text long taken to be a Roman creation, reflecting Roman rites, is in fact an entirely Frankish *ordo*. The dependence on the Gelasian of the Eighth Century, which was not known in Rome and which has always been acknowledged as a Frankish compilation, makes this plain. Indeed, further evidence can be found in the language of the *ordo*, which uses the terms *matrina* and *patrinus* (*Ordo* 11, n.12) for the godparents, which only appear in Frankish sources, and were not widely used before the ninth century.[147] This text thus cannot be taken to reflect a Roman social milieu or Roman attitudes to baptism, except in the core of Gelasian prayers and homilies (and these latter texts had already seen some adjustment in Gaul, as de Puniet has noted). We can probably state that Rome therefore had never known seven scrutinies at this point.[148] This is reflected in the Roman *Capitulare evangeliorum* (lists of gospel readings) even those from the time in which Andrieu placed the redaction of *Ordo* 11 (in the seventh century), which preserve notice of only three scrutinies, with different readings from those given by *Ordo* 11.[149]

---

[146] Phelan, *The Formation of Christian Europe*, p.206: 'a broad consensus . . . not uniformity of practice but in harmony of world view'; Cramer, *Baptism and Change*, pp.56, 187.

[147] Joseph Lynch, *Godparents and Kinship in Early Medieval Europe* (Princeton, 1986), pp.170–171.

[148] Hazarded by Pierre de Puniet, 'Catechumenat', *Dictionnaire d'archéologie chrétienne et de liturgie*, vol. II (1910), col.2609.

[149] For example BAV Pal.lat.46; see Theodor Klauser, 'Ein vollständiges Evangelienverzeichnis der römischen Kirche aus dem 7. Jahrhundert, erhalten im Cod. Vat. Pal. lat. 46', *Römische Quartalschrift für christliche Altertumskunde und Kirchengeschichte*, 35 (1927), pp.113–134.

Evidence from the Expositiones

This can also make a small contribution to the question of the origins of the Old Gelasian Sacramentary. Chavasse neatly solved the question of the Old Gelasian's contradictions with papal practice by suggesting it was, in fact, a 'presbyterial' Roman Sacramentary, one used by a priest in the urban *tituli* rather than by the Pope himself. It was still, thus, 'essentially' Roman, and we saw that Chavasse believed its baptism ritual to be Roman as well.[150] But the rubric I began this chapter with in order to question the Roman origin of *Ordo* 11 is, in fact, to be found among the very few rubrics in the Gelasian:

> cum omni ordine sacerdotum ... ante eum notariis cum duobus cereis ardentibus, cum turabulis et timiamateribus.[151]

As we began by saying, this does not look like the Roman ceremonial of baptism at all: it looks like the practice at a standard cathedral outside Rome. Gamber had already raised this possibility.[152]

Gamber believed the Old Gelasian to have come from Ravenna, which cannot be verified, but what has been laid out in this chapter does lend further strength to ongoing arguments about what exactly the Old Gelasian is. Coeburgh argued against Chavasse that non-Roman clerics from Italy had created the Old Gelasian Sacramentary from material in the Roman archives.[153] This would allow us to make sense of what happened in the book's scrutiny ritual, which would then lend further support to his reconstruction. As de Puniet had originally argued, the spoken elements of the ritual (homilies and prayers) in the Old Gelasian, and certainly the creeds in Latin and Greek, all do go back to the Roman practice. But it seems that the *rubrics* were added in the transmission and adaptation of the Old Gelasian outside Rome, thus representing (as we have said) practices in a North Italian cathedral with neighbouring baptistery.

It was in the same vicinity that these rubrics were repeatedly enhanced and added to, with most experimentation taking place within the fertile Gelasian of the Eighth Century. We see a number of stages of this

---

[150] Jean-Paul Bouhot, 'Trois rituels occasionnels du baptême dans le sacramentaire gélasien', *RevBen*, 122 (2012), pp.125–152 indicates the Gelasian baptism ritual to be complex and composite.

[151] *Liber sacramentorum*, Eizenhöfer *et al.* (eds.): 'with every order of priests . . . before him the notaries with two burning candles, with thuribles and incense carriers'.

[152] Gamber, 'Fragmenta liturgica IV', pp.207–208: 'Die Heimat unseres Skrutinienritus (*Ordo* 11) ist vielmehr dort zu suchen, wo das sog. Gelasianum entstanden ist, da in ihm dieser Ritus erstmals bezeugt ist . . . dass weder im Text des Gelasianums noch in den Rubriken des *Ordo* XI irgend ein Hinweis zu finden ist, der auf Rom als Entstehungsort dieser Skrutinien hinweist'; *CLLA*, vol. II, pp.188–189.

[153] Coeburgh, 'Le sacramentaire gélasien ancien'.

176   The *Ordo Romanus* of the Baptismal Scrutinies

experimentation beginning in France, though unfortunately the witnesses from Italy are too fragmentary to give a clear idea of the perhaps even more complex and rich experiments taking place there.[154] The addition of seven scrutinies was seen in French books, as was the removal of the *ordo* from Lent itself, but the *ordo* was fully completed, on the basis of a text like that of Godelgaudus, with placement of the scrutinies, readings and chants, probably in a Gelasian plenary missal from Italy in the late eighth century. In fact, Paulinus of Aquileia (d.804) on the banks of the Danube in 787 commanded that people must be instructed over at least seven days in Lent (as part of his missionary activity).[155] This would indicate that Gamber, as so often, was on the right track despite the fact that his conclusions about the *origins* of the baptismal ritual went too far into speculation, given his argument that the Old Gelasian could be located precisely to Ravenna, and much earlier than any manuscript evidence. The Gelasian was adapted in Northern Italy into a text like *Ordo* II, but this was actually on was the basis of an already fully achieved form of the Gelasian of the Eighth Century from France, one like the Sacramentary of Godelgaudus. The text likely came to Metz from Northern Italy (as part of a stock of characteristically North Italian material) and was incorporated into Collection A, after being extracted from the Sacramentary. This recorded an updating of previous practice in Metz under Chrodegang, which had involved only three scrutinies on three Sundays, according to his station list, an updating that likely took place under his successor, Angilram.

Given that *Ordo* II was not Roman, and did not address the same priorities as *Ordines* I or 34 (though it shares many of the same liturgical characters and terminology as *Ordines* 24 and 26, of course), why incorporate it? There is another vital element here, which is already visible in Chrodegang's station list. The scrutinies were integral to a stational Lent.[156] With their system of announcements to the people, movements back and forth across churches in Lent, and the gradual drawing back towards the *matris ecclesiae* (as *Ordo* 15 put it) on Holy Saturday itself, the scrutinies present themselves in Francia as instances of intensive management of the ecclesiastical space. To those who understood the ritual as 'Roman', or were specifically encouraged to understand it as such by the presentation of *Ordo* II right next to the stational Mass par excellence of

---

[154] For example Gamber's notices of *CLLA*, vol. II, pp.1280, 1285.

[155] *MGH* Concil. Aevi karolini I p.175: 'per septem tantum illius dies . . . indictio ieunio catecizantur cotidie'.

[156] Antoine Chavasse, 'L'organisation stationale du Carême romain, avant le VIIIe siècle. Une organisation "pastorale"', *Revue des sciences religeuses*, 56 (1982), pp.17–32.

Evidence from the Expositiones   177

Ordo I, this management of sacred space would allow the kinds of connections that liturgy in the Frankish realms inculcated and inspired through the use of Roman liturgy in particular. With time, as in Amalarius or the Pontifical of Paris, the term *ordo romanus* was applied to *Ordo* II too. Thus, the baptistery might indeed be the Lateran Baptistery, not literally (as Andrieu said) but rather in the more imaginative mode with which these rites were clearly being read.

CHAPTER 7

Ordines *for Special Occasions, Ordination and the Ember Days: The Contribution of Arn of Salzburg*

Processions of the Year

Many *ordines* dealt only with extraordinary annual liturgical events; the 'long recension' of *Ordo* 1 was set at Easter, though, of course, was intended to be adapted for other days as well. *Ordines* 15, 16 and 17 saw an annual structure as a way to compile varied texts and comments describing varied rituals, perhaps some of which circulated originally independently. Other rare *ordines* described specific and special liturgical events, such as *Ordines* 20 (Candlemas), 21 (the Great Litany) and 38 (Ember Saturday). These texts, for the most part, are found only in single, widely dispersed manuscripts. *Ordines* 20 and 21 are found only in the Collection of St Amand on spare folios of Paris BnF lat.974. *Ordo* 38 appears earliest in Vienna ÖNB cod.ser.n.2762, the pontifical made for Regensburg. This is a witness Andrieu did not know, which contains some key differences from his edited form of this text. There are some indications, however, that these three *ordines*, coming from opposite sides of the Empire, were actually closely related.

Andrieu already highlighted a certain identity of expression between *Ordo* 20/21 and *Ordo* 38.[1] Because Andrieu only knew *Ordo* 38 as a much later text, he assumed the former two *ordines* were among the sources for the latter. But given that *Ordo* 38 actually appears first in a manuscript that is earlier than the surviving manuscript of the Collection of St Amand, it is quite possible that, in fact, these *ordines* might all go back to a common collection. Andrieu hypothesised that the whole Collection here preserved went back to a single author, a monk or cleric in the late eighth century.[2] These select few *ordines* were copied by chance into the Paris manuscript of

---

[1] *Les Ordines*, vol. IV, pp.259–262.
[2] *Les Ordines*, vol. II, pp.138–139; *Les Ordines,* vol. III, p.239: 'Les nombreuses phrases et expressions qu'il (*Ordo* 21) a en commun avec *Les Ordines* IV et XX montret que cet ensemble de textes est l'oeuvre d'un même rédacteur'.

178

Augustine, using all the available space at the beginning and end, but the source, perhaps almost a century old by the time the Paris manuscript was copied (hence the need to preserve some of its contents), might have had a number of other texts too, perhaps concerning other particular solemnities.[3] Notably, *Ordo* 20 refers directly to *Ordo* 21: *sicut alibi scriptum est*.[4] *Ordo* 38, for example, could have been an obvious accompaniment. All of these texts are concerned with the organisation and topography of the stational processions that occurred in Rome on given feast days.[5] If a single author or group of related authors can be assumed, these texts were clearly redacted by someone who knew Rome and had observed the ceremonies there, and who knew quite well, and was particularly interested, in the stational system of Rome. Close knowledge is indicated by the use of specialised vocabulary such as the presence of the *stauroferes*.

Another text which could have suited this same context is *Ordo* 22, which concerns the organisation of the stational processions on Ash Wednesday and in Lent, which can be found in St Gallen 614 and its copy, St Gallen 140 (as well as in two eleventh-century manuscripts, including Montecassino, Archivio della Badia, MS 451 from a Mainz exemplar). It is certainly true that both St Gall manuscripts presents the same identities of expression that Andrieu had signalled concerning the above texts.[6] Here the experience

---

[3] *Les Ordines*, vol. I, p.493: 'Mais nous n'avons peut-être, de notre copie du IXe siècle, qu'une partie de la collection primitive. Puisque des *ordines* spécieux sont consacrés à la Purification et à la Litanie majeure, il est probable qu'on avait fait place à d'autres importantes solennités de l'année liturgique.'

[4] *Ordo* 20, n.11; the reference is for the text of the litany given in *Ordo* 21, n.17.

[5] The original orthography of the manuscript is maintained. For example, *Ordo* 20, n.1: 'Ipsa autem die, aurora ascendente, procedunt omnes de universas diaconias sive de titulis cum letania vel antiphonas psallendo et cerea accensa portantes omnes in minibus per turmas suas et veniunt in ecclesia sancti Adriani martyris et expectant pontificem'; *Ordo* 20, n.7: 'Interim egrediuntur cruces VII, portantur a stauroforo permixti cum populo. Deinde presbiteri vel diaconi. Deinde pontifex cum diaconibus . . . . Deinde subsequitur scola pontificem psallendo antiphonas'; *Ordo* 20, n.9: 'Cum autem adpropinquaverint atrium sanctae Dei genetricis ecclesiae innuit pontifex scola ut dicatur letania'; *Ordo* 21, n.1 'Quando letania maior debet fieri adnuntiat eam diaconus in statione catholica et dicit: *Feria tale ueniente, collecta in basilica beati Illius; statio in basilica sancti illius*'; *Ordo* 21, n.10: 'Et interim egrediuntur omnes de ecclesia. Primitus enim pauperes de xenodochio, cum cruce lignea picta, clamando *Kyrie eleison*, deinde *Christe eleison*, inde *Christe audi nos*, deinde *Sancta Maria ora pro nobis*, et ceteros. Et post Ipsos egrediantur cruces VII stacionarias, portantes ab stauroforos, habens in unaquaque III accensos cereos. Deinde secuntur episcopi vel presbiteri et subdiaconi: deinde pontifex cum diaconibus et due cruces ante eum, portantes a subdiaconibus et timiamasteria portantur a mansionariis ecclesiae et scola post pontificem psallendo.'

[6] *Ordo* 22, n.4: 'Ut autem finita fuerit antiphona, stans pontifex a dexteris altari, directus ad populum, dicit: *Dominus vobiscum;* deinde regirat se ad orientem, dicit : *Oremus*; diaconus: *Flectamus ienua*, deinde: *Levate. Sequitur oratio*'; nn.7–8: 'Ut autem ingressi fuerint ecclesiam, pontifex ingreditur in secretarium. Scola pergit decantando usque ad altare. Ut autem finierint letaniam, post paululum incipiunt antiphonam ad introitum.'

180 *Ordines* for Special Occasions, Ordination and the Ember Days

by an outsider of Rome is signalled more blatantly, given the mention of Pope Hadrian (as above), but the text also signals directly to other bishops and priests (*'ceteri vero episcopi aut presbiteri'*).[7]

Directly after that, the text also offers an interesting appendix, addressing the performance of the Mass in a list of asides, with advice on the *Gloria* (quoted from the Gregorian Sacramentary *Ordo* 22, n.16), the responsory, alleluia, laying down and moving of candles.[8] Its final point addresses the offertory, noting that the Pope (*domnus papa*) would chant it twice in a single Mass, something we do not otherwise know much about.[9] These asides closely resemble diverse appendices in the 'pontifical', Weissenburgenses 91, and even concern similar topics.[10] It is therefore true that the makers of a circle of somewhat related manuscripts (Vienna ÖNB cod.ser.n.2762, St Gallen 614, Paris BnF lat.974 and Wolfenbüttel Weissenburgenses 91) saw nothing wrong with presenting more general advice to Frankish readers in the form of such appendices alongside, and in direct continuation from, *ordines* that described specifically Roman ceremonies. Andrieu hypothesised repeatedly the presence of lost Roman documents behind these texts, but this is not strictly necessary. Direct observation of the ceremonies, as well as access to the Pope and his staff to question them, as we know the Franks did, would have sufficed.

We seem to have here signs of one or more closely linked Collections of *ordines romani* perhaps stemming from a connected circle of people but subsequently dispersed and adapted within their new contexts, addressing various such occasions, situated ambiguously between norms specific to Rome and adapted Frankish ones. Put together into a narrative along the course of the year, the group of such texts would look much as we have in the later *Ordo* 50, present in manuscripts from the eleventh century, which drew on a number of similar texts, switching between Roman and Frankish details.[11] Of course, there are also more contemporary witnesses to the existence of exactly such kinds of texts. *Ordines* 15, 16 and 17, while briefer, are basically made up of strings of *ordines* on the structure of the year. They address a number of the same occasions (Candlemas, Ember Days, Ash

---

[7] *Ordo* 22, n.15.   [8] *Ordo* 22, nn.16–20.

[9] *Ordo* 22, n.21: 'De offertorio seu et versu ipsius duobus vicibus ad unum missam domno pape cantatur.'

[10] Appendix to *Ordo* 24: 'In pascha usque in octabas ad omnes cursus non cantatur responsum nec lectio recitatur sed **versum pro versu, id est ad tertiam, sextam nonamque sed tantum Resp. Grad.** *Haec dies* dicantur primam; sine *Kyrieleison* autem fac totum officium in ipsa ebdomada, nisi tantum in missa dic *Kyrieleison*. Feria II ad *Venite* et per totam ebdomadam ant. *Surrexit dominus uere alleluia.*'

[11] Edited in *Les Ordines*, vol. V.

Wednesday). *Ordo* 15, in particular, assumes a stational framework with specific mentions of the stational churches; the partial copy of this text informally added at the end of the *Ordo* section in Weissenburgenses 91 is particularly outstanding in that regard, for example mentioning Santa Sabina as the station for Ash Wednesday.[12] These texts even have very similar asides and appendices to those we have noted elsewhere placed around the *ordines*, and even addressing some of the same matters, such as the *Gloria*.[13]

Ordinations and the Ember Days

While lower clergy might be ordained whenever there was need, deacons and priests were only to be ordained on one of the four Ember Days.[14] We have already seen that these Ember Days were a time of particular identification with Rome for the Franks, since they were fixed points of stational observance that punctuated the year, with the same locations applied in each case: Wednesday at Santa Maria Maggiore, Friday at Santi Apostoli, and Saturday, the time of ordination itself, at St Peter's Basilica. Even before the Carolingian period, Frankish legislation had concerned itself with these days.[15] The critical meeting of prelates at Mainz in 813 commanded the observation of Ember Days in detail:

> Constituimus ut quattuor tempora anni ab omnibus cum ieiunio observentur, id est in Martio mense ebdomada prima, feria IIII et VI et sabbato veniant omnes ad eclesiam hora nona cum laetaniis ad missarum sollemnia; similiter et in mense Iunio ebdomada II., feria IIII et VI, et sabbato ieiunetur usque ad horam nonam et a carne ab omnibus abstineatur; similiter et in mense

---

[12] *Ordo* 15, n.79: 'Postea quidem die secondo mense februario Ypapanti, quod est IIII nonas ipsius mensis, colleguntur omnes tam clerus romanae ecclesiae quam et omnes monachi monasteriorum cum omni populo suburbano seu et copiosa multitudo peregrinorum de quacumque provintia congregati, venientes ad ecclesiam beati Adriani mane prima et accipiunt de manu pontificis unusquis cereum unum'; *Ordo* 15, n.83: 'Primum autem ieiunium IIII feria ad sanctam Savinam publicae agitur cum cruce et turabulis simul cum laetaniis, id est post Lma et ante XLma, necnon et VI feria similiter faciunt ieiunium publica'; *Ordo* 15, n.84 'In XLma uero, prima ebdomada, si in mense martio uenerit, IIII et VI feria seu et sabbato, omnes publicas stationes faciunt ad Sanctum Petrum in XII lectionibus. Sin autem minime in martio mense prima ebdomada uenerit, in alia uel tertia ebdomada quando pontifex iudicauerit, XII lectiones agenda sunt et ordinantur qui ordinandi sunt.'

[13] For example *Ordo* 15, nn.152–156: 'Diebus autem quadragissime, ad missas, non cantant Gloria in excelsis Deo usque in sabbato sancto . . . De pascha uero soluta totis quinquagenta diebus usque in pentecosten responsurium ad missas non cantatur apud Romanos . . . .'

[14] See Thomas J. Talley, 'The Origin of the Ember Days: An Inconclusive Postscript', in Paul de Clerck and Eric Palazzo (eds.), *Rituels: mélanges offerts à Pierre-Marie Gy, o.p.* (Paris, 1990), pp.465–472; G. G. Willis, *Essays in Early Roman Liturgy* (London, 1964), pp.53–54.

[15] Council of Estinnes (743) in *PL* 89, col.823.

182 *Ordines* for Special Occasions, Ordination and the Ember Days

> Septembrio ebdomada III, et in mense Decembrio ebdomada, que fuerit plena ante vigiliam natalis Domini, **sicut est in Romana aecclesia traditum**.[16]

The enjoining of a procession 'with litanies' to a Mass in church is plainly a signal to a form of stational observance on each of the three days, as it was observed in Rome. *Ordo* 21 gives us the form of such litanies in Rome.[17] However, the timing of the Ember Days the council enjoined was not precisely that followed by Rome itself. In a letter to Hilduin of St-Denis (died *c.*855), Amalarius of Metz said he was confused to learn from Abbot Peter of Nonantola during their voyage to Constantinople in 813 that the first Ember Day in Rome was not fixed to the week in the first month, which he had previously believed was a *romanum usum*, but rather that the Roman custom held it in the first week of Lent, no matter which month that fell in.[18] Likewise, the second Ember Day was also fixed to Pentecost week in Rome, and not the second week of June.[19] Amalarius' confusion apparently came from texts he read in Francia, and reveals the possibility that even an expert, though this was early in his career, might be misled. Is it possible the participants at Mainz were likewise confused? The three most senior participants at Mainz (Arn of Salzburg, Richulf of Mainz and Bernharius of Worms) had all been to Rome, and, as I have suggested, showed distinctive interest in Roman liturgy. Yet if the clause 'sicut est in Romana aecclesiae traditum' is applied only to the fourth Ember Day in December, the text would be accurate nevertheless (since on that day there is no divergence from Rome). If so, the clerics at Mainz were applying Roman tradition in the same qualified and selective way that Keefe suggested they had used the term *ordo romanus* as regarded baptism in the earlier canon.[20] As there, these conciliar pronouncements, which have long been used to suggest the uniform and wholesale imposition of Roman liturgy, become much more qualified when we examine them more closely.[21] Notably, in Amalarius' later works, he continued to repeat the Frankish placement of the Ember Days, and made

---

[16] *MGH* Conc.II.1, p.269: 'We lay down that the Ember Days should be observed by everyone with fasts, which is to say, on Wednesday, Friday and Saturday in the first week of March, everyone should come to church at the ninth hour with litanies to a solemn celebration of mass, and the same should be done in the second week of June. On Wednesday, Friday and Saturday everyone should fast until the ninth hour, and abstain from all flesh. The same should be done in the third week of September and in December, in the week before the Christmas vigil, as it is the tradition of the Roman Church.'

[17] *Ordo* 21, n.17.   [18] Hanssens (ed.), *Opera omnia*, vol. I, p.341; *MGH* Epp. V, p.247–248.

[19] *Les Ordines*, vol. IV, pp.218–225.   [20] Keefe, *Water and the Word*, vol. I, pp.67–69.

[21] Arnold Angenendt, 'Die Liturgie und die Organisation des kirchlichen Lebens auf dem Lande', in *Cristianizzazione ed organizzazione ecclesiastica delle campagne nell'alto medioevo*, Settimane di studio 28 (Spoleto, 1982), pp.173ff.

Ordinations and the Ember Days 183

no mention of his previous confusion, seeming to make thereby a similar choice as the bishops at Mainz.[22] Nevertheless, association of the Ember Days with the Roman locations in which these three days were celebrated continued to be a constant element of Frankish use.

Ordo 15, for example, makes particularly plain the identity between the Ember Days (here correctly located in Roman tradition), the Roman stations and the ordination ceremonies that ideally would fall upon them. At n.84:

> Prima vero ebdomada in Quadragesima IIIIta et VI feria et sabbato, **staciones publicas** faciunt et XII lectiones in ipso sabbato consumantur. Et si fuerit ipso sabbato de marcio mense, ordinationis sacerdotum faciunt.[23]

In the case of Weissenburgenses 91's extracts from *Ordo* 15, the use of St Peter's Basilica as venue for the ordinations on Saturday is expressly mentioned.[24]

There is also an additional *ordo* for the Ember Saturday that makes much the same connections, *Ordo* 38. Andrieu discovered this text in a number of manuscripts from the eleventh century and later (some associated with Salzburg), so he deemed it a contemporary creation to his *Pontifical Romano-Germanique* (*c*.950), and to be of Frankish origin.[25] It can, in fact, be found in a ninth-century manuscript, Vienna ÖNB ser. n.2762, the *Kollektar-Ponitifikal* made for Regensburg, which is more than a century earlier, dating from the first half of the ninth century. While Unterkircher suggested the text in the Vienna manuscript was 'inhaltlisch identisch mit OR XXXVIII', there are significant differences.[26] In the Vienna manuscript the text is entitled AD XII LECTIONES AGENDAS. It appears in a miscellaneous section linked to the *Kollektar* portion of the manuscript, with the blessing of the candles on Candlemas soon following, again associating these two occasions of processions, just as the Collection of St Amand does. The text of the *ordo* envisages a stational Ember Saturday. It begins in a church *facta collecta* (the collect being the

---

[22] Hanssens, *Opera omnia*, vol. II, pp.199–201: 'Primi aposotolici semper in decembre mense ... Secunda consecratio est in quarto mense secunda sabbati ... Tertia consecratio celebratur in septembre tertia sabbati ....'

[23] *Les Ordines*, vol. III, pp.115–116: 'On the Wednesday, Friday and Saturday in the first week of Lent, they celebrate a public station each day, and the twelve lections are to be undertaken on that same Saturday. And if it should be that Saturday of the month of March, they perform the ordination of priests.'

[24] *Ordo* 15, n.84: 'In XLma vero prima ebdomada si in mense martio venerit IIII et VI feria seu et sabbato omnes publicas stationes faciunt ad Sanctum Petrum in XII lectionibus ... et ordinantur qui ordinani sunt.'

[25] *Les Ordines*, vol. IV, p.263.

[26] *Kollektar-Pontifikale*, Unterkircher (ed.), p.91: 'identical in terms of content'.

184 *Ordines* for Special Occasions, Ordination and the Ember Days

gathering before procession to the station according to Roman terminology) where a first prayer is said. Images of the cross and candles are lifted, and the people and clergy process with an antiphon 'ad sanctum petrum quo statio fieri debet'.[27] St Peter's was, of course, the correct Roman station for the Ember Saturday, yet the text is actually not a description of the Roman ceremony since it prescribes the singing of the *Benedicite*, a Frankish custom on the Ember Saturday.[28] Notably, the text begins with a note on the timings of the Ember Days, linked to their months as in Frankish custom.[29] This *ordo* is thus something quite similar to a text we find in Collection B, *Ordo* 37.

Ordination

As we have seen, there was a choice of texts available in Francia which explicitly described ordination as it was practised in Rome, probably all written by Frankish observers: *Ordo* 34 (of Collection A), *Ordo* 36 (of St Gallen 614's pilgrim dossier) and *Ordo* 39 (of the Collection of St Amand). While *Ordo* 34 and 36 describe a sequence of grades, *Ordo* 39 is concerned only with the ordination of titular priests in Rome, taking place on the Ember Days. As far as the ninth century is concerned, none of these texts was widely copied beyond the original setting. *Ordo* 34 is found almost only in Collection A manuscripts, with the earliest being BAV Pal.lat.487, while *Ordo* 36 was copied from St Gallen 614 into St Gallen 140. *Ordo* 39 is only witnessed in the single manuscript of the Collection of St Amand, Paris BnF lat.974. The two Frankish texts, *Ordo* 36 and 39, devote particular attention to the stational framework of the ritual.[30] *Ordo* 34 is more circumspect about those details. In this text, the *domnus apostolicus* leads the ceremonies, and the 'aula beati Petri apostoli' (*Ordo* 34, n.18) is the location

---

[27] *Ibid.*, p.92: 'To Saint Peter's, where the station should be done.'

[28] *Ibid.*, p.92: 'sequitur lectio: Angelus domini quam ipse legit qui benedicite cantat. Interim uero dum cantatur benedicite, nullus in ecclesia audeat sedere'.

[29] *Ibid.*, p.91: 'Incipiunt agi duodecim lectiones, in prima mense, hora sexta. In mense quoque quarto, hora tertia, in septimo uero et decimo hora quarta.'

[30] *Ordo* 36, n.5: 'Fit enim conventus populi et congregatio regionum primum ad sanctum Adrianum et inde pergit pontifex una eum populo, precedente solito apparatu, id est, cruces, turibula vel tale, usque ad sanctam Mariam ad presepem'; *Ordo* 36, nn.12–13: 'Deinde advocantur VI feria ad sanctos Apostolos, eo tenore ut supra. Sabbato vero egreditur pontifex ad sanctum Petrum et universae regiones cum eo laetaniam canendo'; *Ordo* 39, title: 'Ordo qualiter in sancta atque apostolica sede, id est beati Petri ecclesia, certis temporibus ordinatio fit, quod ab orthodoxis patribus institutum est, id est mense primo, IIII, VII, X, hoc est in XII lectiones'; *Ordo* 39, n.2: 'Deinde IIII feria, statio in sancta ecclesia sancta Dei genetricis Maria; et procedunt electi seu et omnis clerus'; *Ordo* 39, n.8: 'VI feria veniete, stacio [*sic*] ad sanctos Apostolos. Et procedunt omnes, tam clerus quam et electi'; *Ordo* 38, n.12: 'Sabbato autem veniente in XII lectiones, statio ad beatum Petrum apostolum. Procedit pontifex hora VII et omnis clerus.'

Ordination

of the episcopal ordination, but the topography of the ceremony is not well illustrated, and the orders below bishop in particular are given a relatively limited treatment. The text gives no information on the questions of the timing of when ordinations had to take place, for example. In *Ordo* 34, acolyte and subdeacon receive only the same simple blessing: '*Intercedente beata et gloriosa semperque sola virgine Maria et beato Petro apostolo, salvet et custodiat et protegat te dominus.*'[31] This may help to explain why *Ordo* 34 was not widely copied in Francia outside the manuscripts of Collection A. Most tellingly, the compilers of Collection B chose to discard *Ordo* 34 entirely.

In the place of *Ordo* 34, the Collection B compilers chose to insert another account of ordination, that which they found in the Gelasian Sacramentary, an alternative sequence of the ecclesiastical grades originating purely in Francia that is entitled generally 'ORDO DE SACRIS ORDINIBUS BENEDICENDIS'.[32] In contrast to the sparse copying of *Ordo* 34 specifically in Collection A, the sequence of grades in this text are found in a wide range of manuscripts and its use appears to be the almost universal choice, in all known 'pontifical' manuscripts, as well as our Collection B texts.[33] While the accompanying material can vary, the general form which this *ordo* takes is a series of short rubrics, one pertaining to each one of the grades, then the prayers that would accompany the ceremony. The ceremonies are somewhat more evocative and varied than those in *Ordo* 34, since each of the minor grades generally received something pertaining to their office, the so-called *traditio instrumentorum*. The text addresses more of the ecclesiastical grades than *Ordo* 34, including (in the Gelasian Sacramentary) the *ostiarius* (doorkeeper), lector, exorcist then after them all the grades which are found in *Ordo* 34: acolyte, subdeacon, deacon, priest and bishop. In fact, as Andrieu identified, the rubrics for this ritual originated in an early Frankish set of canons, the *Statuta Ecclesiae Antiqua*, a fifth-century collection from Southern France, where the list also included the psalmist as the lowest grade.[34] Notably, this

---

[31] *Ordo* 34, n.2: 'With the intercession of the blessed and glorious ever virgin Mary and the blessed apostle Peter, may the Lord save and keep and protect you.'

[32] See, for example, *Gellonensis*, Dumas (ed.), p.381: 'The *Ordo* of the Blessings, for the Sacred Orders'; Thompson, 'Ordination Masses'.

[33] For example the two MSS edited by Metzger, *Zwei karolingische Pontifikeln*, 4*–18*; also in BAV 7701, for which: Roger Reynolds, 'The Ritual of Clerical Ordination of the Sacramentarium Gelasianum Saec. VIII: Early Evidence from Southern Italy', in de Clerck and Palazzo (eds.), *Rituels: mélanges offerts*, pp.437–444; repr. in Reynolds, *Clerical Orders*.

[34] *Les Ordines*, vol. III, pp.615–619; Vogel, *Medieval Liturgy*, pp.175–176; Reynolds, 'Clerics in the Early Middle Ages: Hierarchies and Functions', in *Clerics Orders*, pp.26–27; Munier (ed.), *Les statuta ecclesiae antiqua*.

186 *Ordines* for Special Occasions, Ordination and the Ember Days

transformation of canonical rulings into liturgical rubrics is an indication of the possible plasticity of these kinds of text. This is important given that we see canonical rulings written alongside our *ordines* and, even, incorporated in this very sequence of ordinations in the Sacramentary.

Though Andrieu chose to edit the text as it stood in its original form in the *Statuta*, the nearly 300 years before it appeared first in Gelasian Sacramentaries had wrought some changes. Prayers had been supplied to be said during the ceremonies, usually two or more for each of the grades. The prayers for the minor orders had originated in Frankish tradition, but the major orders had an initial core of prayers that were Gregorian, thus from Rome. But to this core were added additional pieces of Frankish redaction, allowing five prayers or even eight texts for the priest, as well as an 'ALLOCUTIO' or 'EXORTATIO AD POPULUM' in the case of both priest and bishop. These additional pieces also accompanied some key rituals that were not part of the Roman customs for the higher clergy such as vesting prayers ('HIC UESTIS EUM CASULAM' for the priest) and the unction of hands or head ('CONSECRATIO MANUUM' prayers conclude the rites for both priest and bishop in the Gelasians).[35] Masses were also given following both the presbyterial and episcopal ordinations. This was much more comprehensive than *Ordo* 34.

In addition, the 'ORDO DE SACRIS ORDINIBUS' tended to contain further commentary of popes. In every manuscript we find an extract from Pope Gregory entitled as such, coming just before the subdeacon's ordination.[36] Of course, such texts directly bore on the regulation of ordinations, but we do have one explicit indication that they might also have had a liturgical role, in the Sacramentary of Drogo, Paris lat.9428. Here the same *Capitulum* of Gregory has the unique title: 'QUANDO ORDINANDI SUNT SUBDIACONI DIACONI ET PRESBITERI DICIT EPISCOPUS.'[37] Thus Gregory's words were actually spoken in the ceremony, in the episcopal church of Metz and perhaps in other places as well, showing

---

[35] Ellard, *Ordination Anointings*.

[36] For example, Cologne 138 fol.35r: 'CAPITULA SANCTI GREGORII PAPAE: Sicut qui inuitatus renuit, quaesitus refugit, sacris altaribus est remouendus, sic qui ultro ambit, uel importunus se ingerit est procul dubio repellendus. Nam qui nititur ad altiora conscendere, quid agit nisi ut crescendo decrescat? Quur non perpenditur, quia benedictio illi, in maledictio conuertitur? Quia ab hoc ut fiat ereticus promouitur?'; *MGH* Epp. II, p.206; *Les Ordines*, vol. I, p.105.

[37] Paris BnF lat.9428, fol.5v: 'WHEN SUBDEACONS, DEACONS AND PRIESTS ARE ORDAINED, THE BISHOP SAYS.'

Ordination 187

the breadth of what could be used or counted as liturgically useful. Moreover, the rubrics were still presented as canons in another manuscript with some *ordines romani*, St Petersburg Q.V.II.n.5, which otherwise lacks a full account of ordination; the rubrics for the *ostiarius* and for the episcopal ordination show up among a set of canons and texts discussing the office of the bishop and his duties, thus showing how the ordination rite illuminated the nature of the office as well.[38]

Finally, the transition from lower grades to higher was marked by an *ordo romanus*, entitled 'ORDO QUALITER IN ROMANA SEDIS APOSTOLICAE ECCLESIA SUBDIACONI DIACONI VEL PRESBYTERI ELEGENDI SUNT'.[39] This is an abbreviated *ordo romanus* that was transmitted via the Old Gelasian Sacramentary, where it appears for the first time attached to the ordination rituals.[40] Thence it became a common accompaniment to the set of grades, and so appears in the manuscripts delineated above. A setting for this *ordo* is given: 'Mensis primi quarti septimi et decimi sabbatorum die in duodecim lectiones ad sanctum Petrum ubi missas celebrantur.'[41] This indicated one of the four Ember Days, the proper time for ordination of the higher grades, and set this firmly in the stational system. However, despite the title and its wide diffusion across ultimately many more manuscripts than most of Andrieu's edited *ordines romani*, the ORDO QUALITER did not accord with true Roman practice in some distinct ways. For example, *Ordo 36* tells us that the scrutiny of the candidates which this *ordo* proposes on Saturday actually happened in Rome on the Wednesday and Friday before the Ember Saturday.[42] We do witness various attempts to adapt details of the 'ORDO QUALITER' within the Sacramentaries by further reference to actual Roman practice. A proportion of them correct the title so that it is only *diaconi* and *presbiteri* who were ordained on the Ember Saturday in St Peter's, leaving aside subdeacons.[43] The Gelasian Sacramentary of Angoulême,

---

[38] Staerk, *Les manuscripts latins*, p.194: 'XCIII Benedictio hostiarii'; p.196: 'Ordo Episcoporum. Episcopus cum ordinatur, duo episcopi ponant . . . .'
[39] 'AN ORDO ON HOW IN THE ROMAN CHURCH OF THE APOSTOLIC SEE SUBDEACONS, DEACONS AND PRIESTS ARE CHOSEN.'
[40] *Liber Sacramentorum*, Eizenhöfer *et al.* (eds.), pp.24–25.
[41] 'On a Saturday of the first, fourth, seventh and tenth months, twelve lections are read at Saint Peter's, where masses are also celebrated.'
[42] *Ordo 36*, nn.5–12; Chavasse, *Le sacramentaire gélasien*, pp.22–27: 'ne peut donc passer pour un *Ordo* d'origine romaine. Il s'inspire certes des rites observés à Rome, mais, avec les anomalies qu'il présente, il n'a pu être rédigé à Rome'.
[43] *Liber Sacramentorum*, Mènard (ed.), p.235: 'Ordo qualiter in Romana Ecclesia **diaconi et presbyteri ordinandi** sunt.'

188   *Ordines* for Special Occasions, Ordination and the Ember Days

notably, adds the detail that the clergy were properly scrutinised on the Ember Wednesday and Friday before the Saturday ordination in St Peter's:

> Mensis primi quarti septimi et decimi **feria IIII et sexta scrutandi sunt ipsi electi secundum canones, si sint digni hoc onus fungi.**[44]

Interestingly a later marginal note in the Sacramentary of Angoulême described the ordination rituals as the practice of a Carolingian bishop, Helias Scotigena (862–875), and framed the sequence as 'secundum ordinem romanum'.[45] In the Sacramentary, therefore, the system of ordinations offered was already a composite and interactive one, drawing on traditions we can today identify as largely Frankish while gesturing to the Roman setting and timing of ordination as a vital component, as well as lacing the canonical words of the popes within.

It is not surprising to see these trends continued and developed in *ordo romanus* manuscripts. The compilers of Collection B may have consulted the original source, the *Statuta Ecclesiae*, because all manuscripts carry the first and lowliest grade, the *psalmista*, which no surviving Gelasian Sacramentary included but which was found in the *Statuta*.[46] If so, it adds to the comprehensiveness of these compilers and the sources they might have used. In the most basic manuscripts of Collection B, notably Verona XCII, Cologne 138 and St Gallen 140, the *Ordo de sacris ordinibus* is made to look more like other *ordines* that precede it since the prayers are merely reduced to *incipits*. Thus, the text appears like a simple list of rubrics. But the sequence does include the accompanying 'ORDO QUALITER IN ROMANA SEDIS APOSTOLICAE' and the 'CAPITULA SANCTI GREGORII'. Interestingly, the prayers accompanying these rubrics applied to the higher grades are also reduced to the basics of the Gregorian, Roman tradition.[47] The additional, Frankish vesting and anointing prayers found in

---

[44] *Engolismensis*, Saint-Roch (ed.), p.316: 'In the first, fourth seventh and tenth month, on the Wednesday and Friday these chosen are examined according to the canons, if they should be worthy to take up this office.'

[45] *Ibid.*, p.312, n.2056: 'Helias Scotigena sic faciebat et episcopus Ugo secundum ordinem romanum: primo dicitur introitus, deinde *Kirrieeleison*, deinde episcopus dicit *oremus* et diaconus *flectamus genua*; collecta de ipso die; deinde ascendit ad sedem et facit quattuor ordines, id est hostiarius, lectores, exorcistas, acolitas; deinde archidiaconus ante episcopum dicat excelsa uoce: *postulat sancta mater ecclesia* et reliqua; deinde erigens se episcopus dicit *auxiliante Domino Deo* et reliqua; deinde altare prosternit se cum ordinandis et dicitur letania; deinde reuertitur ad sedem et facit tres *ordines* id est subdiaconos, diaconos et presbiteros; quibus expletis stant omnes in ordo suo et legit subdiaconus lectione; deinde dicitur responsorium et cetera sicut solitum est et expletum est.'

[46] For example Cologne 138, fol.34r: 'Psalmista id est cantor postea quam ab archidiacono instructus fuerit potest absque scientia episcopi sola iussione presbiteri officium suscipere: Uidete ut quod ore cantatis corde credatis et quod corde creditis operibus probetas.'

[47] For example, Cologne 138, fol.35v.

Ordination

the Gelasian tradition are thus not present. But, again defying the expectation that they might thereby be intending to represent a 'pure' Roman tradition, the compilers of Collection B also addressed ordination in another text which is often found right before the 'ORDO DE SACRIS ORDINIBUS', the *ordo romanus* edited by Andrieu as *Ordo* 37, which appears in Collections A and B.[48]

Entitled 'ORDO QUATTUOR TEMPORUM', it has three basic parts addressing three gaps in the ordination sequence. The first part (nn.1–4) addresses the timing of the Ember Days in the four times of the year, in the same Frankish style as the Council of Mainz: the first week in the first month (March), the second in the fourth month (June), the third in the seventh month (September) and the fourth in the tenth month (December) in the week before Christmas. The second part (nn.5–11) comprises another *ordo* of the Ember Saturday, clearly a Frankish text. It again concerns the ordination of the deacons and priests which would take place. Here the central element is the vesting of those to be ordained deacons in 'orarios et dalmaticis' and those to be ordained priests in 'orarios et planetas' (*orarium* is the stole, not worn by Roman deacons, here with Roman terms for dalmatic and chasuble).[49] There follows a litany, and the pontiff then consecrates them. The final portion of the *Ordo* (nn.12–13) has its own title, 'SABBATO PENTECOSTEN IN XII LECTIONIBUS STATIO AD SANCTUM PETRUM'. This text specifically addresses a foreseen clash between the third Ember Day (of June) and the Saturday of Pentecost, since that day had its own detailed office. Again, this clash would not happen in the Roman system. The placement of *Ordo* 37 before the 'ORDO DE SACRIS ORDINIBUS' suggests that this text was put together to respond to the particular gaps in that text. We should envision that both texts were read in conjunction, and the layout informs us that the Sacramentary usually had to be employed as well. In ordination, as elsewhere, Collection B suggests that readers might draw on a sequence of such texts and various sources to put together a coherent account of the individual ceremonies, whether they required such an account to perform the rituals or sought to understand them. For example, a marginal note adds an unattributed quote from Amalarius below *Ordo* 37A in St Gallen 140, one manuscript of Collection B: 'XII Lectiones propter XII lectores dicuntur non propter XII uarietates sententiarum.'[50] In another case, one

---

[48] *Les Ordines*, vol. IV, pp.209–254.   [49] *Ibid.*, pp.129–136.

[50] St Gallen 140, p.328: '[Called] 12 readings because they are said by 12 lectors, not on account of 12 separate extracts'; Hanssens, *Opera omnia*, vol. II, pp.197, apparently six readings were read in Greek and in Latin 'ab antiquis Romanis'.

190 *Ordines* for Special Occasions, Ordination and the Ember Days

manuscript, Munich Clm 14510 has a unique accompaniment, a further list of rubrics of actions undertaken in ordination, placed oddly between the *ostiarius* and *lector*. Many of them agree with the 'ORDO DE SACRIS ORDINIBUS', but for the deacon and the priest some further details of the ceremony were here attested: 'A diacono ponit pontifex orarium super collum eius' and 'Ad presbiterum uero benedicit pontifex manus cum chrisma super altare'.[51]

Different individual manuscripts of Collection B, therefore, could easily approach this sequence with differing priorities than the original compilers. Several, for example, returned to the Sacramentary as a source and replaced prayer texts that had been removed. In the surviving portions of Zurich Car. C 102, the full prayers are given and align fully with those found in the Gelasians of the Eighth Century, including for example the 'PRESBITERORUM CONSECRATIO MANUUM' (fol.32v). Munich Clm 14510 also consulted a Sacramentary and filled in the prayers, but it appears to have used a more diverse, local tradition. For the episcopal Mass, for example, the 'POST COMMUNIONEM, *Plenum Quaesumus domine*' and the 'SECRETA '*Suscipe domine*' are both only found in the Old Gelasian Sacramentary's episcopal Mass, and not in any known Gelasians of the Eighth Century at all.[52] Surviving fragments suggest that this kind of Sacramentary was known and used in Regensburg.[53] But, though this might suggest the adaptation of the ordination to local tastes, Munich Clm 14510 also extracted something else from the Sacramentary, placed just before the episcopal ordination:

> AD PONTIFICEM ORDINANDUM QUAE ADDI DEBEAT IN CONSECRATIONE CUIUS INITIUM EST *Deus honorem omnium* ad locum *et idirco huic famulo tuo quem apostolicae sedis presulem et primatum omnium* . . ..[54]

This was the final formula in the Gregorian Sacramentary as it had come from Rome, and therefore it must have been specifically sought out and

---

[51] Munich Clm 14510, fol.65r; *Les Ordines*, vol. I, pp.234–235: 'To the deacon, the pontiff places the stole over his shoulder. But to the priest the pontiff blesses his hand with chrism over the altar.'

[52] *Liber Sacramentorum*, Eizenhöfer *et al.* (eds.), 773, p.122.

[53] Carl I. Hammer, 'The Social Landscape of the Prague Sacramentary: The Prosopography of an Eighth Century Mass Book', *Traditio*, 54 (1999), pp.44: 'In eighth-century Bavaria, sacramentaries of the Old Gelasian type were probably the norm'; the fragments have been edited by Petrus Siffrin, 'Zwei Blätter eines Sakramentars in irischer Schrift des 8. Jahrhunderts aus Regensburg (Berlin, Preußische Staatsbibliothek. Ms. lat. fol.877)', *Jahrbuch für Liturgiewissenschaft*, 10 (1930), pp.1–39.

[54] Munich Clm 14510, fol.70r: 'AT THE ORDINATION OF THE POPE THESE MUST BE ADDED IN THE CONSECRATION WHOSE BEGINNING IS: *Deus honorum omnium* at this place: *et idcirco huic famulo* . . ..'

Ordination 191

placed here by the Regensburg compiler.[55] As the wording concerning the apostolic see shows, this was the adjustment made to the episcopal ordination only when the bishop being ordained was the Pope himself. It therefore had no direct applicability in the case of the ordinations as they had been recorded in this manuscript, but must be more understood as telling us something about how ordination was supposed to be understood as linked to the Pope's special status. We have already seen the papal ordination described in *Ordo* 40 which is found likewise associated with the 'ORDO DE SACRIS ORDINIBUS' in Cologne 138, another copy of Collection B.

It is also true that two manuscripts of Collection B, Cologne 138 and Paris BnF 14088 which is very close to it, presented the additional text, *Ordo* 37 in quite a different way (edited by Andrieu as *Ordo* 37B); it later passes into several eleventh-century manuscripts, generally from Bavaria, in this form.[56] The first part (nn.1–4), with the timing of the Ember Days, is largely maintained but the third part with the details of the Pentecost Saturday, is absent entirely. There are several new elements too. The text explicitly links the Ember Days to the Saturday 'IN XII LECTIONES' and the Mass for that occasion is to complete the fast.[57] Then the *ordo* added two details about Roman practice:

> Sacros ordines in aecclesia romana de eis qui dicuntur cardenales tradi consuerunt (ad introitum).[58]

There follows:

> Et in ipsis quattuor superscriptis mensium temporibus qualicumque die domnus apostolicus voulerit, ad sacros ordines parrochianos clericos per omnes aecclesias si necessitas fuerit benedicit.[59]

The *Ordo* for this ceremony is then introduced 'ET HIC EST ORDO'. The Frankish elements of the ordination rite which the other Collection

---

[55] *Le sacramentaire gregorien*, Deshusses (ed.), 1018, p.348.   [56] *Les Ordines*, vol. IV, pp.241–254.

[57] *Ordo* 37B, n.5: 'Et si vigilia natalis domini in sabbato evenit, in antecedente ebdomada suprascriptum ieiunium die sabbati <celebratur>, quando XII lectiones leguntur et cum missis et oblationibus ipsa ieiunia consummantur.'

[58] *Les Ordines*, vol. IV, p.250: 'The Holy Orders in the Roman Church are kept to be handed over by those who are called cardinals (at the Introit)'; in Paris BnF lat.14008 fol.115r the words *ad introitum* appear here, but they are not given in Andrieu's edition. They may be an attempt to harmonise with the *Ordo Qualiter Romana Aecclesia* which is part of the following text, the *Ordo de sacris ordinibus*, but seems correct and make sense of the text.

[59] *Ibid.*, p.250: 'And in these four above said times of the months on whatever of the days the Lord Apostolic should wish, he blesses parish clergy to the holy orders for all the churches, if there should be necessity'; Cologne 138, fol.33v; the reading here is better than that given in *Les Ordines*, vol. IV, p.250.

192 *Ordines* for Special Occasions, Ordination and the Ember Days

B manuscripts offered, for example the vesting of the new clergy in their stoles and chasubles left on the altar overnight, are also removed from *Ordo* 37B. The text thus ends by pointing its reader directly to the Sacramentary.[60] In these manuscripts, the Roman institutions are foregrounded in this section, and the papal ordination follows, presenting a very Roman introduction and context to the following sequence of Frankish rites.

In order to understand how such texts might function, other manuscripts which make a similar blend of Roman and Frankish rituals present us with some possibilities. In addition to Collection B, but independently, another manuscript extracted the full sequence of the 'ORDO DE SACRIS ORDINIBUS' from the Sacramentary: Wolfenbüttel Weissenburgenses 91 fols.77v–83r.[61] As we have seen, this manuscript had access to Collection A and used it to construct a manuscript that presents itself both as a 'pontifical' for the use of a bishop and a document of the Roman liturgical past and present. Like Collection B, but independently of it, Weissenburgenses 91's creators employed the Sacramentary at several instances, and one of these was the addition of the full sequence of the 'ORDO DE SACRIS ORDINIBUS'. The absence of the *psalmista* from the sequence is one of the key indications that Weissenburgenses 91 did not depend on Collection B but extracted the text independently from the Sacramentary, where the psalmist does not appear, though (like Collection B) it also reduced the prayer texts to *incipits*.[62] The *ostiarius*, *lector* and *exorcistae* present the rubrics plainly, in sequence, but when we come to the acolyte something different occurs (the bold letter is highlighted in the text).

> Acolytus cum ordinatur primum ab episcopo doceatur qualiter in officio suo agere debeat . sed ab archidiacono accipiat cereofarium cum cereo ut sciat se ad accendenda ecclesiae luminaria mancipari. Accipiat et orciolum uacuum ad suggerendum uinum in eucharistia corporis Christi. **D**um missa celebrata fuerit induunt clericum illum planeta et orario dumque uenerit episcopus aut ipse domnus apostolicus ad communicandum faciunt eum uenire ad se et porregit in ulnas suas sacculum super planeta et prosternit se in terra cum ipso sacculo et dat ei orationem sic: Intercedente beata et gloriosa semperque sola uirgine maria et beato petro apostoli salute et custodiat et protegat te dominus. Respondet

---

[60] *Ordo* 37B, n.8: 'Prosequitur sacerdos orationem sicut in Sacramentorum continet.'

[61] *Les Ordines*, vol. I, pp.456–457; vol. III, p.538.

[62] Another clue is the prayer for the subdeacon 'Exhibeatur in conspectus episocopi patena et calix uacuus et dicat episcopus: Uide cuius ministerium ibi traditur . . .'; while found in Gelasians, it was not taken up by Collection B manuscripts, but appears in Weissenburgenses 91 in full.

Ordination 193

omnes amen. Item oratio *si uis. Domine sancta pater omnipotens aeterne deus usque uirtute confirma per.*[63]

From 'Acolytus cum ordinatur' to 'eucharistia corporis Christi', the text is the usual rubric from the Sacramentary's 'ORDO DE SACRIS ORDINIBUS'. But then, with a small capital separating it, the text offers the section of *Ordo* 34 pertaining to the acolyte, *Ordo* 34 nn.1–2. The prayer provided 'if you wish' in incipit is the usual Gelasian blessing for the acolyte.[64] Thus, the Roman rite of ordination indicating the presence of the *domnus apostolicus* is sandwiched between the two elements of the Frankish, Gelasian rite where only a Frankish *episcopus* was present.

The subdeacon and deacon are presented quite similarly, coming after the 'ORDO QUALITER' text. The former (fol.79r–v) has the Gelasian rubric 'Subdiaconus cum ordinatur . . .' and the full formula of the handing over of a chalice and paten (not found in Collection B either), then the heading 'SEQUITUR', the *Ordo* 34, n.3 concerning the subdeacon in Rome, then 'Deinde sequitur benediction' and the two Gelasian prayers in incipit. The deacon (fols.79v–80r) has the rubric 'Diaconus cum ordinatur . . .', and following it *Ordo* 34, nn.4–9 with the Gelasian prayer given in incipit where it was left unspecified in the original text.[65] Something similar is done for the priest (fol.80r–v) with *Ordo* 34, nn.10–13. For the case of the bishop, the short rubric of the 'ORDO DE SACRIS ORDINIBUS', 'Episcopus cum ordinatur . . .', is presented as introduction to the long two-day ceremony of election and consecration given in *Ordo* 34, nn.14–45, where the Pope checks the suitability of the candidate, in the aula 'beati Petri apostoli', and blesses him.

While it is difficult to get a sense of it from Andrieu's edition, this sequence is quite strange and confusing. It does not really present a coherent or usable account of ordinations. The focus and setting of the ceremonies in *Ordo* 34 is

---

[63] Wolfenbüttel Weissenburgenses 91 fol.78r–v: 'The acolyte when he is ordained first by the bishop should be taught how in his office he should act, then from the archdeacon he receives the candlestick with a candle so he should know to care for the lighting of the lights of the church. He also receives an empty cruet for carrying the wine in the eucharist of the body of Christ. Then, when the Mass is to be celebrated, the cleric clothes himself in the dalmatic and stole and when the bishop or Lord Apostolic comes to communicate they lead him and he places over his arms the purse over the dalmatic and the cleric prostrates himself on the earth with this purse and the bishop gives to him a prayer thus: *Intercedente beata et gloriosa semperque sola uirgine maria et beato petro apostoli salute et custodiat et protegat te dominus.* Everyone responds: Amen. Then the prayer if you wish: *Domine sancta pater omnipotens aeterne deus* until *uirtute confirma per.*'

[64] For example, *Gellonensis*, Dumas (ed.), p.383.

[65] See *Ordo* 34, n.9 var.9: 'et statim dat ei orationem consecrationis <Adesto quaesumus omnipotens Deus honorum datur, ordinum distributor, officiorumque dispositor, usque: potiore capere mereatur. Per dominum>, et reliquae orationes'.

194 *Ordines* for Special Occasions, Ordination and the Ember Days

entirely different from the Gelasian rubrics now interrupting it, and the place which those rubrics would take in the full unfolding is very unclear. The protagonists shift repeatedly between the *episcopus* and the *domnus apostolicus*. Marginal notes possibly alluded to this confusion, adding the letter R at each point the text shifts to *Ordo* 34 for the subdeacon and deacon (fol.79v), and the priest (fol.80v), which usually meant 'Require' and indicated the need to check the examplar.[66] In any case, it can only be assumed that the compilers knew their readers would not be reading the *ordines* for step-by-step instructions to follow, but rather expected that they would be able to sift from this what was valuable and useful. The complexity of this arrangement demanded the attention of a self-conscious and informed reader before it came to be put into practice. Adding to the resources that were expected to be marshalled, Weissenburgenses 91 also includes several references pointing to the Sacramentary.[67] Nevertheless, the fact that the Roman rites performed by the *domnus apostolicus* here appear in direct continuity and sequence with the Frankish rites that the bishop would actually practise is surely no accident, and the set-up in, for example, Cologne 138 with *Ordo* 37B and the papal ordination preceding the Frankish 'ORDO DE SACRIS ORDINIBUS', offers very similar resources for the same process, allowing a sense of direct descent by ordination, even through liturgical variation. A similar drawing together of *Ordo* 34 with the 'ORDO DE SACRIS ORDINIBUS' can be found in the Pontifical written in Milan, likely of the tenth century but drawing on earlier French sources.[68] This manuscript has the full 'ORDO DE SACRIS ORDINIBUS' as in the Gelasian Sacramentary, beginning with the *ostiarius*. Here it is only from the deacon onwards that rubrics from *Ordo* 34 are added to the texts for each grade.[69] We thus encounter the same addition of rubrics to the texts for the presbyterial ordination.[70] Therefore the idea of presenting the Roman *Ordo* 34 as part of a sequence with the Frankish rites, despite the

---

[66] Steinová, *Notam superponere studui*, p.220.

[67] *Ordo* 34, n.12 var.6: 'Et tunc illi dante orationem consecrat illum presbiterum sicut Sacramentorum continent'; *Ordo* 34, n.40, var.6: 'Completa vero laetenia surgent et tunc benedicet eum <sicut in Sacramentorum continent>.'

[68] Milan, Biblioteca del capitolo metropolitano, cod.D.I. 12, ed. In *Pontificale in usum ecclesiae Mediolanensis*, Marco Magistretti (ed.) (Milan, 1900), pp.1–92; see Rasmussen, *Les pontificaux*, pp.422–423. The Canon of the Mass copied here has only Frankish saints listed as in the Gelasian (Hilary, Martin, Benedict and Gregory), and no Milanese ones, nor does the manuscript reflect Ambrosian rituals.

[69] *Pontificale*, Magistretti (ed.), p.43: 'Dum uero consecratus fuerit induitur stola et dalmatica et dat osculum episcopo et sacerdotibus; et stat ad dexteram episcoporum'; compare *Ordo* 34, n.10.

[70] *Ibid.*, p.45: 'Tuncque tenens eum archidiaconus ducit extra rugas altaris, exuit cum dalmatic et reducit ad episcopum sive ipse sive presbyter'; p.49: 'Et dat osculum episcopo et sacerdotibus et stat in ordine presbyterorum'; compare *Ordo* 34, nn.11–12.

The Ordination Rite of Arn of Salzburg

strangeness of the combination at first glance, occurred to Franks as a way to make use of the rarer text and preserve the Roman details. Presumably, a negotiation could be made between these two rites in practice.

The Ordination Rite of Arn of Salzburg

Excerption was made of Roman rites and examples of Roman canonical authority to build up and buttress the writing down of Frankish rites. In Vienna ÖNB ser.n.2762, the *Kollektar-Pontifikale* written for Regensburg in the first half of the ninth century, now fragmentary, there are some significant advances in these trends. Along with the other rites it contains (church dedication, ordination of an abbot and abbess), the Regensburg Pontifical also contains an unusually developed and (indeed) precocious example of the sequence of ordination rituals. Its text began with a dossier of accompanying texts on ordination as a sort of introduction, including prayers for tonsure and 'AD CLERICUM FACIENDUM' from the Sacramentary, a copy of one of the Ordinals of Christ (now lost except for the title 'DE OFFICIIS VII GRADUM'), the canon of Innocent, the citation of Timothy, the *Capitulum* of Gregory the Great, and the Gelasian 'ORDO QUALITER IN ROMANA ECCLESIA PRESBITERI DIACONI VEL SUBDIACONI ELEGENDI SUNT', here placed before the sequence of ordinations actually began.[71] Another text presented here is new, entitled: 'CANON SANCTI GREGORII DE SACRIS ORDINIBUS', giving some diverse regulations about ordination of priests, monks and abbots.[72] These texts are actually extracts from the so-called Penitential of Theodore of Canterbury.[73] The ordination rites in the Vienna Pontifical were thus introduced by a varied set of canons that dealt with wide-ranging questions, as well as pieces of rituals whose exact place in the sections following was unclear. Again, place was made in this liturgical book for various pieces of

---

[71] *Kollektar Pontifikale*, Unterkircher (ed.), pp.100–103.

[72] *Ibid.*, p.102: 'CANON SANCTI GREGORII DE SACRIS ORDINIBUS. In ordinatione presbiteri vel diaconi oportet episcopus missam cantare. Similiter et greci faciunt quando abbatem eligunt uel abbatissam. In monachi ordinatione abbas debet missam cantare et tres orationes complere super caput eius et septem dies uelet caput suum et septimo die abbas tollat uelamen, sicut in baptismo presbiter septimo die uelamen infantum absulit, ita et abbas debet monacho quia secundus baptismo est uel iuxta iudicium patrum et omnia peccata dimittuntur, sicut in baptismo. In abbatis ordinatione episcopus debet missam complere et eum benedicere inclinato capite cum duobus uel tribus ex fratribus suis et dat ei baculum et pedules.'

[73] T. M. Charles-Edwards, 'The Penitential of Theodore and the Iudicia Theodori', in Michael Lapidge (ed.), *Archbishop Theodore: Commemorative Studies on His Life and Influence*, Cambridge Studies in Anglo-Saxon England 11 (Cambridge, 1995), pp.141–74.

196 *Ordines* for Special Occasions, Ordination and the Ember Days

contextual information, explaining what the grades were and what they meant. The following liturgical texts could be read in much the same way.

The text here begins with the lowliest grade; 'Psalmista id est cantor . . ..' The presence of the psalmist indicates the consultation of the original source, the *Statuta Ecclesiae Antiqua*, not just the Sacramentary. The succeeding grades remain very fragmentary until part of the way through the acolyte. Deviations from *Ordo* 34 in both following texts have been put in bold.

> . . . **uestimenta officialia et** faciant illum uenire **ante episcopum, et** porrigit ei **archidiaconus** sacculum super planetam et prosternit se in terra cum ipso et dat ei **pontifex** orationem hanc: ***Domine sancte pater omnipotens aeterne deus*** . . ..[74]

Thus, we have here something closely resembling *Ordo* 34 but, instead of the Roman prayer from *Ordo* 34, '*Intercedente beata* . . .', the normal Gelasian blessing for the acolyte is given as the prayer. A second rubric comes afterwards, opening the subdeacon's grade.

> **Et si ibi ad prasens eum** uoluerit ad subdiaconatus **ordinem promouere, tollatur ab eo sacculus quem ab archidiacono iam dudum susceperat, et stet in medio apud archidiaconum,** et iuret i**pso tangente super** sancti Christi quattuor euangelia secundum canones. **ITEM DE SUBDIACONO. ORDINATIO SUBDIACONI Subdiaconus cum ordinatur** . . ..[75]

The subdeacon's ordination continues from there with the Gelasian preface, until it is cut by the lacuna in the text. As is made clear here, the general idea of *Ordo* 34 is followed, but already the text has been adjusted to a new setting. Instead of the *domnus apostolicus*, the celebrant is the episcopus or *pontifex*. Klaus Gamber and the editor of the Vienna manuscript, Franz Unterkircher, related these rubrics to the complete text *Ordo* 35, today only known in London BM Add.15222, the eleventh-century copy of Collection A in a 'pontifical' of Besançon.[76] The same adjustments to *Ordo* 34 for the acolyte and subdeacon appear there. Andrieu interpreted *Ordo* 35 as a Roman text redacted in the late tenth century, but there are significant problems with this reconstruction, not least that some pieces of the same

---

[74] *Kollektar-Pontifikale*, Unterkircher (ed.), p.103: 'in his official vestments and they should make him come before the bishop, and the archdeacon should vest him in the pouch over his chasuble and he should prostrate himself in the earth with him and the pontiff gives him this prayer: *Domine sancte pater omnipotens* (etc.)'.

[75] *Ibid.*, p.104: 'And then if he should wish to promote the man to the subdiaconate, the archdeacon should take from him the pouch which he had once given him, and he should stand in the middle with the archdeacon, and he should swear, touching him with the four Gospels of Holy Christ according to the canons.'

[76] *Ibid.*, pp.40–41.

The Ordination Rite of Arn of Salzburg

text appear here in the Vienna manuscript, written in the first half of the ninth century in Bavaria.[77]

For the presbyterial ordination and bishop's ordination which appear next, however, *Ordo* 34 was rejected entirely and instead we find the Frankish rites, in both cases expanded beyond the Gelasian rubric to a much fuller presentation of the ritual. For the priest this includes a page-long rubric including the Frankish rite of vesting.[78] The bishop has a much longer text, comprising an evaluation and a consecration on the next day. It is compared in the Unterkircher edition to Andrieu's *Ordo* 35B. In the Vienna manuscript, however, it is undertaken not by the *domnus apostolicus*, as in *Ordo* 35, but by the *domnus metropolitanus*.[79] Regensburg was of course not a metropolitan see, and thus its bishop when the manuscript was compiled, Baturich, would never have led this ceremony. This text has nothing of the specific Roman details of *Ordo* 34. The series of questions are different, and directed only to the person to be ordained bishop and not (as in *Ordo* 34) in parallel to the representatives of the city to which he is to be ordained (their consent is briefly dealt with at the end: *cum consensu clericorum et laicorum*). The shape of the ceremony of ordination does follow the same general pattern as *Ordo* 34: procession to the church, introit (here *Benedixit te hodie deus*), no *Kyrie*, the first prayer (*Adesto supplicationibus nostris . . .*), the reading of the epistle (1 Timothy in *Ordo* 34, Titus in Vienna), the gradual, the clothing of the metropolitan, announcement to the 'Clerus et plebs', litany, benediction, alleluia, gospel reading and a final Mass. However the climax of the ceremony in the Vienna manuscript is the ceremony from the 'ORDO DE SACRIS ORDINIBUS', where the metropolitan holds a hand over the new bishop's head and blesses him, here 'lenta voce', and two other bishops hold the book of Gospels over his shoulders, while other bishops standing around place their hands there as well.[80] This was foreign to Rome, except in the papal ordination. Interestingly, the text also diverges sharply from

---

77 For *Ordo* 35, *Les Ordines*, vol. IV, pp.3–46; Westwell, 'Content and Ideological Construction'.

78 *Kollektar-Pontifikale*, Unterkircher (ed.), p.105: 'Post lectionum autem et tractum parato electo qui presbiter ordinandus diaconi more absque orario tamen . . . accipiens orarium et casulam inponens ei, eoque inclinator, inponet manum super caput eius et omnes presbiteri qui adsunt pariter cum eo, et ille dans orationem super eum.'

79 *Ibid.*, p.108: 'Episcopus cum ordinatur, primo progreditur domnus metropolitanus cum cuncto clero ad ecclesiam, ubi ipsam fieri uult ordinationem . . . Interim autem innuit domnus metropolitanus . . . .'

80 *Ibid.*, p.109: 'Finita letania elevat ipsum electum domnus metropolitanus et ponit caput eius super altare, et duo episcopi ponant se teneant evangelium super verticem eius. Reliqui ergo omnes qui adsunt episcopi manus super caput eius ponant et domnus metropolitanus infundens benedictionem super eum dicens lenta uoce: DOMINUS UOBISCUM. Propitiare domine . . . .'

198 *Ordines* for Special Occasions, Ordination and the Ember Days

the peculiarities of the other 'pontifical' associated with Baturich of Regensburg, Munich Clm 14510, since there are no signs of the Old Gelasian prayers in the episcopal Mass. This is because the text certainly represents the copy of an exemplar from elsewhere.

The metropolitan rite described here is a startlingly early version of the text that later appears in some manuscripts which Andrieu categorised as the *Pontifical Romano-Germanique*. Among those manuscripts, many are associated with Salzburg. As identified by Unterkircher, the series of interrogations of the new bishop are found otherwise in Andrieu's *Ordo* 35B, which is taken from an eleventh-century manuscript, Rome, Biblioteca Alessandrina, cod.173. That manuscript was, however, clearly copied from a Salzburg exemplar.[81] Our manuscript precedes this manuscript by at least a century and a half. The Vienna manuscript reveals that this text was in fact a Carolingian invention, something Andrieu could not have known since the Vienna manuscript was not available to him. But where or for whom did this invention take place? Since it concerns rites performed by a metropolitan, it is unlikely the text was written originally for the bishop of Regensburg, Baturich. Instead, a monk from a monastery he owned, Mondsee near Salzburg, appears to have copied this text, and more likely the whole of the manuscript, Vienna, ÖNB, MS 2762, working from an exemplar originally written for a metropolitan church. The obvious choice is the metropolitan church of Bavaria, Salzburg. In fact, the most likely candidate for the creation of the ordination rite here written, and for designing the format and content of the exemplar of the Vienna manuscript, is the first metropolitan of that see, Arn of Salzburg, who was perhaps a relative of Baturich.[82] A number of indications add up to compelling evidence:

1) Like Sankt-Emmeram in Regensburg, the community of the Abtei Sankt Peter in Salzburg was under the leadership of the city's bishop, who was simultaneously abbot there.[83] The unusual format of the *Kollektar-Pontifikale* was explained by Unterkircher and Gamber by relation to this double office, which applied just as well to Salzburg as to Regensburg.

---

[81] *Les Ordines*, vol. IV, pp.79–110 at *Ordo* 35B, n.12; the interrogation contains a new question not found in the earlier, Vienna MS: 'Vis sanctae Iuvavensi ecclesiae et michi et successoribus meis fidem et subiectioneum exhibere?', meaning this Italian (Roman?) book had used a Salzburg exemplar.

[82] Wilhelm Störmer, 'Eine Adelsgruppe um die Fuldaer Äbte Sturmi und Eigil und den Holzkirchener Klostergründer Troand', in *Gesellschaft und Herrschaft, Festgabe für Karl Bosl* (Munich, 1969), pp.25ff.

[83] Heinz Dopsch, 'Salzburg zur Zeit Erzbischofs Arns', in Niederkorn-Bruck and Scharer (eds.), *Erzbischof Arn von Salzburg*, pp.27–29; the analogous situation in Regensburg and Salzburg is noted by Gamber's comments in *Kollektar-Pontifikale*, Unterkircher (ed.), p.42.

The Ordination Rite of Arn of Salzburg
199

2) The uniquely early copy of *Ordo* 38, which would subsequently show up in much later Salzburg manuscripts, gives a church of Saint Peter as the locus of the Ember Saturday Mass. The cathedral of Salzburg had that dedication, just as the Cathedral of Regensburg does. The text also records 'vexilla sanctae crucis' leading the procession, a specific detail edited out in the later copies. Salzburg famously possessed an object, the *Rupertkreuz*, that fulfilled this very function.[84]

3) Arn has already been shown above to have been an author of *ordines* specifically for metropolitan functions. He seems to have created an *ordo* for a council also led by the *domnus metropolitanus*.[85] Despite being non-Roman, the text carries the title 'ORDO ROMANUS' (a version of it is found in Cologne 138).[86]

4) The *Kollektar-Pontifikale* carries two collects for the feast day of Saint Emmeram, taken from Alcuin's Mass for a patron saint which was variously adapted to the local saint as needed.[87] Alcuin's Mass is otherwise only known in Bavaria for the feast day of Rupert of Salzburg in the deposit of Alcuin's Masses in the Trent Pre-Hadrianic Gregorian Sacramentary, a copy from a Salzburg exemplar Alcuin shared with Arn himself.[88] Arn therefore knew Alcuin's Mass. Baturich's scribe probably had access to the collect from Arn and had it changed from Rupert to Emmeram in the copying. The presence of a vigil of All Saints among the collects would also point to Alcuin's recommendation of this feast to his friend, Arn.[89]

Adding to its comprehensiveness, the Vienna manuscript also contained the Canon of the Mass, a direct borrowing from the Sacramentary that is

---

[84] Dopsch, 'Salzburg zur Zeit Erzbischofs Arn', p.39.

[85] Schneider, *Konzilsordines*, p.56; Herbert Schneider, 'Karolingische Kirchen- und Liturgiereform. Ein konservativer Neuaufbruch', in Christoph Stiegemann and Matthias Wemhoff (eds.), *Kunst und Kultur der Karolingerzeit. Karl der Große und Papst Leo III in Paderborn*, vol. II (Mainz, 1999), pp.772–781, 779.

[86] Martin Klöckener, 'L'importance des sources liturgiques pour la connaissance de la pensée et des mentalités médiévales', in Hélène Bricout and Martin Klöckener (eds.), *Liturgie, Pensée Théologique et Mentalités Religieuses Au Haut Moyen Âge: Le témoignage des sources liturgiques* (Münster, 2016), pp.13–47.

[87] *Kollektar-Pontifikale*, Unterkircher (ed.), p.67: 'Deus qui nos deuota beati Emmer<am>i martyris tui atque pontific<is>': Deshusses, 'Les anciens sacramentaires de Tours', pp.287–288.

[88] Trent Castello del Buoncosiglio Cod.M.N.1590, see Ferdinando dell'Oro, Bonifatius Barrofio, Ioseph Ferraro, Hyginus Rogger (eds.), *Monumenta Liturgica Ecclesiae Tridentinae*, vol. II/a: Fontes Liturgici. Libri Sacramentorum (Trent, 1985), p.368: 'Deus qui nos devota beati Hrodperthi confessoris ...'; Deshusses, 'Le sacramentaire grégorien de Trente'; Klaus Gamber, 'Ein Salzburger Sakramentarfragment des 10. Jahrhunderts mit zwei Rupert-Messe', *Heiliger Dienst*, 15 (1961), pp.81–91.

[89] *Kollektar-Pontifikale*, Unterkircher (ed.), p.66; *MGH* Epp. IV, 321; Arn would also legislate the celebration of All Saints' at Rispach in 798, *MGH* Conc.II.i, p.197.

200 *Ordines* for Special Occasions, Ordination and the Ember Days

unusual in pontificals.[90] The Canon is placed with prayers for the Mass following an ordination of a bishop, making ordination central in this manuscript. Moreover, it seems that before the redaction of this rite in this form there may not have existed a full *ordo* of the episcopal ordination as practised in Francia. Certainly, no other has survived until some time later.

That is also the impression we receive from a later letter of Hincmar of Reims (bishop 845–882) to Bishop Adventius of Metz (bishop 855–875).[91] It seems Adventius had asked Hincmar for an example of the *consecrationem episcopi* to help him with the consecration of a new archbishop of Trier in 869/870, and Hincmar sent him a full narrative recording how he was accustomed to consecrate and how he himself had been consecrated in 845 ('qualiter ordinationem agamus episcopi et qualiter in me acta fuerunt').[92] Andrieu noted correctly that the rite Hincmar describes to Adventius does not accord with his *Ordo* 34 at all but, since he did not know the Vienna manuscript, he could not compare it to a witness close to Hincmar's own day. But the shape of the ritual clearly shares a great deal with the Vienna manuscript, and there are some particularly important moments of overlap which show us that the Vienna *Ordo* is a new, written version of what Hincmar was describing from memory, representing the ritual as it had already been shared by the metropolitans and bishops of Francia.

One of the most important overlaps is the mention of the Council of Carthage in the preliminary Saturday session, detailing that the new bishop should know the Catholic faith.[93] The very same Council was appealed to in the opening formula for the Saturday session in our Vienna manuscript (the page concerned is lost and the Vienna manuscript begins at *trinitatis*, but the text is easily reconstructed since it is identical to that found in other

---

[90] *Kollektar-Pontifikale*, Unterkircher (ed.), pp.94–97, commentary on p.41; the Milanese Pontifical also copies it, but few others.

[91] Michel Andrieu, 'Le sacre épiscopal d'après Hincmar de Rheims', *Revue d'histoire ecclésiastique*, 48 (1953), pp.22–73. The Liege manuscript from which Sirmond originally published this letter is now lost, seeming to be a collection of Hincmar's liturgical compositions including his coronation *ordo*, *Ordines coronationis Franciae*, Jackson (ed.), vol. I, pp.73–74; for Adventius: Michèle Gaillard, 'Un évêque et son temps, Advence de Metz (858–875)', in Hans-Walter Herrmann and Reinhard Schneider (eds.), *Lotharingia. Eine europäische Kernlandschaft um das Jahr 1000. Referate eines Kolloquiums vom 24. bis 26. Mai 1994 in Saarbrücken* Veröffentlichungen der Kommission für Saarländische Landesgeschichte und Volksforschung, 26 (Saarbrücken 1995), pp.89–119.

[92] *Ibid.*, p.72: 'How we undertake the ordination of a bishop, and how this act was done for me.'

[93] Andrieu, 'Le sacre épiscopal', p.31: 'examinandus est idem electus ab episcopis secundum capitulum Carthaginensis concilii, quo manifestatur qualis debeat ordinari episcopi so ita credat et simplicibus uerbis catholicam fidem profiteaetur, sicut ibidem scriptum habetur'.

The Ordination Rite of Arn of Salzburg

manuscripts used by Andrieu).[94] In fact the reference here is to a part of the *Statuta Ecclesiae Antiqua*, which circulated under this false attribution to Carthage in, among other places, the Pseudo-Isidorian Collection.[95] Indeed, in one of our manuscripts also including *Ordo* 17, BAV, Pal. lat.574, the *Statuta* appears within the canonical collection as a SYNODUS AFRICANUS (fols.18v–25r), including the ordination rubrics.

Before the ordination texts employed as the 'ORDO DE SACRIS ORDINIBUS', the *Statuta* had a long preface describing what a bishop should be able to assent to, which was then adapted to the explicit series of questions in our Vienna manuscripts. Hincmar had in mind a similar series of questions using the same preface. As the attribution to Carthage circulated and spread, it is clear that the ordination rites in the 'ORDO DE SACRIS ORDINIBUS' also described there would gain currency as authoritative. Liturgical use and pseudo-canonical authority fed off each other. The creator of the ordination rite sequence in the Vienna manuscript, likely to be Arn himself, certainly had direct access to the *Statuta* probably under the name of the Council of Carthage, for he added the rite of the psalmist which was there, and not in the Sacramentary. The climax of this ritual, the holding of the Gospel Book over the bishop elect as he is consecrated, is identical in Hincmar's description.[96] Hincmar does embellish the ritual in some ways. In his description, the bishop is anointed with oil during the consecration, receives the ring and staff after it, and then is led to the throne before the Mass.[97] Our Vienna manuscript does not prescribe these elements, but it has the crosses that Hincmar mentioned.[98]

---

[94] *Kollektar-Pontifikale*, Unterkircher (ed.), p.105; we can also use a later manuscript of Regensburg, in Verona Biblioteca Capitolare LXXXVII, *Das Sakramentar-Pontifikale des Bischofs Wolfgang von Regensburg*, Klaus Gamber (ed.) (Regensburg, 1985), p.277: 'Antiqua sanctorum patrum institutio docet et praecepit ut is qui ad ordinem episcopatus elegitur maxime ut legimus in canone kartaginensi antea diligentissime examinetur cum omni caritate de fidei sanctae **trinitatis** . . . .'

[95] *Decretales pseudo-Isidoranae et Capitula Angilramni*, Paul Hinschius (ed.) (Leipzig, 1863), pp.301–306: CONCILIUM CARTHAGINENSE QUARTUM; *ibid.*, pp.303–304 contain the ordinations.

[96] Andrieu, 'Le sacre épiscopal', p.38: 'Ut autem clerus inceperit dicere: *Agnus dei* erigant se episcopi et qui fundet consecrationem accipiat quatuor evangelia et aperiat per medium et incurvato ipso electo ante altare, mittat ipse evangelia super collum et cervicem eius et teneant ipsa evangelia super eum duo episcopi, unus ex una parte, alter ex altera, et tam consecrator quam omnes episcopi teneant manus dextras suas super caput ordinandi et dicat consecrator: *Oremus. Propitiare domine supplicationibus nostris.*'

[97] *Ibid.*, p.39: 'in quibus sunt cruces signatae accipiat consecrator uas chrismatis in sinistra manu et cum dextera police cantans quae ibidem continentur, per singula loca faciat crucem in uerticem consecrandi'; p.54 'Et mittet anulum in dextrae manus digito . . . Deinde donet illi baculum.'

[98] With the aid of Wolfgang's Pontifical, the rubric introducing the Consecration that *Kollektar-Pontifikale*, Unterkircher (ed.), p.109 could not make out is easily reconstructed as: 'Qua expleta altiori uoce dicit hanc orationem.'

202 *Ordines* for Special Occasions, Ordination and the Ember Days

These components of the ritual are only written down in later liturgical manuscripts, often as additions in the margins of the ordination rite. Among the minor differences, Hincmar has the reading of the letter to Timothy only after the ordination had finished, whereas in the Vienna manuscript the apostle is read before and (as in *Ordo* 34) the ordinations begin only after the gradual is sung.[99] In a somewhat obscure ending to the letter, Hincmar suggested that he did not himself have the text of the *consecrationem episcopi*, which would go some way to explaining the differences.[100] If the majority of episcopal ordinations had hitherto proceeded from memory, with perhaps only the short rubric of the Gelasian Sacramentary as the climax, and constructed based on the kinds of discussions, collaborations and communications between bishops that we see in Hincmar's letter, the fact that Arn chose to write down an *Ordo* for this ceremony, perhaps for the first time, was a significant choice.

Arn also would have certainly had a need to redact and share such texts. He was himself appointed as an entirely new metropolitan in 798, and the accession of Salzburg had not passed without resistance among the other Bavarian dioceses.[101] It would not only make sense that Arn might therefore have had written new *ordines* for the most distinctive aspects of his new office (councils, ordination of fellow bishops) but that he might also have shared them with allies in the dioceses under his control. Arn's conciliar order was described by Schneider as a 'mirror for a bishop' (*Bischoffspiegel*), so his description of the ordination of the bishop in the same way stressed the place of the bishop, his duties and, of course, his obedience to and direct dependence from the metropolitan.[102] Arn also formalised texts for the letters which would be exchanged to concern the election of a bishop, as well as those to a pope and to an archbishop, which make plain how he conceived the episcopal office in very high terms.[103] The role of coronation *ordines* in political legitimisation is well known, so it is not so strange to consider that a new archbishop might have employed these texts in a similar way to legitimise his office.[104] It is therefore very probable that it was to Arn we owe the redaction of the metropolitan rite, the entire

---

[99] Andrieu, 'Le sacre épiscopal', p.63.

[100] *Ibid.*, p.72: 'Decretum autem et consecrationem episcopalem quae ibi memoratur, ego non habui, quae tamen vos habere posse cognosco.'

[101] Dopsch, 'Salzburg zur Zeit Erzbischofs Arns', pp.36–37.

[102] Schneider, *Konzilsordines*, pp.56, 337–341.

[103] *Salzburgisches Formelbuch*, in Ludwig Rockinger (ed.), *Quellen und Eröterungen zur bayerischen und deutschen Geschichte*, vol. VII (Munich, 1856), pp.1–168, at pp.100–104.

[104] Janet Nelson, 'Ritual and Reality in the Early Medieval *Ordines*', in Derek Baker (ed.), *The Materials, Sources and Methods of Ecclesiastical History* (Oxford, 1975), pp.41–52.

The Ordination Rite of Arn of Salzburg

sequence of ordinations that precede it including *Ordo* 38 and the unique manuscript format Baturich had copied at Sankt-Emmeram, which survives in the *Kollektar-Pontifikale* in Vienna. This would be the most obvious explanation as to why the earliest example appears in the non-metropolitan see of Regensburg.

I would hypothesise an earlier version of the entire Baturich *Kollektar-Pontifikale* in the distinctive script of the 'Arn-Stil' written either in Salzburg or, like other examples of this script, at Arn's monstery of St Amand, as the direct exemplar of the Vienna manuscript.[105] This may also make sense of the fact that the scribe of the Vienna manuscript was from Mondsee, as concluded by Bischoff, and not Sankt-Emmeram itself, despite mentions of Emmeram in the texts.[106] While acquired by Baturich himself for Regensburg in 833 (a *terminus post quem* for the manuscript?), Mondsee is very close to Salzburg, and a scribe from the monastery could easily have copied a Salzburg exemplar for his bishop. As with Bernharius of Worm's book, Weissenburgenses 91, which ends up in his monastery of Wissembourg, Mondsee would certainly later come to possess the Vienna manuscript, as it was recovered from bindings of that monastery. Since the version of the ordination rite written here would have a long history, and came back to Rome itself in the Alessandrina Pontifical, Arn's contribution to the liturgy in his choice to formulate a written version of the episcopal ordination by a metropolitan, and perhaps a deliberate campaign to disseminate it, would be one of the more significant Carolingian contributions to the liturgy.

---

[105] For the 'Arn-Stil', Bischoff, *Schreibschulen*, vol. II, pp.61–73.
[106] *Ibid.*, p.218; *Kollektar-Pontifikale*, Unterkircher (ed.), pp.35, 38–39.

PART III

Format and Script of the Manuscripts

CHAPTER 8

Layout, Script and Language of the Ordo Romanus *Manuscripts*

Since *ordo romanus* manuscripts represent one among a number of new liturgical manuscript types originating in the Carolingian period, examining how the manuscripts were put together physically shows us how Carolingian scribes chose to frame and organise an innovative form of manuscript. Unlike the case of the Sacramentary or lectionary, here there was no model or precedent for how to format and present the texts. We have already seen the freedom with which they reinterpreted the surrounding content. This question can also contribute to our discussion of what exactly these manuscripts are and for whom they were compiled. Did the design and layout of such manuscripts present them as 'for use' or do they disclose other functions? In his analysis, Andrieu did not take account of these aspects in a systematic way, though he implied a certain attention to it in his designation of the *petits pontificaux*. In general, the length of such manuscripts is between fifty-two folios (the original length of Cologne 138 – one quire is today missing) and seventy-one (the length of Verona 92) or seventy-four (the length of the concerned section of Munich Clm 14510). Notably, Verona 92 has a very irregular quire structure, but is exceptional in this respect; the other manuscripts tend to be structured simply in quaternions.[1] These lengths tend to be comparable to the other identified 'pontificals' of the era, since Freiburg UB 363 is fifty-three folios and BAV lat.7701 is seventy-three folios. More variation is to be found in the size of the manuscripts. Verona 92 is a particularly small manuscript at 183 × 120mm, while Cologne 138 is significantly larger at 240 × 195 mm, Munich Clm 14510 in the middle at 227 × 140 mm. Outside Collection B, Weissenburgenses 91 shows somewhat smaller dimensions, at 208 × 125 mm. Here there is a more distinct difference in these particular manuscripts, since an alternative 'pontifical', Freiburg 363, is larger than

---

[1] *Les Ordines*, vol. I, p.368: 'Aucun cahier n'est un quaternion régulier composé de quatre feuilles doubles.'

207

208   Layout, Script & Language of *Ordo Romanus* Manuscripts

any of these manuscripts, at 262 × 158 mm. Indeed, holding these manuscripts in person, the impression of them as being portable is the first and most striking one.

From most of these surviving manuscripts, the hypothetical existence of *libelli* each containing a single *ordo* cannot be easily verified. In the case of his 'pontificals', Rasmussen stressed the division of different rites between quires of the surviving manuscripts as signs of a pre-existing division of such rites into easily circulated *libelli* each concerned with a single rite, and a subsequent union of these originally separate elements into the 'pontifical'.[2] This is certainly applicable in some manuscripts. In BAV lat.7701, for example, Arn's conciliar *ordo* begins on a new quire and is distinctly differently written and conceived, and was probably subsequently united to the other elements of the pontifical (ordination, church dedication and the episcopal blessings).[3] In our Verona manuscript, the irregular quire structure does correspond exactly with texts. For example, *Ordo* I comes to an end on the final leaf (fol.21v) of Quire 3, which has only six folios. Meanwhile, the last folio of Quire 5 (fol.37r–v) was left entirely blank, meaning Quires 4 and 5 contain only the text of *Ordo* II; *Ordo* 28 begins on new quire, Quire 6 at fol.38r. Quire 7 only has three folios, so that *Ordo* 28 ends at the end of the quire too (fol.48v). The last quire, 10, was devoted only to the *laudes*, until more additions were made. According to Rasmussen's reconstruction, this would make it quite likely that Verona XCII was, in fact, among the earliest manuscripts of Collection B, combining what were possibly originally distinct *libelli* for the first time.

But this applies less well to other manuscripts Rasmussen did not treat in the same detail, such as the early pontifical, Freiburg 363, where the individual rites do not correspond to separate quires at all.[4] Like this manuscript, most *ordo romanus* manuscripts do not show an obvious correlation between content and quire boundaries. This could not be said of the earliest manuscripts, like BAV Pal.lat.487, the Lorsch manuscript of Collection A.[5] Originally circulating in manuscripts like this, Collection A was a modest treatise of only twenty-four folios in three quires. The similarly early Murbach manuscript today in fragments was probably equally brief. Commonalities are strongly suggested by their similar dimensions, 210 × 110 mm for the Murbach fragments and

---

[2] Rasmussen, *Les pontificaux*; Vogel, *Medieval Liturgy*, p.227.
[3] Westwell, 'The *ordines* of Vat.lat.7701'.
[4] See the manuscript description at http://dl.ub.uni-freiburg.de/sammlung7/werk/pdf/hs363.pdf.
[5] *Les Ordines*, vol. I, pp.319–320. The original manuscript is three quarternions, but *Ordo* I occupies 1r–9v, *Ordo* II is 9v–15v, *Ordo* 24 is 15v–22r and *Ordo* 24 22r–24r.

Layout, Script & Language of Ordo Romanus Manuscripts 209

210 × 130 mm for BAV Pal.lat.487, but the script of Murbach is more generously spaced out, so was probably longer. Nevertheless, this is still not a *libellus* as strictly defined, since such booklets were supposed to be only concerned with a single ritual each.[6] In any case, it is true that the specialised Roman Collection was initially disseminated in books of much more modest dimensions, more easily circulated and handled, than the manuscripts of Collection B, pontificals 'for use'.

But perhaps the key comparative relationship of these latter manuscripts, not seriously treated by either Andrieu's or Rasmussen's accounts of the 'pontifical', is that with the Sacramentary, and here the differences in dimensions are stark. A representative manuscript of a Carolingian Sacramentary, such as the *Hadrianum* Gregorian Sacramentary in Cambrai, Bibliothèque Municipale 164, for example, is 245 folios, 302 × 110 mm. An important part of the story of the Roman Sacramentary in Francia as reconstructed in standard literature was the inadequacy of the *Hadrianum* for 'liturgical use' by the Frankish clergy. We cannot explain the reception of the *Hadrianum* merely by its supposed imposition by Charlemagne, which no surviving text has actually recorded. Significant proportions of the book, like the stational notices for much of the year, the ordination of the Pope that ends it, and, notably, the authenticating title attributing it directly to Gregory the Great, met for the Franks the same devotional orientation to Rome which the *ordines romani* attested.[7] In any case, Supplementation of the Gregorian Sacramentary to meet the liturgical needs of the Franks made the books even larger and more unwieldly. A good example of the *Hucusque* Supplement, Autun BM S 19 (19bis) has a length of 199 folios, with dimensions of 340 × 235 mm.[8]

Excerption from the larger Sacramentaries is a defining characteristic of the *ordo romanus* manuscripts defined as 'pontificals' (Collection B, Weissenburgenses 91). Along with the texts that were commonly employed, like the 'ORDO DE SACRIS ORDINIBUS' for ordination with the indication of the prayers in incipit, there were also individual selections made of certain blessings and prayers, seemingly according to the preference and selection of the compilers. A number of such prayers concern more mobile liturgical occasions, that might take place in sacred sites other than the bishop's own cathedral, or even outside a church at all; these include visitations to the dead and to institutions such as monasteries, ordeals or blessings of violated fonts, or of rediscovered antique vessels and so on.

---

[6] Pierre-Marie Gy, 'The Different Forms of Liturgical "Libelli"', in Niels Krogh Rasmussen and Gerard Austin (eds.), *Fountain of Life* (Washington, DC, 1991), pp.23–34.
[7] Schieffer, 'Redeamus ad fontem'.   [8] Bischoff, *Katalog*, vol. I, p.37.

The *ordines* selected for these manuscripts also have such a character. The dedication of a new church naturally proceeded at the site itself. As we have seen, the Ember Days and scrutinies were tracked onto the stational calendars of cities, as happened in Rome, and made use of many churches and the streets of the city themselves. Elements of all of these rites were taken directly out of the Sacramentary, and rewritten in this new, more easily transportable and consultable format. The relation of the *ordines* to the Sacramentary is more consequent than the hypothetical *libelli*, which were taken as the purer representation of their original state. This relationship included a mutually reinforcing deepening of the perception and understanding of both texts' Roman-ness, something of demonstrable value to Carolingian compilers. Brussels 10127–10144 is a particularly potent expression of this interrelation between *Ordo* and Sacramentary, since it has an extract of several Masses listed as an 'EXCARPSUS LIBER SACRAMENTORUM', and a selection of canon law was also extracted. Interestingly, Brussels 10127–10144, which was characterised as a 'local priest's handbook' on account of a supposedly scrappy and summary character, significantly goes beyond a number of the manuscripts described as 'pontificals' in its length: at 137 folios in its present form, though two quires are missing.[9]

This allows us to move beyond the reconstruction that such 'pontificals' were created simply to be easier to use, and use is their main explanation. The sacralisation of the city streets and mapping of new topographies through stational processions and rites was a dynamic these manuscripts certainly activated, and the placement of the more complex text, *Ordo* I, in first place (as well as the presence of other notes of Roman practice which were not so easily usable) makes it plain that this sacralisation preceded through the 'paraphrase' of Rome. This expansiveness and elasticity in liturgical function helps to explain manuscripts such as Zurich Car. C 102 (279 × 187 mm and ninety-three folios in its current form with the *ordines* of Collection B covering originally thirty-nine folios) or St Petersburg Q. V. I, n° 34 (190 × 152 mm). These manuscripts showed a similar consultation of the Sacramentary, with Zurich Car. C 102 being particularly closely related to it, extracting several Masses which most other Collection B manuscripts did not. But much of their content was also varied *expositiones* of Mass and baptism. That they were created for monasteries, Nonantola, and the St Petersburg manuscript likely for Corbie, suggests that the space assumed as the site of the sacralisation

---

[9] Hen, 'Knowledge of Canon Law'.

Script and Style 211

was not the literal city, but rather the monastic basilica reimagined as city space (as in the description of Fulda's Mass by Theotroch). The 'portability' of all *ordo romanus* manuscripts therefore was intimately related not only to their presence in the liturgical act itself as a directive, but also their consultation prior to the liturgical act, and their power analogous with the power of 'relics' to make Rome real.

Script and Style

There is a certain range in the presentation of *ordines romani* in their manuscripts. Some are much more complex, elaborate and creative in their employment of various forms and styles of script. It is these on which we can focus more, because of their potential to disclose what copyists wished to emphasise and highlight in the text, as well as the potential ideological messages disclosed in the choices they made. A number of the manuscripts reflect the more general tendencies of their *scriptoria*. For example, Montpellier 412 follows the general style of Tours manuscripts of a similar age (early ninth century). Clear division is here made of *Ordo* 15, from *Ordo* 1 and the beginning of Collection A with *Ordo* 1, marking out clearly that *Ordo* 15 was an addition from another exemplar to the Collection itself. Each section possesses an uncial heading in red, and an ornamented initial which covers three-quarters of the page in the first case and a third of the page in the other, and the first line of each text contains some uncial letters, before the rest of the *ordines* texts are written out in the rigorous and fine minuscule of this period, with titles in red uncial. The format can be seen in the plates provided by Rand.[10] This layout does not differ at all from the Augustine text proceeding the *ordines*. Likewise, manuscripts such as St Gallen 446 do not show a distinction in their representation of *ordines* from the *expositiones* that accompany them, both being in minuscule with rubricated titles in rustic capitals, but without other embellishment. But the manuscripts which show the most creativity in their deployment and use of the *ordines* often have the most interesting features of script as well. This study will therefore proceed through a number of manuscripts that have previously been the subject of attention for their content, revealing how the physical presentation is integral to understanding the ways the texts thus collected were compiled and intended to be read and received.

[10] Edward K. Rand, *Studies in the Script of Tours. I: A Survey of the Manuscripts of Tours* (Cambridge, MA, 1929), p.93ff, Taf.20.1–4.

212   Layout, Script & Language of *Ordo Romanus* Manuscripts

In the early manuscripts of Collection A, BAV Pal.lat.487 and the fragments from Murbach today in Munich, Regensburg and Sankt-Paul, there is not much effort to differentiate and highlight individual parts of the *ordines* as we would see later. For example, there is no use of rubrication in these manuscripts. However, some important graphic conventions were already established, showing that, despite the small and scrappy appearance of the books, their compilers were already employing the resources of script to imbue the texts with the desired appearance of authority.[11] In BAV Pal. lat.487, the first page opens with *Ordo* 1, with the title in large, somewhat elongated rustic capitals. The first line of the text follows in capitalis written to a smaller scale, then the text continues in minuscule. A master scribe may have written the first half of the page, since there is a change of hand halfway through the word 'seruata'.

This suggests that particular effort was made to present the opening of the Collection, and of *Ordo* 1 in particular, with rustic capitals, a script that was associated with Roman-ness and with a textual hierarchy (see Fig. 8.1). The first line of *Ordo* 11 is also in very fine capitals (fol.10r) The minuscule scripts for the body of the *ordines* are quite varied: see the change of hand to a much more compressed proportions in Figure 8.1 at *seruata unicuique*. Those for the first portion of the manuscript (fols.1r–22r) fall within Bischoff's 'ältere Lorscher stil', and most of their characteristics can be found in his treatment of this style.[12] This scribe also writes out KYRIE ELEISON in Greek capitals, in contrast to the scribe who wrote *Ordo* 27, who did not. The Alcuin *Credimus* text and *Ordo* 29, added later, are written in Bischoff's 'jüngere Lorsch stil' of the first half of the ninth century.[13]

Unique among the *ordo romanus* manuscripts in the Murbach fragments of Collection A, but not unknown elsewhere, is the employment of Anglo-Saxon minuscule alongside a pre-Caroline minuscule, a juxtaposition visible in the fragments in Regensburg Staatliche Bibliothek.[14] Although we now lack the pages where the change of hand took place, it is clear that the script changed mid-quire partway through *Ordo* 27, so there was apparently no link in the minds of these scribes between the two separate scripts and quires, or scripts and separate texts. Uncial is used for the heading 'DE SABBATO

---

[11] Bernhard Bischoff, *Latin Palaeography: Antiquity and the Middle Ages*, trans. Daibhm O. Cróinin and David Ganz (Cambridge, 1990), p.60.

[12] Bischoff, *Die Abtei Lorsch*, pp.21–22: 'Der ältere Lorscher Stil'.

[13] *Ibid.*, p.22: 'von fol.24r an in jüngerem Stil, saec IX1, fortgesetzt'.

[14] More on these fragments and images in Arthur Westwell, 'Rome on the Danube: Papal Liturgies at St Emmeram in the Carolingian Period. The Saint-Emmeram Gloss on the Fermentum', in Harald Buchinger and David Hiley (eds.), *Liturgie und Musik in Sankt-Emmeram* (Regensburg, 2022), pp.39–55.

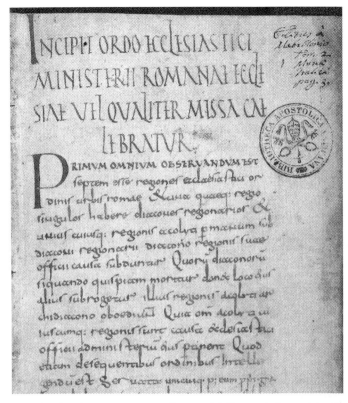

Fig. 8.1 Title of *Ordo Romanus* I in Lorsch copy of Collection A (late eighth century). Biblioteca Apostolica Vaticana Pal.lat.483 fol.1r. © 2023 Biblioteca Apostolica Vaticana.

SANCTO' on the verso of the rightmost folio of this same fragment. The pre-Caroline miniscule used in the main script is somewhat neater than that in the Lorsch manuscript, generously spaced (in eighteen lines in contrast to the twenty-five to thirty in the similar-sized Lorsch manuscript), with fewer ligatures. Notable is, for example, a much more open letter form known as the two-c **a**. Contrasting is the Holy Week *ordo* added to the end in a much more ligatured and heavily abbreviated script. More attention was therefore paid in this copy of Collection A to the clarity of the presentation, and we can imagine that the original manuscript would consequently have had many more pages than BAV Pal.lat.487. The late manuscript of Collection A in Copenhagen GKS 3443 8° is similarly undeveloped in its manner of presentation, using mixed capitals for the titles of ordines, but little else in the way of

214   Layout, Script & Language of *Ordo Romanus* Manuscripts

elaboration.[15] This manuscript is particularly tiny, with dimensions of only 160 × 75/95 mm.

In manuscripts of Collection B, some of these trends are maintained, and others further developed. Verona XCI uses an exceptional capitalis quadrata for the new title of *Ordo* 1 on fol.5v, which is particularly epigraphic in character. Since the manuscript actually begins with *Ordo* 13B, which is not distinguished with such a title, this use of the Roman script once again singles out *Ordo* 1 in particular as Roman. The other *ordines* are introduced only with half-uncial. In this manuscript, we see the beginning of new attempts to highlight different parts of the *Ordo* texts, which is here done with a yellow wash behind the text. The titles of the prayers from the Sacramentary are marked out in this way too. The technique is used only sparingly in *Ordo* 1, on fol.6v for the days of the week in which the different regions of Rome would celebrate. But from fol.22r, on which *Ordo* 11 begins, the technique is then applied more comprehensively. Here the wash is applied specifically where a new person or actor does something in the ritual; for example, on fol.23r **'Item dicit diaconus'** and fol.23v **'Tunc uenit accolitus'** and **'adnuntiat diaconus dicens'** are thus marked out. That this was a particular concern of the creators and users of the manuscripts is made clear by the marginal notes in many of the same points of the text, which repeat the people involved as mentioned in the main text itself; for example, in fol.24r, 'alius acolitus', 'diaconus' and 'tertius acolitus' are all in the margin next to where they perform an action in the *ordo*. There is a significant addition, since in the *ordo* it is simply described that a presbyter would say each of the homilies concerning the gospels as part of the third scrutiny, 'IN AURIUM APERTIONEM'. The marginal notes have a new feature whereby seemingly nine separate priests take one of the homilies each, with their title and number in the note next to where the speech begins: on fol.26v 'presbyter I', on fol.28r 'II presbyter', on fol.28v 'presbyter III' and 'IIII', on fol.29r the numeral 'V', on fol.29v the numeral 'VI', on fol.31r 'presbyter VII', on fol.32r 'presbyter VIII' and on fol.34r the numeral 'VIIII'. These notes reveal further evidence that the narrative of the *ordines* was a starting point that would be developed, according to the resources and expectations of the church using it. In *Ordo* 11, originally nine separate priests are not envisaged, but it is implied here. But they also show the preoccupation of the compilers with the arrangement of the personnel, distinguishing between and making clear the specific roles of clergy. This aspect continues to be highlighted in the subsequent *ordines* of the manuscript, for example **'duo diaconi'** or **'presbiteri uero duo priores'** in *Ordo* 28, but the

---

[15] Digitised at: www5.kb.dk/permalink/2006/manus/101/eng/.

wash is also used to signal moments of transition during the ceremony, the start of a new day or when people move to a new part of the church: on fol.43v '**Post horam tertiam sabbato procedunt qui** baptizandi sunt ad ecclesiam' or on fol.45r '**Deinde ascendit** lector in ambone' and '**Tunc deinde scola** descendit ad fontes', and so on. The instruction *seruat de sancta* on Maundy Thursday is also highlighted as an instruction of interest. These preoccupations cohere with the priorities of compilers we have already seen. They imply the close relation of the texts as received by copyists to the use and (re)interpretation of ecclesiastical topography.

A closely related North Italian manuscript, Cologne 138, uses a red capitalis quadrata on the first page, 1v, to begin *Ordo* 13B, but gave the other titles in uncial. For the conciliar *ordo*, the rubrics are marked out in a recognisable way from the prayers, being in red, but this is not pursued elsewhere. In Munich Clm 14510 we can specifically distinguish between the *ordo* and non-*ordo* content in the use of rubrication, which has become more sophisticated for the former. The sermons opening the collection are simply titled in red mixed majuscules (with capital and uncial letters). *Ordo* 1 is again singled out, being entitled in rustic capitals. Then the *ordines* begin in minuscule, and red is employed in specific cases, in the first case the stational instructions concerning the regions of Rome: '**Nam primo** Oportet ut post numerus ecclesiasticarum sciat quo uoluerit numerum dierum per ebdomadam quo ordine circulariter obsequantur.' Sometimes arrangement of the clergy is concerned in these red sections, but the responses of the people 'AMEN' are also thus highlighted, for example on fol.39v. The fact that speech could be highlighted in red against the black of the actions is an interesting inversion of the usual practices of rubrication, and shows the flexibility of these tools for scribes. There was not yet one established practice. It occurs again throughout the manuscript (see Figure 8.2), in *Ordo* 49 where the

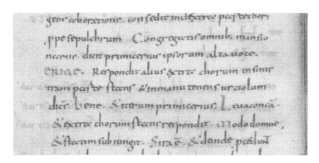

Fig. 8.2 Highlighting of speech in the Regensburg copy of Collection B (824–827). Bayerische Staatsbibliothek München Clm 14510, fol.41v.

speech of the primicerius is thus highlighted and also in uncial '**ERIGE**' (seemingly to represent graphically the *alta uoce* in which the word is supposed to be pronounced), and throughout in *Ordo* 11, where individual speeches of the various actors are given in red (for which see Figure 8.4). Again moments of transition in the ceremony are also highlighted, for example on fol.57r: '**Expletas** lectiones ... **Tunc** deinde scola etc.'; on fol.60v: '**Iterum** ipse pontifex uadit de ipso altare'; and on fol.66v '**Et post**modicum interuallum mox incipiant omnes kyrieeleison cum letania. **Haec** expleta ascendunt ipsi electi ....'

More expressive still are some of the copies of *ordines* 15 and 17 found in canon law manuscripts. In BAV Reg.lat.1127 (see Figure 8.3), *Ordo* 15 is introduced with capitalis quadrata and uncial, in the same way as the writings of the popes that surround it (the rest proceeds without much rubrication). The manuscript containing *Ordo* 17 in a similar context, Pal.lat.574, likewise introduces the text with capitalis quadrata and uncial.

But here red uncial is subsequently used to highlight passages of the *Ordo* itself, standing out starkly against the black minuscule. In the Mass *Ordo* (see Figure 8.5), we see evidence of this script being used to mark important moments of transition in the ritual: '**ET INGREDITUR** lector ... **DEINDE** diaconus inclinet caput ... .**ASCENDENS** in

Fig. 8.3 Title of *Ordo Romanus* 15 in the Canonical Collection from the Tours area (early ninth century) Vatican City. Biblioteca Apostolica Vaticana Reg.lat.1127, fol.52v. © 2023 Biblioteca Apostolica Vaticana.

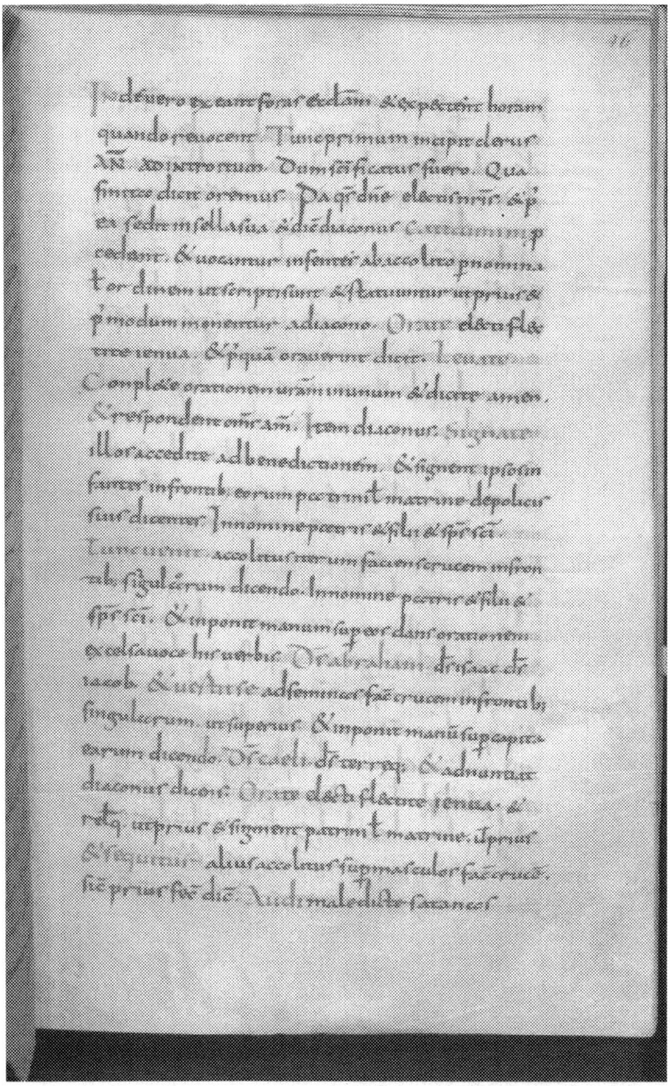

Fig. 8.4 Use of rubrication in the Regensburg copy of Collection B (824–827). Bayerische Staatsbibliothek München Clm 14510, fol.46r.

grado . . .' etc. Likewise it might draw attention to a moment of significance: 'et communicant **OMNES CORPUS** et sanguinem domini' (on fol.164v). This technique was not taken up in the manuscript which was copied from Pal.lat.574, Gotha Membr.I.85, from Wissembourg.

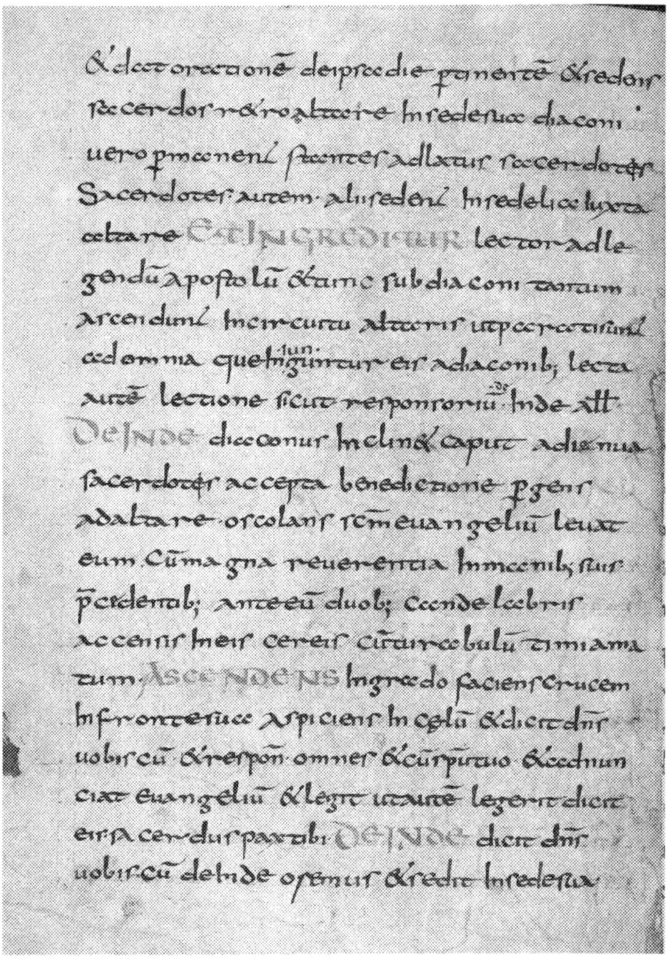

218 Layout, Script & Language of *Ordo Romanus* Manuscripts

Fig. 8.5 Use of rubrication in the copy of *Ordo Romanus* 17 added to a canonical collection from the Rhine area (end of the eighth century). Vatican City Biblioteca Apostolica Vaticana, Pal.lat.574 fol.156v. © 2023 Biblioteca Apostolica Vaticana.

The manuscript attributed to Bernharius of Worms, Wolfenbüttel Weissenburgenses 91, is also particularly preoccupied with the presentation of the *ordines*. The manuscript begins with a full page in splendid ornamental mixed majuscules drawn in hollow outline, the line of text alternating black and red, then uncial, introducing the letter of Pseudo-Clement (fol.25v). Mixed majuscules subsequently introduce the following sections of the papal historical introduction to the *ordines* (fols.35r, 39v), and then the *ordines* themselves, beginning with *Ordo* I, which also has its first lines in red ornamental mixed majuscules (fol.42v), for which see Figure 8.6, as likewise does *Ordo* II (fol.53v). Subsequently the individual scrutinies have their own titles in red mixed majuscules too, a unique feature of this manuscript. The unadorned and unfilled initials drawn in outline in black and red on fol.25v are very close in appearance to those of a manuscript of the *Liber Pontificalis* copied during Bernharius' episcopacy and also at Wissembourg later (indicating the relationship of the two manuscripts, probably copied at the same scriptorium).[16]

As we saw in Pal.lat.574, individual phrases are marked out with red within the *ordines* themselves, but here both capitalis and half-uncial are

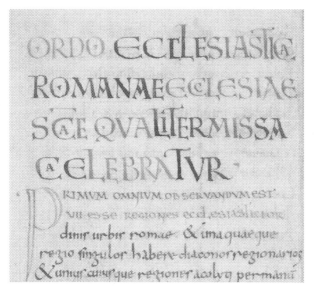

Fig. 8.6 Title of *Ordo Romanus* I in the Ordines Romani Collection of Bernharius of Worms (early ninth century) . Herzog August Bibliothek Wolfenbüttel, Weissenburg 91, fol.42v.

---

[16] Wolfenbüttel, HAB Cod. Guelf. 10. 11 Aug. 4°; online at HAB – Handschriftendatenbank – Handschrift 10–11-aug-4f; Bischoff, *Mittelalteliche Studien*, vol. III, p.93.

used (on fol.45v, 'PONTIFEX' is in mixed majuscules, and at the bottom 'DEINDE' is in uncial). Again we can mark out moments of transition in the text (e.g. fol.48r '**DEINDE** pergente diacono ad altare ... **PONTIFEX** autem descendit ad senatorium') and spoken texts of particular significance (fol.49v: '**SANCTUS SANCTUS SANCTUS** dominus deus sabaoth ... dicens **PER IPSUM ET CUM IPSO** usque per omnia saecula saceulorum ...'; or the dialogues introducing the chrism consecration on fol.61r: 'Dicit Pontifex **Sursum corda. Resp.** Habemus ad dominum. **Gratias agamus domino deo nostro** R. dignum et iustum est'; and the font consecration on fol.64r likewise). As in Munich Clm 14510, this feature is particularly prominent in *Ordo* 11, where the deacon's pronouncements are marked out in red throughout (fol.54r), for which see Figure 8.7.

The mention of objects such as chrism and candles are marked out, as for example on fols.63v or on 83v: '**tres** portiones corporis domini intus in confessionem **Et tres** de incenso'. Stations are highlighted, as they might have been in an antiphoner from which the text came, in the Vespers text of *Ordo* 27, on fol.70v. Interestingly, Greek letters are used for the *Kyrie eleison* here, in the Vespers of *Ordo* 27, for example on fol.69v, *Ordo* 42 on fol.84r and in *Ordo* 34, for example on fol.82v. Greek letters are also used on fol.81r for the word ἀνθρώπω for the prohibition on homosexual relations (translated to 'masculum' in the margin). Since Pal.lat.487 also

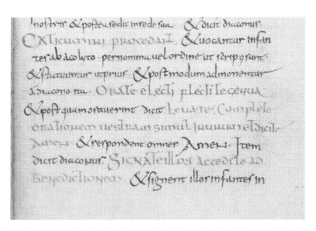

Fig. 8.7 Use of rubrication in the Collection of Bernharius of Worms (early ninth century). Herzog August Bibliothek Wolfenbüttel, Weissenburg 91, fol.54r.

uses Greek letters for *Ordo* 34 alone, it suggests that some early *ordines* had Greek elements which their scribes chose to copy (the Copenhagen manuscript of Collection A does too). Since these techniques are never used in the Roman historical texts of the same manuscript, it would be correct to say that scribes and compilers saw *ordines* as a particular venue to experiment with the potential of different colours and scripts to mark out significant moments, guiding the reader's experience of the text. The 'moments of transition' indicated were the same moments which theorists like Amalarius also focused upon, because, as he repeatedly showed (particularly in Book 3 of the *Liber Officialis* with its Mass *ordo*), the movement and position of clergy in the church were themselves constitutive of the meaning of the varied zones in the church, and Amalarius envisaged that these would even teach the laity observing. This same process, too, is fundamental to the *ordines romani*, as they allowed clergy to interpret the church as the 'paraphrase' of the stational Rome, as they themselves moved in the person of the Pope and his staff through it. Thus the manuscripts which seem particularly preoccupied with this process are most engaged in the graphic highlighting of the most significant moments in which it might be activated.

The Language(s) of the *Ordines*

In terms of the primary language of the *ordines*, Latin, there are related questions to pursue, which help to give a picture of the ways in which Carolingian compilers and scribes approached the task of presenting the texts in these manuscripts, as well as relating to the broad picture of what priorities scribes, correctors and readers brought to these manuscripts. There is the initial question of what kind of Latin the *ordines romani* were written in originally, and the subsidiary question of what corrections individual scribes made in copying the texts. Andrieu used Latin variants of individual manuscripts in his treatment of single examples of the *ordines*, in order to uncover lucidly the sequence of their genealogy and so be able to represent which manuscripts were most closely related to the 'original'. He paid less consideration to what might be learned from a more holistic consideration of the manuscripts. For example, in his particularly thorough consideration of the manuscripts of *Ordo* 1, Andrieu suggested that among the 'best' manuscripts which were closest to the original were St Gallen 614 (the 'short' recension), Bern 289, Albi 42, Wolfenbüttel Weissenburgenses 91 and BAV Pal.lat.487.[17] It is useful to consider more closely the Latin used through the whole

---

[17] *Les Ordines*, vol. II, pp.28–29.

222   Layout, Script & Language of *Ordo Romanus* Manuscripts

manuscripts, particularly given the reconstruction of the 'renaissance caro-lingienne' as a phenomenon, assumed to have had a singular effect upon Latin in a sudden and decisive shift, an assumption that also appears in Andrieu's assessment of the Latin of the *ordines*.[18] This reconstruction relied upon the characterisation of pre-Carolingian Latin orthography and morph-ology in exactly the terms Andrieu assumed, as faulty and base. Reassessment has begun to establish that such characterisations do not do justice to the character of this form of late Latin, which can often better be characterised as a fully legitimate development of Latin as a spoken, still-living language of the time, rather than artificially measured against the canonical classical forms of Latin from generations earlier.[19]

Early manuscripts display traits of these forms of Latin. For example, Brussels 10127–10144 displays in some of what Andrieu calls it faults, the consistent use of an ablative with 'ad' (*Ordo* 24, n.5, var.2: 'ingrediuntur ad missis'; *Ordo* 2, n.4, var.23: 'ad caeteris presbiteris'), with 'post' (*Ordo* 24, n.29 var.5: 'post orationis') and 'in' (*Ordo* 24, n.45, var.5: 'in fonte'; *Ordo* 26, n.12, var.2: 'in fine'), 'infra' (*Ordo* 26, n.6, var.6: 'infra civitate romana'), 'per' (*Ordo* 3, n.1, var.8: 'per has quattuor solemnitatis'), or even the dative with 'de' (*Ordo* 2, n. 3, var.2: 'de altari').

There are a number of orthographic peculiarities in Brussels 10127–10144 as well. These include the use of:

> rc instead of rt: *Ordo* 24, n.8 var.2: 'tercia'; n.22, var.2: 'ora tercia'; n.51: 'spacio'; *Ordo* 26, n.3, var.9: 'excuciunt'; n.13, var.3: 'inicio'; var.12: 'tercia'
> s for x: *Ordo* 24, n.16 var.5: 'comistam'
> ae for e: *Ordo* 24, n.41 var.3: 'caerei'; *Ordo* 26, n.2, var.7: 'caena'; n.6, var.1, 4, 5: 'ignae', 'cearum', 'diae'; *Ordo* 2, n.4, var.2: 'aegritudo'; var.29: 'agaere'.
> d for t: Appendix to *Ordo* 24, var.12: 'ebdomatam'
> v for b: *Ordo* 26, n.8: 'In octabas'.

---

[18] *Ibid.*, p.32.

[19] Roger Wright, *Late Latin and Early Romance in Spain and Carolingian France* (Liverpool, 1982); *Missale Gothicum*, Els Rose (ed.), CCSL 159D (Turnhout, 2005), pp.23–187; Els Rose, 'Liturgical Latin in Early Medieval Gaul', Mary Garrison, Arpad P. Orbán and Marco Mostert (eds.), *Spoken and Written Language: Relations between Latin and the Vernacular Languages in the Earlier Middle Ages* (Turnhout, 2013), pp.303–313; Els Rose, 'The Sanctoral Cycle of the Prague Sacramentary', in Maximilan Diesenberger, Rob Meens, and Els Rose (eds.), *The Prague Sacramentary: Culture, Religion and Politics in Late Eighth-Century Bavaria* (Turnhout, 2016), p.122; Els Rose, 'Emendatio and Effectus', in Meens *et al.* (eds.), *Religious Franks*, pp.137–141; Mostert '"... but they pray badly"', in Meens *et al.* (eds.), *Religious Franks*, pp.122–126; Arthur Westwell, 'Correction of Liturgical Words, and Words of Liturgical Correctio in the *Ordines* Romani of Saint Amand', in Vincent Debiais and Victoria Turner (eds.), *Words in the Middles Ages/Les Mots au Moyen Âge*. Utrecht Studies in Medieval Literacy 46 (Turnhout, 2020), pp.69–87.

The Language(s) of the Ordines

More rarely these appear in other manuscripts too, in particular St Gallen 614 *Ordo* 24 n.15, var.9: 'dependencia' and *Ordo* 24 n.29, var.7: 'spacio'; *Ordo* 2, n.3: 'tercio'. Some of the grammatical peculiarities appear occasionally in St Gallen 614 too: *Ordo* 2, n.8: 'in ipsius manu'; n.3, var.15: 'mittit in calice'.

In the case of the Collection of St Amand, a number of the same features we have already noted in Brussels 10127–10144 present themselves consistently. First, in the orthography:

> *Ordo* 4, n.18 and n.24: 'oracione'; n.43: 'oblaciones'; n.48 with 'oblacio-narium' and 'oblacionarius'; n. 49: 'oblacionario'; n. 114: 'adnunciat' and 'stacione'.
> *Ordo* 39, n.7: 'oracio'.
> *Ordo* 21, n.7: both 'oracionem' and 'orationem'.
> *Ordo* 30B, nn.2, 27: 'benediccionem', n.9: 'oracionem'.
> *Ordo* 30B, n.31: 'leccio'.
> *Ordo* 4, n.28 and n.31, n.33: 'aevangelium'
> *Ordo* 39, n.4: 'aelecti'.
> *Ordo* 39, n.29: 'aegreditur'.
> *Ordo* 20, n.4: 'Exsurge', rather than 'Exurge'.
> *Ordo* 21, n.9: 'scola' not 'scholae'.
> *Ordo* 30B, nn.1, 41, 68: 'secuntur' rather than 'sequuntur'.
> *Ordo* 4, n.52: 'discit' rather than 'dicit'.
> *Ordo* 33B, n.47: 'conpleta' rather than 'complete'.
> *Ordo* 39, n.15: 'conpleverit' rather than 'compleverit'.
> *Ordo* 4, n.9, 27, 99; *Ordo* 43, n.15: 'planita' for the chasuble rather than 'planeta'.

In the same way as he spoke of Brussels manuscript, Andrieu characterised the grammar of this manuscript thus: 'les règles d'accord les plus élémentaires sont constamment violées'.[20] What this means is generally quite similar to what we have seen in Brussels 10127–10144, since the most common and consistent error is the use of the ablative again very consistently with prepositions of movement: *Ordo* 4, n.28: 'et vadit ad altare'; n.32: 'deinde psallit in ambone'; n.33: 'descendit de ambone'; n.34: 'ponunt ea retro altare'; n.39: 'ponit eas in sindone'; n.51: 'et ponit eum super altare'; n.61: 'et revertitur scola in presbiterio, in parte sinistra'; n.71: 'et vadunt in dextra parte altaris'; *Ordo* 20, n.1: 'Et veniunt in ecclesia'; n.5: 'ascendens ante

---

[20] *Les Ordines*, vol. II, p.138: 'The most elementary rules of agreement are constantly violated.'

224 Layout, Script & Language of *Ordo Romanus* Manuscripts

altare'; *Ordo* 21, n.2: 'et ingreditur pontifex in sacrario'; n.7: 'Et venit ante altare'; *Ordo* 30B, n.8: ascendat ad altare'; n.71: 'veniunt usque ad altare', etc.

Even though Paris lat.974 is perhaps a century later than the Brussels manuscript, both were certainly produced in the same region (the Brussels manuscript can be located to the part of the North France/Belgium where St Amand lies), and we know that Paris lat.974 derived from a significantly earlier exemplar, perhaps one contemporary with Brussels 10127–10144 itself. This would attest to a significant level of transmission of certain *ordines* in which such features were present just before and around the year 800. Andrieu was adamant that these features must place this original exemplar prior to the 'Carolingian literary renewal'.[21] Brussels 10127–10144 appears to represent an intermediary form of the *ordines*, preserved in St Gallen 614, in the form in which they were transmitted into the regions of Gallica Belgica (*Ordo* 3, 24 and 26, to which *Ordo* 1 and 2 were probably on lost folios), then put to use in the creation of the Collection of St-Amand. Figures who could be assumed to have taken part in this transmission, such as the abbot of St Amand, Arn of Salzburg, might have been close to individuals such as Alcuin, traditionally characterised as the leaders of efforts to reform Latin, but this did not mean that they saw the copying of *ordines* as inseparably linked to a 'classical' Latin idiom, judged to be correct in the terms Andrieu had characterised it. Scribes writing in Arn's 'Arn-stil', for example, in Salzburg and St Amand, do not display consistent or 'correct' Latin.[22]

An early transmission of the *ordines* occurred in such late forms of Latin. Other sets of *ordines* which could have been copied in the same initial transmission (*Ordo* 15, 16, 17) are characterised by Andrieu in very similar terms.[23] Many of the same traits in the Latin certainly appear in the varied copies of *Ordo* 15, and in the Collection that accompanies it in St Gallen 349.[24] Andrieu's similar verdict on the copy of *Ordo* 17 in Pal.lat.574 shows

---

[21] *Les Ordines*, vol. II, p.138: 'Ni le vocabulaire ni le style ne trahissent encore la moindre influence de renouveau littéraire carolingien . . . ne peuvent guère embrasser que les dernières decades du VIIIe siècle.'

[22] Donald Bullough, 'A Neglected Early-Ninth-Century Manuscript of the Lindisfarne "Vita S. Cuthberti"', *Anglo-Saxon England*, 27 (1988), pp.105–137, at p.108, n.12.

[23] *Les Ordines*, vol. III, p.15: 'Le style même de ce plaidoyer final est bien celui auquel on peut s'attendre de la part d'un moin franc, à la fin de cette période de longue décadence qui précéda la renaissance carolingienne. La pauvreté du vocabulaire,l'incertitude de l'orthographe, l'ignorance des règles d'accord les plus élémentaires caractérisent pareillement, nous l'avons vu, la collection d'*ordines* dite de Saint-Amand.'

[24] Orthography: *Ordo* 15, n.1: 'iniciantur'; n.3: 'leccionibus'; n.12: 'stacio'; 'spacium'; n.14: 'oracionem'; n.32: 'probrias episcoborum'; n.78: 'secuntur'; n.83: 'staciones'; n.86: 'ora tercia'; grammar in *Ordo* 15, n.12: 'prope gradu'; n.15: 'peraccedit ad altare'; n.16: 'transit post altare'; n.31: 'ponent eas super altere'; n.55: 'levans calicem de altari'.

The Language(s) of the Ordines 225

us yet another manuscript with the same distinctive variations.[25] Interestingly, in this latter case, a corrector has gone through and provided corrections above a number of errors in grammar and spelling made by the first scribe (see Figure 8.5), but he left the peculiarities of late Latin intact.[26] He seemingly understood a difference between 'real' errors and the commonly used Latin of the original scribe, in a way Andrieu did not acknowledge.

Rather than being entirely the result of a lack of education that would be remedied at one stroke by the 'Carolingian Reform', it is possible that this form of Latin continued to be seen as quite appropriate for the copying of *ordines*. It is certainly telling that what has been characterised as an effort to 'reform' liturgy was still, up to 800, conducted in Latin that modern scholars would dismiss as in need of 'reform'. A proof that writers were aware of the Latin they used is that the writer of the Collection of St Amand was explicit, even self-conscious, of these features of the Latin. The Collection opens with the long title of *Ordo* 4, which says the author expounded his theme 'non grammatico sermone, sed aperte loquendo veritatem indicare'.[27] While both the scribe and later copyist of the Collection certainly made some errors, this admission and the consistency in the use of these exact forms of grammar and orthography suggests that he deployed a form of Latin deliberately, conscious that an alternative form might be more 'grammatical'. It is further quite possible that this idiom was viewed as particularly suited to texts broadly concerned with liturgy.[28] Our manuscripts show the use of it in Alsace and Alemmania through to Northern France.

This interesting feature of the early transmission was largely dispensed with in the copies of the *ordines* from the ninth century itself. Montpellier 412, notably, corrects *Ordo* 15 systematically in both the orthography and the grammar.[29] St Gallen 140 does the same to St Gallen 614.[30] Likewise

---

[25] *Les Ordines*, vol. III, p.158: 'Il doit son aspect d'archaïsme plus prononcé, moins à l'écriture elle-même, qui est assez soignée, qu'à l'incertitude des formes orthographiques et à l'abondance des irrégularités grammaticales'; See for example, *Ordo* 17, n.23: 'spacium'; n.66: 'octabas'; n.69: 'adque'; n.120: 'gracias.

[26] For example, *Ordo* 17, n.31 'latus sacerdotes' corr. 'sacerdotis'; n.56: 'de ipsam oblationem' corrected to 'de ipsa oblatione' etc.

[27] *Ordo* 4, tit.: 'not in grammatical language, but speaking openly to indicate the truth'.

[28] Els Rose, 'Liturgical Latin in the Bobbio Missal', in Rob Meens and Yithak Hen (eds.), *The Bobbio Missal: Liturgy and Religious Culture in Merovingian Gaul* (Cambridge, 2004), pp.67–78; copies of *expositiones* in the same period such as the ubiquitous text *Dominus uobiscum* show similar traits; Rose and Westwell, 'Correcting the Liturgy and Sacred Language'.

[29] *Les Ordines*, vol. III, p.49; for example *Ordo* 15, n.12, var.11: 'stacio denunciate' becomes 'denuntiata statio', var.16: 'prope gradu' becomes 'prope gradum' etc.

[30] *Ordo* 2, n.3: 'Tercio' becomes 'Tertio'; n.7: 'confrangit' becomes 'confringent'; n.8: 'in ipsius manu' becomes 'in ipsius manum'.

226   Layout, Script & Language of *Ordo Romanus* Manuscripts

the Gotha copy of *Ordo* 17 from Pal.lat.574 has removed some of the first text's peculiarities, sometimes in quite interesting ways, including a change of mood from indicative to subjunctive throughout; for example, 'faciunt' to 'faciant' (*Ordo* 17, n.3, var.3 and n.8, var.1) and 'ingredientur' for 'ingrediuntur' (*Ordo* 17, n.12, var.1 etc.).[31] That no other corrector thought the subjunctive was appropriate suggests a certain diversity of approach to the grammar of *ordines*, which highlights the ambiguity of their relation to practice. Are they descriptive or prescriptive?

Much less extensively, and without the distinctive orthography quite so evident, Pal.lat.487 (our earliest copy of Collection A) shows an inclination for the ablative, which is in some cases verified by Wolfenbüttel Weissenburgenses 91 as part of an initial transmission of the *ordines* from Collection A.[32] As with *Ordo* 15, Montpellier 412 reveals a corrected form of the Collection where this penchant was largely erased.[33] In keeping with traditional visions of how 'Carolingian Reform' of Latin was supposed to have proceeded, Andrieu linked this correction to Tours, where Montpellier 412 was written.[34] But the other early manuscript of the Collection from Murbach in fragments already contains these corrections.[35] Interestingly, in these cases of correction, the new Latin was not regarded as inextricably linked to the new minuscule, since the Murbach manuscript has pages in Anglo-Saxon minuscule. Again, the approaches in monastic institutions, here Lorsch and Murbach, to Latin language of the *ordines* could vary, even though both manuscripts were copied at a similar time. That Wolfenbüttel Weissenburgenses 91 continued to display traits that went back to early copies shows that certain copyists were less concerned to update the text of the *ordines* even as late as the first quarter of the ninth century. In

---

[31] For other examples, in *Ordo* 17, n.6, var.7 'tercium' becomes 'tertium'; n.110, var.11, 'solempnia' becomes 'solemnia'; n.17, var.5, n.41, var.5, n.108, var.6, 'in sacrario' becomes 'in sacrarium'; and at n.94, var.1, 'in ecclesia' becomes 'in ecclesiam'. A nominative absolute in *Ordo* 17, n.46, 'nullus alius audiente', is made ablative: 'nullo alio audiente'.

[32] *Ordo* 27, n.12, var.11: 'iusta consuetudine'; n.71, var.4: 'salutat primus scolae archidiacono'; *Ordo* 34, n.7,var.7: 'ad sacro ordine' (a reading also seen in Wolfenbüttel Weissenburgenses 91); n.42, var.3: 'super omnes episcopis'; see *Les Ordines*, vol. III, pp.538–539.

[33] *Ordo* 27, n.12: 'iuxta consuetudinem'; n. 71: 'Post hos versus, salutat primus scolae archidiaconum' etc.

[34] *Les Ordines*, vol. III, p.49: 'dans un milieu où la réforme alcuinienne portait déjà tous ses fruits'.

[35] Andrieu noted this with respect to *Ordo* 34 and the Sankt Paul fragment, *Les Ordines*, vol. III, p.538: 'Le fragment du ms. De Saint-Paul de Lavanthal (K) se rattache aussi à la même famille ... une particulière parenté ave le couple MQ.'; *Ordo* 27, n.51, the manuscript gives Holy Saturday a title DE SABBATO SANCTO and at n.54, var.7: 'et ut ventum fueri ad Agnus Dei', the addition otherwise peculiar to Montpellier.

The Language(s) of the Ordines

general, the manuscripts of Collection B show a broad agreement with the correctness of the Latin established by the Montpellier manuscript.

However, one striking exception, manuscript Zurich Car. C 102, shows that *ordines* were still being copied in diverse forms of Latin orthography well into the ninth century. Andrieu's assessment alerts us to the peculiarities.[36] Here his explanation was different since the manuscript postdated the assumed watershed of the 'Carolingian Reform', so he supposed that Zurich Car. C 102 could have been written to dictation by a less accomplished Latinist.[37] We might here usefully distinguish errors which all the copies of Collection B make in certain places, with a distinctive orthographic preference; for example, ci over ti, very similar to early manuscripts.[38] This applies equally in the *expositiones* portion of the manuscript, though these features were not recorded in Hanssen's editions; for example, fol.78r *leccionis* in the introduction to the *missa expositionis geminus codex*.[39] The hands which added content including three scrutiny Masses to Gregorian Sacramentary Modena *Biblioteca Capitolare* O.II.7, whose script is similar to the Zurich manuscript, notably have exactly the same traits to the same pronounced degree.[40] This evidence proves that the singular features of the Zurich manuscript were not the result of deficiencies in that manuscript's transcription alone, but can be regarded as a tradition in the handling of liturgical material in the group of scribes or scriptorium who write in both manuscripts, the evidence suggesting this was in Nonantola. Equally expressive that accident cannot fully explain the use of Latin in the Zurich manuscript is a related manuscript, Paris BnF, lat.1248, which likewise offered a selection of *ordines* and xpositions, such as the *Eglogae de ordine romano*, and occasionally has similar spellings.[41]

One other language played a significant role in the transmission of the *ordines* in Francia. I suggested briefly that the use of Greek letters for the

---

[36] *Les Ordines*, vol. II, p.20: 'est sorti des mains d'un copiste peu lettré ... les menues fautes de transcription sont nombreuse'; vol. III, p.379: 'Le ms. de Zurich est le plus entaché de graphies vicieuses.'

[37] *Ibid.*, p.379: 'Il semble avoir été écrit, sous la dictée d'un lecteur par un mediocre latiniste.'

[38] Strikingly in the titles of texts, for which see *Les Ordines*, vol. I, pp.458–464: 'Incipit Ordo vel denunciacio', 'Oracio ad missa', 'Benediccio crucis'; also for example: *Ordo* 28, n.11, var.2: 'tercia', n.72, var.2: 'benediccionem'; *Ordo* 42, n.4, var.6: 'substanciam', var.9: 'propicius', var.15: 'benediccionis', n.8, var.6: 'dominacionis' etc.

[39] Hanssens, *Opera omnia*, vol. I, p.255.

[40] Modena, Biblioteca Capitolare O.II.7, fol.9r–v: 'Miseracio', 'oblacionem', 'miseracionis', 'generacione', etc.

[41] 'benediccionem' on fol.82r, an extract from *Ordo* 28 not identified by Andrieu; Andrieu, *Les Ordines*, vol. IV, p.210: 'Il (Zurich) a quelques affinités avec le Parisianus.1248.'

228   Layout, Script & Language of *Ordo Romanus* Manuscripts

Kyrie Eleison in some early copies of Roman *ordines* was maintained in some cases as a sign of the authenticity of the copy, and expressive of its ability to embody the particularity of Rome's liturgical practices, with which Greek in liturgical use could itself be associated by the reading of the *ordines* themselves. The earliest copies of the baptismal order, going back to the Old Gelasian Sacramentary, assumed the choice of a Greek or a Latin Creed to be recited on the day 'IN AURIUM APERTIONEM'. In the Old Gelasian Sacramentary, the Greek Creed is written out in Latin letters, but the interrogation prior to it was in Latin, not Greek (which may already suggest a movement away from the actual practice in Rome).[42] The Creed in Greek itself is supplied with an interlinear gloss in Latin. However, this basic setting was clearly not the only format circulating in Francia. In the first *ordo* of the Sacramentary of Gellone, the dialogue that precedes the recitation of the Creed is written out in something approximating the Greek language, in Latin letters but employing the Greek *phi* and *omega*, and with more extensive rubrication.[43] The Greek Creed in Latin letters also follows here. A better sense of what this dialogue originally would have consisted of can be seen in the edition of the destroyed Godelgaudus Sacramentary, which probably presented this section in the same way as Gellone.[44] The editors of this Sacramentary have manifestly corrected and supplied accents to the text, so it is difficult to say how 'correct' the Greek was originally here. The Godelgaudus Sacramentary, however, did not give the recited Creed in full, either in Latin or Greek,

---

[42] *Liber Sacramentorum*, Eizenhöfer *et al.* (eds.), pp.48–50: 'Post haec accipiens acolyte unum ex ipsis infantibus masculum, tenens eum in sinistro brachio ponens manum super caput eius. Et interrogat ei praesbiter: Quae lingua confitentur dominum iesum Christum? Respondet: Graecae. Iterum dicit praesbiter: Adnuntia fidem ipsorum qualiter credant. Et dicit acolytus symbolum Graecae decantando, tenens manum super caput infantibus in his uerbis ....' Much the same is given in *Engolismensis*, Saint-Roch (ed.), p.104: 'FILII CARISSIMI AUDISTIS SYMBOLUM GRAECE AUDITE ET LATINUM. Et dicis: qua lingua confitentur Dominus nostrum Iesum Christum. RESPONDIT : LATINE ADNUNCIANT FIDEM IPSORUM.'

[43] *Gellonensis*, Dumas (ed.), pp.68–69: 'Post haec accipiens unum ex ipsis infantibus acolitus masculum tenens eum in sinistro brachyo, ponens manum super caput eius. Et interrogat ei presbyter grece: Lyo sacolr feminaos πτοcπvy moπo thocython Kyron monin xpm. Respondit acolitus: Eainnityn. Iterum dicit presbyter: πnπnτynmhtinii ictyn πuiωntuiti octuc theukcyn. Et dicit acolitus symbolum greci decantando, tenens manum supra caput infantum, his uerbis: Pisteuo his sena theon patera ....'

[44] *Sacramentaire et martyrologie*, Chevalier (ed.), p.349: 'Post haec accipiens acolitus unum ex ipsis infantibus masculum tenens eum in sinistro brachio, ponens manum super caput eius et interrogat praesbyter graece: Ποία γλῶττη ὁμολογοῦιν τὸν Κύριον ἡμων Ιησῦν Χπιστὸν ? Respondit acolitus: Ἑλληνιστί . Item dicit presbyter. Ἀνάγγειλε τὴν πιστιν αὐτῶν πῶς πιστευόσιν. Et dicit acolitus Symbolum graece, decantando, tenens manum super caput infantis. Hoc finito iterum accipiens alter acolitus ex ipsis infantibus foeminam, sicut supra. Et interrogat presbyter latine, qua lingua confiteatur Dominum nostrum Iesum Christum. Respondet acolitus: Latine. Iterum dicit presbyter: Adnuncia fidem ipsorum qualiter credent. Ponens manum acolitus super caput infantis dicit Symbolum decantando.'

The Language(s) of the Ordines   229

merely suggesting this would be said. The exact same configuration is to be seen in the Pontifical of Constance, once Donaueschingen 192 (again showing the close dependence of this late 'pontifical' on a Gelasian of the Eighth Century which was like Godelgaudus).[45] This probably gives us a better sense of what the original Reims Sacramentary probably transmitted. In the Constance Pontifical, an original woeful attempt at writing in Greek letters was then corrected by a second-hand which was much more able. In these two related examples, and in the Sacramentary of Gellone, there is a distinct movement away from the original sense of the rite of dividing a Latin- and Greek-speaking populace. In these examples, the Greek interrogation is given to a child that is specifically *masculum*, while the Latin is specifically a *feminam*. This could be the Frankish interpretation of the original Roman text. Nevertheless, the Greek dialogue (however mangled by Gellone) perhaps indicates a layer of the rite as it was actually performed in Rome that the Old Gelasian itself had lost.

In *Ordo* 11 too, this preceding dialogue is still in Latin, but the more sophisticated rubrication sets out the rite with division by language, then secondly by sex.[46] This is an obvious implication of how the rite in two languages might have been supposed to have been performed. However, *Ordo* 11 did not offer the full written version of the Greek Creed, with the exception of a single manuscript, Wolfenbüttel Weissenburgenses 91, that has the complete Greek and Latin forms (both writing the Niceno-Constantinopolitan Creed as we see in the Sacramentary).[47]

As in its representation of Roman topography and history, here Bernharius' manuscript represents itself as a particularly sophisticated endeavour, and one (once again) that directed itself to numerous needs and expectations beyond the simple use as a 'pontifical'. We know that the compilers of Weissenburgenses 91 consulted a Gelasian Sacramentary specifically in their writing of *Ordo* 11, since the prayers and homilies are filled in. Notably, the Greek of Weissenburgenses 91 (see Figure 8.8) is remarkably

---

[45] *Zwei karolingische Pontifikalien*, Metzger (ed.), p.92*; likewise the 'Pontifical of Paris', *Il cosiddetto pontificale di Poitiers*, Martini (ed.), pp.63–66.

[46] *Les Ordines*, vol. II, pp.434–435: 'Ipsa expleta, tenens acolitus unum ex ipsis infantibus masculum in sinistro brachio et interrogat eum presbiter dicens: Qua lingua confitentur dominum nostrum Iesum Christum? Resp. Graece – Adnuntia fidem ipsorum qualiter credant. Et dicit symoblum graece decantando in his uerbis: Pisteu his ena theon. Hoc expleto vertit se ad feminas et facit similiter. Iterum acolitus alter accipiens ex latinis infantibus unum in sinistro brachio ponens manum dextram super caput ipsius et interrogat eum presbiter: Qua lingua confitentur sicut prius. Et respondit Latina. Dicit ei presbiter: Adnuntia fidem ipsorum qualiter credant. Et ille cantat symbolum. Credo in unum Deum patrem omnipotentem factorem caeli et terrae uisibilium.'

[47] Wolfenbüttel Weissenburgenses 91, fols.57v–58r.

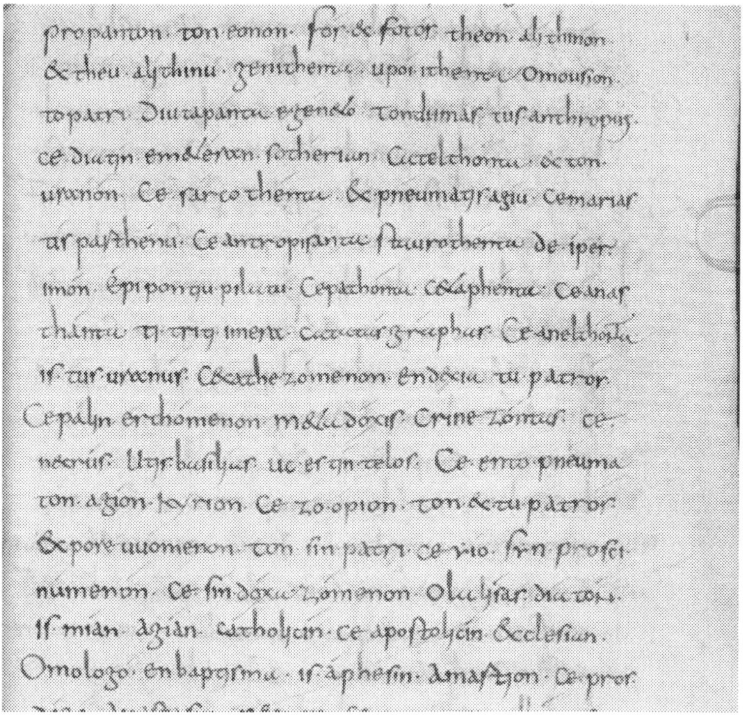

230 Layout, Script & Language of *Ordo Romanus* Manuscripts

Fig. 8.8 The Greek Creed in the Collection of Bernharius of Worms (early ninth century). Herzog August Bibliothek Wolfenbüttel, Weissenburg 91, fol.58r.

correct in word separation and in reflecting contemporary pronunciation, particularly when compared to the Gelasian Sacramentaries (e.g. the use of 'ce' rather than 'kae' for the Greek καὶ; 'yion' rather than 'ion' for γίὸν; a distinction of theta from tau; the recognition of a soft breathing in εἰς as 'eis', not 'his').[48] Uniquely, the scribe has also added accents to aid the

---

[48] *Les Ordines*, vol. II, p.434: 'Pisteuo his enan theon patera pantocratoran, poiitin uranu ce gis, oraton ce panton ce aoraton, ce is enan kyrion ihm xpm, ton yion tu theu ton monogenin, ton ec tu patros genithenta pro panton ton eonon, fos ec fotos, theon alithinon ec theu alithinu, genithenta u poiithenta, omousion to patri, diu ta panta egeneto, ton di imas tus anthropus ce dia tin emeteran sotherian catelthonta ec ton uranon, ce sarcothenta ec pneumatis agiu ce Marias tis parthenu, ce antropisanta staurothenta de iper imon epi Pontiu Pilatu, ce pathonta, ce taphenta, ce anasthanta ti triti imera cata tas graphas, ce anelthonta is tus uranus, ce cathezomenon en dexia tu patros, ce palin erchomenon meta doxis crine zontas ce necrus, u tis basilias uc estin telos ; ce en to pneuma ton agion, kyrion ce zoopion, ton ec tu patros ecporeuomenon, ton sin patri ce yio synproscinumenon, ce sindoxazomenon, o lalisas dia ton [profiton]; [ce] is mian, agian, catholicin ce apostolicin

recitation, and words are carefully separated by a point. We certainly might wonder if Bernharius had checked the Greek Creed against what he could have heard in Rome on one of his visits. Or did he have direct access to an original source for *Ordo* 11, our hypothetical North Italian missal?[49]

The other use of Greek associated with a Roman occasion was during the Roman Easter Vespers where Greek alleluias were sung, described in the second half of *Ordo* 27, but also preserved in a separate tradition in Weissenburgenses 91 (see Figure 8.9).[50] We have in this manuscript the chants at *Ordo* 27, n.74: '*O kyrius. Versus Kecharis*'; *Ordo* 27, n.81: '*Alleluia o pymemonton Israhel. V. Ampelon ex aegypton*'; n.84: '*Alleluia. Prosechyte laos mu. V. Anisaan. V. Uetiuia*'; n.93: '*Uranu diigunthe doxan theu V. imerati imera*'; and n.94: '*Alleluia Deute a gallea sometuto kyrio V. Proftharomen . to prospon autun V. Othi theus megas kyrius.*' Most interesting is the use of Greek abbreviations for *kyrius* and *kyrio* with Greek omega and sigma in the latter chant. Once again, the relative expertise with which the Greek is handled is noteworthy for this manuscript. Yet the Greek chants are more

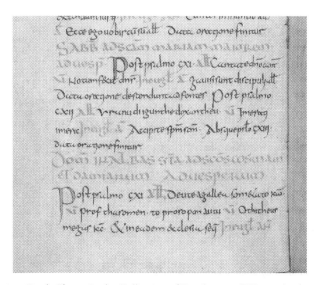

Fig. 8.9 Greek Chants in the Collection of Bernharius of Worms (early ninth century). Herzog August Bibliothek Wolfenbüttel, Weissenburg 91, fol.70v.

---

ecclesian. Omologo en baptisma is aphesin amartion ; ce prosdogo anastasin necron, c zoin tu mellontos eonos. Amin.'

[49] *Les Ordines*, vol. II, pp.373–374.   [50] Van Dijk, 'Medieval Easter Vespers'.

abbreviated in Weissenburgenses 91, compared with the manuscripts of Collection A where they are given in full, instead of just incipits.[51] There is evidence that the Franks both knew that Romans used Greek also at other points during Holy Week (*Ordo* 30B, 23), and aspired to sing in Greek themselves (*Ordo* 33 and the Institution of Angilram of Metz).

Readers and Correctors

We have already drawn attention to forms of correction of the *ordines romani* manuscripts, such as where a correcting hand has checked the grammar and orthography for identifiable errors soon after the completion of the manuscript in the same scriptorium, or where a subsequent copyist in the same or a different scriptorium might correct mistakes in the process of copying. More expressive forms of interaction by readers with the text do however survive in some manuscripts. One manuscript of Collection B, Verona XCII, displays the traits of a particularly interesting corrector, identifiable by his paler ink (see Figure 8.10). It is also interesting that

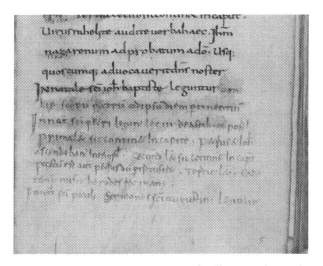

Fig. 8.10 Correcting hand in the Verona copy of Collection B (814–817). Verona Biblioteca Capitolare XCII fol.5r.

---

[51] For example, *Ordo* 27, n.181: 'Deinde post psalmo CXII sequitur Alleluia. Q pymenon ton Jsrael proches, o dyugo o si probaton then Eosyph. O chatimenosio ophy ton cerebin enphanethi, enantynonu Effrem ce Dianamin che Manasse. V[ersus] Ampelon ex Egypton ineteras enim meteras; exebalas etinnia chathefytheusas tusizasi auti. Odonpyisas enprosten autis ce aephyros intingit.'

Readers and Correctors

this corrector uses a more ligatured and idiosyncratic minuscule than the main hand, such as commonly employing uncial d (compare his hand with one of the main hands in the substantial addition to *Ordo* 13B). The nt eg and ec ligatures, for example, are never used by the main hands.

We have seen this corrector add notices of the people involved in the rite to the margin to *Ordo* 11. He also uses signs to add passages which the initial scribe left out, and corrects the latter with interlinear additions. However, in the case of Verona XCII, this corrector had access to an alternative manuscript, which Andrieu identified as similar to Cologne 138, probably the exemplar for the latter.[52] From this source, the later hand added, for example, the Supplement *Ordo* 3 on fol.21v after *Ordo* 1. Like Cologne 138, the version of *Ordo* 1 in this example had already removed some of the specific identifiable features of Collection B, replacing the very specific Roman details that had been removed, and removing the additions made to *Ordo* 1 in manuscripts of Collection B. The narrative of *Ordo* 1 was compared to that of Collection B found in Verona XCII by the corrector, and the additional pieces added marginally, while the pieces not found in this example were marked out with a line. There was therefore some interest in alternative versions of the text, and the expectation that readers would want to know this. The interest of the corrector in representing alternative traditions is further expressed in his addition of Canon 46 of the Council of Laodicea in the blank lower part of fol.64v.[53] As Amalarius also noted, this canon contradicted *Ordo* 11 by saying that the catechumens should recite the Creed on Maundy Thursday, and not in the scrutiny during Lent, *de aurium apertionem*, and, according to him, some people followed this tradition.[54] The corrector of Verona XCII shows how *ordines* were being read widely with the same methodology as Amalarius, without the expectation that they would give the single definitive shape to ritual, but bearing in mind the viable alternatives in the diverse liturgical tradition, and weighing these up actively with the narratives, perhaps even one or more alternative traditions of the *ordines* where these were available.

---

[52] *Les Ordines*, vol. II, pp.17–20.

[53] Verona XCII fol.64v: 'Concilium laudicense titulus XLVI. Quod oporteat eos qui ad baptisma [*sic*] ueniunt symbolum discere et V feria septimane maioris episcopo aut presbiteris reddere'; Hefele-Leclercq (ed.), *Histoire des Conciles*, p.1021.

[54] Hanssens (ed.), *Opera omnia*, vol. II, p.66: 'In ea die paenitentes veniunt ad solutionem, et apud quosdam redditur symbolum a catecuminis, ut in canone Laodicensis concilii continentur. Nos tamen, Romanum ordinem sequentes, hanc redditorem servamus usque in Sabbato Sancto.'

234   Layout, Script & Language of *Ordo Romanus* Manuscripts

The annotator of Verona XCI has been identified as Pacificus of Verona, archdeacon of the episcopal church.[55] Tradition has tended to attribute a greater significance to Pacificus than can be verified, but he was certainly active in Verona at the time the manuscript was written: the two documents signed by him which are the only incontrovertible evidence of his writing are from 809 and 814.[56] It is certainly also true that the traits of the hand in Verona XCII are closely comparable with those in other manuscripts whose marginalia were also identified as the hand of Pacificus.[57] Three such manuscripts have very similar ligatures and other traits, such as the uncial d, comparable with our manuscript.[58] In general, I have assumed a process of construction of the 'pontifical' whereby the manuscripts can be directly attributed to and planned by the individual bishop, but it should be admitted that archdeacons were also very likely planners of these manuscripts. The duties of archdeacons included teaching junior clergy about their ecclesiastical duties, including liturgy, and they certainly took a leading role in the new canonical communities set up around cathedrals, including at Verona in the time of Bishop Ratold.[59] The functions of the

---

[55] Teresa Venturini, *Ricerche Paleografiche intorno all'Archidicono Pacifico* (Verona, 1929), pp.85, 125; Meersseman *et al.*, *L'orazionale dell'archidiacono Pacifico*, p.5, suggest Verona XCI, which they call 'un pontificale embrionale, uno dei primi tentative del genere' was 'certainly written in the hand of Pacificus' but there is actually no evidence that he was the main hand or the main scribe of the other liturgical manuscripts here mentioned. This opinion is a misinterpretation of Venturini's more cautious verdict.

[56] Cristina La Rocca, 'A Man for all Seasons: Pacificus of Verona and the Creation of a Local Carolingian Past', in Yitzhak Hen and Matthew Innes (eds.), *The Uses of the Past in the Early Middle Ages* (Cambridge, 2000), p.250; G. P. Marchi, 'Per un restauro della biografia di Pacifico, humilis levita Christi', in Dorothee Walz (ed.), *Scripturus vitam. Lateinische Biographie von der Antike bis in die Gegenwart. Festgabe für Walter Berschin zum 65. Geburtstag* (Heidelberg, 2002), pp.379–392.

[57] Bischoff noted with the opinion 'Marginalien von Pacificus' a number of manuscript examples, such as Bischoff, *Katalog*, vol. II, p.242, 3077 for Munich Clm 6407. A complete list is found in the index volume: Bischoff, *Katalog*, vol. IV. p.158.

[58] Berlin Phillipps 1829 is in colour at http://bvmm.irht.cnrs.fr/consult/consult.php?mode=ecran&p anier=false&reproductionId=4559&VUE_ID=993508&carouselThere=false&nbVignettes=tout&p age=1&angle=0&zoom=petit&tailleReelle= ; Munich Clm 6407 (from microfilm) at http://daten .digitale-sammlungen.de/~db/0003/bsb00036088/images/index.html?seite=00001&l=de. A large collection of manuscripts also remained in Verona, seen in *CLA*, vol. IV, for example, p.25; Munich Clm 6407 fol.31r can be employed as example. Here, Pacificus uses an **nt** ligature in the middle of a word 'pronuntiatur' (with a pro abbreviation), and the second **n** is an uncial form. He also uses the two-c **a** form, but the minuscule **a** form has a pronounced slant (Berlin 1829 165v; compare stella with main text). Rather than using the Caroline minuscule **d** consistently, Pacificus often uses the sloping uncial **d**, as fol.14v of the same manuscript on 'ordinanda' (which also has an uncial **n** on the first **n**), where the second **d** is a particularly striking almost diagonal on the ascender (also on the word 'Theodosius' in Berlin, fol.157r). When in ligature, his **r** goes below and above the line (as in 'oratio' in Clm 6407, fol.314 with an **ra** ligature).

[59] A. Amanieu, 'Archidiacre', in *Dictionnaire du Droit Canonique*, vol. I (Paris, 1935), cols. 948–1004; Barrow, *Clergy in the Medieval World*, pp.49–51.

Readers and Correctors   235

ordo manuscripts to deepen the meaning and explain the rationale of the rituals they described, as well as the focus of the individual texts on the arranging and placements of the hierarchy of the church itself, would fall within the archdeacon's remit. In particular, the Roman archdeacon had a very pronounced liturgical presence in a number of these texts, most notably in *Ordo* 1, including in pieces which Pacificus specifically adds in the margin to Verona XCII.[60] Acting in the person of the Roman archdeacon liturgically would enhance the prestige of a Frank in this position. For example, the archdeacon announces the station in Frankish additions to *Ordo* 1 in both *Ordo* 15 and in Wolfenbüttel Weissenburgenses 91.[61] Few archdeacons are known as well as Pacificus, so in most other cases their possible involvement in copying and using *ordines*, and in setting up liturgical celebration, remains speculation.

[60] Verona Biblioteca Capitolare, XCII, fol.39v upper margin: 'ita confirmatur ab archidiacono'; *Les Ordines*, vol. II, p.102.
[61] See above.

Conclusion
Who Copied the Ordines Romani, *and Why?*

While Andrieu pushed back the transmission of the *ordines romani* from Rome into Francia to the very early eighth century, manuscript evidence has never been uncovered to substantiate this. With manuscripts only appearing at the end of the eighth century, and the immediate flurry of adaptation that accompanied them from the moment they first appear, we cannot reasonably accept a widespread transmission of such texts prior to 750. They thus appear as a consummately Carolingian phenomenon, and require explanation as such. A number of the *ordines* can reasonably be linked to personal exchanges and experiences of Rome by certain elite clergymen of the Carolingian Church, and the thirst to take back a certain piece of the city upon one's return. As 'textual relics', as much as liturgical models, they served the personal and institutional needs of those who copied them.[1] Notably, the appearance of Collection A in Lorsch manuscript BAV Pal.lat.487, and the presence of *Ordo* I in the early Bern fragment from Metz with the *Regula Canonicorum* that he authored, point clearly to Chrodegang of Metz as a possible transmitter (inventor?) of one or more of the earliest *ordines romani*. Chrodegang was in Rome in 753. He also had a clear motivation to begin to invent such texts, since he was engaged in a liturgical project in Metz that involved the imitation of forms he identified with Rome.[2] His *Regula* for canons refers to the example and 'order' of Rome on several occasions. Chrodegang was also probably responsible for a revival or renewal of the stational system in Metz, for which the group of *Ordo* I ('short recension') 2, 24 and 26 could have suited as a model.

In those activities which brought elements of Rome into life in Metz, Chrodegang provided a model that subsequent bishops of the era would pursue in their own cities. His programme included architectural modification, the seeking out of relics of Roman martyrs, and the foundation or

---

[1] Schieffer, 'Redeamus ad fontem'.   [2] Claussen, *Reform of the Frankish Church*, pp.213–287.

Conclusion

reinterpretation of liturgical structures such as the stational systems.[3] When he explicitly invoked the Roman model in relation to the canons of his cathedral, Chrodegang used it as a means to better arrange and distinguish between them, with a particular focus on their clothing. If Chrodegang wrote and circulated *ordines*, this was something else in which subsequent bishops would also emulate him.

Nevertheless, the lack from elsewhere of such rich documentation as we possess for Metz should not make us emphasise the example of Chrodegang above and beyond all others. Another set of early *ordines* seems to have begun to be disseminated from another post-Roman city with a powerful and historic episcopacy, Tours. Previous attempts to locate *Ordo* 15 and the tradition which developed out of that text to monasteries such as Luxeuil or the Roman basilical monasteries have not been satisfactory.[4] Nor would *Ordo* 15 adequately suggest association with Chrodegang of Metz.[5] Instead, the Basilica of St Martin at Tours presents itself as by far the most likely place of redaction of *Ordo* 15. The creation of this text may have been inspired by Chrodegang in some respects, since the creator knew the 'short recension' of *Ordo* 1, here simplified as the text's first Mass *Ordo*.[6] Related texts, *ordines* 15, 18 and 19, may represent a trio of Tours products, possibly a kind of 'customary' of the Basilica of St Martin, or a collection of useful bits and pieces of knowledge. If so, the compilers of such texts in Tours were as interested in the Roman stational system as Chrodegang was in Metz, and we can posit a similar early Carolingian revival or reinterpretation of that system, which already had a local history recorded in Gregory of Tours.[7] But, as would happen in the first surviving manuscripts of Collection A, Tours' *ordo* lays the scene for an ambiguous use of the Roman liturgical inheritance in which manuscripts engage through the entire period. They make claims to reflect Roman practice, while they contradict papal decree and Roman custom.

Another useful indication of the circulation and use of texts like these *ordines* is the *Institutio* of Angilbert. Linked to Tours by his close friendship with Alcuin, he created a text quite similar to *Ordo* 15, but one that was more complex and developed, and likewise rooted in a 'stational' framework.

---

[3] Heitz, 'La groupe cathedral du Metz'.
[4] *Les Ordines*, vol. III, pp.20–21; Peter Jeffrey, 'The Early Liturgy of Saint Peter's'; Hallinger, 'Die römischen *ordines*'.
[5] Claussen, *Reform of the Frankish Church*, p.270.
[6] *Les Ordines*, vol. III, pp.67–68; Van Dijk, 'Urban and Papal Rites', p.458 is not convincing when he suggests this Mass *ordo* is an early Roman one because of its simplicity.
[7] Häußling, *Mönchskonvent und Eucharistiefeier*, p.198.

238   Conclusion

Once the first *ordines* had been created, a secondary transmission took place emanating from some of Francia's most powerful monasteries. Lorsch and Murbach offer us the first witnesses of a preliminary form of Collection A. It was only later completed with *Ordines* 13A and 42, the complete form that can be seen in the Montpellier manuscript . The two *ordines* added to the Collection for the first time in the Montpellier manuscript do seem to reflect additional resources present particularly in France. This sequence of manuscripts therefore suggests that an early version of Collection A circulating in the Rhine/Alsace region was then completed by copyists in Northern France, at the same time as Collection B began to circulate in parallel in Italy and Alemannia. In all these manuscripts of Collection A, the 'long recension' of *Ordo* 1 which is present in this Collection gives us a reinterpretation of the earlier 'short recension' that is even more focused on the particularities of Roman topography, something the full Collection elsewhere somewhat sporadically engaged with (e.g. in the Easter Vespers portion of *Ordo* 27 newly taken out of the Antiphoner). While this makes the 'use' of the text as a straightforward model for the replication of stational services in Francia more complex, it allows us to see that our conception of liturgical 'usefulness' does not capture the full range of what such texts might mean to their copyists. Indeed, the principally monastic circulation of Collection A (and the common presence of it and other *ordo romanus* manuscripts in monastic library lists, e.g. in Reichenau) reveals that monks could be invested in liturgical models that were not directly applicable to them. In these monasteries, the incorporation of alternative *ordines* such as *Ordo* 29 (a monastic reworking of *Ordo* 27 in BAV Pal.lat.487) into the same manuscripts suggests that monks understood and used texts which were divergent from the Roman practice in many of their details, and retooled for use in a monastery not an urban church. The note attached to this text concerning a consultation with Pope Hadrian I (r.772–795) shows that the relation to Rome embodied in these manuscripts was perceived as a still living one for the monks of his day, renewed in the present as they now followed the Pope's instructions.

The connection with Rome was persistent, even as the text diverged from actual Roman practice in details. This helps to explain why the complete Collection A is more complex than is designation as the 'Roman Collection'. Much like the 'fraudulent' *Ordo* 15, the Collection as a whole can be seen to shift between accurate observations of Roman practice and what we know to be non-Roman usages, such as the sevenfold scrutinies described in *Ordo* 11. The exact boundaries of where one ended and the other began may not have concerned Frankish copyists as much as

Conclusion 239

they do modern researchers, since it appears that compilers understood that texts we identify as belonging to separate traditions and origins were able to offer complementary descriptions of rituals, all of which might be rational and useful in their own way. How far later copyists were aware of this ambiguous relation to Rome is reflected in Amalarius of Metz's occasional confusion over whether something was done in Rome or not; yet, as the thundering epilogue in St Gallen 349 stated, if there were doubts, they should go to Rome itself and observe the liturgies there, as these texts attest quite a number must have done.[8] Certainly, even once he had been to Rome and pestered the Roman clergy about their ritual practices at length, Amalarius still saw value in the customs that diverged from Rome.[9]

The ample evidence from St Gallen reveals to us further that a single monastery was not limited by the constraint that a single manuscript would offer all useful liturgical information from all perspectives, or that a single *ordo* would tell you everything you needed to know about a ritual. Only here do we find the complete copy of Tours text, *Ordo* 15, but side by side with a monastic reinterpretation *Ordo* 16 in St Gallen 349. Both *Ordo* 16 and 17 claim to mediate between the Roman tradition and the Rule of St Benedict.[10]

Additionally, judging by the somewhat later manuscript, St Gallen 614, the monastery of St Gallen must have also had access to the 'short recension' of *Ordo* 1, and its two Supplements, a configuration that principally aims to propagate and explain stational usages but which nowhere else survives complete, here presented with early Holy Week *Ordo* 24 and 26 (also sources for Collection A). One early manuscript, Brussels 10127–10144, may have originally witnessed or harked back to something similar, known about in the manuscript's home of North-Eastern France, since here is found *Ordo* 3, one of the two Supplements, but without *Ordo* 1 (two quires are missing which might have contained this text originally) and the two Holy Week *ordines*, *Ordo* 24 and 26, as well as a set of Masses from the Sacramentary each provided with their stational notice. There are also stations noted in the Gradual which the manuscript

---

[8] *Ordo* 19, n.34: 'vadat sibi ipse Roma aut, si piget, missa suo fidele in suo loco transmittat et inquerat diligenter si est ita aut non est, quod de pluerbus [*sic*] patrum conscripsemus, aut si non ita ibidem celebratur, vel si bene cum sancta intentione vel devotione inquesierat et adhuc in centuplum melius, unde in opera Dei proficiat, invenerit.'

[9] Jones, *A Lost Work*, pp.66–68.

[10] *Ordo* 16, tit.: 'incipit instruccio ecclesiastici ordinis, qualiter in coenubiis fideliter domino servientes tam iuxta auctoritatem catholice atque apostolice romane ecclesie quam iuxta dispositione et regulam sancti Benedicti'.

240   Conclusion

contains, making this manuscript also a 'stational guideline'.[11] In St Gallen 614, the early stock of texts (in the order *Ordo* 1, 2, 24, 26, 3 at pp.184–213) is placed alongside what I described as a 'pilgrim dossier' (*Ordo* 22, the appendix to *Ordo* 28, 12, 36 and 8 at pp.213–230), which was (at least in part, if not fully) the fruit of an intimate observation of Roman practice by a Frankish enthusiast, which can be placed in the reign of Leo III (r.795–816). The observations of this Frankish enthusiast would have been just prior to the copying of the manuscript, apparently in the first or second quarter of the ninth century, but would constitute a later source than the preceding section (which had already been adapted into Collection A by the turn of the ninth century). The manuscript appears thereby to combine at least two separate booklets of *ordines*, stemming from two separate compilers, pre-serving for the monastery various strata of *ordines* describing Roman prac-tices available to them, which in some cases overlap in their subjects (e.g. Holy Saturday is treated in the appendix to *Ordo* 28, as well as *Ordo* 24 and 26). The earlier of the two booklets, the 'stational' programme, could well go back to Chrodegang, and would have suited his agenda. Councils such as Attigny in 765, where Chrodegang led bishops and abbots from all over the kingdom, including Northern France, might have provided a venue for distributing and recommending such texts.[12] The second dossier belongs with a circle of bishops in the next generation, who had followed in Chrodegang's footsteps.

Arn of Salzburg (*c.*740–821) was the leader of this circle. Arn's creation of several *ordines* is to be linked to his status as the newest metropolitan of the kingdom. He seems to have conceived two texts dealing with the metropolitan responsibilities of holding councils and ordaining bishops, and probably the text *Ordo* 38 which describes the stational celebration of the Ember Saturday and may be correctly set on the streets of Salzburg. His text, specifically called an 'ORDO ROMANUS' for the leadership of a council, is known in the ninth century from Italy, attesting to Arn's wide distribution of the texts (to his suffragen bishop in Säben perhaps?). A version of it appears with Collection B of the *ordines romani* in Cologne 138, but the most distinctive version with citations of Alcuin's letters collected by Arn is known only in BAV lat.7701, another 'pontifical' from the bishopric of Chieti, which is also not a metropolitan see.[13] Arn's *ordo* for ordaining bishops appears in a copy of a *Kollektar-Pontifikale* copied in Regensburg under a direct suffragan,

---

[11] The stational Masses are edited in C. Coeburgh and Pierre de Puniet (eds.), *Liber sacramentorum excarsus*, CCCM 47 (Turnhout, 1977), pp.81–110; the gradual is edited in *Antiphonale Missarum sextuplex*, Hesbert (ed.), as the 'Antiphonaire de Mont-Blandin', pp.xv–xviii.

[12] *MGH* Conc.II.1, pp.72–73.   [13] For the manuscript, Westwell, 'The *ordines* of Vat.lat.7701'.

Conclusion 241

probably Baturich of Regensburg (r.817–847). This manuscript shows that Arn also innovated in the way he presented and contextualised the *ordines*. If, as seems convincing, the exemplar of the *Kollektar-Pontifikale* today in Vienna goes back to Arn, he chose to set his copy of the metropolitan *ordo* for ordaining a bishop and his copy of *Ordo* 38 describing the Ember Days in this innovative format. Like other 'pontificals', which survive from the first decades of the night century, the same manuscript also carries the *ordo* for church dedication, similar to *Ordo* 41, and a baptism *ordo*.[14] Very fragmentary pieces indicate that the original manuscript also had an *ordo* describing Holy Week in detail, though unfortunately too little survives to determine much of its nature.[15] The 'pontifical' conceived by Arn would be another early version of such a book, contemporary with other manuscripts identified as such like Cologne 138. This identification led scholars to evaluate such manuscripts based on their closeness to the genre as it exists today, a book that is defined by its exclusive orientation to practice. But the continual association of these early books with the *ordines romani* shows that the manuscripts were formulated to answer numerous other expectations, that interacted with and supplemented any use made of this manuscript.

To their creators, such books were not inadequate pontificals, as they would later be defined. Judging by the way these manuscripts are put together, Carolingian copyists did not see other practices of reading as irreconcilable with liturgical 'usefulness' in the way Andrieu and others supposed in the distinction they drew between 'true liturgical books' and 'library books'. Indeed, the manuscripts present such additional practice of reading as, in fact, indispensable to the Carolingian understanding of liturgical 'usefulness', something that requires us to abandon our preconceptions of what the creators of these manuscripts were setting out to do and how their readers approached the books. In the case of Arn, his 'pontifical' functions additionally as a manifesto of his metropolitanate. In particular, the description of the ordination of a bishop, in its level of detail, goes far beyond what is found in other early manuscripts (which generally include only the single rubric for the climax of the rite from the *Statuta*), demonstrating that this was one of Arn's focuses. The copy made in Regensburg might either stem from Arn's own initiative to distribute this manifesto to

---

[14] *Kollektar-Pontifikale*, Unterkircher (ed.), pp.114–120, 121–126; compare the MSS in *Zwei karolingische Pontifikalien*, Metzger (ed.).

[15] Fragmente I in *Kollektar-Pontifikale*, Unterkircher (ed.), pp.130 for example: 'et intrat eodem sono in consecrationem maiorem ... emundationem quam lauandis poss ...'; the latter quote, though identified tentatively by Unterkicher with Maundy Thursday's foot washing, is actually from the blessing of the font, *Le sacramentaire grégorien*, Deshusses (ed.), vol. I, p.187.

242   Conclusion

his suffragans as emblematic of his authority, or from the desire of the bishop of Regensburg to obtain a copy of it in order to illuminate his own episcopal office as one that was dependent on Arn's, passed down in the ceremony here described and, through Arn, going back to Rome.

Intrinsic to the presentation of Arn's metropolitan office in the Vienna manuscript is the dependence of his office on Rome and the papacy, his metropolitan status being directly granted by Pope Leo III. Thus, the defence of this office was maintained through an ongoing link with Rome which the manuscript posits. The ordination rituals are, in this case, the heart of the manuscript (the Roman Canon of the Mass was written within the *Kollektar-Pontifikale* as part of the ordination Mass for a bishop as well), and the manuscript formulates this apostolic dependence in familiar ways including the assumption of a stational system in *Ordo* 38, whose 'station at St Peter's' is clearly to associate Salzburg Cathedral with the Vatican, accompanied by canons and pronouncements of popes, real and pseudonymous. The weaving of elements of *Ordo* 34 into the sequence of grades would certainly have led readers who were familiar with this text to see these Frankish rites, no matter how they differed in their conception of ordination, as being in seamless continuity with the Roman rites which *Ordo* 34 described.

Given Arn's interests and his repeated visits to Rome, it is far from unlikely that other *ordines* describing Roman practice could have been formulated and put into circulation by him and his circle. Very likely candidates are the *ordines* for specific ceremonies in the 'Collection of St Amand', *ordines* 20 and 21, which show some textual kinship with the Vienna text of *Ordo* 38.[16] As stated previously, these texts were copied on blank folios in Paris BnF lat.974 at the end of the ninth century, most likely from an earlier manuscript (or a series of *libelli*?) which was falling apart or in danger of destruction. The copying happened at St Amand, where Arn had been abbot. The monastery had been his most important *scriptorium*, and copied liturgical books for him. If Arn had made a collection of *ordines romani*, St Amand would most likely have written it down and stored that copy, until it was copied later to be preserved in spare folios of the Paris manuscript. The Sacramentary known as the Colbertine fragments from St Amand (Paris BnF lat.2296) in the 'Arn-Stil' even shows similar orthographical peculiarities as the *ordines* of this Collection, perhaps placing them both in a similar stage of the *scriptorium*'s development![17] Given the state of the Collection now, it

[16] See above.
[17] Edward Kennard Rand, James A. Mc.Donough and Thomas J. Wade, 'An Unrecognised Sacramentary of Tours', *Harvard Studies in Classical Philology*, 60 (1951), pp.244–245; Sieghild Rehle and Klaus Gamber (eds.), *Sacramentarium Gelasianum mixtim von Saint-Amand* (Regensburg, 1973).

Conclusion

is not possible to determine how many of the *ordines* here preserved might have been originally conceived by Arn.

It is tempting to wonder if *Ordo* 4, a complete Frankish reworking of the stational Mass of *Ordo* 1, might have represented Arn's practice at one stage in his career. Whoever was behind this text knew *Ordo* 1 in the 'short recension', as well as *Ordo* 2 and 3, the same set as we find, for example, in St Gallen 614. We know that *ordines* circulated early in the regions of St-Amand, where Arn would have chosen to have these *ordines* written down. Brussels 10127–10144, from Northern France or Belgium, far from being a 'local priest's handbook', could have been among the sources used by Arn here, since it carries the specialised Supplement *Ordo* 3, and probably originally other *ordines* as well. A relationship of Brussels 10127–10144 to Arn's St Amand is strengthened by the curious title of the Sacramentary excerpt with stations which the Brussels manuscript appends to its *ordines*: 'INCIPIT LIBER SACRAMENTORUM EXCARSUS' (fol.125r). The Colbertine fragments of a Gelasian Sacramentary in the 'Arn-Stil' use the same unusual term: 'INCIPIT LIBER SACRAMENTORUM ROMANE ECCLESIAE ORDINE EXSCARPSUS.'[18] If the Collection of St Amand was also written originally in the 'Arn-Stil', it would suit Andrieu's diagnosis that the later copyist was working from a minuscule with which he was not fully familiar:

> Les fautes dont il fourmille montrent que le scribe n'a pas toujours su lire exactement le modèle qu'il avait sous les yeux. Ce dernier devait présenter un grand nombre d'abréviations, ou plutôt de ligatures, comme on en trouve dans les diverses écritures nationales antérieures à la réforme carolingienne.[19]

Along with its Frankish recension of the pontifical Mass, the Collection of St Amand also has the following texts:

Roman styles of ordination in *Ordo* 39
Ordo 43, for church dedication, which made use of both Frankish *Ordo* 41 and Roman *Ordo* 42
Ordo 30B, which combined *Ordo* 30A, a Frankish source available in the region of St Amand, with some Roman details, concerning both the stations and Eucharistic customs.

---

[18] Paris BnF lat.2296, fol.4v.
[19] *Les Ordines*, vol. II, p.138: 'The faults with which it swarms show that the scribe could not always read the model he had before his eyes. This latter must have presented a great number of abbreviations, or more likely ligatures, as one finds in the diverse national scripts before the Carolingian Reform.'

244   Conclusion

If the St Amand collection can be traced to a single author, that author was quite comfortable weaving specifically Roman traces and terminology among Frankish rites.

The surviving wealth of legislation and advice with which Arn was involved reveals a career-long preoccupation with liturgy, and there is even more evidence for his liturgical preoccupations than we can find for Chrodegang. Roman tradition is a constant refrain in the Council of Reisbach he led in 798, including baptism 'secundum ordinem traditionem Romanorum'.[20] Even more eloquent is his Council which met repeatedly at Reisbach, Freising and Salzburg in the year 800, at which the Bavarian bishops including Baturich's predecessor in Regensburg, Adalwin (bishop, 791–816) were present.[21] The council's rulings are buttressed by papal and conciliar legislation, including citations of the liturgical injunction to perform the peace from Innocent's letter to Decentius, and the Decretal of Zosimus which is excerpted in the *Kollektar-Pontifikale*.[22] In the preface in an early Freising copy of the council not reproduced in the *MGH* edition, Arn specifically recalled his promotion to a metropolitan by Leo III 'ad limina petri'.[23] A series of canons provide clear witness to the coherence of Arn's programme with many of the existing *ordines romani*.[24] For the most significant, Canon 43, the *MGH* edition gives a reading that is very difficult to interpret liturgically, not helped by unclear punctuation.[25] However, consultation of the early and more complete Freising manuscript not known to this editor at the time, Munich BSB

---

[20] *MGH* Conc.II.i, pp.197–201: 'Et hoc considerat episcopus ... ut secundum traditionem Romanae aecclesiae possint instruere ... missas secundum consuetudinem caelebrare, sicut Romana traditione nobis tradidit. Baptismum publicum constitutis temporibus per II vices in anno faciat, in Pascha, in Pentecosten; et hoc secundum ordinem traditionis Romanae debet facere ... sapientem doctorem, qui secundum traditionem Romanorum possint instruere ....'

[21] *Ibid.*, pp.205–219.

[22] *Ibid.*, p.208: 'De non ordinandis presbiteris et diaconibus nisi in legitimis temporibus sicut in decretis Zosimi papae continetur kap.III ... .Ut pacem omnibus inperetur custodiri sicut in capitulo I. continetur regulae Innocentii papae.'

[23] Munich BSB Clm 28135, fol.iv: 'Idcirco per misericordiam diuini muneris direxit humillum uirum arnonem episcopum ad limina sanctissimi petri principis apostolorum seu et apostolicum uirum Leonem papam ut ipse dignaretur iamdictum uirum ad maius quam ante fuerat culmen eleuare ... Ita etiam pallium ei largire dignatus est ....'

[24] *MGH* Conc.II.i, pp.205–219: 'XXXIII Ut infra quadragesima singulis ebdomadibus ternas faciant laetanias, id est II. Feria, IIII. Feria, VI Feria.'; 'XLI Ut missa sanctae Dei genetricis Mariae quarter in anno sollemniter celebretur, id est purificatio IIII. Non. Febr. et conceptio, quod est VIII. Kalendarum Aprilium, et assumptio, quod est XVIII Kal. Septembris, et nativitas eius, quod est VI Id. Septemb.'; 'XLII Ut feria. IIII ante initium Quadragesime, quam Romani caput ieiunii nuncupant, sollemniter celebretur cum laetania et missa post horam nonam.'

[25] *MGH* Conc.II.i, p.212: 'XLIII Ut, si vobis videtur usum Romanum habere velle, fer.IIII ante cenam Domini orationes, quae scriptae sunt ad fer.VI Parasceue, ab episcopis vel presbiteris hora tertia diei supradictae fer.IIII dicuntur in ecclesia cum genuflexione nisi tantum pro Iudaeis, similter et in

Conclusion 245

Clm 28135, gives us a reading that is more correct in format, dividing this text edited as a single canon into two:

> XLII Ut si vobis videtur usum Romanum habere velle, fer.IIII ante cenam Domini orationes maiores, quae scriptae sunt ad feria quinta (sic. sexta) Parasceue, ab episcopis vel presbiteris hora tertia diei supradictae fer.IIII dicuntur in ecclesia cum genuflexione nisi tantum pro Iudaeis, similiter et in Parasceve hora nona, ut Romani faciunt
>
> XLIII Ubi in missale habetur orationem ad collectam secundum Romanam consuetudinem faciamus.[26]

As Andrieu noted, Canon 43 is firmly in agreement with the text of *Ordo* 24, nn.1–3, and was perhaps directly based upon it, because details such as not genuflecting in the prayer for the Jews are first attested in this text.[27] The recovered Canon 44 makes it clear that Arn was enjoining stational observances on the Roman model, since the '*collecta*' mentioned is the Roman one indicated, as the canon says, in the Sacramentary for certain feasts, a gathering at a previous church before one processed to the station for the Mass.[28] It is not used like the term 'collect' is used today for the first prayer of the Mass, known in the Early Middle Ages simply as *oratio*. This is the terminology and tradition which *Ordo* 20, 21, 22 and 38 all use for particular days on which the *collecta* was used in Rome: Candlemas, Ash Wednesday and the Ember Days.[29] The Vienna manuscript even copies an *Oratio ad collectam* from the Gregorian Sacramentary with this title for both Candlemas and Annunciation, as well as correct stational notices for the Easter Vespers and the Great Litany.[30]

Parasceve hora nona, ut Romani faciunt, sicut in missale habetur, orationem ad collectam secundum Romanam consuetudinem faciamus.'

[26] Munich Clm BSB 28135 fol.9r–v: '43 That if it seems to you to intend to have the Roman use, on the Wednesday before Maundy Thursday should be said in church by bishops and priests at the third hour of the aforementioned day the Great Prayers, which are written down at Good Friday, with genuflection except for the prayer for the Jews. Do similarly on Good Friday, at the ninth hour as the Romans do. 44 Where in the Missal is found orationem ad collectem, we should do this according to Roman custom.'

[27] *Les Ordines*, vol. III, pp.287–288.

[28] For example *Le sacramentaire grégorien*, Deshusses (ed.), pp.123, 131; Richard Hierzegger, 'Collecta und Statio: Die römischen Stationsprozessionen im frühen Mittelalter', *Zeitschrift für katholische Theologie*, 60 (1936), pp.511–554.

[29] *Ordo* 21, n.1: 'Quando letania maior debet fieri adnuntiat eam diaconus in statione catholica et dicit: Feria tale ueniente, collecta in basilica beati Illius; statio in basilica sancti illius'; *Ordo* 22, n.1: 'Feria IV initium quadragesimae collegunt omnes ad ecclesiam sanctae Anastasiae'; n.15 'Ceteri vero episcopi aut presbiteri, qui collectam non faciunt . . .'; *Kollektar-Pontifikale*, Unterkircher (ed.), p.92: 'pronuntiante ecclesia facta collecta'.

[30] *Ibid*.: 'Oratio ad collectam. Erudi quaesumus . . .'; pp.58–59: 'Sabbato ad sanctum Johannem ad . . . [. . .]brum . . . Die dominica ad sanctos Cosmas et Damianum; p.60 Ad sanctum Laurentium in lucina . . . Ad sanctum Ualentinum.'

246   Conclusion

These conspicuous uses of Roman tradition are in addition to the cases already cited in the 813 Council of Mainz, at which we know Arn sat with Richulf of Mainz and Bernharius of Worms. The Great Litany was also here enjoined (the reference in several manuscripts to the custom 'sicut sancti patres nostri instituerunt' accords with the title of the Collection of St Amand's *Ordo* 4: 'sicut investigatum a sanctis patribus').[31] Arn's characterisation of these specific occasions as Roman tradition would suggest he may have written and circulated certain *ordines* that gave the details of what this meant, for example showing what a '*collecta*' in the Roman tradition was, and how one performed it. Arn therefore could be a very likely author of several of the texts edited by Andrieu, based on his own observation and record of Roman practice. The 'Collection of St Amand' is a later copy which preserves an early collection of *ordines*, while the Vienna *Kollektar-Pontifical* seems to be a copy of another, later (?) liturgical book he had made once he was metropolitan in which he made use of similar texts. In both cases, Arn's use of Roman *ordines* does not imply the simple replication of Roman liturgical norms in Salzburg; rather, his use of these texts was a spur to innovation in formatting and presenting liturgical texts, also a lively expression and vindication of his office, which was founded and depended on the links to Rome these books present.

It is telling about the nature of what has been characterised as Carolingian liturgical 'reform' that none of the bishops associated with Arn used the *ordines romani* in exactly way that Arn did. Their 'pontifical' manuscripts are quite different from Arn's, and they made use of different texts and traditions. The injunctions made by the councils were not therefore interpreted by those involved in drafting and disseminating them as suggesting a uniform interpretation, or the uniform use of the same texts in the same ways. The way in which these recommendations were put into practice, judging by the manuscripts, was shaped by resources present in these other institutions, and also by the individual agenda of those involved in copying them. We have 'pontificals' that can be associated with two of Arn's contemporaries, both copied in the early ninth century.

Munich BSB Clm 14510, dated 824–827, specifically names Baturich of Regensburg, who was suffragen under Arn, and would, in fact, have been

---

[31] *MGH* Conc.II.1, p.269: 'De laetania maiore XXXIII. Placuit nobis, ut laetania maior observanda sit a cunctis Christianis diebus tribus'; Munich Clm 5541 gives: 'Placuit nobis ut laetania maior observanda sit a cunctis christianis in uno die, id est VII. Kal. Maii ut sicut sancti patres nostri constituerunt, non equitando nec preciosis vestibus induti, sed discalciati, cinere et cilicio induti, nisi infirmitas impedierit.'

Conclusion 247

consecrated by Arn according to Arn's own ritual. Baturich's monastery of St-Emmeram copied Collection B, which had begun to circulate in Northern Italy, and may have been created in that region, perhaps at Verona, given the earliest manuscript Verona 92 was copied there in the 810s. There is repeated evidence of the transmission of liturgical books between Northern Italy and Bavaria (including Arn's conciliar *ordo*). Collection B presents itself as a Frankish reconceptualisation of the *ordines romani*, including adjustments made to *Ordo* 1, and the replacement of Roman *Ordo* 34 with the Frankish ordination rites from the Gelasian Sacramentary. The same basic form of Collection B is known late in the century in manuscript St Gallen 140, presenting the monasteries of Alemannia as the possible thoroughfare for the text to cross into Bavaria. In Regensburg, Baturich developed the Collection further in his own interests, including further material from the Sacramentary to enhance the liturgical comprehensiveness but he also included *Ordo* 44, a pilgrim's description of ceremonies at St Peter's Basilica which were specific to that basilica.

Bernharius of Worms (*c.*799–826) sat at the Council of Mainz with Arn, and had also made several journeys to Rome on official business. His instigation can realistically explain the creation of the manuscript which today comprises part of Wolfenbüttel Weissenburgenses 91, created at the beginning of the ninth century. A recent description of this manuscript as a 'chaotic and often contradictory compromise' reflects the ongoing difficulty to characterise the achievements of these Carolingian copyists according to categories of modern scholarship.[32] In fact, the wide range of its contents and the beauty of its presentation reflect a fully conceived, ideologically rich project, on which considerable thought and work was deployed. The creator of this manuscript knew Collection A, and added elements from the Sacramentary which would also be used in the confection of Collection B, such as church dedication and ordination rites, as well as additional *ordines* of Frankish manufacture. Langlois also characterised the compilers as 'antiquarian', a term that has also been applied to Amalarius' search among sources for the 'ratio' of liturgy.[33] In neither case was this antiquity for antiquity's sake, but both Amalarius and the Wolfenbüttel manuscript constituted wide-ranging attempts to understand and contextualise the liturgical practices they actually knew, with historical examples.

---

[32] Laura Albiero, '"Secundum romanum consuetudinem": La riforma liturgica in epoca carolingia', in Ileana Pagani and Franceso Santi (eds.), *Il secolo di Carlo Magno: Istituzioni, Letterature e cultura del tempo carolingio* (Florence, 2016), pp.151–176 at p.166.
[33] Langlois, 'Le manuscript W', pp.53–54; Jones, *A Lost Work*, p.63.

248   Conclusion

This parallel, independent reinterpretation of Collection A reveals a similar reuse of the *ordines romani* by bishops, and permits us to hypothesise some common practices of reading, inspiration and collaboration in this more or less closely linked circle of bishops during the first decades of the ninth century. But once again, none of the compilers make the choices that modern scholarship imposed. These compilers did not see themselves constrained to 'compromise' with Frankish usages. Rather their purposes for the understanding of the ecclesiastical offices and the individual liturgical rites were fully realised in these books, intended to present ritual as common and continuous. In this respect, the fact that the book opens with the dossier on papal history, going back to the imagined past of Peter and Clement, Damasus and the conciliar decisions of Gregory of the Great, is decisive in how the *ordines* should be understood. Evaluation of the manuscript as a 'pontifical', purely assessed by its 'use', therefore misses the ideological use it made of the *ordines*, something that surely shaped how they were read in practice.

In fact, the relation of the *ordines* to the most important texts of papal history is a constant refrain that is key to understanding the copying and presentation of the *ordines romani* within this circle of related manuscripts. Recent scholarship on the copying of the document of papal history, the *Liber Pontificalis*, in the Frankish realms has emphasised how it served Frankish ideological and devotional interests. Like the *ordines romani*, the *Liber Pontificalis* appears from this period in surviving Frankish manuscript copies and excerpts, not Roman ones. On the one hand, these copies emphasise a continuity of the present Frankish church with papal history back to St Peter.[34] They also guided readers through a 'mental map' of Rome, as it was described in the text.[35] One of the principal focuses of the *Liber Pontificalis* is liturgy, since it aims to show how the popes had shaped by decree the cultic life of the church, giving to them a particular responsibility to care for liturgical life into the present.[36] This theme was another one in which the Franks showed particular interest, not merely in the explicit and repeated citation of the *Liber Pontificalis* by theorists such as Amalarius and Walahfrid Strabo, but also in their abbreviations of the *Liber Pontificalis*, which tend to emphasise this aspect.[37]

---

[34] McKitterick, *Rome and the Invention of the Papacy*, pp.210 ff.   [35] *Ibid.*, pp.57–61.
[36] *Ibid.*, pp.133–145.
[37] *Ibid.*, pp.158–169; for example, *Liber Officialis*, Hanssens (ed.), *Opera omnia*, vol. II, p.237: 'Stephanus, natione Romanus, ex patre Iobio, ut legitur in Gestis episcopalibus, constituit sacerdotibus levitisque vestes sacratas in usu cotidiano, non uti, nisi in ecclesiae.'

Conclusion
249

Along with these, the *ordo romanus* manuscripts reveal how much the assertions of the popes to a historical and ongoing authority on liturgical matters, propagated in the *Liber Pontificalis*, had been accepted in Francia as answering a need that was felt there. The excerption of the Life of Clement from this text in Weissenburgenses 91 is direct proof of a relationship in the eyes of certain Carolingian compilers. Likewise, in Tours, the canonical manuscripts into which *Ordo* 15 was copied also preserved the Felician Epitome of the *Liber Pontificalis*.[38] Other manuscripts go even further than the *Liber Pontificalis* itself, either revealing the ongoing care of the popes for liturgical questions into the present (Pope Hadrian I is cited in BAV Pal.lat.487, and in St Gallen 614's pilgrim dossier), or in citations of historical interventions that were either invented or part of a tradition we cannot access (in Munich BSB Clm 14510, *Ordo* 1 begins by describing the seven regions of Rome 'secundum constitutionem beatissimi ac sanctissimi Silvestri summi pontificis Romae Urbis', something that the *Liber Pontificalis* actually credits to earlier popes Clement, Fabian and Gaius; and there is also the list of popes and abbots of St Peter's who intervened in the liturgy in St Gallen 349).[39] Whether such copyists knew the *Liber Pontificalis* or not, its assertions about the authority of the Papacy over liturgy had been wholeheartedly absorbed. It is therefore not surprising that a significant proportion of copies of the *Liber Pontificalis* we possess come from many of the same places and people as our *ordo romanus* manuscripts. At St Amand in the time of Arn was made one important copy of the C family of the text, Leiden, Bibliothèque de l'Université, Voss. Lat.60 (dated *c*.790), perhaps from an exemplar acquired in Italy. A manuscript of the *Liber Pontificalis* was copied in very similar style to Weissenburgenses 91, today Wolfenbüttel HAB Guelf.10.11 Aug 4° (dated *c*.810), whose marginal annotations add Frankish events to the story.[40] Arn's copy in Leiden and the Wissembourg copy draw on the same version of the *Liber Pontificalis*, the Lombard version, perhaps acquired by Arn in Italy and shared with friends such as Bernharius, as he shared *ordines romani*.

Ellenhart, a scribe of Sankt-Emmeram at the time of Baturich, was responsible for one copy of a Frankish epitome of the text (Munich Clm 14387, fols.8v–14v), which places the text after the Pseudo-Clementine

---

[38] McKitterick, *Rome and the Invention of the Papacy*, p.197.
[39] *Ordo* 1, n.1, var.5: 'According to the constitution of the most blessed and holy Pontiff of the city of Rome, Silvester'; list at *Ordo* 19, nn.36, these popes and abbots are described generically 'ededit', 'ordinavit' or 'conscripsit', without specific details.
[40] McKitterick, *Rome and the Invention of the Papacy*, pp.181, 208, 219.

250 Conclusion

Epistles (also copied in the Wissembourg *ordines romani* manuscript).[41] A very early copy of the *Liber Pontificalis* was in Verona in the early ninth century, today Verona Biblioteca Capitolare XXII, and annotated in a hand very similar to that which annotates our Collection B manuscript, Verona 91. Both annotating hands have been identified with the prodigious figure of Archdeacon Pacificus.[42] Nevertheless, we need not accept the dubious accounts of Pacificus' achievements to notice that similar practices of notation and correction were made in both the *Liber Pontificalis* and the *ordines romani* in Verona, including (as we have seen) the addition of more specific Roman details to the latter.

It is certainly true that all of these sees and their bishops, therefore, were specifically interested in making use of Rome's history for their own purposes. They drew on a common stock of texts, in which the *Liber Pontificalis* had a particular importance. Among others are the Pseudo-Clementine Epistles and the Pseudo-Gelasian *De libris recipiendis*, both of which appear, for example, in Bernharius' Weissenburgenses 91. The latter text was frequently transmitted in association with *ordines* for readings, giving the Pope's sanction to the apocrypha, for example. These texts, for example, emphasise in parallel two themes of the *Liber Pontificalis*: the succession of the papacy from the apostles transmitted by ordination, and the ability of the popes to validate and authenticate liturgical usages. The *ordines romani* were another resource. Like the canons of Church Councils, the *ordines* did not have to be followed literally in every particular for the story they told to be useful to Carolingian authorities. The breadth of sources for the intensity of this preoccupation with Rome, for Arn, in particular, is further demonstrated by two manuscripts that go back to his time, probably copied in St Amand for his use in Salzburg. Martyrologies copied in the time of Arn (e.g. Vienna ÖNB 387) are extraordinary in the extent to which early popes appear among the saints to be commemorated: ninety-two of the ninety-seven popes of the *Liber Pontificalis*, in contrast to only fifteen included in the martyrology of Bede.[43] Secondly, in Vienna ÖNB 795, one of his collections of Alcuin's letters, Arn also had copied two pilgrim itineraries of Rome, respectively entitled *Ecclesiae quae intus Roma habentur* and the *Notitia ecclesiarum urbis Romae*.[44] Not only are

---

[41] *Ibid.*, p.202; digitised at: www.digitale-sammlungen.de/de/view/bsb00046515?page=1.

[42] McKitterick, *Rome and the Invention of the Papacy*, p.201; La Rocca, 'A Man for all Seasons'.

[43] Meta Niederkorn-Bruck, 'Das Salzburger historische Martyrolog aus der Arn-Zeit und seine Bedeutung für die Textgeschichte des Martyrologium Bedae', in Niederkorn-Bruck and Scharer (eds.), *Erzbischof Arn von Salzburg*, pp.155–171, especially pp.168–170.

[44] *Itineraria et alia geographica*, P. Geyer, O. Cuntz, A. Francheschini, R. Weber, L. Bieler, J. Fraipont and Fr. Glorie (eds.) (Turnhout, 1965), pp.321, 310.

Conclusion

there certain indications that these texts, for which this manuscript is the earliest known witness, were enhanced (if not conceived) by Arn based on his own observations of Rome during one of his visits, but the use of such texts in their Frankish copies was the tracing of a 'virtual Rome' for devotional and intellectual purposes, something for which, as we have seen, the *ordines romani* were also eminently suited.[45] At Fulda, common practices of reading these kinds of texts in conjunction with each other were made explicit, since the manuscript today in Einsiedeln 110 copied *Ordo* 33 along with its famous itineraries, clearly representing a pilgrim narrative of the Holy Week which a reader could retrace in the 'virtual' Rome. Having such texts at hand was clearly regarded as valuable in bringing something of the power and sacredness of Rome over the Alps. They would help contextualise and layer meaning upon the processions and stational observances bishops actually performed.

While the results of the programme in which bishops engaged were as varied as the manuscripts they produced, other elements of this Rome-centred episcopal self-assertion have been observed by modern scholars, including architectural adjustments to cathedrals and monasteries that recalled the basilica of St Peter. It is important to note that building *more romano* did not mean the mechanical replication of the Roman model, but inspired its own innovations and reconceptualisation of the meaning and forms of architecture, including layering new meaning on existing local structures.[46] Chrodegang and Richulf of Mainz rebuilt their churches *more romano*, as did Simpert of Regensburg at St Emmeram, himself likely to have overseen the transfer of an *ordo romanus* manuscript from Murbach to Regensbug (the fragments of Collection A).[47] These new buildings had ring crypts in imitation of the Basilica of Saint Peter's, but adapted to the Frankish plan, rather than straightforward replication. In another illustration of the diversity of responses, some communities, such as St Martin of Tours, preferred not to rebuild *more romano*, and maintained the Merovingian structure.[48]

The power to invoke Rome was part of the arsenal of bishops in their self-assertion. We see this specifically in Arn, a new metropolitan, creating the *ordines* that would define his office liturgically. Apostolic succession is

---

[45] Maximilan Diesenberger, 'Rom als virtueller Raum der Martyrer. Zur gedanklichen Aneignung der Roma suburbana in bayerischen Handschriften um 800', in E. Vavra (ed.), *Imaginäre Räume. Sektion B des internationalen Kongresses: 'Virtuelle Räume. Raumwahrnehmung und Raumvorstellung im Mittelalter', Krems an der Donau, 24. bis 26. März 2003* (Krems, 2004), pp.43–68.

[46] Emerick, 'Building *more romano* in Francia'.

[47] Werner Jacobsen, 'Saints' Tombs in Frankish Church Architecture', *Speculum* 72 (1997), pp.1107–1143, at p.1135.

[48] *Ibid.*, pp.1141–1142.

252   Conclusion

the key element here. The *Liber Pontificalis* numbers exhaustively the ordinations of bishops, priests and deacons performed by each of the popes. These specifically and repeatedly linked to their proper timing on the Ember Days, a feature the Franks often maintained in their excerptions of the text despite its seeming tediousness.[49] Ordination is a particular focus in the three *ordo romanus* manuscripts that can be associated with Baturich, Bernharius and Arn, but is not dealt with in the same way by any of them. Arn could and did appeal directly to his promotion by Leo III and, through him, a bishop like Baturich was linked to Rome. While we do not know exactly where the manuscript Cologne 138 was written (probably North Italy: it is certainly linked to Verona), the inclusion of a papal ordination ritual in that manuscript suggests that other bishops were fully aware that the papal office was a powerful symbol of which they could make use. The flurry of greatest creativity in making *ordines* is certainly to be associated with the episcopal self-confidence and definition of the office that was ongoing at this time.[50] The best and most creative manuscripts of the *ordines romani* would belong to this period. It also seems that this flourishing would subsequently dim somewhat. There is significantly less evidence of such creativity in the use of *ordines* through the rest of the ninth century. Eleventh-century manuscripts identified as 'pontificals', however, would make a repeated reclamation of this Carolingian heritage, at another time of episcopal self-promotion.

Nevertheless, *ordines* continued to be copied, often in monasteries. The monasteries at Reichenau and St Gallen continued to copy *ordines romani* throughout the period, including St Gallen 140 and St Gallen 446. The latter was copied in South Germany (now Bamberg lit.131), showing that the passage of liturgical manuscripts into Bavaria from these monasteries did happen, sufficient to explain Collection B's presence in Regensburg via Reichenau. These manuscripts both also recorded and passed on a great variety of the latest liturgical thinking, including texts by Amalarius and Walahfrid Strabo, as well as hosts of anonymous *expositiones* dealing with diverse subjects from various perspectives. Placing the *ordines* in this context invited synthesis: the construction of a complex set of associations surrounding liturgical actions and rites without distinguishing strictly between 'use' of an *ordo* and 'use' of an *expositio*. There was no single answer as to how to understand these actions: involving the *ordines* in these

---

[49] McKitterick, *Rome and the Invention of the Papacy*, pp.83, 135–136.
[50] Steffan Patzold, *Episcopus: Wissen über Bischöfe im Frankenreich des späten 8. bis frühen 10. Jahrhunderts* (Ostfildern, 2008), especially, pp.72–83, 519–521.

Conclusion

253

diverse and complex contexts suggests that readers did not expect them to reflect a single complete and comprehensive understanding of how a rite should be performed and understood. In Nonantola, texts by theorists on liturgy were collected with a developed version of Collection B, including, in the case of Zurich Car. C 102, full texts extracted from the Sacramentary. It should be acknowledged that in such cases compilers could be interested in the full representation of rites, including spoken elements, without necessarily intending to use these rites themselves. Given that the foundation of the *expositiones* is the assumption of liturgy as a coherent system whose individual elements might interpret each other, the creation of 'pontifical' books which synthesised these varied elements would certainly allow reading of the rituals in this way. A crowning achievement is the Pontifical of Paris, produced in a monastery near the city *c.*870 and now in the Bibliothèque de l'Arsenal. While providing exhaustive depth in its representation of rituals, including and expanding available *ordines romani*, it offers these rituals in a context of the wider Church, including a full stational map of Holy Week in Rome, citation of the contemporary pope, Nicholas I, and even a reference to practice in Jerusalem from pilgrim accounts.[51] This manuscript proves that even at this late date there were still innovative usages to be made of *ordines*, and monasteries might continue to cultivate interest in some of the same preoccupations that the bishops had shown in their compilation of such manuscripts earlier in the century.

The 'use' which copyists might have made of *ordines romani*, and the key to their copying of the texts, therefore is not to be resolved by the strict binaries imposed in modern scholarship: 'use' excluding 'study', or indeed the stricter conception of 'liturgical' as applied to modern liturgical books. It is certainly very plausible that the reading of such texts led to the adjustment of a liturgical performance of a ceremony. For example, stational observances at Mass in many of Francia's great episcopal cities were inspired by the circulation of *Ordo* I, while *Ordo* II's specific recommendation of seven scrutinies was at least recognised as a theoretical ideal by thinkers such as Amalarius or Engilmodus of Soissons. The same texts might also have functioned to help introduce and guide the performance of ceremonies such as the Great Litany, where these were newly enjoined in councils. But the acknowledgement of how the *ordines* are presented, and their relationship to the parallel literature, the *expositiones*, requires the acceptance that the copying of a text of an *ordo romanus*, and the identification of one's own practice as 'secundum ordinem romanum', still

---

[51] Westwell, 'Content and Ideological Construction'.

254   Conclusion

permitted significant personal input in the actual performance of the ceremony described, and, potentially, significant divergence from the letter of the text itself. Carolingian authors did not expect *ordines* to give them a complete picture of the ceremony, which they would follow exactly. We cannot, therefore, expect liturgical manuscripts like these to tell us how rituals were performed in every detail, nor can we assume that the copying of a liturgical manuscript necessarily entailed the 'reform' of local liturgical practice in accordance with it.

In these texts, we can also see the combination and harmonisation of many interests of the Franks. Some of these reflect much broader shifts in the period, such as the thirst to understand the 'ratio' for rituals, in their individual elements and in the unfolding of a complete ceremony, witnessed also in the *expositiones*. Another is the need to make Rome present, to create a virtual Rome on the manuscript page, which would interact with other texts and the memory and imagination of the reader to 'activate' a recollection of Rome for a reader, even one who had never been there. Such manuscripts were used in conjunction with other available individual and institutional resources, and were never expected to provide a single process or meaning that would be applied universally. In other cases, and often simultaneously, manuscripts reflect more immediate, contingent needs, as exemplified by Baturich's manuscript, Munich Clm 14510, containing the coronation texts, or Arn of Salzburg's need to establish himself as the Empire's newest metropolitan bishop.

The intensification of theatricality of the liturgy under the Carolingians is intimately linked to these many layers of meaning.[52] Again and again, what Frankish adaptation of the *ordines* chose to highlight and intensify were references to changes in the tone and sound of spoken words, movements of lights, treatment of the Eucharist, genuflection, and symmetry in the numbering of deacons, subdeacons and acolytes. Even the use of Greek had a theatrical element; the Franks probably enjoyed its beauty and mystery.[53] Of course, the 'paraphrase' of Rome was always, in a way, a theatrical performance, and the gestural and tonal imitation of the *domnus apostolicus* a 'play' of a sort. Indeed, the *ordines* are perhaps 'stage directions' from this perspective, though my Introduction rejected this

---

[52] Christine Catharina Schnusenberg, *Das Verhältnis von Kirche und Theater Dargestellt an ausgewahlten Schriften der Kirchenvater und liturgischen Texten bis auf Amalarius von Metz (a.d. 775–852)* (Frankfurt-am-Main, 1981), English trans. in *The Relationship Between the Church and the Theatre: Exemplified by Selected Writings of the Church Fathers and by Liturgical Texts Until Amalarius of Metz, 775–852 AD* (Lanham, 1988).

[53] Kaczynski, *Greek in the Carolingian Age*, p.112.

Conclusion

255

designation. Yet this theatricality was not an empty vessel. Instead, *expositiones* like those of Amalarius poured meaning into it. Despite seeming initially opaque, the aspiration was there that such details would help instruct the people too, at least according to Amalarius. He claimed, for example, that the symmetry of the cantor would teach the people the unity of worship, even deaf people, who would be able to see it in the arrangement.[54] Thus, what may seem to us like quibbling over details or extravagance in theatricality to them was really a serious matter. Of course, which came first, the 'meaning' or the liturgical act, is difficult to say. Probably, as the manuscripts would suggest, both mutually influenced one another. The interrelation of *ordo* and *expositio* helps to show why these same preoccupations recur again and again; these dramatic features were actually intended to 'teach' something, or act as the spur to the question of their meaning. Writing down the *ordo*, and pondering it outside a liturgical ceremony, helped one prepare to see and understand the ceremony in the right way. Even if one actually did things differently in practice, the written text of the *ordo* suggested what one should look out for and how to set the text.

As has been underlined elsewhere of Carolingian 'Reform', the point of the copying of such texts was an invitation to understand the rituals more deeply rather than in a singular way: education not standardisation. The *ordines romani* helped to unlock a new plane of understanding, by layering the Roman context over the ritual, as it was performed, imagined or conceived. In some cases, that new insight might lead to specific changes so that the rituals were ever more intimately associated with Rome as the imaginative model which the Franks prized, but such changes were often, as in the stational liturgy or the sevenfold scrutiny, the spur to ever more innovation in practice and understanding, rather than the unthinking imposition of any 'authorised' version. The *ordines* are best seen within networks of the people who shared and compiled them, as collaborative texts. Many may have begun life as letters, reports, even oral reminiscence.

An inevitable conclusion of my study is that the Romans did not generally seem to have written *ordines* at all (or any detailed descriptions of their liturgical practices). The sparseness of rubrication (any description of the gestures and movements during a ritual) in the Roman Gregorian Sacramentary is a useful counterpart to this conclusion. Sacramentaries

---

[54] *Liber Officialis*, Hanssens (ed.), *Opera omnia*, vol. II, p.267: 'Hinc tractent cantores quid significant simphonia eorum; ea ammonent plebem ut in unitate unius Dei cultus perseverent. Etiamsi aliquis surdus affuerit, idipsum statu illorum in choro ordinatissimo insinuant, ut qui auribus capere non possunt unitatem, visa capiant.'

compiled by the Franks, like the Gelasian of the Eighth Century, enclose, in contrast, extensive rubrication and even complete *ordines*. Though the Gregorian had stational notices for the setting of Masses (of which the Franks made innovative use as spurs to their own stational observances), it gave no detailed descriptions of gestures and actions, save a few rubrics in Holy Week. Likewise, the unambiguously Roman ordines, *Ordo* 13A and 14, are simply lists of readings, without any elaboration. This need to have texts describing the movements, placements, gestures and settings of ritual was therefore a feature of Frankish devotional life and response to their religious priorities, and not one that originated in Rome at all. Rome was not particularly interested in spreading or sharing its liturgical life in this period. The initiative came from Franks who made the journey to the city, and who penned the narratives that we study here. This turns the idea of 'reform', or the so-called Carolingian adoption of the 'Roman Rite', on its head. As with Arn of Salzburg's ordination rite for the bishops under him, some Frankish *ordines* had a lasting future as descriptions of rites that would became standard from the eleventh century. They were even received and copied in Rome itself, since by this time the ancient, unwritten Roman traditions attenuated and were lost.

The *ordines romani* should be interpreted from the outset as a Carolingian phenomenon. These texts did not begin, therefore, as directories for Roman clergy for practical purposes. They were formulated to meet Frankish needs, and the vision of Rome they impart to us is therefore filtered through these needs. This Frankish need to put liturgical rites into textual form was not the same as the desire for codification in the sense of standardisation or fossilisation of form and meaning, but itself allowed even more creativity in thinking about liturgy by drawing liturgical texts into a broader culture of the interpretation of text where they could be parsed and interpreted.

Bibliography

Manuscripts

Albi, Bibliothèque Municipale, MS 42.
Autun, Bibliothèque Municipale, MS S 184.
Bamberg, Staatsbibliothek, MS Lit.131.
Barcelona, Biblioteca Central de la Diputación, MS 944.
Berlin, Staatsbibliothek, MS Phillipps 1829.
Bern, Burgerbibliothek, MS 289.
Brussels, Bibliothèque royale, MS lat.10127–10144.
Cambrai, Bibliothèque Municipale, MS 164.
Cambrai, Bibliothèque Municipale, MS 465.
Cologne, Dombibliothek, MS 138.
Copenhagen, Kongelige Bibliotek, MS Gl. kgl. 3443.
(Formerly) Donaueschingen, Fürstliche Fürstenbergische Hofbibliothek, MS 192.
Douai, Bibliothèque Municipale, MS 14.
Dusseldorf, Universitätsbibliothek, MS D1.
Einsiedeln, Stiftsbibliothek, MS 110.
Einsiedeln, Stiftsbibliothek, MS 326.
Erlangen, Universitätsbibliothek MS 2000.
Freiburg im Breisgau, Universitätsbibliothek cod.363.
Friuli, Museo archeologico nazionale LXXXV.
Leiden, Bibliothèque de l'Université Voss.Lat.60.
Gotha, Forschungsbibliothek Membr.I.85.
Göttingen, Universitätsbibliothek Cod. Theol. 231 ('The Sacramentary of Fulda').
The Hague, Museum Meermanno Westreeanium cod.10.B.4.
Kassel, Universitätsbibliothek 2° MS astron. 2.
Laon Bibiliothèque Municipale 201.
London British Library Add.MS.15222.
Metz, Bibliothèque Municipale 134 (destroyed 1944).
Milan, Biblioteca del capitolo metropolitano, cod.D.I. 12.
Montecassino, Archivio della Badia, MS 451
Montpellier, Bibliothèque de la Faculté de Médecine 412.
Monza, Biblioteca Capitolare b-23/141.

Bibliography

Munich, Bayerische Staatsbibliothek, ANA 553 (*Nachlass* of Bernhard Bischoff).
Munich, Bayerische Staatsbibliothek Clm 6398.
Munich, Bayerische Staatsbibliothek Clm 6407.
Munich, Bayerische Staatsbibliothek Clm 14082.
Munich, Bayerische Staatsbibliothek Clm 14379.
Munich, Bayerische Staatsbibliothek Clm 14387.
Munich, Bayerische Staatsbibliothek Clm 14470
Munich, Bayerische Staatsbibliothek Clm 14510.
Munich, Bayerische Staatsbibliothek Clm 14659.
Munich, Bayerische Staatsbibliothek Clm 14655.
Munich, Bayerische Staatsbibliothek Clm 14747.
Munich, Bayerische Staatsbibliothek Clm 28135.
Munich, Bayerische Staatsbibliothek Clm 29300(29).
Padua, Biblioteca Capitolare MS D 47 ('Paduensis Sacramentary').
Paris Bibliothèque de l'Arsenal 227 ('The Pontifical of Poitiers').
Paris, Bibliothèque national de France, MS latin 816 ('The Sacramentary of Angoulême').
Paris, Bibliothèque national de France latin 974.
Paris, Bibliothèque national de France latin 1248.
Paris, Bibliothèque national de France latin 2296 ('The Colbertine Fragments').
Paris, Bibliothèque national de France latin 2399.
Paris, Bibliothèque national de France latin 2449.
Paris, Bibliothèque national de France latin 3836.
Paris, Bibliothèque national de France latin 9421.
Paris, Bibliothèque national de France latin 9428 ('The Sacramentary of Drogo').
Paris, Bibliothèque national de France latin 12048 ('The Sacramentary of Gellone').
Paris, Bibliothèque national de France latin 12500 ('The Sacramentary of St Eloi').
Paris, Bibliothèque national de France latin 12507.
Paris, Bibliothèque national de France latin 14008.
Paris, Bibliothèque national de France latin 17436 ('The Antiphoner of Compiègne').
Reims, Bibliothèque Municipale 1.
Regensburg, Staatliche Bibliothek fragm.2.
Rome, Biblioteca Nazionale Sessorianus 52.
Rouen, Bibliothèque Municipale 26.
Rouen, Bibliothèque Municipale 369 ('The Benedictional of Archbishop Robert').
Sankt Paul im Lavantthal, Stiftsbibliothek, MS 979 (formerly MS 24.4.9).
St Gallen, Stiftsbibliothek, MS 11.
St Gallen, Stiftsbibliothek, MS 140.
St Gallen, Stiftsbibliothek cod.150.
St Gallen, Stiftsbibliothek cod.225.
St Gallen, Stiftsbibliothek cod.236.
St Gallen, Stiftsbibliothek cod.349.
St Gallen, Stiftsbibliothek cod.446.
St Gallen, Stiftsbibliothek cod.614.

Bibliography

St Petersburg Rossijskaja Akademija Nauk, Institut Istorii West-European Section 3/625.
St Petersburg, National Library of Russia Q. V. I, n° 34.
St Petersburg, National Library of Russia Q.v.I.n° 35 ('The Pontifical of Sens').
St Petersburg, National Library of Russia Q. V. I, n° 56.
St Petersburg, National Library of Russia Q. V. II, n° 5.
Trento, Museo Provinciale d'arte del Castello del buonconsiglio, MS M.N.1590.
Vatican City, Archivum Apostolicum Vaticanum, Misc., Arm. XI,19.
Vatican City, Biblioteca Apostolica Vaticana lat.4770.
Vatican City, Biblioteca Apostolica Vaticana lat. 6018.
Vatican City, Biblioteca Apostolica Vaticana lat. 7701.
Vatican City, Biblioteca Apostolica Vaticana Pal.lat.46.
Vatican City, Biblioteca Apostolica Vaticana Pal.lat.47.
Vatican City, Biblioteca Apostolica Vaticana Pal.lat.277.
Vatican City, Biblioteca Apostolica Vaticana Pal.lat.493.
Vatican City, Biblioteca Apostolica Vaticana Pal.lat. 574.
Vatican City, Biblioteca Apostolica Vaticana Pal.lat.487.
Vatican City, Biblioteca Apostolica Vaticana Pal.lat.1341.
Vatican City, Biblioteca Apostolica Vaticana Reg.lat.235.
Vatican City, Biblioteca Apostolica Vaticana Reg.lat.316 ('The Old Gelasian Sacramentary').
Vatican City, Biblioteca Apostolica Vaticana Reg.lat.567.
Vatican City, Biblioteca Apostolica Vaticana Reg.lat.1127.
Vercelli, Archivio Capitolare 183.
Verona, Biblioteca Capitolare XXII.
Verona, Biblioteca Capitolare LXXXV ('The *Veronense* Sacramentary').
Verona, Biblioteca Capitolare XCII.
Vienna, Österreichische Nationalbibliothek, MS 387.
Vienna Österreichische Nationalbibliothek cod.701.
Vienna Österreichische Nationalbibliothek cod.795
Vienna Österreichische Nationalbibliothek cod.Ser.n.2762.
Wolfenbüttel, Herzog August Bibliothek Cod. Guelf. 10. 11 Aug. 4°.
Wolfenbüttel, Herzog August Bibliothek, Weissenburgenses 91 (4175).
Würzburg, Universitätsbibliothek, M.p.th.o.1.
Zurich, Zentralbibliothek Car. C 102.
Zurich, Zentralbibliothek Rh. 30.

Printed Primary Sources

Alcuin of York, *Confessio Peccatorum Pura*, PL 101, cols.524D–226A.
    De fide Sanctae Trinitatis et de incarnatione Christi. Quaestiones de Sancta Trinitate, Erik Knibbs and E. Ann Matter (eds.), CCCM 249 (Turnhout, 2012).
    De Psalmorum Usu, PL 101, cols.466B–C.

260   *Bibliography*

Amalarius of Metz, *Ad Hilduinum abbatem*, Jean-Michel Hanssens (ed.), *Amalarii episcopi opera liturgica omnia*, vol. I (Vatican City, 1948), pp.339–358.

Ad Petrum abbatem Nonantulanum, Jean-Michel Hanssens (ed.), *Amalarii episcopi opera liturgica omnia*, vol.I (Vatican City, 1948), pp.227–231.

Liber Officialis, Jean-Michel Hanssens (ed.), *Amalarii episcopi opera liturgica omnia*, vol. II (Vatican City, 1948); English translation in Amalar of Metz, *On the Liturgy*, Eric Knibbs (ed.), 2 vols. (Cambridge, MA, 2014).

Missae expositionis geminus codex, Jean-Michel Hanssens (ed.), *Amalarii episcopi opera liturgica omnia*, vol. I (Vatican City, 1948), pp.253–281.

Angilbert of St-Riquier, *Institutio*, Edmund Bishop (ed.), *Liturgica Historica* (Oxford, 1918), pp.322–332.

Annales Bertiniani, G. Waıtz (ed.), *MGH, Scriptores rerum Germanicum* 5 (Hanover, 1883), pp.1–154.

Annales Breves Fuldenses, Georg Heinrich Pertz (ed.), *MGH*, Scriptores rerum Sangellensium. Annales, chronica historiae aevi Carolini (Hanover, 1829), p.237.

Annales Regni Francorum, Friedrich Kurz (ed.), *MGH*, Scriptores Rerum Germanicarum, vol. VI (Hanover, 1895).

Antiphonale Missarum sextuplex, René-Jean Hesbert (ed.) (Brussels, 1935).

Augustine of Hippo, *Enchiridion ad Laurentium*, Ernest Evans (ed.), in M. P. J. Van den Hout, E. Evans, J. Bauer, R. Vander Plaetse, S. D. Ruegg, M. V. O'Reilly, R. Vander Plaetse and C. Beukers (eds.), *De fide rerum invisibilium. Enchiridion ad Laurentium de fide et spe et caritate. De catechizandis rudibus. Sermo ad catechumenos de symbolo. Sermo de disciplina christiana. De utilitate ieiunii. Sermo de excidio urbis Romae. De haeresibus*, CCSL, 46 (Turnhout, 1969).

De Agone Christiano, J. Zycha (ed.), Corpus Scriptorum Ecclesiasticorum Latinorum, 41 (Vienna 1900), pp.99–138.

De gratia et libero arbitrio ad Valentinum, A. Goldbacher (ed.), Corpus Scriptorum Eccleisasticorum Latinorum, 57 (Vienna, 1911), pp.380–96.

The Benedictional of Archbishop Robert, Henry Wilson (ed.), HBS 24 (London, 1903).

The Benedictionals of Freising (Munich, Bayerische Staatsbibliothek Cod.lat.6430), Christopher Hohler, B. J. Wigan and Robert Amiet (eds.), HBS 88 (London, 1974).

The Bobbio Missal: A Gallican Mass-Book, E. A. Lowe (ed.), 2 vols., HBS 58 and 61 (London, 1920–24; repr. in one volume, Woodbridge, 1991).

Catologi bibliothecarum antiqui, Gustav Becker (ed.), vol. I (Bonn, 1885).

Charlemagne, *Ad Ghaerbaldum Episcopum Leodiensem Epistola*, Alfred Boretius (ed.), *MGH, Capitularia Regum Francorum* I (Hanover, 1883), pp.241–242.

Chrodegang of Metz, *Institutio Canonicorum*, Jerome Bertram (ed.), *The Chrodegang Rules* (Aldershot, 2005).

Concilium Attiniacense, Albertus Werminhoff (ed.), *MGH*, Conc. II: *Concilia aevi Karolini*, vol. I (Hanover, 1906), pp.72–73.

Concilium Liptinense, *PL* 89 cols.809–824.

Concilium Moguntinense, Albertus Werminghoff (ed.), *MGH, Conc. II: Concilia aevi Karolini*, vol. I (Hanover, 1906), pp.258–273.

Bibliography

Concilium Neocaesariense, Jean Hefele-Leclercq (ed.), *Histoire des Conciles d'après les documents originaux*, trans. Henri Leclerq, vol. I, 2 (Paris, 1907), p.332.

Concilium Rispacense, MGH, Conc. *II: Concilia aevi Karolini*, vol. I (Hanover, 1906), pp.196–201.

Concilium Rispacense, Frisingense, Salisburgense, Albertus Werminhoff (ed.), *MGH*, Conc. II: *Concilia aevi Karolini*, vol. I (Hanover, 1906), pp.205–219.

Concilium Ticinense, Wilfried Hartmann, Isolde Schröder and Gerhard Schmitz (eds.), *MGH, Conc. V: Die Konzilien der karolingischen Teilreiche (875–911)* (Hanover, 2012), pp.19–24.

Il cosiddetto pontificale di Poitiers: (Paris, Bibliothèque de l'Arsenal, cod. 227), Aldo Martini (ed.) (Rome, 1979).

Decretales pseudo-Isidoranae et Capitula Angilramni, Paul Hinschius (ed.) (Leipzig, 1863).

Deprecatio quam Papa Gelasius pro Universali Ecclesia Constituit Canendam Esse, PL 101, cols.560–561.

De vestimentis sacerdotalibus, Martin Gerbert (ed.), *Monumenta veteris liturgiae Alemannicae*, vol. II (St-Blaise, 1779), p.290.

Divi Gregorii Papae Huius Nominis Primi Cogonomento Magno Liber Sacramentorum, Hugh Mènard (ed.) (Paris, 1642).

Dominus Uobiscum, Jean-Michel Hanssens (ed.), *Amalarii episcopii opera liturgica omnia*, vol. I (Vatican City, 1947), pp.283–336.

Egeria, *Itinerarium*, in Aet Franceschini and R. Weber (eds.), *Itineraria et alia Geographica*, CCSL 175 (Turnhout, 1965), pp.27–103; also Pierre Maraval, *Égérie. Journal de voyage (Itinéraire)* (Paris, 1982); English translation in Anne McGowan and Paul F. Bradshaw (eds.), *The Pilgrimage of Egeria* (Collegeville, MN, 2018).

Die Einsiedler Inschriftensammlung und der Pilgerführer durch Rom (Codex Einsidlensis 326). Facsimile, Umschrift, Übersetzung und Kommentar, G. Walser (ed.) (Stuttgart, 1987).

Das fränkische Sacramentarium Gelasianum in alamannischer Überlieferung, Leo Cunibert Mohlberg (ed.) (Münster, 1971).

Gregory the Great, *Decretum ad Clerum in Basilica Petri Apostoli*, Paul Ewald and Ludwig Hartmann (eds.), *MGH, Epistolae, I, Gregorius I Papae Registrum Epistolarum* 1 (Berlin, 1891), pp.362–367.

Denuntiatio pro septiformi letania, Ludwig Hartmann (ed.), *MGH, Epistolae, II, Gregorius I Papae Registrum Epistolarum* 2 (Berlin, 1899), pp.365–367.

Gregorius Augustino Episcopo, Ludwig Hartmann (ed.), *MGH, Epistolae, II, Gregorius I Papae Registrum Epistolarum* 2 (Berlin, 1899), pp.332–343.

Gregorius Syagrio, Etherio, Vergilio et Desiderio Episcopis a Paribus Galliarum, Ludwig Hartmann (ed.), *MGH, Epistolae, II, Gregorius I Papae Registrum Epistolarum* 2 (Hanover, 1899), pp.205–210.

Pope Gregory II, *Gregorius II Papa ad varias Bonifatii consultations rescribit*, Ernst Dümmler (ed.), *MGH, Epistolae III, Epistolae Merowingici et Karolini Aevi*, vol. I (Berlin, 1892), p.275–277.

262   *Bibliography*

Gregory of Tours, *Liber in gloria martyrum*, B. Krusch (ed.), *MGH Scriptores Rerum Merovingicarum, vol. I: Gregorii Turonensis Opera*, pt.2 (Hanover, 1885), pp.34–111.

Pope Hadrian I, *Epistola Carolo Regi*, Ernst Dümmler (ed.), *MGH, Epistolae III, Epistolae Merowingici et Karolini Aevi*, vol.I (Berlin, 1892), pp.632–636.

Haito of Basel, *Capitulary*, P. Brommer (ed.), *MGH, Capitula Episcoporum* I (Hanover, 1984), pp.203–219.

Hincmar of Rheims, *Capitula Presbyteris Data Anno 852*, Wolf-Dieter Runge (ed.), *MGH, Capitula Episcoporum* II (Hanover, 1995), pp.8–90.

Epistola XXIX, Ad Adventium episcopum Metensem, PL 126, cols.186–188.

Hrabanus Maurus,*De institutione clericorum*, D. Zimpel (ed.), 2 vols. (Turnhout, 2006).

Innocent I, '*Epistle 25*', Robert Cabie (ed.), *La lettre du Pape Innocent Ier à Decentius de Gubbio* (Louvain, 1973).

Itinereraria et alia geographica, P. Geyer, O. Cuntz, A. Francheschini, R. Weber, L. Bieler, J. Fraipont and F. Glorie (eds.) (Turnhout, 1965).

Das Kollektar-Pontifikale des Bischofs Baturich von Regensburg (817–848) (Cod. Vindob.ser.n.2762), Franz Unterkircher (ed.), *Spicilegium Friburgense*, 8 (Freiburg, 1962).

Leo the Great, *Epistola XII: Ad Episcopos Africanos Provinciae Mauritaniae Caesariensis, PL* 54, cols.645–663.

Epistola XV: Leo Episcopus Turribio episcopo, cols.678–692.

Pope Leo III, Epistolae 9: *Riculfo episcopo Moguntino*, Ernst Dümmler (ed.), *MGH Epistolae 5, Karolini Aevi* 3 (Berlin, 1899), pp.67–68.

Liber Diurnus Romanorum Pontificum, Hans Foerster (ed.) (Bern 1958).

Le Liber Pontificalis: Texte Introduction et Commentaire, Louis Duchesne (ed.), 2 vols. (Paris, 1886–1892).

Liber Sacramentorum Augustodunensis, Otto Heiming (ed.), CCSL, 159B (Turnholt, 1984).

Liber Sacramentorum Engolismensis, Patrick Saint-Roch (ed.), CCSL, 159C (Turnhout, 1987).

Liber sacramentorum excarsus, C. Coeburgh and Pierre de Puniet (eds.), CCCM, 47 (Turnhout, 1977).

Liber Sacramentorum Gellonensis, Antoine Dumas (ed.), 2 vols., CCSL, 159–159A (Turnhout, 1981).

Liber Sacramentorum Paduensis, Alcestis Catella, Ferdinandus dell'Oro and Aldus Martini (eds.), Monumenta Italiae Liturgica, vol. III (Rome, 2005).

Liber Sacramentorum Romanae Aeclesiae Ordinis Anni Circuli (Cod. Vat. Reg. lat. 316/Paris Bibl. Nat. 7193 41/56), Leo Eizenhöfer, Leo Cunibert Mohlberg and Petrus Siffrin (eds.), Rerum Ecclesiasticarum Documenta. Series Maior, Fontes 4 (Rome, 1960).

Les Ordines Romani du haut moyen Âge, Michel Andrieu (ed.), 5 vols., Spicilegium Sacrum Lovaniense, Études et Documents, 11, 23–24, 28–29 (Louvain, 1931–1961).

Bibliography 263

Manuale Ambrosianum ex codice saec. XI olim in usum canonicae vallis Travaliae, Marco Magistretti (ed.), vol. 2, Monumenta veteris liturgiae Ambrosianae, 3 (Milan, 1905).

Missae Expositionis Geminus Codex, Jean-Michel Hanssens (ed.), *Amalarii episcopii opera liturgica omnia,* vol.I (Vatican City, 1947), pp.255–286.

Missale Gothicum, Els Rose (ed.), CCSL 159D (Turnhout, 2005).

Mittelalterliche Bibliothekskataloge Deutschlands und der Schweiz, Paul Lehmann (ed.), vol. I (Munich, 1918).

North Italian Services of the Eleventh Century, Cyrille Lambot (ed.), HBS, 67 (London, 1931).

Ordo Romanus de officio Missae, Georges Cassander (ed.) (Cologne, 1561); reprinted in *Georgii Cassandri Belgae Theologi impp. Ferdinando I et Maximiliano II a consiliis, Opera quae reperiri potuerunt Omnia* (Paris, 1616), pp.87–145.

'*Ordines* aevi regulae mixtae (post seac.VIII. med.)', Josef Semmler (ed.), in Kassius Hallinger (ed.), *Corpus Consuetudinum Monasticarum,* vol. I, *Initia Consuetudinis Benedictinae: Consuetudines Saeculi Octavi e Nonni* (Wiesbaden, 1962), pp.3–76.

Ordines coronationis Franciae: Texts and Ordines for the Coronation of Frankish and French Kings and Queens, Richard Jackson (ed.), vol. I (Philadelphia 1995).

Ordines de celebrando concilio, Herbert Schneider (ed.), *Die Konzilsordines des Früh- und Hochmittelaters, MGH* (Hanover, 1996).

Ordo Foroiuliensis, Bernard de Rubeis (ed.), *Duae Disserationes de Rufino et ritibus Foroiuliensis provinciae* (Venice, 1754), pp.228–246.

Ordo Romanus Antiquus, Melchior Hittorp (ed.), *De divinis catholicae ecclesiae officiis et mysteriis varii vetustorum aliquot Ecclesiae Patrum ac scriptorium ecclesiasticarum libri* (Cologne, 1568; repr. Paris, 1610), pp.10–116.

Paulinus of Aquileia, *Conventus Episcoporum ad ripas Danubii,* Albert Werminghoff (ed.), *MGH, Conc. 2, pt. 1: Concilia Aevi Karolini* I (Hanover, 1906), pp.172–176.

Paul the Deacon, *Gesta Episcoporum Mettensium,* Georg Heinrich Pertz (ed.), *MGH, Scriptores rerum Sangellensium. Annales, chronica historiae aevi Carolini* (Hanover, 1829), pp.260–268.

The Plan of St. Gall: A Study of the Architecture & Economy of, & Life in a Paradigmatic Carolingian Monastery, Walter Horn and Ernest Born (eds.), 3 vols. (Berkeley, CA, 1979).

Pontificale in usum ecclesiae Mediolanensis, Marco Magistretti (ed.) (Milan, 1900).

Paenitentiale Theodori, PL 99, cols.927A–936 C.

Pseudo-Clement, *Epistola Prima Clementis ad Jacobum, PL* 130, cols.19–27B.

Epistola Clementis Papae ad Jacobum Fratrem Domini, PL 130, cols.37–44.

Pseudo-Gelasius, *Decretum de libris recipiendis et non recipiendis,* Ernst von Dobschütz (ed.), *Das Decretum Gelasianum de libris recipiendis et non recipiendis* (Leipzig, 1912).

Pseudo-Germanus, *Expositio Antiquae Liturgiae Gallicanae,* Edward Craddock Ratcliff (ed.), HBS 98 (London, 1971), 14.

264 *Bibliography*

Pseudo-Germanus of Paris, *Expositio antique liturgiae gallicanae*, Phillippe Bernard (ed.), *Transitions liturgiques en Gaule carolingienne* (Paris, 2008).

Pseudo-Stephen, *Epistola I, PL* 3, 1034–1038.

Le sacramentaire grégorien: ses principales formes d'après les plus anciens manuscrits, Jean Deshusses (ed.), 3 vols., Spicelegium Friburgense 16, 24, 28, 3rd ed. (Freiburg, 1971–1982).

Les statuta ecclesiae antiqua: Édition, études critiques, Charles Munier (ed.) (Paris, 1960).

Sacramentarium Abbatiae S. Remigii Remensis, Ulysse Chevalier (ed.), *Sacramentaire et martyrologie de l'Abbaye de Saint-Remy* (Paris, 1900), pp.305–357.

Sacramentarium Arnonis, Sieghild Rehle and Klaus Gamber (ed.) (Regensburg, 1970).

Sacramentarium Fuldense seaculi x, Gregor Richter and Albert Schönfelder (eds.), repr. HBS 101 (London, 1980).

Sacramentarium Gelasianum mixtum von Saint-Amand, Sieghild Rehle and Klaus Gamber (eds.) (Regensburg, 1973).

Sacramentarium Rhenaugiense Handschrift Rh 30 der Zentralbibliothek Zürich, Anton Hänggi and Alfons Schönherr (ed.) (Freiburg, 1970).

Sacramentarium Tridentinae, Ferdinando dell'Oro, Bonifatius Barrofio, Joseph Ferraro and Hyginus Rogger (eds.), *Monumenta Liturgica Ecclesiae Tridentinae*, vol. II/a: Fontes Liturgici. Libri Sacramentorum (Trent, 1985).

Sacramentarium Veronense (Cod.Bibl.Capit. Veron.LXXXV(80)), Leo Cunibert Mohlberg (ed.) (Rome, 1994).

Das Sakramentar-Pontifikale des Bischofs Wolfgang von Regensbur, Klaus Gamber (ed.) (Regensburg, 1985).

Salzburgisches Formelbuch, in Ludwig Rockinger (ed.), *Quellen und Eröterungen zur bayerischen und deutschen Geschichte*, vol. VII (Munich, 1856), pp.1–168.

Theodulf of Orleans, *Capitula ad Presbyteros Parochiae Suae*, P. Brommer (ed.), *MGH, Capitula Episcoporum*, I (Hanover, 1984), pp.73–184.

Theotrochus Diaconus, *Qualiter officium missae agatur in monasterio Fuldae*, Albert Schönfelder (ed.), 'Bruchstück eines Fuldaer *Ordo* missae aus dem frühen Mittelalter. Mit einer Einleitung', *Quellen und Abhandlungen zur Geschichte der Abtei und der Diözese Fulda* 5 (1910), pp.97–105; and with French translation in Eric Palazzo, 'Les fastes de la liturgie. Lettre du diacre Theotrochus sur la messe à Fulda', in Olivier Guyot-Jeannin (ed.), *Autour de Gerbert d'Aurillac, le pape de l'an mil. Album de documents commentés* (Paris, 1996), pp.216–223.

Walahfrid Strabo, *Libellus de exordiis et incrementis quarundam in observationibus ecclesiasticis rerum*, Alice Harting-Correa (ed.), Mittellateinische Studien und Texte, 19 (New York, 1996).

Zwei karolingische Pontifikalien vom Oberrhein, Max Metzger (ed.) (Freiburg, 1914).

Pope Zosimus I, *Ad Hesitium Episcopum Solonitanum, PL* 84 col.673–676.

Bibliography

Secondary Literature

Albiero, Laura, '"Secundum romanum consuetudinem": La riforma liturgica in epoca carolingia', in Ileana Pagani and Francesco Santi (eds.), *Il secolo di Carolo Magno: Istitituzioni, Letterature e cultura del tempo carolingio* (Florence, 2016), pp.151–175.

Amanieu, A., 'Archidiacre', in *Dictionnaire du Droit Canonique*, vol. I (Paris, 1935), cols.948–1004.

Amelli, Ambrosius, *Spicilegium Casinense: Analecta sacra et profana*, vol. I (Monte Cassino, 1888), pp.337–41.

Andrieu, Michel, 'Le sacre épiscopal d'après Hincmar de Rheims', *Revue d'histoire ecclésiastique*, 48 (1953), pp.22–73.

'L'origine du titre de cardinal dans l'Église Romaine', *Miscellanea Giovanni Mercati*, vol. V (1946), pp.113–144.

'Quelques remarques sur le classement des sacramentaires', *Jahrbuch für Liturgiewissenschaft*, 11 (1931), pp.46–66.

'Règlement d'Angilramne de Metz (768–793) fixant les honoraires de quelques fonctions liturgiques', *Revue des sciences religeuses*, 10 (1930), pp.349–369.

'Les messes des jeudis de carême et les anciens sacramentaires', *Revue des sciences religeuses*, 9 (1929), pp.343–375.

Immixtio et Consecratio. La consecration par contact dan les documents liturgiques du moyen-âge (Paris, 1924).

'La cérémonie appelée « Diligentia » à Saint-Pierre de Rome au début du IXe siècle', *Revue des sciences religeuses*, 1 (1921), pp.62–68.

'Notes sur une ancienne rédaction de l' «*Ordo Romanus* Primus »', *Revue des sciences religeuses*, 1 (1921), pp.385–401.

Angenendt, Arnold, 'Keine Romanisierung der Liturgie unter Karl dem Großen?: Einspruch gegen Martin Morards "Sacramentarium immixtum" et uniformisation romaine', *Archiv für Liturgiewissenschaft*, 51 (2009) pp.96–108.

'Die Liturgie und die Organisation des kirchlichen Lebens auf dem Lande', in *Cristianizzazione ed organizzazione ecclesiastica delle campagne nell'alto medioevo*, Settimane di studio 28 (Spoleto, 1982), pp.169–226.

Aubert, Edoard Henrik, 'When the Roman Liturgy Became Frankish: Sound, Performance and Sublation in the Eighth and Ninth Centuries', *Études Grégoriennes*, 40 (2013), pp.57–160.

Baldovin, John F., *The Urban Character of Christian Worship*, Orientalia Christiana Analecta, 228 (Rome, 1987).

Barrow, Julia, *The Clergy in the Medieval World* (Cambridge, 2015).

'The Ideas and Application of Reform', in Julia M. H. Smith and Tom Noble (eds.), *The Cambridge History of Christianity*, vol. III, *600–1100* (Cambridge, 2008), pp.345–362.

Bauckner, Arthur, *Mabillons Reise durch Bayern* (Munich, 1910).

Bauer, Franz Alto, 'Das Bild der Stadt Rom in karolingischer Zeit: Der Anonymus Einsidlensis', *Römische Quartalschrift für christlichen Altertumskunde und Kirchengeschichte*, 92 (1997), pp.190–228.

Bibliography

Bernard, Phillippe, *Transitions liturgiques en Gaule carolingienne* (Paris, 2008).

de Blaauw, Sible, 'Contrasts in Processional Liturgy: A Typology of Outdoor Processions in Twelfth-Century Rome', in Nicolas Bock, Peter Kurmann, Serena Romano and Jean-Michel Spieser (eds.), *Art, cérémonial et liturgie au Moyen Âge: actes du Colloque de 3e Cycle Romand de Lettres, Lausanne-Fribourg, 24–25 mars, 14–15 avril, 12–13 mai 2000* (Rome 2002), pp.357–396.

Black, Jonathan, 'Psalm Uses in Carolingian Prayerbooks: Alcuin's Confessio Peccatorum Pura and the Seven Penitential Psalms', *Mediaeval Studies*, 65 (2003), pp.1–56.

'Psalm Uses in Carolingian Prayerbooks: Alcuin and the Preface to De psalmorum Usu', *Mediaeval Studies*, 64 (2002), pp.1–60.

Bischoff, Bernard, *Katalog der festländischen Handschriften des neunten Jahrhunderts (mit Ausnahme der wisigotischen)*, 4 vols. (Wiesbaden, 1998–2017).

Latin Palaeography: Antiquity and the Middle Ages, trans. Daibhm O. Cróinin and David Ganz (Cambridge, 1990).

Mittelalterliche Studien: ausgewählte Aufsätze zur Schriftkunde und Literaturgeschichte, vol. III (Stuttgart, 1981).

Die Südostdeutschen Schreibschulen und Bibliotheken in der Karolingerzeit, 3rd ed., 2 vols. (Wiesbaden, 1974–1980).

Die Abtei Lorsch im Spiegel ihrer Handschriften (Munich, 1974).

(ed.), 'Panorama der Handschriftenüberlieferung aus der Zeit Karls des Großen', in *Karl der Große. Lebenswerk und Nachleben, Bd. 2: Das geistige Leben* (Dusseldorf, 1965), pp.233–254, reprinted in Bernhard Bischoff, *Mittelalterliche Studien: ausgewählte Aufsätze zur Schriftkunde und Literaturgeschichte*, vol. III (Stuttgart, 1981), pp.5–38.

Bobrycki, Shane, 'The Royal Consecration *ordines* of the Pontifical of Sens from a New Perspective', *Bulletin du centre d'études médiévales d'Auxerre*, 13 (2009), pp.131–142.

Borella, Pietro, 'I sacramenti nella liturgia ambrosiana', in Mario Righetti (ed.), *Manuale di storia liturgica*, 4 (Milan, 1959), pp.555–610.

'Influssi carolingi e monastici sul Messale Ambrosiano', in *Miscellanea L. Cuniberti Mohlberg*, vol. I (Rome, 1948), p.73–115.

Bouhot, Jean-Paul, 'Trois rituels occasionnels du baptême dans le sacramentaire gélasien', *RevBen*, 122 (2012), pp.125–152.

'Un florilège sur le symbolisme du baptême de la seconde moitié du VIIIe siècle', *Recherches augustinniennes*, 18 (1983), pp.151–182.

Bourque, Emmanuel, *Étude sur les sacramentaires romains*, 3 vols. (Rome and Montreal, 1949–1958).

Bullough, Donald, 'The Carolingian Liturgical Experience', in R. N. Swanson (ed.), *Continuity and Change in Christian Worship*, Studies in Church History, 36 (1999), pp.29–64.

'Roman Books and Carolingian *Renovatio*', in *Carolingian Renewal: Sources and Heritage* (Manchester, 1991), pp.1–38.

'A Neglected Early-Ninth-Century Manuscript of the Lindisfarne "Vita S. Cuthberti"', *Anglo-Saxon England*, 27 (1988), pp.105–137.

Bibliography

Butzmann, Hans, *Kataloge der Herzog August Bibliothek Wolfenbüttel: Neue Reihe*, vol. X, *Die Weissenburger Handschriften* (Frankfurt am Main, 1964).

Capelle, Bernard, 'Le rite de la fraction dans la messe romaine', *Revue Bénédictine*, 53 (1941), pp.5–40.

Ó Carragáin, Éamonn and Carol Neumann de Vegvar (eds.), *Roma Felix: Formations and Reflections of Medieval Rome* (Aldershot, 2007).

Charles-Edwards, T. M., 'The Penitential of Theodore and the Iudicia Theodori', in Michael Lapidge (ed.), *Archbishop Theodore: Commemorative Studies on His Life and Influence*, Cambridge Studies in Anglo-Saxon England, 11 (Cambridge, 1995), pp.141–74.

Chavasse, Antoine, *Le sacramentaire dans le groupe dit 'Gélasiens du VIIIe siècle. Une compilation raisonnée, Études des procédés de confection et Synoptiques nouveau modèle*, 2 vols. (The Hague, 1984).

'L'organisation stationale du Carême romain, avant le VIIIe siècle. Une organisation "pastorale"', *Revue des sciences religeuses*, 56 (1982), pp.17–32.

'La discipline romaine des sept scrutins prébaptismaux', *Recherches de science religieuses*, 48 (1960), pp.227–240.

Le sacramentaire gélasien (Vaticanus Reginensis 316): Sacramentaire presbyteral en usage dans les titres romains au VIIe siècle (Tournai, 1957).

'A Rome, le Jeudi-saint au VIIe siècle d'après un vieil *Ordo*', *Revue d'histoire ecclésiastique*, 50 (1955), pp.21–35.

Chelini, Jean, 'Alcuin, Charlemagne et Saint-Martin de Tours', *Revue d'histoire de l'Église de France*, 144 (1961), pp.19–50.

Claussen, Marty A., *The Reform of the Frankish Church: Chrodegang of Metz and the Regula Canonicorum in the Eighth Century* (Cambridge, 2004).

Coeburgh, C., 'Le sacramentaire gélasien ancien', *Archiv für Liturgiewissenschaft*, 7 (1961), pp.46–88.

Collins, Samuel, *The Carolingian Debate over Sacred Space* (New York, 2012).

Connell, Martin, *Church and Worship in Fifth-Century Rome The Letter of Pope Innocent I to Decentius of Gubbio* (Cambridge, 2010).

Connolly, R. H., 'Liturgical Prayers of Intercession', *The Journal of Theological Studies*, 21 (1920), 219–232.

Cramer, Peter, *Baptism and Change in the Early Middle Ages (c.200–1150)* (Cambridge, 1993).

Davis, Jennifer, *Charlemagne's Practice of Empire* (Cambridge, 2015).

Davis, Raymond, *The Book of Pontiffs* (Liverpool, 1989).

Dekkers, Eligius '"Benedictiones quas faciunt Galli": Qu'a voulu demander saint Boniface?', in Albert Lehner and Walter Berschin (eds.), *Lateinische Kultur im VIII. Jahrhundert. Traube-Gedenkschrift* (St Ottilien, 1989), pp.41–46.

dell'Oro, Ferdinando, 'L'Iniziazione cristiana a Novara da V al XI Secolo', *Rivista Liturgica*, 1 (1978), pp.678–718.

Deshusses, Jean, 'Les anciens sacramentaires de Tours', *Revue Bénédictine*, 89 (1979), pp.281–302.

'Le sacramentaire grégorien du Trente', *Revue Bénédictine*, 78 (1968), pp.264–266.

Bibliography

Dey, Hendrik, *The Afterlife of the Roman City: Architecture and Ceremony in Late Antiquity and the Early Middle Ages* (Cambridge, 2015).

DiCenso, Daniel, 'Revisiting the Admonitio generalis', in Daniel DiCenso and Rebecca Maloy (eds.), *Chant, Liturgy and the Inheritance of Rome: Essays in Honour of Joseph Dyer* (London, 2017), pp.315–372.

Diesenberger, Maximilan, 'Rom als virtueller Raum der Martyrer. Zur gedanklichen Aneignung der Roma suburbana in bayerischen Handschriften um 800', in E. Vavra (ed.), *Imaginäre Räume. Sektion B des internationalen Kongresses: 'Virtuelle Räume. Raumwahrnehmung und Raumvorstellung im Mittelalter', Krems an der Donau, 24. bis 26. März 2003* (Krems, 2004), pp.43–68.

van Dijk, Stephen J. P., 'The Medieval Easter Vespers of the Roman Clergy', *Sacris Erudiri*, 19 (1969–70), pp.261–363.

'Urban and Papal Rites', *Sacris Erudiri*, 12 (1965), pp.450–465.

Dondeyne, Albert, 'La discipline des scrutins dans l'église latine avant Charlemagne', *Revue d'histoire écclesiastique*, 28 (1932), pp.5–33, 751–787.

Donkin, Lucy, 'Suo loco: The *Traditio evangeliorum* and the Four Evangelist Symbols in the Presbytery Pavement of Novara Cathedral', *Speculum*, 88 (2013), pp.92–143.

Dopsch, Heinz, 'Salzburg zur Zeit Erzbischofs Arns', in Meta Niederkorn-Bruck and Anton Scharer (eds.), *Erzbischof Arn von Salzburg* (Munich, 2004), pp.27–29.

Dorn, Johann 'Stationsgottesdienste in frühmittelalterlichen Bischofsstädten', in Heinrich M. Gietl (ed.), *Festgabe für A. Knöpfler* (Freiburg, 1917), pp.43–55.

Duchesne, Louis, *Origines du culte chrétien*, 5th ed. (Paris, 1920); English translation, *Christian Worship: Its Origins and Evolution*, trans. L. McClure (London, 1919).

Dyer, Joseph, 'City Streets as Sacred Space: The Typology of Processions in Medieval Rome', in Harald Buchinger and David Hiley (eds.), *Prozessionen und ihre Gesänge in der mittelalterlichen Stadt – Gestalt, Hermenutik, Repräsentation* (Regensburg, 2017), pp.13–33.

Emerick, Judson, 'Building *more romano* in Francia During the Third Quarter of the Eighth Century: The Abbey Church of Saint-Denis and Its Model', in Claudia Bolgia, Rosamond McKitterick and John Osborne (eds.), *Rome Across Time and Space: Cultural Transmission and the Exchange of Ideas, c.500–1400* (Cambridge, 2011), pp.127–150.

Fisher, J. D. C., *Christian Initiation: Baptism in the Medieval West* (London, 1965).

Flicoteux, Emmanuel, 'Un Problème de littérature liturgique: Les «Eclogae de officio Missae» d'Amalare', *Revue Bénédictine*, 25 (1908), pp.304–320.

Ellard, Gerard, *Ordination Anointings in the Western Church Before 1000 AD* (Cambridge, MA, 1933).

Gaillard, Michèle, 'Un évêque et son temps, Advence de Metz (858–875)', in Hans-Walter Herrmann and Reinhard Schneider (eds.), *Lotharingia. Eine europäische Kernlandschaft um das Jahr 1000. Referate eines Kolloquiums vom 24. bis 26. Mai 1994 in Saarbrücken* Veröffentlichungen der Kommission für

Bibliography

269

Saarländische Landesgeschichte und Volksforschung, 26 (Saarbrücken 1995), pp.89–119.

Gamber, Klaus *Codices Liturgici Latini Antiquiores*, 2nd ed., 2 vols. (Freiburg, 1968), Supplement (Freiburg, 1988).

'Fragmenta Liturgica IV', *Sacris Erudiri*, 19 (1969/70), pp.198–260.

'Fragmenta Liturgica III', *Sacris Erudiri* 18 (1967), pp.306–332.

'Teile eines ambrosianischen Messbuches im Palimpsest von Monza aus dem 8. Jh.', *Scriptorium*, 16 (1962), pp.3–15.

'Ein Salzburger Sakramentarfragment des 10. Jahrhunderts mit zwei Rupert-Messe', *Heiliger Dienst*, 15 (1961), pp.81–91.

'Frammento Ratisbonense di un messale Ambrosiano', *Ambrosius*, 35 (1949), pp.51–54.

Garrison, Mary, 'The Missa pro principe in the Bobbio Missal', in Yitzhak Hen and Rob Meens (eds.), *The Bobbio Missal: Liturgy and Religious Culture in Merovingian Gaul* (Cambridge, 2004), pp.206–218.

Gerard, Pierre, 'Le Cartulaire de Saint-Sernin de Toulouse et ses problèmes: l'église de Martres-Tolosane, le culte de saint Vidian et la légende de Vivien d'Aliscans', in Ellis Roger, René Tixier and Bernd Weitemeier (eds.), *The Medieval Translator. Traduire au Moyen Age: Proceedings of the International Conference of Göttingen (22–25 July 1996). Actes du Colloque international de Göttingen (22–25 juillet 1996)* (Turnhout, 1998), pp.114–133.

Gerbert, Martin, *Monumenta veteris liturgiae alemannicae* (St-Blaise, 1779).

Gittos, Helen, 'Researching the History of Rites', in Helen Gittos and Sarah Hamilton (eds.), *Understanding Medieval Liturgy: Essays in Interpretation* (Aldershot, 2015), pp. 13–37.

Gittos, Helen and Sarah Hamilton (eds.), *Understanding Medieval Liturgy: Essays in Interpretation* (Aldershot, 2015).

Goldberg, Eric, *Struggle for Empire: Kingship and Conflict under Louis the German* (Cambridge, 2006).

Grosse, Rudolf (ed.), *Althochdeutsches Wörterbuch*, vol. IV, *G–J* (Berlin, 1986).

Gullotta, Giuseppe, *Gli antichi cataloghi e i codici della Abbazia di Nonantola*, Studi e Testi, 182 (Vatican City, 1995).

Gy, Pierre-Marie, 'The Different Forms of Liturgical "Libelli"', in Niels Krogh Rasmussen and Gerard Austin (eds.), *Fountain of Life* (Washington, DC, 1991), pp.23–34.

Hallinger, Kassius, 'Die römischen *ordines* von Lorsch, Murbach und St Gall', in Ludwig Lenhart (ed.), *Universitas: Dienst an Wahrheit und Leben. Festschrift für Bischof Dr. Albert Stohr*, vol. I (Mainz, 1960), pp.466–477.

Hamilton, Sarah, 'The Early Pontificals: Anglo-Saxon Evidence Reconsidered from a Continental Perspective', in David Rollason, Conrad Leyser and Hannah Williams (eds.), *England and the Continent in the Tenth Century* (Turnhout, 2011), pp.411–428.

Hammer, Carl I., 'The Social Landscape of the Prague Sacramentary: The Prosopography of an Eighth Century Mass Book', *Traditio*, 54 (1999), pp.41–80.

270 *Bibliography*

Hartmann, Wilfried, *Die Synoden der Karolingerzeit im Frankreich und in Italien* (Schöningh, 1989).

Haubrichs, Wolfgang, 'Das althochdeutsch-lateinische Textensemble des Cod. Weiss. 91 (Weißenburger Katechismus) und das Bistum Worms im frühen neunten Jahrhundert', in R. Bergmann (ed.), *Volkssprachig-lateinische Mischtexte und Textensembles in der althochdeutschen, altsächsischen und altenglischen Überlieferung: Mediävistisches Kolloquium des Zentrums für Mittelalterstudien der Otto-Friedrich-Universität Bamberg am 16. und 17. November 2001* (Heidelberg, 2003), pp.131–173.

Hauke, Hermann, *Katalog der lateinischen Fragmente der Bayerischen Staatsbibliothek München*, vol. I (Wiesbaden, 1994).

Häußling, Angelus Albert, *Mönchskonvent und Eucharistiefeier. Eine Studie über die Messe in der abendländischen Klosterliturgie des frühen Mittelalters und zur Geschichte der Meßhäufigkeit*, Liturgiewissenschaftliche Quellen und Forschungen, 58 (Münster, 1973).

Heitz, Carol, '*More romano*: problèmes d'architecture et liturgie carolingiennes', in *Roma e l'etá carolingia. Atti della giornale di studio 3–8 Maggio 1976 a cura dello Istituto di Storia dell'arte dell'universitá di Roma* (Rome 1976), pp.27–34.

'La groupe cathedral du Metz au temps du Saint Chrodegang', in *Saint Chrodegang, communications présentées au Colloque tenu à Metz à l'occasion du douzième centenaire de sa mort* (Metz, 1967), pp.123–131.

Recherches sur les rapports entre architecture et liturgie à l'époque carolingienne (Paris, 1963).

Helmer, Friedrich, Julia Knödler and Günter Glauche, *Katalog der lateinischen Handschriften der Bayerischen Staatsbibliothek München. Die Handschriften aus St. Emmeram in Regensburg*, vol. IV, *Clm 14401–14540* (Wiesbaden, 2015).

Hen, Yitzhak, 'When Liturgy Gets out of Hand', in Elina Screen and Charles West (eds.), *Writing the Early Medieval West* (Manchester, 2018), pp.203–212.

The Royal Patronage of Liturgy in Frankish Gaul to the Death of Charles the Bald (877), HBS, Subsidia 3 (London, 2001).

'The Knowledge of Canon Law among Rural Priests: The Evidence of Two Manuscripts from around 800', *Journal of Theological Studies*, 50 (1999), pp.117–134.

'Unity in Diversity: the Liturgy of Frankish Gaul before the Carolingians', *Studies in Church History*, 32 (1995), pp.19–30.

and Meens, Rob (eds.), *The Bobbio Missal: Liturgy and Religious Culture in Merovingian Gaul* (Cambridge, 2004).

Hierzegger, Richard, 'Collecta und Statio: Die römischen Stationsprozessionen im frühen Mittelalter', *Zeitschrift für katholische Theologie*, 60 (1936), pp.511–554.

Hlawitschka, Eduard, 'Ratold, Bischof von Verona und Begründer von Radolfzell', *Hegau. Zeitschrift für Volkskunde und Naturgeschichte des Gebietes zwischen Rhein, Donau und Bodensee*, 42 (1997), pp.5–44.

Hofmann, Josef, 'Verstreute Blätter eines deutsch-insularen Sakramentars aus Neustadt am Main', *Mainfränkisches Jahrbuch*, 9 (1957), pp.133–141.

Bibliography

Hubert, Jean, 'Rome et la Renaissance carolingienne', in *Roma e l'età carolingia. Atti della gioranle di studio 3–8 Maggio 1976 a cura dello Istituto di Storia dell'arte dell'università di Roma* (Rome 1976), pp.7–14.

Huglo, Michel, 'Notes sur l'origine du 'Pontifical de Poitiers' (Paris Bibliotheque de l'Arsenal MS 227)', in A. Andrée and E. Kihlman (eds.), *Hortus Troparium: Florilegium in Honorem Gunillae Iversen* (Stockholm, 2008), pp.176–188.

Hummer, Hans, *Politics and Power in Early Medieval Europe: Alsace and the Frankish Realm, 600–1000* (Cambridge, 2006).

Irving, Andrew, 'Mass By Design: Design Elements in Early Italian Mass Book', in Barbara A. Shailor and Consuelo W. Dutschke (eds.), *Scribes and the Presentation of Texts (from Antiquity to c. 1550). Proceedings of the 20th Colloquium of the Comité international de paléographie latine* (Turnhout, 2021), pp.251–274.

Jacobsen, Werner, 'Saints' Tombs in Frankish Church Architecture', *Speculum*, 72 (1997), pp.1107–1143.

Jeffrey, Peter, 'The Early Liturgy of Saint Peter's and the Roman Liturgical Year', in Rosamond McKitterick, John Osborne, Carol M. Richardson and Joanna Story (eds.), *Old Saint Peter's, Rome* (Cambridge, 2013), pp.157–176.

'Eastern and Western Elements in the Irish Monastic Prayers of the Hours', in Margot Fassler and Rebecca A. Baltzer (eds.), *The Divine Office in the Latin Middle Ages* (Oxford, 2000), pp.99–146.

'Rome and Jerusalem: From Oral Tradition to Written Repertory in Two Ancient Liturgical Centers', in Graeme A. Boone (ed.), *Essays on Medieval Music in Honor of David G. Hughes* (Cambridge, MA, 1995), pp.207–248.

Jones, Christopher, *A Lost Work by Amalarius of Metz: Interpolation in Salisbury Cathedral Library MS 154* (London, 2001).

'The Book of the Liturgy in Anglo-Saxon England', *Speculum*, 73 (1996), pp.659–702.

Kaczynski, Bernice M., *Greek in the Carolingian Age: The St Gall Manuscripts* (Cambridge, MA, 1988).

Kantorowicz, Ernst, *Laudes Regiae: A Study in Liturgical Acclamations and Medieval Ruler Worship* (Berkeley and Los Angeles, 1946).

Kasten, Brigitte, *Adalard von Corbie: Die Biographie eines karolingischen Politikers und Klostervorstehers* (Dusseldorf, 1986).

Keefe, Susan, *Water and the Word, Baptism and the Education of the Clergy in the Carolingian Empire*, 2 vols. (Notre Dame, 2002).

'The Claim of Authorship in Carolingian Baptismal Expositiones: The Case of Odilbert of Milan', *Fälschungen im Mittelalter. Internationaler Kongreß der Monumenta Germaniae Historica, München 16–19 September 1986*, vol. V (Hanover, 1988), pp.355–401.

Kéry, Lotte, *Canonical Collections of the Early Middle Ages (ca. 400–1140). A Bibliographical Guide to the Manuscripts and Literature* (Washington, DC, 1999).

Bibliography

Klauser, Theodor, *Das Römische Capitulare Evangeliorum: Texte und Untersuchungen zu seiner ältesten Geschichte*, vol.i, 2nd ed. (Münster, 1972). 'Die liturgischen Austauchsbeziehungen zwischen der römischen und der fränkisch-deutschen Kirche vom achten bis zum elften Jahrhundert', *Historisches Jahrbuch*, 53 (1933), pp.169–189.

'Eine stationsliste der Metzer Kirche aus dem 8. Jahrhundert, wahrscheinlich ein Werk Chrodegangs', *Ephemerides Liturgica*, 44 (1930), pp.162–193; Reprinted in *Gesammelte Arbeiten zur Liturgiegeschichte, Kirchengeschichte und christlichen Archäologie* (Munich, 1924), pp.22–45.

'Ein vollständiges Evangelienverzeichnis der römischen Kirche aus dem 7. Jahrhundert, erhalten im Cod. Vat. Pal. lat. 46', *Römische Quartalschrift für christliche Altertumskunde und Kirchengeschichte*, 35 (1927), pp.113–134.

Klöckener, Martin, 'L'importance des sources liturgiques pour la connaissance de la pensée et des mentalités médiévales', in Hélène Bricout and Martin Klöckener (eds.), *Liturgie, Pensée Théologique et Mentalités Religieuses Au Haut Moyen Âge: Le témoignage des sources liturgiques* (Münster, 2016), pp.13–47.

'Eine liturgische Ordnung für Provinzialkonzilien aus der Karolingerzeit der "Ordo romanus qualiter concilium agatur" des Cod. 138 der Dombibliothek Köln, liturgiegeschichtlich erklärt', *Annuarium Historiae Conciliorum*, 12 (1980), pp.109–182.

Koch, Hadrian W., *Kloster Frauenberg in Fulda* (Fulda, 2009).

Kottje, Raymond, 'Einheit und Vielfalt des kirchlichen Lebens in der Karolingerzeit', *Zeitschrift für Kirchengeschichte*, 76 (1965), pp.335–340.

Kuttner, Stephen, 'Cardinalis: The History of a Canonical Concept', *Traditio*, 3 (1945), pp.129–214.

Langlois, Bernard, 'Le manuscript W de l'*Ordo Romanus* XL (édition M.Andrieu), un *Ordo* de la dédicace des églises, est-il un mauvais manuscript?', *Studia Patristica*, 26 (1993), pp.47–58.

Latham, Jacob, 'Inventing Gregory the Great: Memory, Authority and the Afterlives of the Laetenia Septiformis', *Church History*, 84 (2015), pp.1–31.

Le Jan, Régine, 'Reichenau and its amici viventes: Competition and Cooperation?' in Rob Meens, Dorine van Espelo, Bram von den Hoven van Genderen, Janneke Raaijmakers, Irene van Renswoude and Carine van Rhijn (eds.), *Religious Franks: Religion and Power in the Frankish Kingdoms* (Manchester, 2017), pp.268–269.

Lehmann, Paul, 'Adalhard', *Neue Deutsche Biographie*, vol. I (Berlin, 1953), pp.48 f.

Leroquais, Victor, *Les pontificaux manuscrits des bibliothèques publiques de France*, vol. I (Paris, 1938).

Levison, Wilhelm, 'Handschriften des Museum Meermanno – Westreenianum im Haag', *Neues Archiv der Gesellschaft für ältere deutsche Geschichtskunde*, 38 (1913), pp.513–518.

Lifshitz, Felice, 'A Cyborg Initiation? Liturgy and Gender in Carolingian East Francia', in Celia Chazelle and Felice Lifshitz (eds.), *Paradigms and Methods in Early Medieval Studies* (New York, 2007), pp.101–117.

Bibliography

Lowe, Elias Avery (ed.), *Codices Latini Antiquiores*, 12 vols. (Oxford, 1934–1971).
Lynch, Joseph, *Godparents and Kinship in Early Medieval Europe* (Princeton, 1986).
Mabillon, Jean, *Iter Germanicum* (Hamburg, 1717).
Museum Italicum, vol. II (Paris, 1689).
Marchi, G. P., 'Per un restauro della biografia di Pacifico, humilis levita Christi', in Dorothea Walz (ed.), *Scripturus vitam. Lateinische Biographie von der Antike bis in die Gegenwart. Festgabe für Walter Berschin zum 65. Geburtstag* (Heidelberg, 2002), pp.379–392.
Martène, Edmond, *De Antiquis Ecclesiae Ritibus Libri*, vol. I (Antwerp, 1736).
Martimort, Aimé-Georges, *Les Ordines, les ordinaries et les cérémoniaux*, Typologie des sources du moyenâge, 56 (Turnhout, 1991).
La documentation liturgique de dom Edmond Martène. Étude codicologique (Vatican City, 1978).
'Un Gélasien du VIIIe siècle: Le Sacramentaire de Noyon', in *Miscellanea Pietro Frutaz* (Rome, 1978), pp.183–206.
'Recherches récentes sur les Sacramentaires', *Bulletin de littérature ecclésiastique*, 73 (1972), pp.28–40.
Martinez-Diaz, Gonzalo, 'Un *Ordo Romanus* in Hebdomada Maiore inédito', *Hispania Sacra*, 15 (1962), pp.192–202.
McKitterick, Rosamond, *Rome and the Invention of the Papacy* (Cambridge, 2020).
'Charlemagne, Rome and the Management of Sacred Space', in R. Große and M. Sot (eds.), *Charlemagne: les temps, les espaces, les hommes. Construction et déconstruction* (Turnhout, 2018), pp.165–79.
'Rome and the Popes in the Construction of Institutional History and Identity in the Early Middle Ages : The Case of Leiden UB Scaliger MS 49', in Valerie Garver and Owen Phelan (eds.), *Rome and Religion in the Early Medieval World: Studies in Honor of Thomas F. X. Noble* (Farnham, 2014), pp.207–234.
'Les Perceptions Carolingiennes de Rome', in Woljciech Falkowski and Yves Sasser (eds.), *Le monde carolingien: Bilan, Perspectives, champs de recherches, Actes de colloque international de Poitiers, Centre d'Études Supérieures de civilisation mediévale, 18–20 novembre* (Turnhout, 2009), pp.83–102.
The Frankish Church and the Carolingian Reforms 789–895 (London, 1977).
Meens, Rob, Dorine van Espelo, Bram von den Hoven van Genderen, Janneke Raaijmakers, Irene van Renswoude and Carine van Rhijn (eds.), *Religious Franks: Religion and Power in the Frankish Kingdoms* (Manchester, 2017).
Meersseman, Giles Gerard, E. Adda and Jean Deshusses (eds.), *L'orazionale dell'archidiacono Pacifico e il carpsum del cantore Stefano: Studie e testi sulla liturgica del Duomo di Verona dal' IX all XI sec.* (Freibourg, 1974).
Meyveart, Paul, 'Diversity within Unity: A Gregorian Theme', *The Heythrop Journal*, 4 (1963), pp. 141–162.

274 *Bibliography*

Mews, Constant, 'Gregory the Great, the Rule of Benedict and Roman Liturgy: The Evolution of a Legend', *Journal of Medieval History*, 37 (2011), pp.125–144.

Mohlberg, Leo Cunibert, *Katalog der Handschriften der Zentralbibliothek Zürich*, vol. I, *Mittelalterliche Handschriften* (Zurich, 1951).

'Milano e Metz nella redazione del Sacramentario di Drogone', *Rediconti della Pontifica Accademia Romana di Archeologia*, 16 (1940), pp.151–155.

Mordek, Hubert, *Bibliotheca capitularium regum Francorum manuscripta* (Munich, 1995).

Moreton, Bernard, *The Eighth-Century Gelasian Sacramentaries. A Study in Tradition* (Oxford, 1976).

'The Liber Secundus of the Eighth Century Gelasian Sacramentaries: A Reassessment', *Studia Patristica*, 13 (1975), pp.382–86.

Morin, Jean, *Commentarius Historicus de Sacramento Poenitentiae* (Antwerp, 1682).

'Notice sur un manuscript important pour l'histoire du symbole', *RevBen*, 14 (1897), pp.481–488.

Morrison, Karl, 'Know Thyself: Music in the Carolingian Renaissance', *Committenti e produzione artistico-letteraria nell'alto medioevo occidentale*, Settimane, 39 (Spoleto, 1992), pp.369–481.

Mostert, Marco, '". . . but they pray badly using corrected books": Errors in the Early Carolingian Copies of the Admonitio Generalis', in Rob Meens, Dorine van Espelo, Bram von den Hoven van Genderen, Janneke Raaijmakers, Irene van Renswoude and Carine van Rhijn (eds.), *Religious Franks: Religion and Power in the Frankish Kingdoms* (Manchester, 2017), pp.112–127.

Mütherich, Florentine, 'Das Godelgaudus-Sakramentar ein verlorenes Denkmal aus der Zeit Karls des Großen', in Piel Friedrich and Jorg Traeger (eds.), *Festschrift Wolfgang Braunfels* (Tübingen, 1977), pp.267–274.

Mundó, Anscharius, 'Adnotationes in antiquissimum ordinem romanum feriae V in cena domini noviter editum', *Liturgica*, 2 (1958), pp.181–216.

Munier Charles, 'L'*Ordo Romanus* qualiter concilium agatur d'après le cod. Coloniensis 138', *Revue de theologie ancienne et medievale*, 29 (1962), pp.288–294.

Nason, Corey, 'The Mass Pericopes for Saint Arnulf's Day from the Drogo Sacramentary', *Revue Bénédictine*, 124 (2014), pp.298–324.

Nelson, Janet, 'Ritual and Reality in the Early Medieval Ordines', in Derek Baker (ed.), *The Materials, Sources and Methods of Ecclesiastical History* (Oxford, 1975), pp.41–52.

Nocent, Adrian, 'Un Fragment de sacramentaire de Sens au Xe siècle. La liturgie baptismale de la province ecclésiastique de Sens dans les manuscrits du IXe au XVIe siècles', in *Miscellanea liturgica in onore di S.E. il cardinale Giacomo Lercaro*, vol. 2 (Rome, 1967), pp.649–794.

Niederkorn-Bruck, Meta, 'Das Salzburger historische Martyrolog aus der Arn-Zeit und seine Bedeutung für die Textgeschichte des Martyrologium Bedae',

Bibliography

in Meta Niederkorn-Bruck and Anton Scharer (eds.), *Erzbischof Arn von Salzburg* (Munich, 2004), pp.155–171.

and Anton Scharer (eds.), *Erzbischof Arn von Salzburg* (Munich, 2004).

Oesterreicher, John, 'Pro Perfidis Judaeis', *Theological Studies*, 8 (1947), pp.80–96.

Oexle, Otto Gerhard, 'Die Karolinger und die Stadt des heiligen Arnulf' *Frühmittelalterliche Studien*, 1 (1967), pp.250–364.

Palazzo, Eric, 'La liturgie carolingienne: vieux débats, nouvelles questions, publications récentes', in Woljciech Falkowski and Yves Sasser (eds.), *Le monde carolingien: Bilan, Perspectives, champs de recherches, Actes de colloque international de Poitiers, Centre d'Études Supérieures de civilisation mediévale, 18–20 novembre* (Turnhout, 2009), pp.219–241.

Histoire des livres liturgiques: Le Moyen Âge des origines au XIIIe siècle (Paris, 1993).

Parkes, Henry, *The Making of Liturgy in the Ottonian Church: Books Music and Ritual in Mainz 950–1050* (Cambridge, 2015).

'Questioning the Authority of Vogel and Elze's PRG', Helen Gittos and Sarah Hamilton (eds.), *Understanding Medieval Liturgy: Essays in Interpretation* (Aldershot, 2015), pp.76–100.

Patzold, Steffen, *Presbyter. Moral, Mobilität und die Kirchenorganisation im Karolingerreich* (Stuttgart, 2020).

Episcopus: Wissen über Bischöfe im Frankenreich des späten 8. bis frühen 10. Jahrhunderts (Ostfildern, 2008).

Paxton, Frederick S., 'Researching Rites for the Dying and the Dead', in Helen Gittos and Sarah Hamilton (eds.), *Understanding Medieval Liturgy: Essays in Interpretation* (Aldershot, 2015), pp.39–56,

Picard Jean-Charles, 'Les origins du mot paradisus-parvus', *Mélanges de l'école française de Rome*, 83 (1971), pp.159–186.

Phelan, Owen, *The Formation of Christian Europe: The Carolingians, Baptism and the Imperium Christianum* (Oxford, 2014).

Plotzek, Joachim M., *Glaube und Wissen im Mittelalter die Kölner Dombibliothek* (Munich, 1998).

Pollard, Richard, 'Libri di scuola spirituale: Manuscripts and Marginalia at the Monastery of Nonantola', in Oronzo Pecere and Lucio Del Corso (eds.), *Libri di scuola e pratiche didattiche. Atti del Convegno Internazionale di Studi (Cassino, 7–10 Maggio 2008)* (Cassino, 2010), pp.379–380.

Preisendanz, Karl, 'Reginbert von der Reichenau. Aus Bibliothek und Skriptorium des Inselklosters', *Neue Heidelburger Jahrbücher* (1952/3), pp.1–49.

de Puniet, Pierre, 'Concelebration Liturgique' *Dictionnaire d'archéologie chrétienne et de liturgie*, vol. III (Paris, 1913/14), col.2476–2477.

'Catechumenat', *Dictionnaire d'archéologie chrétienne et de liturgie*, vol. II (Paris, 1910), col.2609.

'Les trois homélies catéchétiques du Sacramentaire Gélasien', *Revue d'histoire écclesiastique* 5 (1904), pp.503–529, 755–786 and 6; (1905), pp.15–32, 304–318.

Raaijmakers, Janneke, *The Making of the Monastic Community of Fulda c.744–c.900* (Cambridge, 2012).

Bibliography

Rabe, Susan, A., *Faith, Art, and Politics at Saint-Riquier: The Symbolic Vision of Angilbert* (Pennsylvania, 1995).

Rand, Edward K., *Studies in the Script of Tours. I: A Survey of the Manuscripts of Tours* (Cambridge, MA, 1929).

James A. Mc.Donough and J. Wade Thomas, 'An Unrecognised Sacramentary of Tours', *Harvard Studies in Classical Philology*, 60 (1951), pp.235–261.

Rankin, Susan, *Writing Sounds in Carolingian Europe: The Invention of Musical Notation* (Cambridge, 2019).

'Carolingian Liturgical Books: Problems of Categorization', *Gazette du Livre Médiéval*, 62 (2016) pp.21–33.

Rasmussen, Niels Krogh, *Les pontificaux du Haut Moyen Âge, Gènese du Livre de l'évêque* (Leuven, 1998).

'Unité et diversité des Pontificaux latins aux VIIIe, IXe, et Xe siècles', in *Liturgie et l'Église particulière et liturgie de l'Église universelle Conférences Saint-Serge, XXIIe Semaine d'études liturgiques, Paris, 30 juin–3 juillet 1975* (Rome, 1976), pp.393–410.

Ray, Maurice, *Les Diocèses de Besançon et de Saint-Claude* (Paris, 1977).

Repsher, Brian, *The Rite of Church Dedication in the Early Medieval Era* (Lewiston, 1998).

Reynolds, Roger, 'Clerics in the Early Middle Ages: Hierarchies and Functions', *Clerics in the Early Middle Ages. Hierarchy and Image* (Aldershot, 1999), pp.1–31.

'The Ordination of Clerics in the Middle Ages', Article XI in *Clerical Orders in the Early Middle Ages. Duties and Ordination* (Aldershot, 1999).

'Pseudonymous Liturgica in Early Medieval Canon Law Collections', *Law and Liturgy in the Latin Church, 5th–12th Centuries* (Aldershot, 1994), pp.67–76.

'The Ritual of Clerical Ordination of the Sacramentarium Gelasianum Saec. VIII: Early Evidence from Southern Italy', in Paul de Clerck and Eric Palazzo (eds.), *Rituels: mélanges offerts à Pierre-Marie Gy, o.p.* (Paris, 1990), pp.437–444; repr. in Roger Reynolds, *Clerical Orders in the Early Middle Ages* (Aldershot, 1999).

'A South Italian Mass Commentary', *Mediaeval History*, 50 (1988), pp.626–670.

'ordines', in Joseph Strayer (ed.), *Dictionary of the Middle Ages*, vol. IX (New York, 1987), p.269.

'Image and Text: A Carolingian Illustration of Modifications in the Early Roman Eucharistic *ordines*', *Viator: Medieval and Renaissance Studies*, 14 (1983), pp.59–75, reprinted as Article VII in *Clerical Orders in the Early Middle Ages* (Aldershot, 1999).

'A Ninth-Century Treatise on the Origins, Office and Ordination of a Bishop' *Revue Bénédictine*, 85 (1975), pp.321–332; reprinted as Article V in Reynolds, *Clerical Orders in the Early Middle Ages* (Aldershot, 1999).

van Rhijn, Carine, 'Manuscripts for Local Priests and the Carolingian Reforms', in Steffen Patzold and Carine van Rhijn (eds.), *Men in the Middle: Local Priests in Early Medieval Europe* (Berlin, 2016), pp.177–198.

Bibliography

277

'The Local Church, Priests' Handbooks and Pastoral Care in the Carolingian Period', *Chiese locali e chiese regionali nell'alto Medioevo*, Settimane di Studio del Centro Italiano di Studi Sull'Alto Medioevo, 61 (Spoleto, 2014), pp.689–709.

La Rocca, Cristina, 'A Man for all Seasons: Pacificus of Verona and the Creation of a Local Carolingian Past', in Yitzhak Hen and Matthew Innes (eds.), *The Uses of the Past in the Early Middle Ages* (Cambridge, 2000), pp.250–79.

Pacifico di Verona. Il passato Carolingio nella costruzione dellamemoria urbana, con un nota di Stefano Zamponi (Rome, 1995).

Romano, John, 'Baptizing the Romans', *Acta ad archaeologiam et artium historiam pertinentia*, 31 (2019), pp.43–62.

Liturgy and Society in Early Medieval Rome (Abingdon, 2014).

'The Fates of Liturgies: Towards a History of the First Roman Ordo', *Antiphon*, 11 (2007), pp.43–77.

Rose, Els, 'Emendatio and Effectus', in Rob Meens, Dorine van Espelo, Bram von den Hoven van Genderen, Janneke Raaijmakers, Irene van Renswoude and Carine van Rhijn (eds.), *Religious Franks: Religion and Power in the Frankish Kingdoms* (Manchester, 2017), pp.137–141.

'The Sanctoral Cycle of the Prague Sacramentary', in Maximilan Diesenberger, Rob Meens and Els Rose (eds.), *The Prague Sacramentary: Culture, Religion and Politics in Late Eighth-Century Bavaria* (Turnhout, 2016), pp.95–122.

'Liturgical Latin in Early Medieval Gaul', in Mary Garrison, Arpad P. Orbán and Marco Mostert (eds.), *Spoken and Written Language: Relations between Latin and the Vernacular Languages in the Earlier Middle Ages* (Turnhout, 2013), pp.303–313.

'Liturgical Latin in the Bobbio Missal', in Rob Meens and Yithak Hen (eds.), *The Bobbio Missal: Liturgy and Religious Culture in Merovingian Gaul* (Cambridge, 2004), pp.67–78.

and Arthur Westwell, 'Correcting the Liturgy and Sacred Language', in Arthur Westwell, Carine van Rhijn and Ingrid Rembold (eds.), *Rethinking the Carolingian Reforms* (Manchester, 2023), pp.141–175.

von Scarpatetti, Beat Matthias, *Die Handschriften der Stiftsbibliothek St. Gallen*, vol. I, pt. IV, *Codices 547–669: Hagiographica, Historica, Geographica, 8–18. Jahrhundert* (Wiesbaden, 2003).

Scherrer, Gustav, *Verzeichnis der Handschriften der Stiftsbibliothek von St. Gallen* (Halle, 1875).

Schieffer, Rudolf, '"Redeamus ad fontem". Rom als Hort authentischer Überlieferung im frühen Mittelalter', in Arnold Angenendt and Rudolf Schieffer (eds.), *Roma – Caput et Fons: Zwei Vorträge über das päpstliche Rom zwischen Altertum und Mittelalter* (Opladen, 1989), pp.45–70.

Schieffer, Theodulf, 'Erzbischof Richulf (787–813)', *Jahrbuch für das Bistum Mainz*, 5 (1950), pp.329–342.

Schneider, Herbert, 'Roman Liturgy and Frankish Allegory: Editions of Fragments of Amalarius', in Julia M. H. Smith (ed.), *Early Medieval Rome and the Christian West: Essays in Honour of Donald A. Bullough* (Leiden, 2000), pp.358–361.

278 *Bibliography*

'Karolingische Kirchen- und Liturgiereform. Ein konservativer Neuaufbruch', in Christoph Stiegemann and Matthias Wemhoff (eds.), *Kunst und Kultur der Karolingerzeit. Karl der Große und Papst Leo III in Paderborn*, vol. II (Mainz, 1999), pp.772–781.

Schnusenberg, Christine Catharina, *Das Verhältnis von Kirche und Theater Dargestellt an ausgewahlten Schriften der Kirchenvater und liturgischen Texten bis auf Amalarius von Metz (a.d. 775–852)* (Frankfurt-am-Main, 1981); English trans. in *The Relationship Between the Church and the Theatre: Exemplified by Selected Writings of the Church Fathers and by Liturgical Texts Until Amalarius of Metz, 775–852 AD* (Lanham, 1988).

Semmler, Josef, 'Chrodegang, Bishof von Metz 747–766', in Friedrich Knöpp (ed.), *Die Reichsabtei Lorsch: Festschrift zum Gedenken an ihre Stiftung 764*, vol. I (Darmstadt, 1973), pp.229–245.

Siffrin, Petrus, 'Zwei Blätter eines Sakramentars in irischer Schrift des 8. Jahrhunderts aus Regensburg (Berlin, Preußische Staatsbibliothek. Ms. lat. fol. 877)', *Jahrbuch für Liturgiewissenschaft*, 10 (1930), pp.1–39.

Silva-Tarouca, Carlo, 'Giovanni « archicantor » di S. Pietro a Roma et l'« Ordo romanus » da lui composta (anno 680)', *Atti della Pontificia Accademia Romana di Archeologia (Serie III) . Memorie*, 1 (Roma, 1923), pp.159–213.

Simperl, Matthias, 'Ein gallischer Liber Pontificalis? Bemerkung zur Text- und Überlieferungsgeschichte des sogenannten Catalogus Felicianus', *Römische Quartalschrift für christliche Altertumskunde und Kirchengeschichte*, 111, 3.4 (2016), pp.272–287.

Smith, Julia M. H. (ed.), 'Old Saints, New Cults: Roman relics in Carolingian Francia', in *Early Medieval Rome and the Christian West: Essays in Honour of Donald A. Bullough* (Leiden, 2000), pp.317–340.

Smyth, Matthieu, *La liturgie oubliée: la prière eucharistique en Gaule Antique et dans L'Occident non romain* (Paris, 2003).

Staab, Franz, 'Erzbischof Richulf (787–813)', in Friedhelm Jürgensmeier (ed.), *Handbuch der Mainzer Kirchengeschichte*, vol. I, *Christliche Antike und Mittelalter*, pt.1., Beiträge zur Mainzer Kirchengeschichte, 6 (Würzburg, 2000), pp.102ff, 138, 144–150 and 841–843.

Stäblein, Bruno, '"Gregorius Praesul", der Prolog zum römischen Antiphonale', in *Musik und Geschichte im Mittelalter. Gessamelte Aufsätze* (Göppingen, 1984), pp.117–142.

Staerk, Antonio, *Les Manuscrits Latins du Ve au XIIIe siècle conservés à la Bibliothèque Impériale de Saint-Pétersbourg*, vol. I (St Petersburg, 1910; repr. Hildesheim, 1976).

Steck, Wolfgang, '"Secundum usum romanum": Liturgischer Anspruch und Wirchlichkeit zur Karolingerzeit', in Christian Schäfer and Martin Thurner (eds.), *Mittelalterliches Denken: Debatten, Ideen und Gestalten im Kontext* (Darmstadt, 2007), pp.15–28.

Der Liturgiker Amalarius: Eine quellenkritische Untersuchung zu Leben und Werk eines Theologen der Karolingerzeit (Munich, 2000).

Bibliography

Stegmüller, F., 'Bischof Angilmodus über die Taufe. Ein Beitrag zur spätkarolingischen Tauftheologie', *Römische Quartalschrift für christlichen Altertumskunde und Kirchengeschichte*, 52 (1957), pp.15–32.

Steinová, Evina, *Notam superponere studui. The Use of Annotation Symbols in the Early Middle Ages* (Turnhout, 2019).

Stenzel, Alois, *Die Taufe: eine genetische Erklärung der Taufliturgie* (Innsbruck, 1958).

Störmer, Wilhelm, 'Eine Adelsgruppe um die Fuldaer Äbte Sturmi und Eigil und den Holzkirchener Klostergründer Troand', in *Gesellschaft und Herrschaft, Festgabe für Karl Bosl* (Munich, 1969), pp.1–34.

Symes, Carol, 'Liturgical Texts and Performance Practices', in Helen Gittos and Sarah Hamilton (eds.), *Understanding Medieval Liturgy: Essays in Interpretation* (Aldershot, 2015), pp.241–244.

Talley, Thomas J., 'The Origin of the Ember Days: An Inconclusive Postscript', in Paul de Clerck and Eric Palazzo (eds.), *Rituels: mélanges offerts à Pierre-Marie Gy, o.p.* (Paris, 1990), pp.465–472.

Tellenbach, Gerd, *Römischer und christlicher Reichsgedanke in der Literatur des frühen Mittelalters* (Heidelberg, 1934).

Thompson, J. D., 'The Ordination Masses in Vat. Reg. 316', *Studia Patristica*, 10 (1970), pp.436–440.

Traube, Ludwig and Rudolf Ehwald, *Jean-Baptiste Maugérard: ein Beitrag zur Bibliotheksgeschichte*. Palaeographische Forschungen 23.4 (Munich, 1904).

Unterkircher, Franz, *Zur Ikonographie und Liturgie des Drogo-Sakramentars: Paris, BnF, Ms. Lat. 9428* (Graz, 1977).

Venturini, Teresa, *Ricerche Paleografiche intorno all'Archidicono Pacifico* (Verona, 1929).

Vigarini, Guido, *Inventario dei Manoscritti dell'archivio capitolare di Modena* (Modena, 2003).

Vogel, Cyrille, *Medieval Liturgy: An Introduction to the Sources*, trans. William G. Storey and Niels Krogh Rasmussen (Washington, DC, 1986).

'La réforme liturgique sous Charlemagne', in Bernhard Bischoff (ed.), *Karl der Große Lebenswerk und Nachleben*, vol. II, *Das geistige Leiben* (Dusseldorf, 1966), pp.217–32.

Volkert, Wilhelm and Friedrich Zoepfl, *Die Regesten der Bischöfe und des Domkapitels von Augsburg*, vol. I (Augsburg, 1985).

Webber Jones, Leslie, 'The Scriptorium at Corbie 1: The Library', *Speculum*, 22 (1947), pp.191–204.

Westwell, Arthur, 'The Lost Missal of Alcuin and the Carolingian Sacramentaries of Tours', *Early Medieval Europe*, 30 (2022), pp.350–383.

'Ordering the Church in the *Ordines Romani*', in Rutger Kramer, Emilie Kurdziel and Graeme Ward (eds.), *Categorising the Church: Monastic Communities and Canonical Clergy In The Carolingian World (780–840)* (Turnhout, 2022), pp.425–445.

'Rome on the Danube: Papal Liturgies at St Emmeram in the Carolingian Period. The Saint-Emmeram Gloss on the Fermentum', in Harald Buchinger and

David Hiley (eds.), *Liturgie und Musik in Sankt-Emmeram* (Regensburg, 2022), pp.39–55.

'Three Ninth-Century Liturgical Fragments Identified as Pontificals in Heidelberg, Douai and Innsbruck', *Revue Bénédictine*, 131 (2021), pp.387–406.

'The Content and the Ideological Construction of the Early Pontifical Manuscripts', *Mélanges de l'École française de Rome – Moyen Âge*, 132 (2020), pp.233–251.

'Correction of Liturgical Words, and Words of Liturgical Correctio in the *Ordines Romani* of Saint Amand', in Vincent Debiais and Victoria Turner (eds.), *Words in the Middles Ages/Les Mots au Moyen Âge*. Utrecht Studies in Medieval Literacy 46 (Turnhout, 2020), pp.69–87.

'The *Ordines Romani* and the Carolingian Choreography of a Liturgical Route to Rome' *Acta ad archaeologiam et artium historiam pertinentia* 31 (2019) pp.64–70.

'The *ordines* of Vat. Lat. 7701 and the Liturgical Culture of Carolingian Chieti', *Papers of the British School at Rome*, 86 (2017), pp.127–152.

Carine van Rhijn and Ingrid Rembold (eds.), *Rethinking the Carolingian Reforms* (Manchester, 2023).

Wiegand, Friedrich Ludwig Leonhard, *Erzbischof Odilbert von Mailand über die Taufe ein Beitrag zur Geschichte der Taufliturgie im Zeitalter Karls des Großen* (Leipzig, 1899).

Winandy, Jacques, 'Un témoignage oublié sur les anciens usages Cassiniens', *Revue Bénédictine*, 50 (1938), pp.254–291.

Willis, G. G., *Essays in Early Roman Liturgy* (London, 1964).

Wilmart, André, 'Le lectionnaire d'Alcuin', *Epherimides Liturgica*, 51 (1937), pp.136–197.

'Un florilège carolingien sur le symbolisme des cérémonies du baptême', in *Analecta Reginensia*, Studi e Testi 59 (Vatican City, 1933), pp.153–179.

'La lettre philosophique d'Almanne et son context littéraire', *Archives d'histoire doctrinale et littéraire du Moyen-Âge*, 3 (1928), pp.285–320.

'Expositio Missae', in Fernand Cabrol and Henri Leclercq (eds.), *Dictionnaire d'archéologie chrétienne et de liturgie*, vol. V (Paris, 1922), col. 1014–1027.

'L'index liturgique de Saint-Thierry', *Revue Bénédictine* 30 (1913), pp.437–450.

Wright, Roger, *Late Latin and Early Romance in Spain and Carolingian France* (Liverpool, 1982).

Zerfaß, Rolf, 'Die Idee der römischen Stationsfeier und ihr Fortleben', *Liturgisches Jahrbuch*, 8 (1958), pp.218–229.

Index

Adalard of Corbie, Abbot, 46
Adventius of Metz, bishop, 200
agnus dei, wax figures, 30
Alcuin of York, 21, 35, 38, 58, 78, 84, 212, 224, 237,
240, 250
Comes of, 108
Mass of Rupert of Salzburg, 199
Almannus of Hautvilliers, monk, 83
Amalarius of Metz, 45, 77, 94, 107, 111, 128, 141,
147, 159, 171, 182, 239, 248, 252–253, 255
eglogae de ordine romano, 78–80, 82, 116,
118, 134
Liber Officialis, 14, 39, 67, 81–82, 118, 127, 136,
172, 221, 233
Andrieu, Michel, 6–9, 15, 19–21, 23, 24, 26–28,
30–33, 35–36, 37, 38–40, 42, 46–47, 49,
53–55, 56, 57, 58, 61, 62, 64–65, 74–75, 88,
91, 96, 98, 105, 110, 113, 116, 117, 118,
121–122, 125, 126, 127–128, 132, 133, 136,
141–146, 150, 151, 156, 160, 162–163, 174,
177–180, 183, 185, 187, 189, 191, 196–198,
200, 201, 207, 221–222, 224–225,
226–227, 233, 236, 243, 245–246
editing of the *ordines*, 12, 22, 52, 62, 186, 193
understanding of liturgical 'use', 67, 69–72,
75–77, 84, 94–95, 100, 103, 129, 133, 241
understanding of the 'pontifical', 53, 129, 209
Angilbert of Milan, archbishop, 170
Angilbert of St-Riquier, Abbot, 46, 237
Institutio, 137–139
Angilram of Metz, bishop, 24, 26, 32–33, 35, 52,
114, 165, 170, 176
Institutio of, 24, 109–111, 232
Antiphoner of Compiègne, 31, 33
archdeacon, 30, 59, 104, 112, 117, 137, 142, 143,
234–235
archiclavius, 130
architecture, *more romano*, 10, 66, 114, 132, 251
Arn of Salzburg, archbishop, 48, 64–65, 66, 140,
182, 198–200, 201, 202–203, 224,
240–246, 254, 256

martyrology, 250
ordo for a council, 98, 199, 208, 240

baptism, 38, 48, 68, 74, 140–177, 244
at Epiphany, 37, 57, 132
exposition of, 14, 36, 48, 77, 78, 82, 83,
169–177, 210
ordo of *See* ordo romanus: 11
Baturich of Regensburg, bishop, 44, 51, 52, 73, 113,
197–199, 203, 241, 244, 246, 247, 249,
252, 254
copy of Collection B *See* manuscript: Munich,
BSB: Clm 14510
kollektar-pontifikale See manuscript: Vienna
ÖNB: ser.n. 2762
Bernard of Italy, King, 46
Bernharius of Worms, bishop, 53, 55, 56, 65–66,
140, 182, 203, 218–219, 231, 246, 247, 249,
250, 252
collection of *ordines romani See* manuscript:
Wolfenbüttel Herzog August Bibliothek:
MS Weissenburgenses, 91
Besançon, 24, 87
Bischoff, Bernhard, 21, 26, 35, 46, 53, 57, 58, 64,
78, 84, 122, 203, 212
blessing, episcopal, 113
Bobbio, monastery, 47

Candlemas *see* ordo romanus: 20
canon law, 88–91, 195, 210, 216, 250
Collectio Laureshamensis, 90
Collection of 'Saint-Blaise', 92
Collection of St-Maur, 90
Dionysio-Hadriana, 90
Statuta Ecclesiae Antiqua, 41, 196
cardinals, 49, 50, 59, 63, 119, 125–126, 136
catalogues, 5, 69, 93, 238
chant, 9, 31, 55, 59, 72, 74, 99, 109, 158, 163, 164,
167, 176
Benedicite, 184
Deus in adiutorum, 37

281

282   *Index*

chant (cont.)
  Dextera domini, 76
  Greek, 31, 62, 231, 232
Charlemagne, 2, 21, 23, 28, 64, 65, 110, 131, 139,
    141, 148, 209
  survey on baptism, 77, 78, 141, 147, 169,
    170, 172
Chavasse, Antoine, 30, 97, 175
Chrism Mass, 76, 96, 97, 119, 121, 123, 129, 220
Chrodegang of Metz, bishop, 22–23, 24, 30,
    60–62, 97, 109, 110, 149–150, 164, 170,
    176, 236–237, 240, 244, 251
  Regula, 22, 61, 109, 136
  stational list *See* manuscript: Paris, BnF:
    lat.268
church
  baptismal, 124
  dedication of *see ordo romanus*: 41
Clement I, Pope, 54, 86, 248, 249
collection
  A of the *ordines romani*, 8, 19–39, 40, 69, 93,
    162, 176, 208, 212, 232, 237, 238, 239, 240
  B of the *ordines romani*, 8, 20, 40–51, 75, 80, 111,
    184, 185–192, 209, 214, 233, 247, 252
    as *petit pontifical*, 70, 75
  Capitulare. *See* manuscript: St-Gall,
    Stiftsbibliothek: cod.349
  of St-Amand *See* manuscript: Paris, BnF:
    lat.974
  of St-Gall *See* manuscript: St-Gall,
    Stiftsbibliothek: cod.614
concelebration, Eucharistic, 125, 136
Corbie, monastery, 35, 46, 77, 88, 95, 210
  ab minuscule script, 97
coronation, 73, 98, 202, 254
council
  Aachen 809, 55
  Attigny 765, 240
  Danube 787, 176
  Mainz 813, 66, 140, 141, 147, 182, 189, 246, 247
  ordo for *See* ordo romanus: for a council
  Pavia 876, 118
  Reisbach 798, 61, 244
  Reisbach, Freising, Salzburg 800, 244
  Rome 595, 54, 86
  Tours 858, 90

de Puniet, Pierre, 146, 158, 174
diligentia
  ordo romanus for *See* ordo romanus: 44
Duchesne, Louis, 5, 114

Egeria, 11
Ember Days, 63, 74, 181–184, 189, 252
Engilmodus of Soissons, bishop, 172–173, 253

Eugenius I, Pope, 44
expositio missae, 36, 77, 83, 118
  Dominus Uobiscum, 36, 77
expositions, liturgical, 13–14, 45, 47, 75–84, 252

fermentum, 124–125, 128
  Saint-Emmeram gloss *See* manuscript:
    Munich, BSB: Clm 14747
Fulda, monastery, 66, 132–137, 251

Gamber, Klaus, 142, 163, 175–176
Gelasius I, Pope, 89
Gerbert, Martin, 5
Greek, 212, 220, 227–232
  Creed, 98, 144, 148, 228–231
Gregory III, Pope, 107
Gregory of Tours, 130, 237
Gregory the Great, Pope, 59
  letter to Augustine of Canterbury, 91
  septiform litany, 88, 138

Hadrian I, Pope, 28, 35, 64, 133, 238, 249
Haito of Basel, bishop, 93
Hariulf of St-Riquier, 137
Häußling, Angelus Albert, 103, 129
Hermingard, empress, 43
Hincmar of Reims, archbishop, 93, 200–202
Hrabanus Maurus, 39, 81
Hugh of Salins, archbishop, 24

immixtion, 126–128, 134
Innocent I, Pope, 85, 88, 124
Isidore of Seville, 78, 131

Jerusalem, 11, 100, 253
Jesse of Amiens, bishop, 171
Judith, empress, 43

Keefe, Susan, 141, 171

Lateran, St-John, 28, 67, 97, 119–120, 129, 132, 138
  baptistery, 31, 143, 177
  patriarchium, 105
Latin, language of the *ordines romani*, 221–227
Laudes Regiae, 41, 42, 112
Leo III, Pope, 55, 64, 65, 240, 242, 244, 252
Leroquais, Victor, 70, 96
libelli, 19, 208
Liber Diurnus Romanorum Pontificum, 47
Liber Pontificalis, 11, 90, 93, 107, 108, 248–250, 252
litany, Great *see* ordo romanus: 21
liturgy
  Ambrosian, 164–165
  Gallican, 7, 130–131
  stational, 11, 60, 104–108, 132, 137, 209, 253, 256

Index 283

Lorsch, monastery, 23, 57, 129, 133, 226, 238
Lothar, Emperor, 95
Louis II, Emperor, 44, 118
Louis the German, King, 44, 51, 73
Lupus of Aquleia
  ordo of *See* manuscript: Museo archeologico
  nazionale, MS LXXXV

Mabillon, Jean, 5, 142
manuscript
  Albi, BM, MS 42, 25, 49, 83, 84, 93, 221
  Autun, BM, MS 184, 130
  Bamberg, Staatsbibliothek, cod.lit. 131, 80, 81,
    93, 252
  Barcelona, Archivio y Biblioteca Capitular de
    la Catedral de Barcelona, MS 64, 172
  Bern, Burgerbibliothek, MS 289, 22, 221, 236
  Brussels, Bibliothèque royale, MS 10127–10144,
    29, 59, 62, 210, 222, 224, 239, 243
  Cologne, Dombibliothek 138, 46, 47, 49–50,
    59, 72–73, 88, 98, 111, 125, 194, 207, 215,
    233, 240
  Copenhagen, Kongelige Bibliotek, MS Gl.
    kgl. 3443, , 26, 213, 221
  Donaueschingen, Fürstlich Fürstenbergische
    Bibliothek, cod.192 (olim), 98, 157, 229
  Douai, BM, MS 14, 25
  Einsiedeln, Stiftsbibliothek
    MS 110, 47, 80, 251
    MS 326, 66, 132
  Frankfurt, Staatsbibliothek MS Bart.181,
    ivory, 126
  Freiburg im Breisgau, UB 363, 207
  Friuli, Museo archeologico nazionale, MS
    LXXXV, 146, 168–169, 171
  Gotha, Forschungsbibliothek, Membr.I. 85,
    57, 87, 90, 217, 226
  Leiden, Bibliothèque de l'Université, Voss.
    Lat. 60, 249
  London, British Library, Add. MS 15222, 24,
    87, 92, 109
  Metz, BM 134 (destroyed in 1944), 91
  Milan, Biblioteca del capitolo metropolitano,
    cod.D.I. 12, 194
  Montecassino, Archivio della Badia, MS
    451, 179
  Montpellier, Bibliothèque de la faculté
    de médecine, MS 412, 24, 38, 56, 84, 211,
    225, 238
  Monza, Biblioteca Capitolare, b-23/141, 164
  Munich, BSB
    Clm 14387, 249
    Clm 14470, 25
    Clm 14510, 44, 48, 73, 84, 112, 198, 207,
      215–216, 246–247, 249

Clm 14747, 124
Clm 28135, 245
Clm 6398, 25
Murbach fragments (Sankt Paul,
  Stiftsbibliothek fragment 979, Munich,
  Bayerische Staatsbibliothek, Clm 14659,
  Clm 14655 and Regensburg, Staatliche
  Bibliothek, fragm.2), 23, 37, 208,
  212–213, 226
Padua, Biblioteca Capitolare, D47, 95, 108
Paris, Bibliothèque de l'Arsenal, MS 227,
  99–100, 118, 128, 146, 149, 158–160, 253
Paris, BnF
  lat. 12051, 95
  lat. 1248, 82, 84, 227
  lat. 14008, 46, 48
  lat. 2399, 38
  lat. 2449, 92
  lat. 268, 60, 149
  lat. 3836, 91
  lat. 816 *see* sacramentary: of Angoulême
  lat. 938, 108
  lat. 9421, 81
  lat. 9428, 89
  lat. 9430, 114
  lat. 974, 8, 59, 62, 65, 114, 125, 178, 179, 224,
    225, 242–244
Reims, BM, MS 1, 25
Rome, Biblioteca Alessandrina, cod. 173, 198
Rome, Biblioteca Nazionale, MS Sessorianus
  52, 44, 50, 146
Rouen, BM, MS 26, 25
St Petersburg, National Library
  lat.Q.v.I, n° 35, 55, 98, 99
  Q. V. I, n° 34, Q. V. I, n° 56 and Q. V. II, n°
    5, 35, 77, 88, 210
St Gall, Stiftsbibliothek
  cod. 1092, 129
  cod. 11, 91
  cod. 140, 58, 62, 67, 89, 106, 116, 179, 225,
    247, 252
  cod. 225, 25
  cod. 348 *See* sacramentary: of Rheinau
  cod. 349, 8, 56, 57, 85, 91, 161, 224, 239, 249
  cod. 446, 46, 50, 78, 80, 93, 211, 252
  cod. 614, 8, 29, 50, 58, 62–64, 89, 106, 116,
    133, 179, 221, 223, 225, 239, 243, 249
The Hague, Museum Meermanno
  Westreeanium cod. 10.B. 4, 38, 90
Vatican City, BAV
  lat. 4770, 157
  lat. 6018, 25, 92
  lat. 7701, 48, 98, 207, 208
  Pal.lat. 1341, 133
  Pal.lat. 277, 91

284   *Index*

manuscript (cont.)
  Pal.lat. 47, 94
  Pal.lat. 487, 22, 33–36, 84, 93, 162, 163, 208,
    212, 220, 221, 226, 236, 249
  Pal.lat. 574, 57, 87, 90, 216, 224
  Reg.lat. 1127, 90, 216
  Reg.lat. 235, 137
  Reg.lat. 316, *see* sacramentary: Old Gelasian
Vercelli, Archivio Capitolare, MS 183, 25
Verona, Biblioteca Capitolare
  LXXXV, 72
  XCI, 72
  XCII, 42–44, 45, 50, 71, 125, 207, 214–215,
    232–234, 247
  XCIV, 49
  XXII, 250
Vienna, ÖNB
  cod. 387, 250
  cod. 795, 250
  cod.ser.n. 2762, 99, 183–184, 195–200, 203,
    240–242, 245
Wolfenbüttel Herzog August Bibliothek
  Ms Guelf.10.11 Aug 4°, 249
  MS Weissenburgenses 91, 31, 52–56, 59, 60,
    64, 68, 73–74, 86–88, 92, 111, 112, 113, 125,
    180, 181, 192–194, 207, 209, 220, 221, 226,
    229–232, 235, 247
Zurich Zentralbibliothek Car C 102, 44, 50,
    75–77, 146, 210, 227, 253
Maxentius of Aquileia, patriarch, 169
Metz, 22, 30, 61, 108, 176, 236, 237
Mondsee, monastery, 198, 203
Montecassino, monastery, 49
Murbach, monastery, 23, 226, 238, 251

Nicholas I, Pope, 44, 99, 253
Nonantola, monastery, 44, 47, 210, 253

Old High German, 36, 116
orationes sollemnes, 60
ordination, rite of
  Frankish practice *See* ordo de sacris ordinibus
  Roman practice *see* ordo romanus: 34
ordo de sacris ordinibus, 41, 54, 89, 99, 185–189,
  192–195, 197
ordo romanus
  1, 21, 22, 40, 47, 54, 79, 83, 93, 104–108, 118, 176,
    178, 210, 214, 247, 253
    'long recension', 21, 27, 105, 117, 126, 128,
      137, 238
    'short recension', 27, 58, 62, 104, 117, 126,
      221, 236–237, 239
    origin outside Rome, 27, 32, 126–128
  2, 58, 106, 125, 223, 236, 243
  3, 47, 54, 58, 59–60, 125–126, 136, 233, 239, 243
  4, 60, 65, 79, 114–116, 126, 223, 225, 243, 246

  6, 110, 136
  7, 95, 127
  8, 62, 240
  9, 78, 79, 116–117
  11, 21, 22, 40, 54, 76, 83, 99, 142–147, 162–166,
    212, 214, 229, 238, 253
    origin outside Rome, 27, 32, 95, 163, 174
  12, 62, 64, 65, 240
  13A, 21, 24, 25–26, 32, 54, 87, 238, 256
  13B, 40, 215
  14, 56, 91, 256
  15, 6, 37–38, 52, 54, 85, 90, 108, 117–118, 127,
    129–132, 137, 160–162, 178, 180, 216, 224,
    225, 235, 237, 239, 249
  16, 56, 178, 180, 224, 239
  17, 57, 87, 90–91, 178, 180, 216, 224, 239
  18, 237
  19, 237
  20, 65, 138, 178, 223, 242, 245
  21, 65, 178, 242, 245
  22, 62, 64, 179, 240, 245
  23, 66
  24, 21, 25, 29, 30, 54, 58, 61, 62, 99, 176, 222,
    236, 239, 245
  25, 54, 74
  26, 21, 25, 31, 52, 54, 58, 62, 99, 176, 222,
    236, 239
  27, 21, 22, 29–32, 93, 212, 238
  28, 40, 54, 76, 82, 214
    Appendix, 62, 240
  28A, 54, 74, 113
  29, 33–34, 36, 133, 212, 238
  30A, 59, 243
  30B, 65, 125, 223, 232, 243
  31, 81
  32, 48, 82
  33, 232
  33B, 223
  34, 21, 22, 27–28, 32, 41, 54, 93, 184, 193–195,
    196–197, 247
  35B, 197
  36, 62, 64, 89, 184, 187, 240
  37, 41, 82, 89, 184, 190
  37B, 49
  38, 178, 183–184, 199, 203, 240, 241, 245
  39, 65, 184, 223, 243
  40, 47, 48, 71
  41, 40, 54, 82, 83
  42, 21, 24, 32, 40, 54, 76, 82, 83, 93, 132,
    238
  43, 65, 243
  44, 48, 247
  50, 180
  51 (of Chavasse), 97, 119–120
  for a council, 47, 98
ostiarius (doorkeeper), 135

Index

285

Pacificus of Verona, archdeacon, 45, 234–235, 250
Parkes, Henry, 100
Paschal I, Pope, 49
Paul the Deacon, 109
Paulinus of Aquileia, patriarch, 176
Peter of Nonantola, Abbot, 45, 77, 182
Pippin III, King, 2
Pippin of Italy, King, 46, 51
pontifical
  of Besançon *See* manuscript: London, British Library, Add. MS 15222
  of Chieti *See* manuscript: Vatican City, BAV: lat.7701
  of Constance *See* Donaueschingen, Fürstlich Fürstenbergische Bibliothek, cod.192 (olim)
  of Milan *See* Milan, Biblioteca del capitolo metropolitano, cod.D.I.12
  of Sens *See* manuscript: Saint-Petersburg, National Library:lat. Q.v.I., n°. 35
  of Turpin of Reims (destroyed in 1776), 96–97
  origins of, 8, 51, 70–71, 75, 96–100, 208–211
  Romano-Germanique, 73, 117, 183, 198
Pope, office, 5, 9, 48, 61, 76, 106, 108, 127–128, 180, 193, 221
  ordination of *see ordo romanus*: 40A
priest, local, 59, 210
Pseudo-Clement, epistles, 54, 86, 87, 219
Pseudo-Damasus, 54, 86
Pseudo-Gelasius, De libris recipiendis et non recipiendis, 86–87, 92
Pseudo-Germanus, 130–131
Pseudo-Isidore, decretals, 92, 201

Rasmussen, Niels Krogh, 70, 98, 208
Ratold of Verona, bishop, 50, 234
reform, concept, 2–4, 6–8, 12, 15, 21, 79, 83, 110, 130, 131, 132, 139, 141, 224, 225–227, 246, 254, 255, 256
Regensburg, 51, 247
Reginbert of Reichenau, librarian, 78, 80
Reichenau, monastery, 51, 78, 80, 93, 116, 252
relics, deposition of *See ordo romanus*: 42
Richulf of Mainz, archbishop, 65, 251
Rome
  'virtual', 248, 251
  Itinerary, 66, 132, 250
  pilgrimage to, 28, 49, 66, 247, 251
  relics from, 10, 66, 132
rubrication, 212, 215–220

Sacramentary, 4, 27, 61, 74, 76, 77, 94–95, 148, 207, 210
  fragment from Neustadt, 155

Gelasian of the Eighth Century, 7, 30, 36, 41, 72, 74, 76, 95, 145, 161, 163, 243
Gregorian, 10, 21, 33, 51, 72, 76, 135, 180, 209, 245, 255
  Supplement, 209
  of Angoulême, 146, 148, 150–151, 153, 187
  of Drogo *See* manuscript: Paris, BnF: lat.9428
  ivory, 114
  of Gellone, 74, 132, 146, 151–154, 167–168, 228
  of Godelgaudus (destroyed in 1776), 146, 151, 158, 160, 176, 228
  of Rheinau, 155
  Old Gelasian, 30, 144, 146, 148–150, 152, 162, 175–176, 187
  Paduense See manuscript: Padua, Biblioteca Capitolare D47
  Veronense See manuscript: Verona Biblioteca Capitolare: LXXXV
Salzburg, 183, 199, 224, 246
Santa Maria Maggiore, basilica, 63, 130, 181
script, Anglo-Saxon minuscule, 154, 212, 226
scrutinies, baptismal, 142–177
  IN AURIUM APERTIONEM, 72, 145, 146, 147, 148, 150, 154, 156, 158, 159, 160, 161, 162, 163, 165, 168, 169, 171, 173, 214, 228
  in Rome, 144–146, 174
Sergius I, Pope, 107
Simpert of Regensburg, bishop, 23, 251
St Amand, monastery, 59, 114, 203, 224, 243, 249
stationarii, clergy, 110
St Emmeram, monastery, 36, 37, 49, 124, 128, 198, 203, 247, 249, 251
St Gallen, monastery, 78, 116, 129, 252
  Plan of *See* St-Gall, Stiftsbibliothek: cod.1092
St Martin of Tours, basilica, 26, 38, 58, 130–131, 237, 251
St Maur-des-Fossés, monastery, 100, 129
St Riquier, monastery, 137

Theodulf of Orleans, bishop, 36, 77, 82, 93
Theotroch of Lorsch, monk, 133–137, 211
Tours, 24, 117, 131, 226, 237, 249

Vatican, Basilica of St Peter, 10, 27, 32, 48, 56, 63, 64, 117, 138, 181, 183, 184, 187, 188, 189, 242, 247, 249, 251
  oratory of St-Martin, 63
Verona, 46, 247
vestments, 62, 89, 109
Vogel, Cyrille, 19–20, 86

Walahfrid Strabo, 12, 80, 107, 248, 252
Wissembourg, monastery, 53, 57, 87, 203
Worms, 112

Zacharias I, Pope, 32

Printed in the United States
by Baker & Taylor Publisher Services